W9-CMH-126

"HAROLD"

THE PEOPLE'S MAYOR

To Richard,
with my very
best wishes —
[illegible]
12-24-88

Other books by Dempsey J. Travis

"Don't Stop Me Now"

"An Autobiography Of Black Chicago"

"An Autobiography Of Black Jazz"

"An Autobiography Of Black Politics"

"Real Estate Is The Gold In Your Future"

an authorized biography of

URBAN RESEARCH PRESS, INC.

Mayor HAROLD WASHINGTON

by

Dempsey J. Travis

840 East 87th Street, Chicago, Illinois 60619

Printed in the United States of America
First Edition
ISBN: 0-941484-08-4
Library of Congress Catalogue Card Number: 88-14225

Library of Congress Cataloging-in-Publication Data

Travis, Dempsey J., 1920–
"Harold," the people's mayor: the authorized biography of Mayor Harold Washington/by Dempsey J. Travis.
p. cm.
Bibliography: p.
Includes index.
ISBN 0-941484-08-4: $19.25
1. Washington, Harold, 1922–1987. 2. Mayors—Illinois—Chicago—Biography.
3. Chicago (Ill.)—Politics and government—1951–
I. Title.
F548.54.W36T73 1989
977.3 I 10430924—dc19
[B] 88-14225
CIP

PHOTO CREDITS

The Arlene Jackson Washington estate: 8, 42, 49, 61
Chicago Sun-Times: 192, 193, 204
Chicago Tribune: 180, 210, 214
Oak Woods Cemetery Association: 289, 290, 291, 292
Roosevelt University: 44, 47, 52
All the other photos are the property of Urban Research Press Inc.

To Roy Lee Washington Sr.
and
Bertha Washington,
the parents of
Harold Washington,
mayor of Chicago, 1983–1987.

ACKNOWLEDGMENTS

On Saturday, April 23, 1983 Harold Washington and the author met in his third floor office suite at 7801 S. Cottage Grove for our initial taped interview. Harold had been elected as mayor of Chicago just 11 days earlier and his inauguration was six days away. The environment was not conducive to an in-depth conversation. We were continually interrupted by a stream of telephone calls.

The mayor was always generous with his time whenever his secretary Delores Woods and I could pin him down to a specific date and hour. Yet, even with a firm confirmation, I could not be certain he could keep the appointment because of the fluidity of his crowded schedule. This biography would not have been possible without his total cooperation, along with assistance from the people he suggested I talk with who had been close to him during various periods of his life.

This personal history is enhanced by the stature of the Black man who became the first reform mayor of Chicago. Equally important is the timing: the biography was completed within one year of Washington's death, while many of his contemporaries are still around to tell the rest of the story. Unfortunately, the structure of this work does not lend itself to naming the contribution that more 100 people have made to this work, though many of them are listed in both the bibliography and index. The story would not have been complete without the contributions of the family of the late Arlene Jackson Washington, Harold's stepmother.

Credits for this work must be bestowed upon Ruby Davis, the senior researcher on the six books I have written, including a children's book. Assisting Mrs. Davis were Jan Brooks, librarian, Government Publications Dept. at the Chicago Public Library; Olivia Chew, librarian, Carter G. Woodson Regional Libary; and Lyle Benedict, reference librarian, Chicago Municipal Reference Library, City Hall.

Catherine Jones, my young and able administrative assistant, has assumed a great deal of the responsibility of keeping the old man and his books on track. She is truly worthy of the very highest accolades. I say this because she is in the unique position of having weathered the storm of assisting me in producing my last two best sellers.

Dorothy Parr Riesen, my editor, keeps me standing on my fingers by grading most of my chapters "excellent" or "superior." However, when she does not give a chapter high marks, I know it is time for me to go back to the drawing board and rewrite it. Dorothy, without a doubt, is one of the best of a breed.

Orville A. Hurt, a creative genius, had the necessary tolerance and patience to work with me on the jackets of my last five books. That takes some doing. Trust me, I know.

The bright lights in my life are my wife Moselynne and my 91-year-old mother, Mittie Travis. On some occasions when I want to declare party time, Moselynne reminds me that I cannot write a book in a crowd. On the other hand, my mother constantly chides me for not getting enough rest. I usually retort, "This is no time for a Black man to sleep."

CONTENTS

FOREWORD

Harold Washington, Chicago's first Black mayor, lives in the minds of millions of people from many races and widely divergent backgrounds.

An accurate and just portrayal of this remarkable man and his political genius requires an author with a personal as well as political sensitivity. This authorized biography by Dempsey J. Travis, *Harold: The People's Mayor,* captures the heart, the spirit and the very essence of Harold Washington and of Chicago politics in a way I had not imagined possible.

HAROLD is written from the point of view of a "buddy," a friend and associate who grew up with Washington in the Chicago of political bosses and the "plantation wards" of the South and West Sides. Yet, in spite of their closeness, Travis writes of his friend with the balance of a trapeze artist. From personal reminiscences, notes and more than 100 hours of taped interviews with Harold, in addition to several hundred hours of taped interviews with other mutual friends and foes who knew the late mayor, Dempsey Travis spins a fast-paced and exciting history of the man who became acknowledged as one of Chicago's great political leaders.

From the 3rd Ward on the South Side of Chicago to the state capitol in Springfield to the House of Representatives in Washington, D.C., and back to Chicago's City Hall, Harold lives again in a biography flavored with his blunt, off-the-cuff remarks and eloquent speeches. For those of us who stayed up all night February 23, 1983 waiting for the results of the primary election in Chicago, Harold's words ring once again—this time from the pages of this personal political history.

Harold Washington's political career sprang from Chicago's Democratic party machine. He inherited both a job at City Hall and a precinct to run when his father died. *HAROLD* is a compelling witness to his evolution from a machine functionary into an independent politician whose strong stands on the "people issues" gained national recognition.

The drive and resourcefulness exhibited by Harold Washington when he worked in the 3rd Ward Young Democrats organization in the early 1950s drew the attention of Mayor Richard J. Daley. But the young man soon learned that the rules were stacked against him and any other Blacks looking for real representation and power in the party. Author Travis recounts incident after incident of the backstabbing and maneuvering routinely carried out by the anti-Black and anti-working class politicians that dominated the Chicago machine for more than five decades. As Harold charged in 1963, "When we get in the game, they change the rules."

This biography is a real find for scholars and laypeople alike. *HAROLD* exposes the foundation of racism, moral bankruptcy and the political corruption that triggered the emergence of a Black independent political movement—a movement that beat the Democratic machine in an aldermanic race in 1963 and culminated in Washington's successful run for mayor in 1983.

The grass roots movement that built Harold's campaign began with the registration of 230,000 voters, the Women for Washington organization, and the emergence of committees in almost every Chicago community. Travis chronicles the roaring, citywide, 12,000-strong rally at the University of Illinois Pavilion that was the culmination of the forces that Harold Washington represented and that carried him to victory.

But, it is also the story of a reluctant Harold Washington. In 1982, he had to be talked into running for mayor. Just days before he finally announced, no one on his committee really knew what his decision would be.

While the massive turnout in the Black community provided the base of victory, it was Harold's genius in building the progressive rainbow coalition that created the necessary margin to win the mayoral race from a white Republican opponent. The dirty tricks, the racist maneuverings of the Vrdolyaks and Byrnes, the use of "Bye, Bye Blackbird" by the Bernard Epton campaign just made good people fight harder.

Harold Washington did become the first bonafide reform mayor of the city of Chicago.

As I read his inaugural speech in this biography by Dempsey J. Travis, I experienced once more the great sense of victory, accomplishment and pride in the man who had led Chicago such a great distance in such a brief period of time.

Harold: The People's Mayor helps us to understand, to continue the struggle, and to be inspired anew by Harold Washington, who is still the leader, in spirit, of the people's party.

Richard G. Hatcher, J.D.
Mayor of Gary, Indiana
1968 to 1988

INTRODUCTION

This biography of Harold Washington is a most significant contribution to contemporary American history for a number of reasons. The life of Harold Washington covered one of the most momentous periods in worldwide developments, including the victory of the Allies over the authoritarian, racist, and inhuman Nazi efforts at world domination; the newly gained freedom from colonial rule of large parts of the world, including many African states from where a large proportion of the United States population's ancestry came as slaves; and—above all—the birth, the struggle, and the ultimate victory of the Civil Rights Movement.

This book is important and should become required reading not only for the lay public, Black and white. It is, unlike many other scholarly books, extremely readable, comprehensive, and well-researched. Its author, Dempsey J. Travis, has developed a well-deserved reputation as a writer, businessman, community leader, and effective advocate for equal opportunity for Blacks.

No one else could have written this biography with the intimate knowledge of Chicago's first Black mayor, or of the post-World War II Chicago as Dempsey J. Travis has. He and Harold Washington were classmates at Roosevelt University in the late 1940s at a time when I served as an assistant professor of economics. Harold was one of my outstanding students and I had an opportunity to watch and vicariously delight in his stellar career from Assistant State's Attorney to State Senator, and ultimately to Mayor of Chicago.

Harold Washington was one of a significant number of Black leaders who found the non-discriminatory environment of Roosevelt University to be the perfect seed bed from which could sprout a cadre of men and women ideally suited to bring pride and overdue recognition to the Black community. In introducing Washington to a student assembly during the 1983 mayoral campaign, I could honestly say that Chicago never had as culturally educated a mayor as Harold Washington was going to be. He had benefited from the teaching of such people as St. Clair Drake, Harold Laski, George Watson, and many other excellent scholars.

The *Chicago Tribune* on Dec. 4, 1987, in commenting about the memorial service at Roosevelt University, said, "Washington's years at Roosevelt were a part of him and Washington continued to be a part of Roosevelt . . . returning frequently and speaking fondly of his days at school." On one such occasion,

Roosevelt University's then Chairman of the Board, Jerome Stone, asked Harold: "What would you like to be remembered for?" His response was: "I don't want to be remembered as the first Black mayor of Chicago but as the first *reform* mayor of Chicago." Indeed, under the Washington administration, Chicago got both affirmative action and a meaningful effort toward merit appointments in lieu of the old machine patronage system.

To get the full benefit from *Harold: The People's Mayor,* I strongly urge the reader to go back in time and to read Dempsey J. Travis' earlier volume, *An Autobiography of Black Chicago,* for a better appreciation of the Black struggle that culminated in the election and re-election of Harold Washington through a coalition of Black and white voters.

At the time of the publication of this volume, there is great uncertainty about who will ultimately inherit the mantle of Harold Washington. But there is no uncertainty in my mind that just as Martin Luther King was unique as a Civil Rights Leader, so Harold Washington always will stand out as a man who permanently changed the political landscape of Chicago.

To understand the life and the significance of Harold Washington, Dempsey J. Travis' volume must be compulsory reading for a broad spectrum of the population. It promises to become a classic in Chicago political history.

Rolf A. Weil
President
Roosevelt University
Chicago, Illinois
August 1988

A 1947 photo of Bertha Washington Price, mother of Chicago's Mayor Harold Washington.

Roy Lee Washington Sr., father of the mayor. The picture was taken on the night that Roy graduated from Chicago Kent College of Law in June 1923.

1. PLACE OF BIRTH
Registration Dist. No. **3104**
STATE OF ILLINOIS
DEPARTMENT OF PUBLIC HEALTH
DIVISION OF VITAL STATISTICS
HEALTH DEPARTMENT'S RECORD
CITY OF CHICAGO

County of COOK
City of CHICAGO
Primary District No.........
CERTIFICATE OF BIRTH
Registered No. 15512 (Consecutive No.)

Street and Number. No..............., ...St., ...Ward. Cook Co. Hospital
(If birth occured in hospital or institution, give its name instead of street and number.)

2. FULL NAME OF CHILD Harold Lee Washington (If child is not yet named, make supplemental report, as directed)

3. Sex of Child M | 4. Twin, triplet, or other?...... | 5. Number in order of birth.... (To be answered only in the event of Plural births) | 6. Legitimate? Yes | 7. Date of birth 4 – 15 – 1922 (Month) (Day) (Year)

FATHER

8. FULL NAME Roy Washington
9. RESIDENCE (P. O. Address) 3341 Prairie Av
10. COLOR Col
11. AGE AT LAST BIRTHDAY 25 Years
12. BIRTHPLACE (City or Place)........
(Name State if in U. S.) Ky
(Name Country, if Foreign)........
13. OCCUPATION
(Nature of Industry) Laborer

MOTHER

14. FULL MAIDEN NAME Bertha Jones
15. RESIDENCE 3341 Prairie Av
16. COLOR Col
17. AGE AT LAST BIRTHDAY 24 Years
18. BIRTHPLACE (City or Place)........
(Name State, if in U. S. Ills
(Name Country, if Foreign)........
19. OCCUPATION
(Nature of Industry) Housewife

20. NUMBER OF CHILDREN OF THIS MOTHER (Taken as of time of birth of child herein certified and including this child) (a) Born alive and now living 4 (b) Born alive but now dead........ (c) Stillborn........

WHAT TREATMENT WAS GIVEN CHILD'S EYES AT BIRTH? ag. No. 3 – 1%

21. CERTIFICATE OF ATTENDING PHYSICIAN OR MIDWIFE*

I hereby certify that I attended the birth of this child, who was born alive at 11 P.M., on the date above stated.

*When there is no attending physician or midwife, then the father, mother, householder, etc., shall make this return. See Sec. 12 of vital statistics law.

22. (Signature) F. B. Lefbert M. D. Midwife (Physician or Midwife)
Address Cook Co. Hosp. Telephone W-4960
Date Certificate Signed 4 – 18 – 1922 (Month) (Day) (Year)

23. Given name added from a supplemental report
June 1 – 22 19.. (Month) (Day) (Year)
M. O. Heckard Registrar

24. Filed MAY 2 - 1922 M. O. Heckard Registrar
Post Office Address........

A copy of the birth certificate of Harold Washington.

CHAPTER

1

From a Cook County Ward to City Hall

The economic winds of the 1920s roared like a lion for white folks, but meowed like a kitten for Black folks. Roy Lee and Bertha Jones Washington moved to Chicago from downstate Illinois just in time to hear the 1920 kitty cat make her last meow. Times were tough for the young couple, but Roy Lee finally got lucky and secured a job in a stockyard slaughterhouse.

The industrial depression that plagued Chicago during the last six months of 1920 caused the layoff of some 20,000 Blacks. Many of them had to seek shelter in pool halls, police stations, and in unheated hallways. During the warmer months, the Lake Michigan shore north of 31st Street was home to thousands of the homeless. The "Village of the Deserted" along the lake shore housed makeshift shanties made of rocks, wooden planks, newspapers and other junk that punctuated Chicago's front door. Although the street people were indigent, most would not accept free transportation to the South, where there was a critical shortage of sharecroppers. They preferred Chicago, where the hopeless could still dream of hope as they huddled around the bonfires under Wacker Drive and on the shores of the City By the Lake.

On April 15, 1922, the Chicago skyline was cloudless and the outdoor temperature was a mild 56 degrees. Shortly before high noon, Bertha and

Roy Lee welcomed their fourth child, Harold, who was born in Cook County Hospital, the commoners' health facility located on Chicago's near West Side at 1835 W. Harrison.

As they had with their other children, the Washingtons bestowed upon their omega child the middle name of Lee. It was Harold, who, by the time he could spell it, rejected the surname of Robert Edward Lee, commander-in-chief of the Confederate army.

William "Big Bill" Thompson, hailed by some as the "20th Century Abe Lincoln," was mayor and Edward "The Iron Master" Wright was serving his maiden term as the first Black ward committeeman of Carl Sandburg's "City of the big Shoulders." Louis B. Anderson had replaced Oscar DePriest, Chicago's first Black alderman, in the 2nd Ward.

The desire to be a person that was somebody drove Harold Washington's dad to attend law school at night while working fulltime for $15 per week on the killing floor at Wilson and Company in the Chicago stockyards.

After the energetic 25-year-old Roy Lee Washington earned a law degree from the Chicago Kent College of Law in June 1923, he joined the other 95 Black lawyers in Chicago, most of whom held full-time jobs as postal clerks in the main post office or worked as Pullman porters for the railroad. He continued the backbreaking work in the stockyards and lived at 3341 S. Prairie Ave. for two years after he received his law degree.

The smells and sounds that crowded Roy Washington's nostrils and ears as he walked through the streets of the stockyards in route to his job at the slaughterhouse were those of screaming hogs and cows being herded by goats to the killing room through the overhead runways crisscrossing the packing companies' yards. Fertilizer fumes were the most dominant among the many foul stockyard odors, along with the rancid odor of the blood of dead animals. The funky, sweaty smell of dirty work clothes worn by men who did not bother to bathe except on Saturday night heightened the malodorous working conditions. On windy days, the stockyard stench carried 10 miles northeast to downtown Chicago.

Nineteen twenty-three was another eventful year for the young family. Roy passed the Illinois bar examination and proudly had his name painted in gold letters on the door of a law office that he shared with attorney James A. Terry at 3456 S. State St. He was ready to serve the public. He was filled with the anticipation of seeing his fortune balloon like Chicago's Black population, which had grown to 109,000 in 1922 from 30,150 in 1900.

In 1924, two years after Harold was born, Adelbert H. Roberts, a three-term state representative, was elected on the Republican ticket as the first Black state senator in Illinois. William E. Dever was elected the Democratic mayor with the assistance of "Big Bill" Thompson, the former two-term Republican mayor, and a coalition of Democrats and Republicans. In the same year, Republican Albert B. George became the first Black lawyer to sit on the bench and preside over a municipal courtroom in Cook County, Illinois.

St. Benedict the Moor, a Catholic boarding school that catered to children of Black professionals, such as entertainers who traveled extensively, and to children of single parents. Harold and his brother Edward were students here from 1926 to 1929.

Bertha Washington was a very beautiful and robust woman who was interested in pursuing a career in the theater. Bertha and Roy attended concerts together in Orchestra Hall, where they were seated high in the peanut gallery, the section reserved for Blacks only. In the summer of 1926, Bertha walked out on Roy and their children. The Washingtons were divorced in 1930.

Roy Lee Washington, lawyer, minister and ex-stockyard laborer, was granted legal custody of their four youngsters. This supports Harold's contention that his dad was an unusual man. The parental breakup caused the Washington siblings to be separated. Roy Lee Jr., the eldest son, was sent to live with his maternal grandparents in Carrier Mills, Illinois. Elizabeth Lee joined her paternal grandparents, Rev. Isaiah and Amanda Washington, in Springfield, Illinois, a city filled with layers of Jim Crowism that paralleled the racism practiced in the bowels of such states as Mississippi, Georgia, Alabama and Louisiana. The father and his two youngest sons, Edward and Harold, moved into the home of Roy's elder sister on the Near South Side in Chicago's 3rd Ward.

In the fall of 1926, Roy sent the small boys to St. Benedict The Moor, a Catholic boarding school for colored children in Milwaukee, Wisconsin. Harold was only four and a half years old, and Edward had just celebrated his sixth birthday.

Six days after they set their feet inside the school of St. Benedict, the free-spirited young brothers became disillusioned by the regimentation and the realization that they were being institutionalized in a strange environment a long way from their father. The lads displayed their disenchantment by running away from the school 14 times within 34 months. Eight times they managed to arrive safely and without an incident at the doorsteps of their aunt's home in Chicago, where their father maintained a single room. On five occasions, they were apprehended by policemen who thought the two little fellows were lost, and once by a Catholic sister who caught them in the act of attempting to thumb a ride. In good and bad weather, they bummed rides in T-Model Fords, Moons, Packards, Hudsons, Pierce Arrows, trucks, horses hitched to wagons and any other moving object that was headed south toward Chicago.

Although Roy Washington always greeted his two young sons warmly, he also tenderly but firmly packed them up and delivered them back to the Catholic sisters in Milwaukee. The sisters frequently told the father that Harold and Edward were both high-spirited, impetuous youngsters who could be nuisances, but were never classified as bad or incorrigible.

Black parents felt safe in leaving their children in the care of the Capucin fathers at St. Benedict The Moor. It was considered an ideal school for the children of Black professionals, such as entertainers who traveled extensively and for children of single parents. At the beginning of each school year, nuns from St. Benedict would go to the Milwaukee railroad station to pick up incoming students, who would be found standing on the platform with their names printed on cards hung around their necks. The famous comedian John "Redd Foxx" Sanford, of the "Sanford and Son" TV series, was a resident at the boarding school during the same period that Harold and Edward were there.

"We taught Black history and Black literature long before it was the stylish thing to do," said Sister Florence Shigo, who began teaching at the school in the 1940s. "It was very strict. The children were . . . I hate to use the word 'herded,' but we kept close tabs on them."

According to an old St. Benedict handbook, students were not allowed to keep spending money, to leave the school without permission, or to have any written material that had not been approved by the teachers. The rector read all the children's incoming and outgoing mail. The handbook warned that "familiarity between older and younger pupils would not be tolerated," and that "all running, jumping, whistling, screaming within the buildings . . . are strictly forbidden." The younger children had to be in bed by 7 p.m. and up by 6 a.m. Morning prayers were at 6:30, breakfast at 7:15, classes from 9 a.m. to 3:30 p.m. and evening prayer at 6:30. These rules implemented the kind of lockstep education that caused Harold and Edward to rebel.

Years after Harold Washington's stay at St. Benedict The Moor, he recalled:

3936 S. Grand Blvd, now Dr. Martin Luther King Drive, is the house where Harold and Edward occupied the front room on the second floor with their father when they returned to Chicago from St. Benedict The Moor in the summer of 1929.

> I was never tamed. I was always a free spirit. I was always a guy who, just relatively speaking, followed his own drum beat. If I liked something, I liked it. I didn't like Catholic school. I didn't like kneeling and praying all day. One of my most perceptive statements in life was made when I was a kid. We had to go to Catholic church three times a day. I recall telling the sisters at St. Benedict The Moor, 'I don't think the Lord wanted little children just to pray all day, he wanted them to play.'

In the winter of 1928, while Harold and Edward were retained at the boarding school, William L. Dawson mustered enough audacity to run for Congress in the 1st Congressional District against Rep. Martin B. Madden. Madden was the great white father and a political savior in the minds of the majority of Chicago's colored folks, but Dawson made an impressive primary showing by garnering 29 percent of the Black Republican votes. Considering the temper of race relations at the time, his success at the polls was unprecedented.

Edward and Harold received written permission from their father to leave the boarding school and return to Chicago the following year. Roy Lee and his two young sons moved into a three-story white stone Victorian mansion owned by his friend Virginia Davis, a widow with a young daughter named Gwendolyn. They lived at 3936 S. Parkway (now Dr. Martin Luther King Drive), directly across the street from the renowned Grand Terrace Night Club. The club was the musical headquarters of the world-famous piano player, Earl "Fatha" Hines, and his orchestra.

The Earl Hines Band of 1929. Left to right: Billy Franklin (singer & trombone), Omer Simeon (sax), Charlie Allen (trumpet), Lawrence Dixon (guitar & cello), George Dixon (vocal, sax & trumpet), Wallace Bishop (drums, chimes, tymps, bells & vibes), Earl Hines (piano), Walter Fuller (vocal & trumpet), Louis Taylor (sax), Quinn Wilson (tuba, string bass, accordion, violin & piano), Darnell Howard (sax, clarinet, violin & trumpet) and Cecil Irwin (sax).

Young Harold spent many evenings looking out of his second-floor bedroom window at white women draped in mink coats and jackets and at white men in tuxedos, tails and top hats. They arrived at the door of the cabaret in their chauffeur-driven cars, eager to be entertained by Earl Hines and his all-star Black orchestra and a jewel-studded colored floor show crowned with shapely mulatto chorus girls.

The plush Grand Terrace was controlled by the Al Capone syndicate, and although it was located in the heart of Chicago's Black Belt, it catered to a "white only" crowd. Occasionally, the owners proclaimed a colored movie celebrity like Hattie McDaniels or a policy king like Ed Jones an "honorary white," a status that allowed them entry to the night club.

Harold learned early in life that the part of Chicago where he lived, known within the Negro community as Bronzeville, was residentially 100 percent Black. The only white folk he saw on a daily basis were the community merchants who had a monopoly on the Black economy and those rich-looking white folk who came nightly to the Grand Terrace to enjoy Black jazz and Black entertainment.

Shortly after the Washington brothers returned to Chicago in 1929, Oscar DePriest, Black Chicago's Republican political hero, became the first Black in the 20th Century to be elected to the U.S. Congress. At the time of the election, Edward and Harold were enrolled in Felsenthal Elementary School, 4101 S. Calumet Ave.

The boys attending Felsenthal were known for their rough and tough behavior. Young Harold, a slender kid, was bait for several of the school's oversized roughnecks who chose him as their punching bag almost every Friday afternoon right after the school bell rang at 3:15. If Harold managed to escape from school without getting whipped by the bullies, Edward, who was a year and a half older and much larger than he, would frequently exercise his fist against Harold's head when he got home.

Harold Washington's head, though a weekly target of the school's toughies, was filled with ideas and information. He started reading before he was four years old and had developed a ferocious appetite for the printed words in newspapers, magazines and books by the time he was seven. Harold was the only person that I knew who read serious books between innings at a baseball game in which he was an active player, and who would continue to read while walking from the player's bench to outfield.

Harold acquired his reading tastes by emulating his father, a reflective man who read avidly, mostly books on power and self-determination.

Young Harold's reading tastes were catholic, though focused on biographies and autobiographies. He was particularly fascinated with "The Letters of Lord Chesterfield to His Son," a compilation of letters written by an 18th Century father to his son away at boarding school.

The Chesterfield letters were a bold contrast to Harold's boarding school days, and the writings perhaps mirrored an education Harold wished he had had. I suspect that young Washington walked vicariously in young Chesterfield's footsteps when deciding which road to travel after his stint at the school in Milwaukee.

One afternoon in the winter of 1932, while reading a dime detective magazine, Harold saw an advertisement by Charles Atlas, the strong man. It pictured a handsome muscular guy kicking sand in the face of a skinny guy who was lying on the beach with his girlfriend, and the girl walking away with the young man with the muscles. The lead line in the ad read, "How Joe's body brought him fame instead of shame." Harold mailed the magazine coupon to Charles Atlas in New York City for a copy of the promotional pamphlet on muscle development.

Apparently, the desire to become a Black Charles Atlas kindled young Harold's entrepreneurial juices—he became self-employed in the heart of the great Depression. The lad solicited window washing jobs from the homeowners and tenants in the 3900 and 4000 blocks of South Parkway every Saturday from sunup to sundown.

Pint-sized Harold was paid a nickel for every two windows he washed, and he saved every penny until he had enough to send for an Atlas instruction course on muscle building. Roy Lee Jr. recalls how his younger brother always wanted someone to feel his muscles after he started practicing the Atlas

The Atlas ad that pushed Harold Washington into becoming a muscle man and turning the tide against the playground bullies at Felsenthal Elementary School.

dynamic tension technique. Harold was very serious about body building, working at it for almost two years until he was both satisfied with his physical development and confident of his ability to acquit himself in combative situations.

Roy Lee Jr. recalls that a day of reckoning arrived one Saturday morning when Edward began his own ritual exercise of beating up his younger brother. Harold shouted: "No! No! You don't fight me anymore!" and successfully employed his muscle training on Edward's head and body. Harold's ability to defend himself at home was transferred to the school yard. After several decisive victories on the playground at Felsenthal, his problems with the school bullies ceased.

In the spring of 1933, William L. Dawson was elected alderman of the 2nd Ward on the Republican ticket. In the early winter of that year, Rev. Roy Washington and his sons, Harold and Edward, moved into a large apartment located in a six-flat building at 4507 S. Vincennes Ave. They shared the walk-up second-floor flat of a distant cousin, Prentiss Wheeler, who owned a newspaper and candy concession at the 47th Street elevator train stop.

The building in which they lived was a three-story brick walk-up next door to the Ebenezer Baptist Church. The church was home base for many of Chicago's famous gospel singers and composers—Mahalia Jackson, Willie Webb, Robert Anderson, Sallie Martin and Thomas A. Dorsey. Mr. Dorsey composed hundreds of sacred works. "Precious Lord," one of his best loved hymns, was the favorite gospel song of Dr. Martin Luther King Jr.

Jerry Sloan, who was a friend of Prentiss Wheeler, young Washington's cousin, was Harold's first regular employer. He was the branch manager at 49th and State Street for William Randolph Hearst's *Chicago Herald Examiner.* Harold was hired as a newspaper carrier in 1933. Sloan indicated that the 11-year-old Harold was prompt on his deliveries of the morning paper regardless of the weather and a good salesman who made $7 to $10 a week. This was a pretty good salary for a kid in those days.

John Cheefus, Washington's lifelong friend, says that they were such good newspaper boys that on some Sundays they would sell out all of their *Herald Examiners,* then go by the *Chicago Tribune* branch and buy additional papers and sell them to make extra money. In addition to their regular paper route, they sold the *Chicago Defender* on Fridays and Saturdays. Harold kept a little tobacco bag in his left hip pocket in which he carried spending money in amounts varying from 50 cents to $1 in small change. In 1933, you could rent a hotel room in first-class surroundings or take 10 kids to the movies for $1.

In 1934, while the Washington family was still residing on Vincennes Ave., Arthur W. Mitchell defeated Congressman Oscar DePriest, the Republican stalwart, in his bid for re-election. Thus, Mitchell became the first Black Democrat in this century to serve in the halls of the U.S. Congress.

Harold's father, an associate minister at Bethel A.M.E. Church for many years under the leadership of Bishop A. Wayman Ward, supported Mitchell as a fellow Democrat in his bid for Congress. Rev. Washington conducted Sunday services at Bethel only about once a year, but was frequently called upon to give the Sunday morning sermons and make political speeches at various African Methodist Episcopal churches on the South and West sides of Chicago. By most accounts, Roy did not have the oratorical talent of his son Harold.

Rev. Washington regularly took young Harold to houses of worship and occasionally to Democratic party rallies. The late Judge Richard Harewood recalled seeing Rev. Washington and his little boy at church and at political rallies on several occasions. Rev. Roy Washington would frequently say, "Son, you need some experience speaking. So here's a nickel. You go to church with me and I will give you a chance to talk." Harold would go to the front of the house of the Lord and say, "I am here with my father to worship and I am putting a nickel in the collection box." His dad would always smile and beam with pride. A smile on the face of Roy Washington was a rarity. He was not the smiling type. Hence, Harold must have inherited that personality trait from his mother.

The ministry was Rev. Roy Washington's first love, and although he wanted Harold to become a minister, he never tried to influence him. In contrast, Rev. Isaiah Washington, Harold's paternal grandfather, definitely tried to persuade him to become a minister, but "Master" Harold resisted.

Harold recalls:

> I always knew what my father's Sunday sermon was going to be about because he would start practicing on me on Monday. Although I was not exactly an inanimate object, I did not do much responding. If you have ever been around preachers, you know they start practicing their sermon on whomever they can get their hands on. Since I was the youngest child, I was his captured audience. He would articulate his sermon to me because that is the way preachers prepare for the next Sunday. I would always listen very carefully just in case he might ask me a question, which he occasionally did. Therefore, I have to credit the extensive knowledge I have about the Bible today to those Bible sessions with my father.

Young Harold Washington had some strong notions about church and his father's influence. Chicago's first Black mayor reflected:

> Although I knew I would never become a minister, I was certain that someday I would finish law school and be a public figure, not necessarily a politician. It never occurred to me to run for office. I don't recall figuring that out. As a matter of fact, I had a tinge of distaste for politics. My old man had a tempering influence on me; he was a good role model. He got his message across to his boys by example.

In 1935, Harold's father met and married Arlene Jackson, who had been both a school teacher and a music instructor in Kansas City, Kansas, before

On the far left is Arlene Jackson Washington, a music instructor and social worker from Kansas City, Kansas, who married attorney Roy Lee Washington Sr. in 1935. She is shown with Beatrice Carter (middle) and Beatrice Turner in the dining room of her second floor apartment at 4941 S. Michigan Ave.

becoming a social case worker for the Children's Home and Aid Society in Chicago. She continued to work there until 1955. The marriage to Miss Jackson enabled Rev. Washington to stabilize his family life in a huge rented apartment at 4444 S. Indiana Ave. The place was large enough to give everybody in the family laughing room—everybody except Elizabeth Lee, who lived with her paternal grandparents in Springfield, Illinois, until she was married.

In the spring of 1936, the Washington family moved around the corner to an even larger apartment at 111 E. 44th St. There Harold met a beautiful girl, Dorothy Nancy Finch. He instantly became infatuated with Nancy, and affectionately nicknamed her "Peaches" because of the peach-like fuzz on her face. It was truly puppy love at first sight. He was bowled over by the appearance of the five-foot-five-inch beige beauty with whom he attended Forrestville Elementary School. In addition to fondly remembering the pretty little girl who lived on the third floor, Harold recalled:

Dorothy Nancy Finch, Harold Washington's childhood sweetheart and the girl that he affectionately nicknamed "Peaches." When she became his wife in May 1941, the groom's father, Rev. Roy Lee Washington, conducted the marriage ceremony.

I was always involved in the political process. When we transferred from the Felsenthal to the Forrestville Elementary School, located at 622 E. 45th St., I was always getting elected to some position, running for some office or serving on some committee. I actually worked in the precinct with my old man before I was 14 years old. I used to help him pass out literature.

Politics was a centerpiece around our house. Before I reached my teens, I was aware of presidents, mayors, governors, aldermen and people of that nature. My father discussed politics at the dinner table almost every night. The only subject that superseded politics in our home was religion. Political personalities such as William L. Dawson, Oscar DePriest, Mike Sneed, Arthur W. Mitchell and C.C. Wimbush were frequent visitors in our home. I was literally raised in a political atmosphere.

Although Harold considered his father an ideal role model, there was a teacher at Forrestville Elementary School who made a big impression on young Washington. He described Charlotte Roland:

> Very matronly, but firm, detached, and warm. She was just a strange kind of woman. She had a common influence on everybody. For example, in her class, there was never any loud talking or sounds. The kids were always orderly, mannerly and courteous. She ran a tight ship but everybody loved her. She was a robust, husky woman; a typical Black woman, an earth mother. I don't recall any other teacher in grammar school having any real serious influence on me. Teachers like Miss Roland are never forgotten.

Miss Roland's influence at Forrestville made Washington's graduation from that institution a meaningful event.

The Thinclads of DuSable High School. Seated in the front row, second from the left is Harold Washington; third is James Tillman. Standing in the third row is: (left to right) Albert Brown, Robert Ray, captain of the team, and Thomas ''Madman'' Jones.

CHAPTER

2

The DuSable High School Years: 1936–39

In January 1936, Harold Washington was a member of the third freshman class to enter the new Wendell Phillips High School at 4934 S. Wabash Ave. in Chicago. The school name was changed in April of that year to Jean Baptiste Point DuSable High School, in honor of a Black man who was Chicago's first non-Indian settler. DuSable founded a trading post in 1779 on the present site of the Chicago Tribune Tower, located on North Michigan Avenue by the Chicago River.

Freshie Harold was one of 3,500 Black students crammed into an educational facility built to accommodate 2,500 pupils. DuSable High School mirrored the sardine-tight, kitchenette living conditions in Chicago's racially restricted Black Belt, where no one but the overworked teachers paid much attention to the overcrowded conditions.

Harold, like most other kids that year, was caught up in the dance craze of trucking and jitterbugging to Fletcher Henderson's hit song "Christopher Columbus." Armies of white musicians and white swing addicts flocked to the Grand Terrace across the street from where Roy Sr., Edward and Harold Washington had roomed two years earlier. The big attraction on Sunday, January 26, was the famous 15-piece orchestra featuring Fletcher's piano and arrangements, Chu Berry on the tenor sax and Roy Eldridge on trumpet.

Present at Fletcher's opening was Earl Hines and his band and several white big band leaders: Jan Garber, "Little" Jack Little, Henry Bussey, Bud Harris, Jack Hilton the Englishman and Benny Goodman's entire orchestra (then appearing at the Congress Hotel downtown). Movie star Louise Beaver

Fletcher Henderson's Orchestra in 1936 at the Chicago Grand Terrace. Left to right: Chu Berry (tenor sax), Joe Thomas (trumpet), Horace Henderson (piano), Sidney Catlett (drums), Dick Vance (trumpet), Teddy Lewis, Buster Bailey (clarinet), Elmer Williams (tenor), Ed Cuffee (trombone), Roy Eldridge (trumpet), Israel Crosby (bass), Fernando Arbello (trombone), Bob Lessey (guitar), Don Pasquall (tenor). Seated at the piano is Fletcher Henderson.

and all-time piano genius Art Tatum enjoyed the music for the show, orchestrated by ex-bandleader Tiny Parham.

Fletcher Henderson's opening was historic for more than one reason. Dave Walker, the manager, had announced in the January 18 *Chicago Defender* that the management of the Grand Terrace had a new policy. Colored patrons would be admitted nightly, on the same basis as whites, for a $1 minimum cover charge.

But we DuSable-lites caught the swinging sound of Henderson's theme song by bending our ears and hugging the radio for the twice-nightly, seven-days-a-week broadcast coming directly from Chicago's own Grand Terrace.

In addition to being a Henderson fan, Harold Washington was a Walter Dyett devotee. Captain Walter Dyett, the DuSable bandmaster, was a former jazz musician. Each year he would stage a "DuSable Hi-Jinks," a musical that gave the students an opportunity to exhibit their talents. Harold and I were sitting front row center the first night of the 1936 Hi-Jinks presentation, which was entitled "Swinging On." We joined the audience in stomping and clapping after hearing Savannah Strong's rendition of "At My Beck and Call." Years later, we reminisced about Elizabeth Hunt Moutoussamy's memorable version of George Gershwin's "Summertime," and Bessie Suttle's show-stopping interpretation of Duke Ellington's "I Let A Song Go Out of My Heart."

DuSable High School was loaded with musically talented students who have appeared in the Hi-Jinks productions. Gifted alumni included: Austin Powell and his Cats and the Fiddle (Powell was both singer and composer

Dr. Mildred Bryant Jones, the chairman and talented music teacher at DuSable High School, told Harold he was a nonsinger but had a pleasant personality. Therefore, she gave him the position of hummer in the DuSable glee club.

of the hit song, "Please Don't Leave Me Now"), the immortal Nat "King" Cole, Dorothy Donegan, Johnny Board, John "Redd Foxx" Sanford, Martha Davis, Johnny Hartman, Johnny Griffin, John Young and hundreds of others.

Harold loved to listen to music and was a good dancer but never showed any real interest in wanting to learn how to play a musical instrument. The closest that he came to learning anything about music was in a class presided over by a harmony and voice teacher at DuSable, Dr. Mildred Bryant Jones. Harold recalled:

> Dr. Jones insisted that I join the glee club although I could not sing a lick, nor was I able to carry a tune. Therefore, she settled on the notion that I could hum. I was the best hummer in the class because I was the only one. The good doctor was a little bit of a lady, but a powerful and inspirational teacher. Dr. Jones was a good friend of Dr. W.E.B. DuBois, a great Black scholar who earned a Ph.D. at Harvard before the turn of the century. She would often mention Dr. DuBois as an excellent role model for her students to follow. She told us about DuBois' scholarly achievements and demanded we pursue excellence the same as he did. I was impressed.

When Harold was not reading or listening to music, he was participating in sports. He has had an interest in sports from the day he was old enough to understand baseball. As a matter of fact, he recalled that the most important Christmas gift he ever received from his father was a baseball glove. Holiday gift giving was never a big thing in the Washington household, but Harold did not appear to be hurt because Christmas was not a big day. He frequently said: "I knew my father was Santa Claus almost as soon as I learned to walk." Since the mechanically inclined lad made all his own scooters, wagons and slides, receiving toys were never high on his agenda.

In a reflective mood, Chicago's first Black mayor recalled:

My main interest in high school was sports. As a matter of fact, Robert Ray, the captain of the DuSable Thinclads, and I were the winners of the city championship in 1939. Ray won the 100-yard dash and the 200-yard dash. I won the 120-yard high hurdle and got second place in the 200-yard low hurdle. We got third place in the relay and won the city title. If you look at us now, you probably would say, how did those cats run? We were both built about the same. Ray was stockier and more muscular than I. Our mutual friend, Albert Brown, placed third in the 880-yard dash.

Cecil Hellman, our coach, was a very decent and pleasant person. He was a big raw-boned Scandinavian, a fatherly-type man who showed great concern about the welfare of the members of the track team. He frequently asked you questions. For example, 'Is there anything I can do for you? Are you doing good? Is there anything bothering you?' Although he was kind, he was not of very much value to me because he did not know anything about hurdling. He was more of a calisthenics man, and my primary interest was track. Therefore, I learned hurdling by reading pamphlets on the subject and through trial and error.

I recall my brother Roy telling me about a Pathe News reel that was showing at the Regal Theater that had a small segment on hurdling. I made a mad dash to the Regal the next day and sat through the movie three times just to see that section of the news reel, which went 'zip!' I also hung around the University of Chicago field house every time there was a meet just to catch the hurdlers. The longest hurdle at the field house, I believe, was 60 yards. That goes in six or seven seconds, and it's over-zip! If you were seated at the wrong angle watching a hurdle meet, you wouldn't get much out of it. And I was always seated at the wrong angle.

I was usually sitting where the hurdlers were coming at me, while in order to get the greatest benefit, you had to see it from the side. My teaching aids were limited to watching news reels at the Regal and Metropolitan theaters and at track meets at the University of Chicago. Nowadays, you can record Foster or Wilson from television on to a VHS or Betamax and play it back 50 times or more if necessary in slow motion. How can you miss?

Carl Denoms, a member of the DuSable Thinclads, remembers Harold Washington as a member of the track team:

I remember Harold as a shy, I mean very shy, guy who just sort of blended in with the landscape. He was never talkative. He just conscientiously worked at becoming a hurdler.

We were all individually responsible for our respective equipment. And since DuSable did not have an indoor or outdoor track, we had to wait until the kids were gone and the halls were clear so we could practice. I watched Harold many a day bring out the hurdle equipment and carefully measure the distance between each hurdle in order to simulate actual track field conditions. I have watched him stand with

The Regal Theater at 4725 S. Parkway is where Harold Washington spent many an hour watching the Pathe News reels repeatedly for the purpose of teaching himself how to run the low and high hurdles.

one foot on the hurdle and then another for periods that seemed like hours in an effort to gauge his stride, because if you break the stride, you are subject to knock the hurdles over and thus disqualify yourself.

To stay qualified, you had to beat the competition. And since I was on the track team when Harold joined, he frequently asked me who his outside competition was because Harold was the best DuSable had. I made known to him the fellow he had to watch was Henry Bledsoe, a model hurdler at Tilden Technical High School. So, every opportunity Harold got he would secretly watch Bledsoe. Bledsoe was a natural

Albert Brown, a 1939 DuSable High School grad, joined the Civilian Conservation Corps with Harold Washington in June of 1939.

hurdler because of his height. Harold became an excellent hurdler by sheer perseverance and a great deal of practice, because he was certainly not tall and sprintly.

Albert Brown remembers when Harold joined the track team in 1937:

> He was a jolly, friendly fellow, who trained hard and had a lot of ability. Harold was big for his age, muscular with a large chest area and big legs. He was the same height at age 16 as he is today. Although young Washington had an outgoing personality, he never discussed his family. None of us knew that Harold's father was an attorney and that his stepmother was a social worker. He selected, for some reason, to hang out with the rough and rugged fellows.
>
> Harold was the best boxer in our group. He was good enough to turn professional. However, Eddie Plique, the Savoy Ballroom boxing promoter, discouraged Harold from turning pro because he felt that he had too much brain power to waste on the canvass of a boxing ring.

Brain power was Harold's long suit. He never carried textbooks home from school. He was a "cafeteria" reader outside of the classroom on subjects stretching beyond textbooks to everything he could get his fingers on. He always had a book in his hand or a magazine sticking out of his hip pocket. Sometimes, he carried small books or magazines in both hip pockets. Even as a member of the neighborhood softball team called the Falcons, his standard equipment as the third baseman was a glove and a book. Harold would read snatches of Edward Bellamy's *Looking Backward, 1887–2000, The Education of Henry Adams,* Henry David Thoreau's *Walden* and magazines such as *Modern Mechanics,* or *The Shadow* while walking from third base to the player's bench between innings. Often he would read short stories from Dostoevsky or Hawthorne while waiting his turn at bat. Some of Harold's teammates included John Cheefus, Frank and Kenneth Titus, Aaron and Al-

Left, Mrs. Anna Sublette, the history teacher who made historical figures come alive and walk right off the pages of the book for Harold Washington. Right, Cecil Hellman, the DuSable track coach; a fatherly type who showed great concern about the welfare of the members of the track team.

bert Hart, Melvin Wilkins, "Red" Christian, Henry Adams, Booker T. Washington, not related, and Edward Washington, Harold's brother, who frequently accused him of eating a dictionary for lunch.

Attorney Roy Washington was a very reflective man and an omnivorous reader, who spent a lot of time talking to his boys, mostly to Harold, the youngest, who could not get away.

Young Harold may not have been able to escape from his father, but women played an important role in his youth, and greatly influenced his direction in life. Years later he reflected:

> Mrs. Anna Sublette was my history teacher, and a woman that I was just fascinated with. She had the most infectious personality of any person I had met in my life. Mrs. Sublette made history come alive. When she explained a historical incident, we could see the characters walking right off the pages of the book. Women influenced me in school. I can't think of a single male teacher throughout my high school days who had any influence on my thinking or behavior.
>
> There was another lady I was very fond of, Mrs. Charlemae Rollins, a librarian at the George Cleveland Hall Library, which is located at 4801 S. Michigan Ave., two blocks from DuSable High School and four blocks from my home. I read through whole sections of that library. Miss Vivian Harsh, the head librarian at the Cleveland Hall Branch, was instrumental in pulling together the most comprehensive collection of books on Afro American history in Chicago. It was in that collection that I was first exposed to Black authors such as Carter G. Woodson, Dr. W.E.B. DuBois, and Booker T. Washington.

Two women who had a great deal of influence on Harold Washington were (left) Mrs. Charlemae Rollins, his favorite librarian at the Cleveland Hall Branch, which was located at 48th and Michigan Ave., and (right) Mrs. Vivian Harsh, head librarian of the George Cleveland Hall Branch, who was responsible for putting together the most comprehensive collection of books on Afro-American history in Chicago. She introduced Harold to great Black literary giants such as Dr. Carter G. Woodson, Dr. W.E.B. DuBois, Arna Bontemps, Sterling Brown, Claude McKay, Langston Hughes and Countee Cullen.

Left, Mrs. Jeannette Tripplett, the English teacher who made young Washington tow the line in her class. Right, Mrs. Mary Herrick, the beloved DuSable civics instructor and Harold's homeroom and study hour teacher.

Reading was an excursion that took me places an urban kid would never see. Reading whetted my appetite. It really wasn't the library but the books. The main value was the joy of reading. I can't imagine life without it.

At this point, I cut off the tape recorder while Mayor Washington took time out to go to the kitchen to get a glass of water. When he returned to the living room, he continued:

I was a good student and I did not really have to work very hard to maintain good grades. My main interest was the track team. I don't think I carried a school textbook home five times during the entire period that I was at DuSable High. I used to do all my homework during the study hour; that was enough. Miss Mary Herrick was my division and study hour teacher. She was a kind person. Miss Herrick did not play favorites with her attention; she was a universal den mother. I probably studied a little better than an hour a day. That was about it. If I took school work home, it was usually for a book report or some other English writing assignment.

I had an English teacher named Jeannette Triplett, who didn't take any stuff. Students had to produce in her class. I remember she was a stickler for punctuation and preciseness. I recall that she gave us a choice for our final paper. We could write about anything we wanted, as long as it was concerning Chicago. Of all things, I wrote about policy, which is the old version of our current daily lottery game. I wrote about it, I guess, because of the economic rationale for the existence of policy, that is the number of people who were employed by the policy barons, how much money was moved around and the glamour that seemed to envelope the individuals who were involved in the policy game. I recall when I got to class on the day the papers were to be turned in, I had to confess that I had not written the paper but that I had an outline and was prepared to deliver my assignment orally.

Mrs. Triplett countered by saying, 'You were supposed to write it.'

I said, 'But I can give it orally; as a matter of fact, I don't mind giving it orally.'

The class then took a vote, and I was allowed to give my presentation orally. When I gave my talk, Mrs. Triplett went into shock. After class, Mrs. Triplett chastised me. She said that giving a paper on an illegal subject like gambling was a horrible thing. My stepmother and Mrs. Triplett were very good friends. Mrs. Triplett even went so far as to tell my stepmother, who was a highly moral person. My stepmother said she thought it was a hideous thing for me to be supporting because it was improper for a person to be an advocate for any activity that was against the law.

My father thought it was funny because he pitched in all those worlds. Although Mrs. Triplett gave me a passing grade, I was not considered one of her favorite people.

DuSable High School was not a challenge to Washington. Shortly after his 17th birthday, he decided to drop out of school and join the Civilian Conservation Corps. Commonly known as the "CCC camp," this was one of President Franklin Delano Roosevelt's New Deal programs that put young men to work in fields and forests around the country. Harold was paid $30 a month for standing either at the end of a hoe or at the end of a shovel. Twenty-five dollars of the $30 he earned was automatically sent home to his family by the Civilian Conservation Corps.

Albert Brown, who, with Harold, was a member of the DuSable 1939 championship track team, was surprised when he saw Washington enlisting in the CCC camp at the same time he did in June 1939. Brown still believes, almost 50 years later, that Harold went into the CCC camp without his parents' consent. Harold contradicted that with:

> I don't really know how my father got me in the Civilian Conservation Corps, but I got in. They may have removed the income level requirements at the time because the CCC camp was very popular during the middle and late 1930s. I was sent up to the camp at Bitely, Michigan, which is close to Baldwin and 40 miles northeast of Muskegon. In addition to a land reclamation program, we planted evergreen trees in that area. After three months, I was shipped out to Stockton, Illinois, which is near the northwest border of the state between Freeport and Galena. I was there for several months. Our job was quarrying limestone, which was heavy, hard and just plain dirty Georgia buggy work. The bad thing about Stockton was the atmosphere. It was a very prejudiced little town.
>
> The limestone that we quarried was given to the farmers free. And the members of the Conservation Corps used it to stop soil erosion. It was a very useful type of work, not the most captivating experience I ever had, but I did not find it unpleasant.
>
> My only real gripe with the Civilian Conservation Corps was the fact that it reminded me of my earlier regimentation experience at St. Benedict The Moor Boarding School. The CCC camp was quasi-military although we did not have to march and drill. The similarities between the army and the CCC camp centered around the fact that we had to wear uniforms and line up for the mandatory reveille before breakfast and retreat before dinner. On balance, it was a mind-opening experience for a 17-year-old boy. I completed my six-month tour of duty and returned to Chicago.

While Harold Washington was planting evergreen trees in Michigan and quarrying limestone in Illinois, William L. Dawson and Chicago Mayor Edward J. Kelly were cutting a political deal that led to Dawson walking out of the Republican party and joining the Democrats. In December 1939, the month Washington completed his duty in the CCC, Pat Nash and Mayor Kelly anointed Bill Dawson with the committeemanship of the 2nd Ward and gave him a bundle of patronage positions for his precinct captains. Earl B. Dickerson, an independent Democrat, had been elected alderman of the 2nd Ward in April of 1939 with the assistance of the then Republican Bill Dawson.

Following his half-year stint in the Civilian Conservation Corps, Washington worked at a series of jobs that paid less than 35 cents per hour. Between January and May of 1940, he worked as a hawker of Cokes, sandwiches and candy aboard Greyhound buses when they made brief stops to pick up passengers at the 79th and Stony Island Avenue bus station. He supplemented that income with part-time jobs as a pin boy at a North Side bowling alley and as a tooth polisher in a downtown dentist laboratory.

The Union Stockyards employed more Negroes from 1918 to 1950 than any other industry in Chicago. The steel mills ranked second in the employment of colored men during that same period.

In June 1940, Harold landed a good job, by ghetto standards, as a laborer working for Wilson and Company, the same firm his father had worked for 20 years earlier. He worked in the freezer department, where he threw frozen hams and slabs of pork bellies onto a train of small metal carts. Every work day he wore several pairs of gloves, high boots, rubber shoes and layers of clothing to protect himself from the subzero temperature maintained in the freezer.

From the freezer, the frozen meat was carted into the sweet pickle department, where it was thrown into a defrosting tank. The author, like his father, worked in the cold and wet sweet pickle (defrosting) section in the early 1940s for approximately a year. Harold's job was even worse than the one I had: the workers in the freezer department had to go outside in the zero temperatures to warm up.

In the spring of 1941, Harold was among the fortunate few to pass the Civil Service examination for a clerkship in the Chicago office of the U.S. Treasury Department, which was located in the Merchandise Mart. At the treasury, he worked in the E-Bond Division, manning data processing machines until November 1942, when he was drafted into the U.S. Army.

In the meantime, Harold proposed to Dorothy Nancy Finch, the young beauty who lived on the third floor at 111 E. 44th St. Since he had just turned 19 and she was 17, they both had to get permission from their parents in order to get their marriage license.

In May 1941, Rev. Roy Lee Washington Sr. performed the wedding ceremony in his living room on the second floor at 111 E. 44th St. Harold recalls, "My future mother-in-law, Mrs. Sally Finch, a very stylish stout woman with a beautiful face, kept asking my father: 'Is this legal Roy? Are you sure this is legal Roy?' "

Rev. Washington retorted, "I marry people all the time."

Mrs. Finch snapped back, "That is not what I asked you, Roy."

The two sweethearts discovered, almost immediately after they had taken vows, that their "non-shotgun" marriage was not made in heaven and that it was going to be a stormy one. Both Harold and Dorothy Nancy were strong-willed people with volatile tempers. It took an Army draft and the separation that followed during World War II to cool them off.

The U.S.S. Arizona was one of the more seriously damaged United States ships at Pearl Harbor on Dec. 7, 1941. Many of the more than 2,000 officers and enlisted men killed at Pearl Harbor were buried alive in ships like the Arizona.

CHAPTER

3

The World War II Period: 1941–46

In the summer of 1941, as the Japanese were invading the French colonies of Indochina, the United States drew its battle lines on the side of the colonies. The U.S. government embargoed scrap iron and oil shipments slated for Japan, and the Japanese, after their supply lines had been cut off, were forced to react before they ran out of petroleum. Pearl Harbor became inevitable and its timetable predictable as a result.

On Dec. 7, 1941, the Japanese bombed Pearl Harbor. The following day, funds belonging to Japanese Americans in California were frozen and banks refused to cash their checks. Milkmen refused to deliver their milk. Grocers refused to sell them food. And insurance companies canceled their policies. The state of California revoked their licenses to practice law and medicine, and dismissed them from civil service jobs in city, county and state offices from Crescent City to San Diego.

Three days after the bombing of Pearl Harbor, Germany and Italy came to the aid of Japan and declared war on the United States. On Dec. 8, 1941, Congress declared that American males from ages 18 to 65 had to register, and those from the ages of 20 through 45 were subject to being drafted. Thousands of white men began to volunteer for service in the Air Corps, the Marines, the Navy and the Army the day after Pearl Harbor. Black men were not permitted to volunteer for any duty except the labor battalions in the Army and were relegated to kitchen or mess duty in the Navy. The status of Blacks in the military evolved through several stages until the Truman administration issued its Freedom to Serve report in 1950.

By November 1942, more than 110,000 men, women and children of Japanese American ancestry—70,000 of them Nisei, or American-born citizens—were herded together like cattle throughout the state of California, and shuttled off to imprisonment in "internment camps" with little or no notice. Although many of the Japanese owned farms, homes and businesses—with an estimated total value of $510 million—they were permitted to carry no more of their worldly goods than they had on their backs and the meager amounts that they could hurriedly stuff into two small suitcases. Most of them were incarcerated for the duration of World War II in places like the flood-damaged land at Relocation, Arkansas, the mountains of Wyoming and the desert land of Western Arizona.

Only the young Nisei, who volunteered for U.S. military duty and heroically defended democracy while fighting in segregated units, escaped internment in the United States. To add to the paradox, German prisoners of war who were brought to America during the same period were permitted to use U.S. Army and civilian facilities that were off-limits to both Black and Nisei soldiers.

The Army accelerated its call for Black soldiers in the fall of 1942 when the United States joined its Western allies in the invasion of North Africa. Harold Washington was sworn into the Army that November, and shipped out of Chicago from Illinois Central Railroad Station at 12th and Michigan Avenue. At Fort Custer, Michigan, near the city of Battle Creek, he was processed through the all-Black 1609th Service Center.

Washington's stay at Fort Custer was approximately 72 hours, during which time he officially became an "old soldier" after receiving his metal dog tag, which bore the serial number 36395331, inoculation shots and a duffle bag full of Army gear. Here he was told that it was mandatory for soldiers to wear their dog tags at all times. This was the Army's means of determining the blood type of wounded soldiers and the identification of dead ones.

Buck Pvt. Washington had undergone some military indoctrination before he was drafted. He had served six months in the Civilian Conservation Corps, and found that the CCC was a mini-Army minus the drills and guns. In 1937, at DuSable High School, Harold had opted to join the Reserved Officers Training Corps (ROTC) instead of taking gym because he thought he got enough gymnastics in his three- to five-hour daily track practice. ROTC at DuSable gave him a leg up for soldiering, for he learned close-order drill and how to man weapons ranging from the M-1 rifle to the 105mm howitzer.

Following the short stay at Fort Custer, Michigan, Pvt. Washington, his high school friend Theodore Davis and approximately 230 other Black recruits were shipped in a Jim Crow car on a troop train to Tonpeah, Nevada, for basic training. After a couple of days at Camp Tonpeah, an Army Air Force base, it became obvious to Washington and the other young soldiers that they had been shipped to the wrong camp because Tonpeah had no infantry basic training facilities. The young recruits simply marked time for several months

Harold Washington was processed into the Army in the 1609th Service Unit at Fort Custer, Michigan. Pictured here are recruits from Chicago and Detroit standing in formation in front of the barracks of the service unit.

until they were shipped to another camp for their initial basic training. Pvt. Washington recalled:

> There was a soldier at Camp Tonpeah with the surname of Shields who was a former Davis Cup tennis player. He asked me to help him recruit a boxing team to participate in the regional Golden Gloves finals, which were to be held in Reno, Nevada, about 100 miles from Camp Tonpeah. We recruited a team of boxers in the upper six weights. Theodore 'Red' Davis, a former co-captain of the DuSable High School football team, was our heavyweight. I was the light heavyweight. Another guy whose name I cannot recall was the middleweight. We trained hurriedly for about three weeks. It was tough because the camp was approximately 6,000 feet above sea level, and none of us were accustomed to that rarified air.
>
> Dawn finally broke, after what seemed like an extremely long night of anticipation, on the day we were to make the trip to Reno, the gambling capital of America. We were told we would be staying at the Hotel Golden. I'll never forget when we arrived at the hotel, we went in through the back door. We didn't stay in a hotel room, but in a converted pantry or storage room where they had set up seven cots and had stacked the hotel supplies into a corner of the same room. They had moved us around to the rear of the hotel so fast we didn't know what was going on. This was a very humiliating experience. During the five days that we were there, we occasionally went out the front door, which was the 'for white only' entrance. (What a privilege for an American soldier in uniform.)
>
> One day, 'Red' said, 'Let's go to Harrah's gambling casino.' I wasn't much of a gambler. I played a little poker, but I wasn't going to play that kind of stuff out there. Anyway, 'Red' gambled a little bit.

"White folks wouldn't like it if we let you use this door."

As I recall, a fellow walked up to us as we were standing there watching a roulette wheel. He said, 'No coloreds allowed.'

I said, 'What?' I really didn't understand him at first.

He repeated, 'No coloreds allowed.'

Then 'Red' said, 'What did you say?'

So we made a game out of it. And the cat finally, in disgust, walked away. After that encounter, to make a long story short, we walked around in the casino with a sort of a braggadocio attitude for about 10 minutes and then split. It wasn't my first encounter with prejudice, obviously, but it was kind of shocking because it was one of my first encounters with prejudice as a soldier. I remember after we got back to

Tech 3 Harold Washington kept himself busy with books and school almost 90 percent of the time he was at March Field in California.

the pantry in the hotel, I was pretty upset about it. I wanted to get the hell out of town. But Shields calmed us down. We went on and fought. 'Red' got beat pretty bad in his bouts. I lost one of my three bouts. Max Baer, the former heavyweight champion of the world, was the referee, and I believe I would have had a better chance if he had not been. 'Red' obviously went along for the trip because he wasn't really a boxer.

Two days after we returned to Tonpeah from Reno, we were shipped to Hammerfield, California, which was a training ground. I stayed there for approximately 13 weeks, after which I went to March Field, California, where I stayed for about a year. While there, I went to every damn school I could think of. I attended the Chemical Warfare School and Administration School, which came in handy later because I was subsequently made a first sergeant. I enrolled in something else that you would never think or imagine, a Soil Technician School, which was a fascinating business. The other school that I attended was the Camouflage School.

At the Soil Technician School, I learned how to test soil, clay and gravel to determine whether or not the ground would support an airfield. When I came out of Soil Technician School at March Field, I was made a technical staff sergeant, the one with "T" in the middle of three stripes up and one stripe down.

Although Tech 3 Harold had been up to his eyes in schools at March Field, there was plenty of opportunity for diversion. There were weekly amateur boxing matches at the base gym, but after the Reno boxing experience, Harold was merely an observer. And, there was a stream of singers, dancers, or-

The Duke Ellington Band visited March Field during Harold's stay there. Left to right: Wellman Broad (bass), Toby Hardwick (saxophone), Duke Ellington, Lawrence Brown (trombone), Joe Nanton (trombone), Rex Stewart (trumpet), Arnie Whetsol (trumpet), Harry Carney (baritone sax), and directly behind Carney is Johnny Hodges, Juan Tizol (trombone), Fred Guy (guitar), Barney Bigard (sax and clarinet), Sonny Greer (drums). Cootie Williams (trumpet) is on stage but is not shown. Rex Stewart (trumpet) is shown to the right of Sonny Greer at the top of the picture.

chestras, movie and radio stars such as Jack Benny and Rochester, Betty Davis, Joan Crawford, John Wayne, Bob Hope, Duke Ellington, Count Basie, Erskine Hawkins, Lena Horne and Benny Goodman, who visited the camp during the year. During the leisure period when there was no structured entertainment—and sometimes when there was—Washington spent his time in the well-stocked base library.

The high point of every week was the March Field Service Club dances. They were well attended by lovely young ladies of every size and shape from Los Angeles, San Bernadino and Riverside. The ladies were chaperoned by Mrs. Claudia Claursal, Mrs. Eleanore Lawe and Mrs. Jeannette Rutland, the operators of the Service Club. However, the epitome of enjoyment for Harold and his fellow Chicagoan, Ted Davis, was Los Angeles, which was too far away for overnight passes. On weekends, the city was saturated with sailors and soldiers from March Field and neighboring camps.

Those good things came to an end in April 1944. Harold Washington and his fellow soldiers were shipped out of March Field, their home for the past year, to Camp Patrick Henry, Virginia, the staging area for the Hampton Roads Port of Embarkation. The soldiers were hot and cramped in the troop train

The high point of the week for Harold and his fellow soldiers was the March Field Service Club dances. Those dances were attended by young ladies from Los Angeles, San Bernardino and Riverside. They were chaperoned, and they came in every size and shape.

during their seven-day trip. Salt Lake City, Denver, Chicago, Baltimore and Richmond were just a few of the cities that the homesick soldiers could barely glimpse through the windows as they passed through.

Upon reaching Camp Patrick Henry, the outfit was hurriedly processed, only to be told by the post commander on the eve of their embarkation for overseas duty to wait for further orders. Those who had relatives in nearby cities and towns and a few other fortunate ones such as Harold and Ted were given short weekend passes to Richmond, Newport, Baltimore or Washington, where they went into their usual intense search for female companionship.

There was another change of destination on April 12 when Harold Washington's battalion was put on alert and then entrained to Greenville Army Air Base, Greenville, S.C. Greenville was the answer to a lonely soldier's dreams. It had an abundance of friendly, singular-minded women who would put Gen. Joseph Hooker's female Civil War camp followers to shame. The Greenville-area women were of the vintage to really know how to sing Cole Porter's standard, "Love for Sale." The lyrics to the Porter classic went as follows:

> Love---for sale, --------appetizing young love for sale. ----Love that's fresh and still unspoiled. Love that's only slightly soiled. Love----for sale.-----Who-----will buy?-----Who would like to sample my supply?---Who's prepared to pay the price for a trip to paradise? Love---for sale.

The hookers were permitted to operate on the campgrounds throughout the day and part of the night, apparently with official sanction. (Since the Civil War, "hooker" has been a synonym for prostitute.)

However, the racial environment was such that most of the men who had never been in the heart of the Confederacy were ready to give up the friendly warmth of the southern female companionship for the colder climate of the North.

Just prior to the surrender of the German government on May 7 and 8, 1945, U.S. troop strength was diverted to the Pacific in an effort to end the island-to-island guerrilla warfare with the Japanese. Unaware that an end to the European operations was imminent, the battalion to which Washington belonged received new marching orders April 26. Telegrams were dispatched to those men on furlough, supplies were packed, and the area cleared. Another cross-country trip was under way, this time going west. Washington and his fellow soldiers rode in Pullman cars on the troop train that passed through South Carolina, Georgia, Tennessee, Indiana, Minnesota, Montana, and Idaho before reaching Fort Lawton in Seattle.

Since no assignments awaited them at Fort Lawton, the men's idle minds began to wander but their thoughts never strayed far from a central theme: female companionship. Fort Lawton, unlike the Greenville camp, did not permit any women in the general area. However, there were some GIs who found a way to circumvent the post restriction.

On May 13, the battalion received its sailing orders. Amid the blare of the military band, and the friendly Red Cross workers passing out hot coffee and donuts, a lot of tearful soldiers boarded the U.S.S. Grant for a destination unknown.

The worst conditions that one could imagine about the troop ship U.S.S. Grant would, if voiced, be the understatement of the year. The quarters were closetlike, dirty and depressing. The food—ill-prepared, unappetizing in appearance and tasting worse—was no better. If it was the intent of the cook to make the men sick, he succeeded. The rocking motion of the boat caused many of the soldiers to be more miserable with bouts of sea sickness.

Blackouts on the U.S.S. Grant were a nightly occurrence that scared the hell out of the men who thought a Japanese air raid was imminent. The shrill peals of the practice alerts in total blackness did not make them feel any easier. Apprehension was ever present, even when the soldiers were gambling, watching a movie, or playing a friendly game of bridge below deck.

Rumors of land being sighted on the seventh day at sea were thick as flies over an open garbage can. Then, on the morning of May 22, Diamond Head, the famous clifflike structure at the entrance of Honolulu Harbor, loomed ahead. The land-starved soldiers hung over the rails of the ship like hungry dogs, eagerly anticipating their first look at a topless Hawaiian female wearing a skimpy grass skirt like those worn by Dorothy Lamour in her many movies about the South Sea islands.

The men were really disappointed when they did not see a single girl when they debarked, and they were immediately directed to board an open

Tent city in Kahuka, Hawaii, which was located at the end of an airstrip runway is where Harold Washington and his colleagues spent their time during their stay on the sunny island of the west.

train. The destination was a tent city in Kahuka, at the end of an airstrip runway. In addition to mosquitoes, the tents were skimmed day and night by B-24 bombers taking off for points west. The battalion had not been on the island a month when it suffered a tragedy. One of the oldest, and in many men's opinion, the most conscientious non-commissioned officers was reported missing. The clothes of Staff Sgt. Ryan J. Coleman, "A" Company supply sergeant, were found on the sands of the Princess Beach. His body was never recovered.

On July 15, the battalion moved to Hickam Field, which the Japanese rendered impotent on Dec. 7, 1941. There the supplies were checked and superfluous material was discarded. The trucks, jeeps and other vehicles were greased, painted and conditioned for the anticipated adverse conditions. Three land ship transports (LSTs) were assigned to the unit, and loading them commenced immediately.

On Aug. 6, the battalion boarded the ship and on August 8 they sailed. Rumors had the boat going everywhere from Sakhalin to Singapore. There were about 50 ships in the convoy, consisting mainly of LSTs, with mine sweepers and destroyer escorts playing a protective role. Secrecy necessitated a zigzag route, but the general direction was south by west toward the Solomon Islands.

The ships were much smaller than the U.S.S. Grant, but living conditions were 100 percent better. Some men occupied bunks below, others had improvised shelters on deck. One large tarpaulin and several smaller ones were used to shelter the deckdwellers from the weather. Others lived under

A letter from Harold Washington to his dad, dated July 3, 1944.

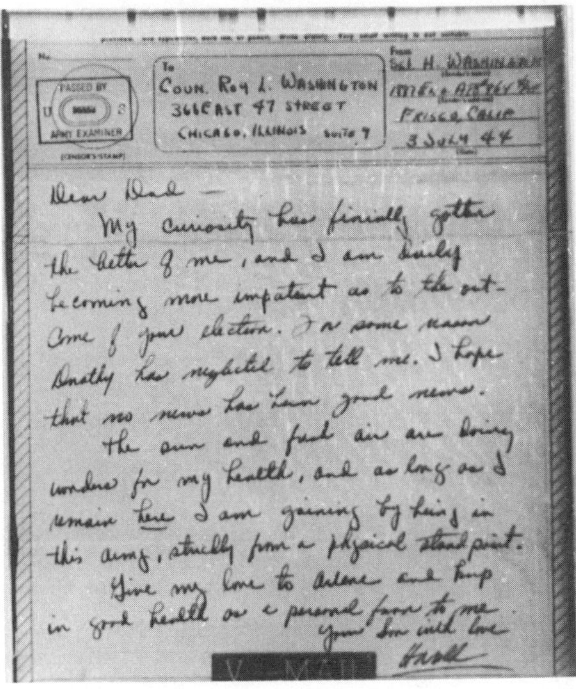
PASSED BY
ARMY EXAMINER
(CENSOR'S STAMP)

To
Coun. Roy L. Washington
366 East 47 Street
Chicago, Illinois Suite 7

From
Sgt H. Washington
Frisco Calif
3 July 44

Dear Dad —
My curiosity has finally gotten the better of me, and I am daily becoming more impatient as to the outcome of your election. For some reason Dorothy has neglected to tell me. I hope that no news has been good news.
The sun and fresh air are doing wonders for my health, and as long as I remain here I am gaining by being in this army, strictly from a physical standpoint.
Give my love to Arlene and keep in good health as a personal favor to me.
Your son with love
Harold

trucks that had been anchored to the deck. For diversion, there was the radio and gambling, but Tech 3 Harold Washington's time was consumed with reading. Books were handled gingerly and passed on; one particularly popular novel, *Sanctuary,* made a complete cycle of every reader on LST 737.

There were numerous submarine alerts throughout the voyage. Frequent practice in aircraft defense and nightly blackouts reminded the men that the game that they were playing was a deadly one. The deficiency of the salt-free water made rationing a necessity. Clothes were washed by the unorthodox method of tying them to a rope and trailing the apparel in the sea, letting friction do the work. There were occasional storms, but the nights on the Pacific were indescribably beautiful.

On Sept. 12, the men were assembled aboard their ships and given the long-awaited orders. The task force was to bombard and invade the islands of Pelelieu and Anguar, in the Palau Group, which were situated at the western extremity of the Caroline Islands.

The 1st Marine Division was to invade Pelelieu on the 15th. The 81st Infantry Division, of which T/3 Harold Washington was a part, was to move in on Anguar, the pear-shaped island on the southern tip, on the 17th. The island, which measured one mile wide and two miles long, was densely forested. The island's defenses were not enumerated. It was expected that the men would encounter a formidable force. And they did.

An invasion of the Phillipine Islands was in the making, and the division was to help pave the road for the invasion by building a bomber strip on An-

Harold Washington and his company, shown on an LST leaving Hawaii for destinations unknown in the South Pacific.

guar, jointly with the 1884th Engineer Aviation Battalion. The convoy arrived at its destination on the night of Sept. 14, 1944. Aerial and naval bombardments started the next day.

On Sept. 19, the task force's survey party began construction of the center line of the runway. Dock detail fell to Company "C," and Sept. 23 saw most of the men landed and part of their equipment unloaded, although a choppy sea created a hazardous blanket of water over the pontoon bridges. Bulldozers pulled equipment over the unstable beach.

A dense jungle growth about 500 yards from the proposed runway was cleared for the battalion area. Foxholes, command posts, and SU offices were immediately set up. Snipers, mosquitoes, humidity and heat, and the steady rumble of artillery made the night one long damnable hell. Everyone wanted a medic to sleep in or near his foxhole. Mingled with the wetness of the forest was the tangible stench of dead bodies.

By Oct. 15, the battalion that included Harold Washington and the 1884th Engineer Aviation Battalion had made the runway serviceable but by no means complete. A C-46 and a C-47 landed on the 17th of that month and the first bomber rolled the length of the strip four days later. For putting this runway in service in an incredibly short time of 20 days, the 1887th and the 1884th engineering aviation battalions received the meritorious Service Unit Award.

Although only half the Japanese on the island were accounted for, the island was declared secured Sept. 20. Those Japanese who remained were

Sgt. Wilbur Rice and Pvt. Bruce Dunn are buried with full military honors on Jan. 3, 1945, at the 81st Division cemetery on the island of Anguar.

bottled up in caves and gorges on the northwestern portion of the island. The infiltration, sniping and food pilferage were a constant worry and danger.

On Sept. 31, several men were seriously wounded by gunfire. Sgt. Wilbur Rice and Pvt. Bruce Dunn died in a hospital that night. They were buried with full military honors on Jan. 3, 1945, at the 81st Divisional Cemetery.

The battalion continued its work until the middle of February 1945, when it was ordered to prepare to move to Guam, in the Marianas. After surmounting the inevitable transport impediments, the troops boarded the U.S.S. Johnson on Feb. 27. The 1887th left behind it an impressive record embracing such completed triumphs as: completion of one runway, two taxiways, and 93 hardstands; erection of two tank forms; and one transit hotel ready for use. When the U.S.S. Johnson plowed away from the shores of Anguar on the morning of Feb. 28th, the men on board realized that they were leaving the scene of a successful mission.

Guam came into view on the morning of March 15, 1945, a cloudy day. The seemingly barren hills in the background gave the island a sinister appearance. Everyone was anxious to get off and give Guam the once-over. Tech Sgt. Harold Washington made the following statement:

> Shortly after we reached Guam, I was made acting first sergeant. It was one of those things. Talent was skimpy. I was the only soil techni-

The merit award was given to the 1887th Engineer Aviation squad for completing a runway in the record time of 20 days.

> cian in the entire area. They shuttled me from island to island periodically to test the soil. There had been a high mortality rate among soil technicians because they were getting bumped off. But I really didn't think too much about getting killed. I must have thought I was Emperor Jones and could only be wiped out with a silver bullet. (Washington roared with laughter after making this statement.)
>
> I did a great deal of structured reading while I was overseas. I must have taken at least 30 correspondence courses. Every 90 days I would report to the company warrant officer, who was our resident teacher for correspondence courses, to take a test in his presence on the material I had completed. I took almost every course listed in the catalogues: history, literature, chemistry, and a great number of English courses. I didn't take any physics courses because the Soil Technician School had been an accelerated truncated course in physics. I devoured all that material. Some people drink and chew gum; I read. All of my correspondence credits were mailed back to DuSable High School by the company warrant officer.

In the fall of 1945, at the time that 1st Sgt. Harold Washington was rushing through correspondence courses in the blazing sun over the Mariano Islands, his wife Dorothy Nancy was pursuing studies at Roosevelt College in Chicago, where she planned to become an elementary school teacher.

Dorothy Nancy frequently wrote Harold love letters in which his bride mentioned something about her academic progress at this new college founded

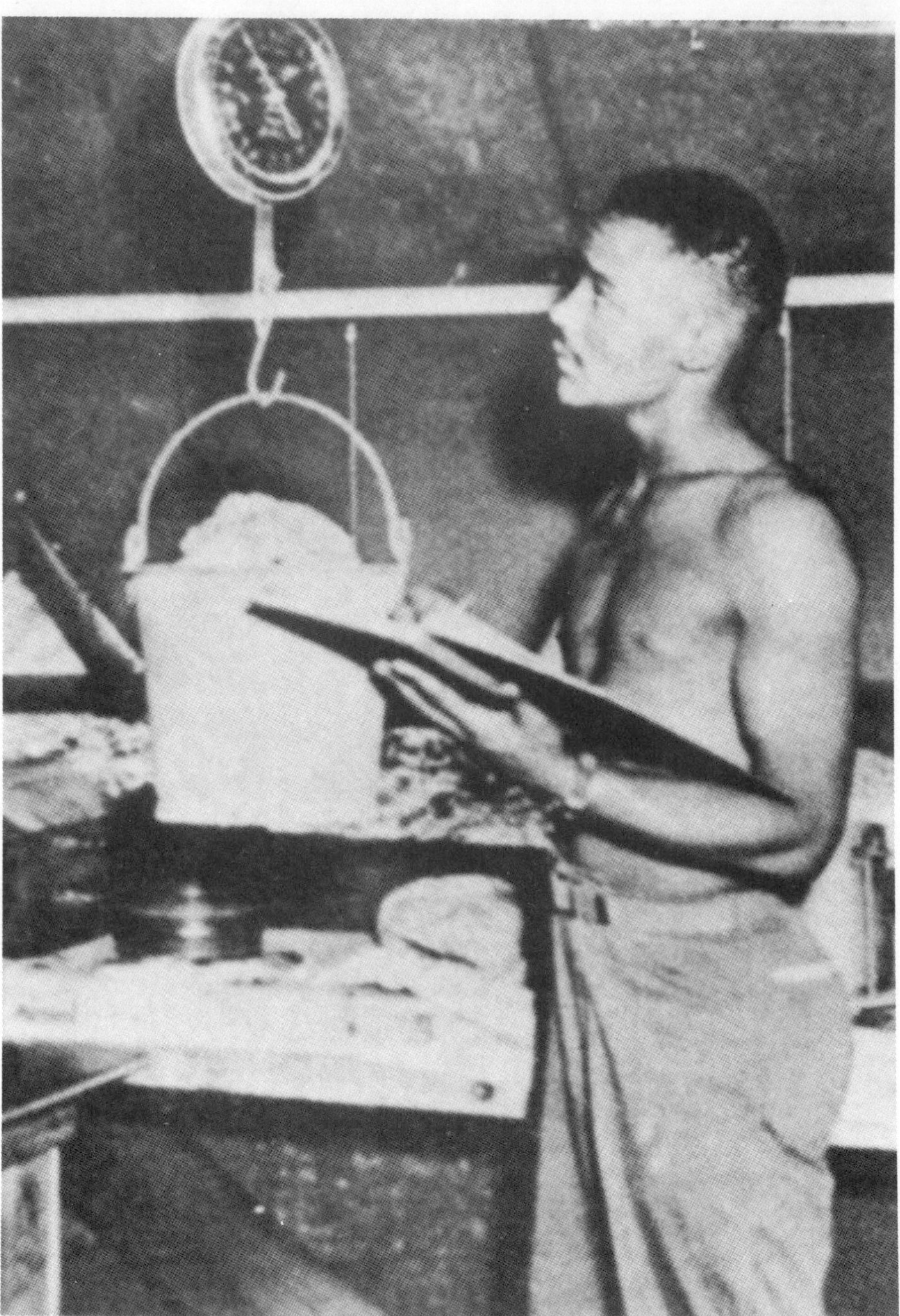

1st Sgt. Harold Washington of Headquarters and Supply Company in the 1887th Engineer Aviation Battalion performing one of his many tasks as a soil technician on the island of Guam in the South Pacific in April of 1945.

A picture of the headquarters and service company units of the 1887th Engineer Aviation Battalion, taken in Guam in November 1945. Standing at the extreme left in the first row is Acting 1st Sgt. Harold Washington.

without quotas for Blacks or other minorities. Harold salivated at the thought of a college without racial walls in his hometown. He cocked his hat to go there with the hope of using the newly passed Servicemen's Readjustment Act, commonly known as the G.I. Bill of Rights. The Servicemen's Act offered the veterans a living allowance, tuition fees, and money for books and supplies. In addition, there was the 52-20 Club, which allowed vets who couldn't find a job to collect $20 a week unemployment compensation for 52 weeks after getting out of the service.

On Jan. 20, 1946, 1st Sgt. Harold Washington was discharged from the U.S. Army. His first observations, after returning to "Sweet Home, Chicago," were:

> After staying in the tropical climate of the South Pacific for a very long period, I forgot how cold and mean the 'hawk' (wind) could be in Chicago in January. To my surprise, when I arrived home, I couldn't find any clothes. I walked around for several months wearing both G.I. and civilian garments because I couldn't find a suit, that is, one within my price range. After an extensive search, I was able to find some trousers and later a sports coat, never two things in the same store. For reasons that I could not understand, I didn't have any trouble finding an overcoat in my size at the Rothchilds' Clothing Store on South State Street.

Harold Washington accumulated enough credits while taking correspondence courses in the Army to qualify for three high school diplomas. He picked up his diploma in June of 1946, several months after he had started his course of studies at Roosevelt University.

Had I known that I was going to have such a difficult time finding clothes, I would have brought a duffel bag full of G.I. garments home with me and used them until I could make an adjustment from Army life to civilian life. The Army actually allowed a soldier 30 days after discharge to get out of uniform. However, I hated the Army with such a passion that I left everything that they ever gave me except the clothes I had on my back and toilet articles such as toothpaste, a brush and a comb. I don't know if I was ever totally acclimated to the regimentation of Army life.

Even before I found decent clothes to wear, I went directly to DuSable and picked up my diploma because I had covered enough academic material in the service to graduate from high school three times. My return to Chicago was paled because my brother Edward, who had been afflicted with leukemia since age 15, died at the age of 26.

AUTHOR'S NOTE

Although Harold Washington frequently stated that he never dreamed of being mayor of the city of Chicago, he never said that he was lacking that particular ambition. The author feels it proper to end this chapter with an article Harold wrote for an Army battalion newspaper when he was on Guam. The article, "Ambition," appeared in the Feb. 14, 1945, issue of the *New World:*

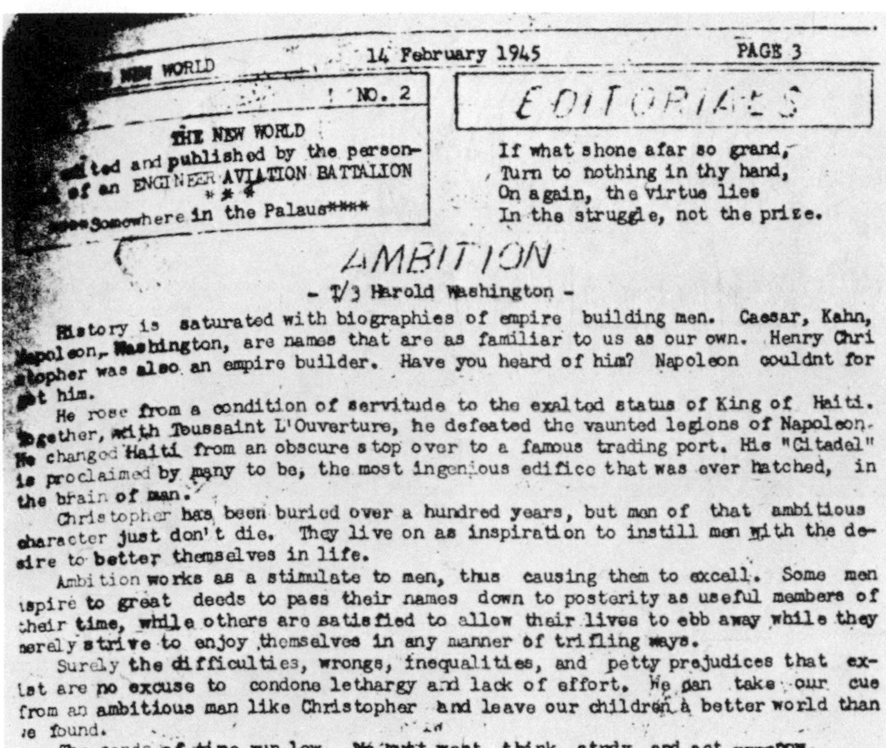

THE NEW WORLD 14 February 1945 PAGE 3

NO. 2

THE NEW WORLD
...ted and published by the person-
of an ENGINEER AVIATION BATTALION
* * *
Somewhere in the Palaus****

EDITORIALS

If what shone afar so grand,
Turn to nothing in thy hand,
On again, the virtue lies
In the struggle, not the prize.

AMBITION

- T/3 Harold Washington -

History is saturated with biographies of empire building men. Caesar, Kahn, Napoleon, Washington, are names that are as familiar to us as our own. Henry Christopher was also an empire builder. Have you heard of him? Napoleon couldnt forget him.

He rose from a condition of servitude to the exalted status of King of Haiti. Together, with Toussaint L'Ouverture, he defeated the vaunted legions of Napoleon. He changed Haiti from an obscure stop over to a famous trading port. His "Citadel" is proclaimed by many to be, the most ingenious edifice that was ever hatched, in the brain of man.

Christopher has been buried over a hundred years, but men of that ambitious character just don't die. They live on as inspiration to instill men with the desire to better themselves in life.

Ambition works as a stimulate to men, thus causing them to excell. Some men aspire to great deeds to pass their names down to posterity as useful members of their time, while others are satisfied to allow their lives to ebb away while they merely strive to enjoy themselves in any manner of trifling ways.

Surely the difficulties, wrongs, inequalities, and petty prejudices that exist are no excuse to condone lethargy and lack of effort. We can take our cue from an ambitious man like Christopher and leave our children a better world than we found.

The sands of time run low. We must want, think, study, and act ----now.

Above left: Roosevelt College was located at 231 S. Wells St. in 1945. Upper right: President Franklin Delano Roosevelt, who died April 12, 1945. Lower right: College President Dr. Edward J. Sparling and Eleanor Roosevelt, President Roosevelt's widow, at the college dedication ceremony in November 1945.

CHAPTER

4

The Roosevelt College Years Plus Three: 1946 to 1952

Harold Washington received his honorable discharge after serving 3 1/2 years in the 1887th Engineer Aviation Battalion of the U.S. Army. The sergeant was anxious to get back to Chicago to the taste, the sights and sounds of 47th and South Parkway (now King Drive), the crossroads of Black America. There is an old saying that if you stood on that once-famous corner during the 1930s and '40s for a single hour, you were bound to see people that you had not seen for years. The author found this to be true. For instance, it was on the southeast corner of that intersection, in front of a Walgreen Drug Store in February 1946, that Harold and I ran into each other for the first time after World War II.

It was some 37 years later, on April 23, 1983, that Harold talked with the writer about that era and commented on his separation from the military service:

> I had no problems at all getting my old job back in the bond department at the U.S. Treasury, which was located in Joseph Patrick Kennedy's Merchandise Mart Building. (Kennedy was the father of the late President John F. Kennedy.) The Chicago branch of the Treasury Department located on Wells at Wacker Drive was only a short hike to 231 S. Wells St., the home of the brand new Roosevelt College. I decided that I would see what the new school was like. After I got there and looked around, I said, 'Hell, this place is as good as any.' Although the structural facilities were a far cry from those at North-

western University, the democratic climate and spirit of the school's faculty and student body seemed unlike any other college or university within the confines of the 48 states.

Marian Despres, wife of former Alderman Leon Despres, remembers when Harold Washington enrolled as a freshman in Roosevelt College in February 1946. She describes the young man who enrolled in her introductory psychology class:

> I remember Harold clearly, and yet I don't remember very many students. Although he was not a physically big person, he had a presence you could not forget and a voice that conveyed an inner confidence and authority. As a teacher, you notice a student who talks up in class; but at the same time, he never talked too much. And he always made a great deal of sense to me.

Harold remembered Marian Despres' psychology class primarily because it was held in a makeshift classroom cram packed wall-to-wall with 50 to 60 students, most of them mature male World Ward II veterans with a "no-nonsense" attitude. He recalled that one afternoon after class, the teacher approached him and suggested:

> The student council is looking for members, and I would like for you to represent our class. I feel that you would make an excellent spokesman in that you would be able to articulate the sentiments of the other members of the class.

Washington's initial reaction to Mrs. Despres' suggestion was negative because he was holding down a full-time job at the Treasury Department and carrying a 16-hour class load. The professor prevailed upon him in her quiet diplomatic manner until he relented. Harold was elected to the student council, and remembers his initial bath in college politics:

> The bottom line was that with Mrs. Despres' support, I was elected to the student council with almost 100 percent of my classmates' votes, and that marked my initial involvement in student government at Roosevelt College. From the council, one thing led to another, and I got more and more involved in student activities. There was no resistance to it. It was the kind of stuff that I was concerned about. In the Army, I was always running lectures on government. I was the education officer, in effect if not in name, because the commissioned education officer was a southern white gentleman who could hardly read. Therefore, he turned the classes over to me, and I did a lot of teaching. I wrote the battalion's newspaper. I drafted the battalion's history. I was just involved in a lot of that kind of stuff. So the student council was sort of an extension. I don't recall any metamorphosis or awakening as a result of sitting on that student body.
>
> However, I must confess that the student council was my first sustained relationship with a large segment of white folk. Like most Black kids on the South Side, my relationship with whites was spasmodic, in-

Harold Laskey, a economist from the London School of Economics, was a visiting professor at Roosevelt University during the spring of 1948. He is shown with a group of student leaders. Left to right: Louis Roundtree, *Torch* reporter; Harold Washington, chairman of the Student Fund Drive; Irving Horwitz, editor of the *Torch;* and Ray Clevenger, president of the Student Council.

volving contact with the grocery man, the butcher, the streetcar conductor, the bus driver and on a job at a Jewish-operated summer camp job in South Haven, Mich.

After being inducted into the segregated U.S. Army, my relationship with whites was limited to white commissioned officers and an occasional contact with white enlisted men at the Army post exchange or in the post theater.

As a young kid, my only contact with whites was either to play ball with them or fight them in what we used to call gang fights. I developed a cosmopolitan attitude about race relations, although I went through the same kind of Jim Crow nonsense that most Black people experienced in Chicago. I lived in an incubator. The South Side was my world. I would get on my bicycle and ride all over the entire South Side and not come in personal contact with a single white person. I really never had any meaningful peer relationships with whites until I attended Roosevelt College.

In 1946, Roosevelt College was an island unto itself, a bold experiment in democracy in education. An open enrollment for Blacks had never been attempted at any non-Black college or university in America. The daring experiment occurred during a period when Blacks were not allowed to eat or sleep in a downtown hotel or any other place outside of the defined Black Belt. All Chicago restaurants outside of the ghetto were off-limits to Blacks, even the most greasy of the greasy spoon variety. The one exception in downtown Chicago was a lunch counter in a Woolworth 5 cents and 10 cents store located on the southwest corner of State and Washington. Even there, the writer learned later, they had special drinking glasses for Blacks. At an earlier period in the same "five and dime," they painted the "for Blacks only" drinking glasses red at the bottom in order to avoid serving whites with glasses that had been used by Blacks.

Louis Roundtree, a fellow student with Harold and the writer at Roosevelt College, recalls that if a couple of white kids and a Black kid were seen walking together along Chicago's State Street or Michigan Avenue, it was a special event. Some people would stop in their tracks, turn, stare and point their fingers at them as though they were freaks in a circus sideshow.

Roosevelt College was not a sideshow. It was the main event. The spirit of brotherhood that permeated the walls of that educational institution was unlike anything the writer had ever experienced. Every morning when I stepped inside those doors, I was enveloped with a feeling of hope for Black people in America. But each afternoon when I stepped outside onto Michigan Avenue to catch the #3 bus going south, I was jarred back into the realization that Roosevelt was not a mirror of the real world.

Some days I would walk north on Michigan to catch the bus in front of the main library on Washington Street. During some of those walks, I would look up at the tall, white-owned office buildings and say to myself, "Those buildings don't even have black smoke coming out of their chimneys." Sometimes, my mind was drenched with the thoughts of Blacks being systematically excluded from the world of commerce. There was ample evidence to support my feelings.

The racial climate outside of Roosevelt College was my barometer and the democratic atmosphere created by the faculty and students within Roosevelt was my thermometer. It was in this milieu, where the placid world of acadamia met the turbulent world of commerce, that Harold Washington's political star began to rise. In 1947, the stellar political science student and leader in student politics at Roosevelt College decided to get into the real world politics. Harold's father who was running for the aldermanic seat in the 3rd Ward.

There were eight aldermanic candidates in the ward that year: Roy L. Washington, Rev. Archibald J. Carey Jr., Oscar DePriest (former congressman of the First Congressional District), Edgar G. Brown (an early civil rights activist), Maj. C. Udell Turpin, Rev. B. H. January, Clinton A. Brown and Homer Lewis.

Third Ward Committeeman Mike Sneed was a hard-headed, tough and rough South Sider who possessed a lot of political savvy and street smarts but was so insecure that he was intimidated by the presence of educated blacks. The well-educated Roy Washington, the only lawyer in the 3rd Ward organization, asked for Sneed's support. Roy had paid his political dues through loyalty to the party and by hard work as a precinct captain, and felt he deserved endorsement from the ward boss.

Attorney Washington first wanted to be a municipal judge, but Sneed supported attorney Wendell Green for that post, and Roy was furious. In a final

ELECT
THE CANDIDATE WHO WILL SERVE YOU BEST!
V O T E for "Well-Informed" ROY J. WASHINGTON
Vote for Continued City PROGRESS
ELECT A FIGHTER . . . ROY J. WASHINGTON . . .
HONEST!
CAPABLE
If you want cleaner alleys . . . Better street lights
If you want to "go ahead" with progressive ideas
If you want a "Real" Representative of the 3rd ward
BY ALL MEANS . . . TURN OUT A HEAVY VOTE FOR
ROY J. WASHINGTON
He's The Man To Get These and Other Things Done
Endorsed by Third Ward Regular Democratic Organization
EDWARD M. SNEED, Committeeman
Election, Tuesday, February 25, 1947
YOU CAN GIVE HIM HIS SEAT ON THIS DAY

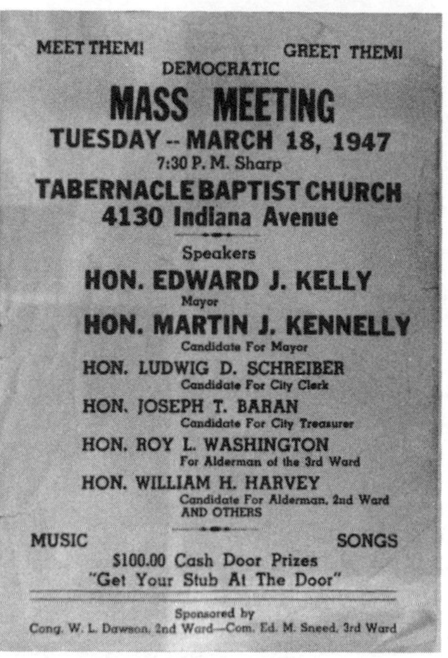
MEET THEM! GREET THEM!
DEMOCRATIC
MASS MEETING
TUESDAY -- MARCH 18, 1947
7:30 P. M. Sharp
TABERNACLE BAPTIST CHURCH
4130 Indiana Avenue
Speakers
HON. EDWARD J. KELLY
Mayor
HON. MARTIN J. KENNELLY
Candidate For Mayor
HON. LUDWIG D. SCHREIBER
Candidate For City Clerk
HON. JOSEPH T. BARAN
Candidate For City Treasurer
HON. ROY L. WASHINGTON
For Alderman of the 3rd Ward
HON. WILLIAM H. HARVEY
Candidate For Alderman, 2nd Ward
AND OTHERS
MUSIC SONGS
$100.00 Cash Door Prizes
"Get Your Stub At The Door"
Sponsored by
Cong. W. L. Dawson, 2nd Ward—Com. Ed. M. Sneed, 3rd Ward

Harold Washington passed out this campaign literature for his father.

effort to get some recognition in the 3rd Ward organization, Roy jockeyed around and, after a great deal of persuading and arm twisting, got 65 of the 90 precinct captains in the ward to support his candidacy for alderman.

In the February 1947 primary, Roy L. Washington polled 4,813 votes while the Republican candidate Rev. Archibald J. Carey Jr. was close on his heels with 4,427. The incumbent, Oscar DePriest, who failed to gain regular G.O.P. backing, polled 3,609. A protest vote of 2,331 went to Edgar G. Brown, and Maj. C. Udell Turpin, who was the husband of my third grade elementary school teacher at Willard, polled 1,066. Rev. B. H. January got 513 votes, Clinton A. Brown received 238 and Homer Lewis, 113. Roy Washington did not have the majority of votes, and was forced into a runoff election with runner-up Carey.

Al Benson, a popular radio disc jockey known as "the old swing master," became Roy's campaign manager. He got lots of help from the candidate's sons, who threw their efforts into the aldermanic campaign. Harold and Roy Lee divided 24 precincts between them. They did not bother to work the other ward precincts, which were Democratic strongholds they knew they had in their hip pocket.

Archibald Carey Jr. beat Roy Washington in the general election on April 1, 1947. Carey received 13,960 votes to Washington's 11,978. An analysis of

Present at the Democratic mass meeting held on March 18, 1947, in the Tabernacle Baptist Church were, (left to right) Roy Washington, mayoral candidate Martin J. Kennelly, the Honorable William H. Harvey (2nd Ward), Mayor Edward J. Kelly, Committeeman Mike Sneed and Congressman William L. Dawson.

Al Benson, campaign manager for Roy Lee Washington, and a popular disc jockey, is shown collecting a political contribution for the aldermanic campaign from Dinah Washington, an international pop and blues singer.

all precincts' votes revealed that Roy had been sold out by Committeeman Sneed, who got some 3rd Ward policy barons to bankroll the Carey campaign, and literally bought the election. Roy knew he had been double-crossed, and was spitting fire and brimstone. Harold described his father's post-election frustration:

> Although my old man was a minister, he started carrying a gun on his hip, and for a period of about three weeks, he looked for Sneed. I had

The Rev. Archibald Carey Jr. defeated attorney Roy Lee Washington by 1,982 votes in the 3rd Ward aldermanic election, which took place on April 1, 1947.

never seen him that mad in my life. I remember asking my father, 'Why are you walking around with that gun?' He knew he was not going to use it. Anyway, Sneed was out of town; I reminded my father that although he had spent $8,000 on the campaign that if he shot Sneed, it would take more than that to get him out of jail. My father intoned, 'I'm going to shoot him, Harold. I'm going to shoot him, Harold.'

Whenever my father called me 'Harold,' he was mad. When he wasn't mad, he called me 'son.' He repeated, 'I'm going to shoot him, Harold.' Finally, while Mike Sneed was still out of town, my old man cooled down. He went downtown and talked with Jacob Arvey, chairman of the Cook County Democratic Committee, and with Mayor Edward J. Kelly and told them that Mike Sneed had ripped him off.

When Sneed came back to town, several things happened. Jacob Arvey took the 3rd Ward committeepost away from Sneed, but let Sneed keep his seat as a Cook County commissioner. They made Sneed give my father $8,000 to repay what he spent on the campaign, and they temporarily released about 15 precinct captains. They put C.C. Wimbush in as the 3rd Ward committeeman early in the summer of 1947. No election was necessary. They simply shifted the patronage from Sneed to Wimbush. Sneed was finished as a power broker in the 3rd Ward.

Christopher C. Wimbush was anointed 3rd Ward committeeman by Jacob Arvey and received the blessings of Congressman William L. Dawson. Wimbush was a Dawson protege and former president of Dawson's 2nd Ward organization. With Wimbush as the 3rd Ward committeeman, Dawson was able

National Association of Delegates from Roosevelt College holding post-mortem on a convention held in Urbana-Champaign, Illinois, on Feb. 7–8, 1948. Members of the delegation: (left to right) Frank London Brown, Ray Clevenger (council president), Harriet Fishman, Harold Washington (council vice president), Charlotte Grossman, Sheldon Periman, Bernard Jaffe and Marshall Dickstein.

to control the patronage activities of the ward. Dawson's political troops then invaded the adjacent 20th Ward in 1948 and made Col. Kenneth E. Campbell the committeeman.

Following his father's disappointing political defeat, Harold immersed himself in student political activity at Roosevelt College. Only 10 months had passed before Harold got another opportunity to exhibit his political talents outside the college walls.

Harold was one of 10 delegates selected to represent the Roosevelt student council at the Illinois Regional National Student Association. The conference was held Feb. 7 and 8, 1948, on the campus of the University of Illinois in Champaign-Urbana. Frank London Brown, Ray Clevenger, Marshall Dickstein, Harriet Fishman, Charlotte Grossman, Bernard Jaffee, John Lewin, Sheldon Perlman, Phyllis Rappin, and of course, Harold Washington, comprised Roosevelt's representatives at the meet.

The knottiest problem facing the National Student Association that season was "securing and eventually eliminating all forms of discriminatory educational systems everywhere in the United States." Proposals presented by the University of Chicago and Roosevelt College were summarily rejected. A "bill of rights" suggested by the U of C was defeated; a substitute proposal by Ray Clevenger was not approved.

Despite the crushing defeats they experienced and the conservative trends taken by the association, the Roosevelt College delegates unanimously agreed that the student organization should be supported.

Harold Washington, undaunted, immediately jumped into the middle of the Henry A. Wallace for President campaign and took charge of a membership drive.

In late March of 1948, Drew Pearson, Washington, D.C. correspondent and radio commentator, launched a contest called, "How to Make Democracy Live." Ray Clevenger (who later became a Michigan state congressman) and Harold Washington, president and vice-president of the all-college council, issued a joint statement:

> At Roosevelt College, we see democracy living everyday. Our examples should furnish much material to Drew Pearson's contest, 'How to Make Democracy Work.' We urge all Roosevelt students to enter the contest so we can help others toward a better understanding of how education at Roosevelt College bears out the principles of democracy.

On Aug. 23, 1948, in Madison, Wisconsin, Harold Washington, president pro-tem of the Roosevelt College student council, was elected vice-president of the Illinois Region of the National Student Association at its first annual convention. His election took place after two days of debate on the methods of eliminating discrimination in higher education and on whether to affiliate with the International Union of Students. The Roosevelt delegation, led by Frank London Brown (who later authored the novel *Trumbull Park*), consisted of Marshall Dickstein, Jerome Gordon, Esther Grunsfeld, Wilberforce Jones, Judith Rawson, and Harold Washington.

Back in Chicago, elections to fill 40 seats in the Roosevelt College Student Council were held Oct. 14, 15 and 16, 1948, climaxing more than two weeks of pre-election debates. The pre-election assemblies were chaired by Harold or one of the other council members.

President Pro-Tem Harold Washington stated:

> The student council here at Roosevelt College enjoys a unique position in comparison with other colleges in the country. It has a greater area of discretion than most schools. It is necessary, therefore, that each student should be aware of this and attempt to maintain this autonomy. This can be done only by familiarizing themselves with issues and candidates and voting for those who they believe will best serve the college community. Any student who fails to do this has no right to censor the student council.

At the new council's first meeting in the fall term on Friday, Oct. 22, 1948, Harold was unanimously elected president. The other officers were Marshall Dickstein, vice president; Phyllis Rappin, recording secretary; Gloria Auerbach, corresponding secretary, and Stewart Schencker, treasurer. A total of 2,185 ballots were cast in the general election, representing approximately 36 percent of the student body.

The Dec. 6, 1948, edition of the *Roosevelt Torch* carried this story:

WASHINGTON CLARIFIES COUNCIL ISSUES

In a letter to Winston Kennedy, editor-in-chief of the Roosevelt College Torch, Student Council President Harold Washington stated, 'The student council appreciates the constructive interest that the Torch has taken in the council, and therefore, welcomed your criticism in Keylines of Nov. 22.'

Washington went on to say, 'However, certain clarifications are necessary in order to do justice to the council that is attempting to implement its stated policy. In the area of student conduct, the council has received needed assistance from the school authorities. The few students who insist upon violating the school regulations shall be made the target of an increment of insistent reminders of their obligations to the student community.

Additional facilities are needed and it must be realized, of course, that the solution of student conduct problems involves not only students' cooperation but also involves cooperation from the school authorities in the form of additional lounge and game room facilities. Such facilities would help solve the problems of crowded, noisy and littered hallways.

A statement by Washington, written or oral, got the attention of both the faculty and the students. Here's one example: Carlisle Bloxom was faculty advisor to the Roosevelt college theater, an instinctive conservative who would not cast a Black in a role that was traditionally played by whites. Winston Kennedy, an Irishman and editor of the *Roosevelt Torch,* took issue with Bloxom's position and wrote an editorial accompanied by a cartoon with a Nazi swastika. Displaying a swastika at a college with a predominantly Jewish student body was asking for trouble. Sure enough, Bloxom took the issue to President Edward J. Sparling and to the faculty senate. He recommended to both that Winston Kennedy be kicked out of Roosevelt College.

The Torch editor was figuratively half way out of the front door when Harold Washington came to the rescue. Washington prevailed upon the faculty senate and President Sparling to give young Kennedy another chance. The outcome was reduced, at the request of the President Sparling, to Kennedy writing a public letter of apology addressed to anyone who might have been offended.

Winston Kennedy, now a successful Hyde Park real estate executive, said, "Harold went to bat for me with President Sparling and the faculty. I have always been grateful to him for that because I think the issue would have tilted the other way without his help."

Harold Washington carried the Roosevelt torch for democracy across the street to a student bar-restaurant hangout called Anne's Rendezvous, which was located at 55 E. Congress St. During the 1930s and '40s, a popular pastime in bars was playing "26," a dice game that could be played for 25 cents. If you throw 26 in three tries, you won $3 in drinks. Washington was in Anne's at the time a Black student, Mildred McNary, was told by the "26" girl that she could not play because she was on a list of people not allowed to play the game. Ms. McNary stated that she had played the "26" before, but the dice girl ignored her.

Washington commented that, "Pat Jones, Bill Jones and I attempted to play '26.' And we were refused with the excuse that the '26' girl was going out for a cup of coffee."

Later that evening, a group of students were refused drinks at the bar because, according to the bartender, they had been drinking too much. Harold Washington disputed the bartender, contending, "No one had any liquor or beer except me."

Subsequently, four whites were served at the bar after the Blacks had been informed that the bar was closed. Rather than create a disturbance, Washington called the police. When the police were told that the bartender had refused to serve them, the officers replied, "Well, they don't have to serve you." Washington then cited the state statutes (Chap. 38, Sec. 125, 126 and 128 of the Illinois Civil Rights Act), which state that service must be given regardless of race or color.

The police then told the bartender to serve the group, which he did.

The following Monday, Washington and four students came to Anne's and requested that the dice girl be fired along with the bartender. The following day, Ralph Metcalfe, of the Chicago Commission on Human Relations, visited with George J. Annes, the owner of the bar. The "26" girl and the bartender were fired.

The Anne's incident was one of the last civil rights activities Harold Washington was involved in before graduating, along with the writer, in the Roosevelt class of August 1949. Washington's grades at Roosevelt were good enough to get him into Northwestern University School of Law, the alma mater of three Illinois governors, Adlai E. Stevenson II, Dan Walker and James R. Thompson, as well as U.S. Supreme Court Justice John Paul Stevens.

The thrill of the undergraduate years at Roosevelt ended when Harold Washington entered Northwestern Law School on Chicago Avenue. No longer was he the big cheese on the campus, no longer the top dog of the student council. The political science and philosophy courses gave way to constitutional law, torts, contracts, conveyances and moot court.

In the fall of 1949, Northwestern's traditional quota system was intact. Washington was the only Black among the 185 students in the freshman class of 185. Chicago treasurer Cecil Partee, a graduate of Northwestern School of Law, class of '46, and Illinois Appellate Court Judge R. Eugene Pincham, a member of the Northwestern Class of 1949, had been the only Blacks in their classes. Washington and Sen. Dawn Clark Netsch stood out in the freshman class of 1949 because she was the only female and he was the only Black.

Washington's law school grades, unlike his college grades, were average, but he was above average in perseverance, attending law school and holding down a job at the same time. Unlike most of the Northwestern law students who lived next door to the law school at Abbott Hall, Washington commuted

This snapshot was taken by the author in the late fall of 1952 shortly after Harold passed the Illinois Bar Examination. Standing in Mrs. Mittie Travis' kitchen from left to right are: Harold Washington, Gus Savage, Willie Wright and Lawrence Halliburton. Seated are Mrs. Travis, mother of Dempsey J. Travis, and Henry G. Fort.

daily from his home in his father's apartment building at 4941-43 S. Michigan Ave.

Going to school was not an easy load for Harold Washington in either undergraduate or law school. He had to supplement his $75 per month G.I. income in several ways. In his junior year at Roosevelt College, he was employed as a part-time assistant in the political science department, which was chaired by Dr. Jerome Watson. He was appointed a full-time assistant instructor to Dale Pontius, one of the college's brilliant political science professors, in his senior year.

Roy Lee Washington Sr. owned several small apartment buildings on Chicago's South Side and it was through working for their father that young Roy and Harold perfected their plumbing, plastering, carpentry and decorating craftsmanship. Harold Washington's paychecks were thin. So the Washington brothers started a decorating and maintenance service on the side. Harold launched his marketing program for their decorating service by advertising the Washington brothers' capabilities on the bulletin boards at Roosevelt College. Soon after, they were inundated with so much work that it was necessary for them to hire additional help.

During a moment of reflection, Harold said:

> We had a lot of decorating gigs. Wilberforce Jones and four or five other guys used to work with Roy and me on the weekends. We scheduled all our work for Saturdays and Sundays. We must have painted half of the homes on North Sheridan Road. In my second year of law school, we made good money.

In spite of his academic and work loads, Harold was elected and served as treasurer of the school's junior bar association. He soon learned that this position was a far cry from the power that he had enjoyed as president of the student council at Roosevelt College. The president of the junior bar association held the power and was the sole contact with the law school dean. The other elected officers simply kept their seats warm.

When Washington graduated from law school in 1952, his employment prospects were better than his father's had been when he received his law degree some 30 years earlier. The difference was that Roy Washington had to continue to work as a laborer in the stockyards after graduating from law school, while Harold had the opportunity to share a small law office with his father at 366 E. 47th St.

It was in that 47th Street building that Washington sat near the throne of politically powerful Alderman Ralph Metcalfe, who had offices directly across the hall. The proximity of those two offices played a big role in Harold Washington's career plans. Attorney Roy Washington frequently told Harold that he should hitch his wagon to Ralph Metcalfe's, because Ralph was young, ambitious and destined to go somewhere.

Left: William L. Dawson, U.S. representative of the 1st Congressional District and Ralph H. Metcalfe, alderman and committeeman of the 3rd Ward.

CHAPTER

5

Harold Washington's Official Political Beginning 1954–1964

Harold Washington had been practicing law for only a little more than a year when his father, attorney Roy Washington, died suddenly on Nov. 7, 1953. In one of their frequent father and son talks, Roy had strongly suggested several months earlier that Harold get to know Alderman Ralph Metcalfe better. Although Harold had unofficially worked with his father in the precincts under several 3rd Ward committeemen over a period of 16 years, he had never formally joined Metcalfe's 3rd Ward Democratic organization.

At age 31, Harold Washington had not really entertained any notions about becoming a professional politician, although his experiences from grade school through college seemed to lead in that direction. Politics was a game of chess with Washington, who took to politics and people movements like a duck takes to water. Throughout his life, Harold found working with and for people such a joy that he never really considered it a job. This probably explains why the man who was grounded in the Protestant work ethic said, "I had no particular interest in politics. As a matter of fact, I have never thought of it as a way to make a living."

Ralph Metcalfe, who was 43 years old, had other ideas. Just two months after Roy's death, Alderman Metcalfe called young Washington. "Harold, can you come across the hall to my office within the hour? I would like to talk with you about some business," he urged.

Harold retorted, "I am wrapping up some business on my father's estate and I will be free shortly."

Harold recalled, "The moment I stepped into Alderman Metcalfe's private office, he looked up from a stack of papers on his desk and asked, 'Are you going to take over your father's precinct and also take his job in the corporation counsel's office?' "

In deference to a father who had been his only hero, Harold accepted both the corporation counsel position and also became the precinct captain. He really didn't consider the precinct work a challenge because he had lived in the 3rd Ward all of his life and had done practically all of the precinct work for his father for the previous two or three years.

In 1954, when Harold went on the city payroll, the corporation counsel's job paid only $4,800, which was a little better than a pedestrian's salary. In 1988 dollars, $4,800 would be equivalent to $19,200 per annum. That salary would not enable Harold to live in the style that he had envisioned for himself, so he continued to practice law on the side.

Washington had worked barely three months in the corporation counsel's office when Ralph Metcalfe, his job sponsor, approached him with a new assignment. The alderman asked Harold to take over the 3rd Ward Young Democrat organization. Congressman William L. Dawson had told Metcalfe that Mayor Richard J. Daley wanted to rejuvenate the Young Democrats organization on the South Side and pool the talents of the young people from the 2nd, 3rd, 4th, and 20th Wards.

Actually, this was Mayor Daley's method for bringing disenchanted middle-class Blacks into the youth organization. Young Blacks from wards throughout the city and suburbs joined the 3rd Ward organization in order to work under the leadership of Harold Washington. By 1960, the youth auxiliary of the 3rd Ward had three times as many members as Metcalfe's 3rd Ward regular organization.

Within eight months, Washington had developed the 3rd Ward Young Democrats into the largest minority political organization in the city, with a membership of 3,000. At its annual affairs, the Young Democrats had a bigger turnout than the 3rd Ward parent organization. The youth group gave between $7,000 and $8,000 a year above expenses to the 3rd Ward.

In addition to running the youth organization, Harold was able to get out a very high percentage of registered voters in his precincts. Never farther down than the fifth-highest vote getter in the ward among the precinct captains, he usually ranked second. Occasionally, he outdistanced J.D. Jones, the fireball and the number one vote getter of the 3rd Ward precinct captains.

Attorney Washington was flying high among the precinct captains of his ward, and flew even higher on Wednesday evening, May 25, 1955, when he shared the dais with such heavyweights as Mayor Daley, Eleanor Roosevelt, and Supreme Court Chief Justice Earl Warren. Both Justice Warren and Mrs.

A picture of Harold and his father, taken in the fall of 1953, shortly before Roy Washington's death. Clockwise, third from left: Attorney Harold Washington: Jeannette Triplett Jones, his DuSable High School teacher; Arlene Jackson Washington, his stepmother; State Representative James Y. Carter; Beatrice Carter and Attorney Roy Lee Washington Sr.

Roosevelt received honorary degrees from Roosevelt University that evening. Justice Warren was presented with the honorary doctorate of law degree for his "vital contribution to the achievement in American society of equality of opportunity, academic freedom and democratic self-government." Mrs. Roosevelt was presented with a doctorate of humanities and lauded as a "eminent American citizen, who in times of uncertainty and crisis, spoke clearly for the principles of social justice and welfare." The occasion was Roosevelt University's 10th anniversary Founders' and Friends' Dinner held in the International Amphitheater at 4220 S.Halsted St. More than 3,000 persons attended the event.

Harold Washington recalled that delightful evening with a smile and these observations:

> I felt good that night for a lot of reasons other than the fact that I was sharing the dais with Mrs. Eleanor Roosevelt and Chief Justice Warren. Mayor Richard J. Daley was my seat mate. Daley had only been in office about six weeks.
>
> Actually, I worked for Daley in the city's law office. He didn't know me and I didn't expect him to. And I didn't know him, although I had worked for him in the campaign. So here we were sitting next to each other. We were making small talk when I was introduced to make my speech. I spoke on behalf of the Roosevelt alumni that night.

The text of Washington's speech was:

Left: Richard J. Daley, mayor of Chicago, April 1955 to December 1976.

Right: Attorney Edith Sampson, trustee of Roosevelt University and a close friend of the Daley family.

Mr. Chairman, Mrs. Roosevelt, Chief Justice Warren, distinguished guests, friends and founders. Tonight mine is a very pleasant task. It is pleasant even though Mr. Burnett cautioned me that I should not speak over four minutes. I could talk about this institution for days and days. But though it's a pleasant task, it's one which I approach with feelings of inadequacy. Because I feel that I might fail to capture the spirit, the warmth and the comfort and the feeling of brotherhood that I've found existing in Roosevelt University. But it is assumed, and correctly so, that the friends and founders, those who as Judge Campbell said, served by paying and paying and paying and paying ad infinitu-it is assumed that they have a right to know what a former student of this great institution feels about it. I would say that Roosevelt University represents to an alumnus an experience in democratic living. Roosevelt University was, I found, in the words of Justice Oliver Wendell Holmes, a 'small laboratory of democracy.'

Let me very briefly relate just what that experience is to me and many others like me. The cornerstone of Roosevelt University is, of course, equality of educational opportunity, not only in terms of admitting a student into the university if he can pass certain objective examinations showing that he has a potential for intellectual development. But this equality of educational opportunity permeates the entire university atmosphere. He finds on all levels of the university people reaching out to help him and assist him. People reaching out to fill whatever gaps they may have had in their backgrounds, which might retard them in their efforts to realize this ultimate development and thus be more useful citizens in our greater democracy. Students find it on the administration level. They find it certainly, to a vast extent, on the faculty level. And even yet, find it on a student-student relationship level. It's a catching, contagious thing. Everyone wants to help everyone else. There's a feeling about the university that no soul, no mind should be lost. And when people feel that way, surprisingly enough, very few minds are lost.

This feeling that you find, this feeling of equality of opportunity that you find in the university has certain definite advantages for the student. Advantages not only for the student who is helped, but also, I think, for the student who helps. One day that student, with this helping hand, this attitude, is able to develop an intellectual capacity to the utmost. And also, the student finds that another benefit accrues. And that is this feeling of identification, a feeling of belonging. Not only in this laboratory that I'm speaking of, but a feeling that this greater democracy in which the student must ultimately find a way and make a path, but this greater democracy reaches out, beckons, solicits the student to develop and come into this greater democracy and make whatever contribution is possible.

But, if to an alumnus Roosevelt University represents freedom of educational opportunity, it also represents something else, which Dr. Sparling has spoken of. It represents freedom of thought and expression. And this freedom of thought and expression, I found, was based on a belief by the administration and the faculty that a student with correct guidance from the faculty can wield a way through a mirage and mire of complicated ideas, facts and data. And also wield a way through conflicting ideals, ideal theories and come out unscathed and come out with a firm and a sturdy belief that the democratic way of life represents the highest form in which an individual could find personal expression and development.

In short, Roosevelt University represents to me, and other alumni like me, experience in democratic living. I think a student comes out of that institution with a firm grasp on certain concepts that are fundamental to our government. Equality of educational opportunity, freedom of expression are not merely names. They have substance and meaning-substance and meaning to take out into the community in which one must live.

So it is with a degree of humbleness and appreciation that I stand before you, the grantors, the friends and founders, the people who have made this experience in democracy possible to so many students over the past 10 years. It is on behalf of those students that I wish to say to you: I thank you for having made it possible.

When Washington sat down after making his speech, Daley said, "You are in the corporation counsel's office." Harold answered, "Yes." Then the new counsel and the mayor conversed more intimately.

Harold had displayed his best oratorical skills that night. The writer was a witness. If applause is a barometer, then everyone in the audience was pleased with his presentation. More than 1,000 Blacks were present that evening, and they seemed to be bursting with pride. They recognized that their neighborhood boy, Roosevelt University's first Black class president, was endowed with a talent for public speaking that could be matched with the best that America had to offer.

Washington did not have the slightest notion of the impact that his speech made on Mayor Daley until his first day back at work the following week. He recalls what occurred that day at City Hall:

When I went into work that Monday, John Melaniphy, the corporation counsel, called me into his office and said, 'Daley is interested in you. He really wants to put you out there.' I asked, 'What's wrong?' He lowered his voice almost to a whisper and mumbled, 'I'll tell you. Confidentially, the city's chief prosecutor is going to be replaced. I think Mayor Daley wants to groom you to be the city prosecutor.'

I was already in the prosecuting division. So sure as hell, for the next six months, I was transferred from one prosecuting section of the city to another, from narcotics to family court, and then to gambling court, all around. They were grooming me for the big job.

I had never quarreled with anybody, but my new position created a lot of animosity in the office. The white folk were trying to get me out because they thought I was Daley's favorite house nigger. I hadn't said a word to them other than, 'How are you feeling?' I hadn't even talked to Daley since the Roosevelt University affair.

The subtle harassment continued. They gave me a hard time. It was really rough in there. It was so bad I finally threatened Judge David Lefkovitz. He came into my office one day talking a lot of B.S. I asked him, 'What are you talking about?' And we got into a real argument. I threatened to throw him out of a closed window. He started yelling and screaming and folks came running into the office.

> Daley heard about the riff and sent attorney Edith Sampson to talk to me. Edith came down and said, 'Daley wants you to know he really likes you. However, you have got to get along with these dudes.' I yapped, 'I couldn't get along with the racist mothers.' I ran all the stuff down to her. Even as my confidant, I shouldn't have told her all of that mess, but I did anyway. And the harassment continued. Finally, after three years, I just left the corporation counsel job. I was young and unsophisticated.
>
> I didn't know how to handle those white folk. Instead of getting rough, I should have jumped cool and bypassed them. Maybe everything happened for the best, so I left in 1958. Daley was concerned. He called me at home one day and asked, 'What happened?' I thanked him for his concern and replied, 'I couldn't handle that thing. It's just not for me.' He wished me well and all of that.

The fact that Mayor Daley had directed corporation counsel Melaniphy to give Washington that special assignment in the city's law department placed Harold a long way up the ladder from the traditional Negro job track in the city law office. Harold's sharp intellect, no-nonsense mannerisms and infectious smile made him a professional threat to the white lawyers in the department. Harold's father had worked in the same law department for 20 years before his death, but Roy had the typical colored assignment of prosecuting attorney at the 48th and Wabash Avenue police station in the heart of the Black Belt. For Harold, three years in the corporation counsel's office were too many.

In 1959, Metcalfe made Harold his aldermanic secretary and appointed him supervisor of the precinct captains. Washington also worked 10 of the precincts himself and taught political science and government operation classes to the Young Democrats, as well as to older 3rd Ward Democrats.

The position of aldermanic secretary was not Washington's idea of getting the highest and best use out of his law degree, but he remembered what his father had told him about getting to know Ralph Metcalfe better. And no one gets to know the boss better between the hours of 8 a.m. and 6 p.m. than the secretary. Through his late father's eyes, Washington perceived the secretarial position as an opportunity to get an overview of the total political operation. Under different conditions, he may have seen the job as a step down, but the political and financial circumstances for Black lawyers in that period made it a step up.

In the summer of 1960, Harold Washington was elevated from the secretarial post, and was appointed an arbitrator with the Illinois Industrial Commission. His function was to adjudicate worker-management disputes involving personal injuries on the job. In effect, he was to serve as a judge without a robe. Lawyers representing the plaintiffs considered Washington to be a very fair hearing officer. He served in that post for four years.

During the period that he was an arbitrator, Harold also kept a guiding hand on the 3rd Ward Young Democrats. Under Washington's leadership, it became one of the most effective vote-getting machines in the city. The 3rd

First row: far left, David Bradshaw; third from left is Richard J. Elrod; Mary Ella Smith; extreme right: William Harris. Second row: third from the right is Margaret Ferguson. Third row: first left, Alvin Robinson; third from the left is attorney Harold Washington.

Ward gave Mayor Daley his largest plurality in the 1963 election. A large part of this success was attributed to Harold because 50 percent of the 3rd Ward regular Democrat precinct captains were products of his Young Democratic political training classes.

The youth organization grew so rapidly that Alderman Metcalfe imagined that it had become a threat to his power. Indeed, the 3rd Ward Young Democrats were beginning to take some independent forays against the white political establishment without Metcalfe's consent. They had challenged the predominately white Cook County Young Democrats, and beat them on more than one occasion. The young Black Democrats under Washington's leadership so dominated the county organization that the county chairman, David Bradshaw, screamed to Mayor Daley for assistance in getting the Blacks to slow down. Daley told Bradshaw, son-in-law of W. Clement Stone, to straighten up his act or resign. Bradshaw completed his term as chairman and was succeeded by Richard J. Elrod.

Sam Patch recalls that he first met the 3rd Ward's youngest political legend in April 1963 at a convention held by Cook County's Young Democrats organization. Patch had gone to see Alderman Metcalfe about getting into

Sam Patch, former administrative assistant to Mayor Harold Washington for Minority Business Enterprise Compliance, and currently director of Intergovernmental Affairs for Acting Mayor Eugene Sawyer.

politics, and Metcalfe had suggested that he go down to the Morrison Hotel and talk with Harold Washington. Harold was the campaign manager for William Harris, the current Building and zoning commissioner of Cook County. In 1963, Harris was a candidate for chairman of the Young Cook County Democrats. Patch vividly recalls his activities that evening:

> I went down to the Morrison Hotel at 9:30 p.m. that Friday night, and I knocked on door number 506. Harold opened the door, and I told him that Ralph Metcalfe had sent me down to see him. He responded, 'Fine. Who are you?' And I said, 'I'm Sam Patch.' We exchanged some pleasantries during what was known as a social hour among the young group, and then Harold told me to pick up some literature, go out in the lobby of the hotel and buttonhole everybody I saw.
>
> I said, 'What do you mean by buttonhole?'
>
> Harold recoiled, 'Just stop everybody you see and tell them how great Bill Harris is and that you would like for them to vote for Harris.'
>
> I followed his instructions and worked until approximately three o'clock in the morning. I then went back to Harold's room because I was tired. I said to Harold, 'I guess I'll go home.'
>
> Washington looked up from a stack of papers and said, 'Wait just a minute. The politicking has just started.'
>
> And I said, 'But it's three o'clock.'
>
> He replied, 'That's when it starts. Now, if you want to be a politician, I'm going to teach you how to be a politician. Now we are going to politic. We're not going to sleep!' I stayed with Washington, talking and buttonholing people until 6 a.m. It appeared to me at that early hour we had everything buttoned down. I told Harold that I was going home and that I'd see him early that afternoon.
>
> He said, 'Oh, no! I want to see you back here between 8:30 and 9:00 this morning.' This was a Saturday. He reminded me that the election was going to be held that evening.

Patch remembers the thoughts that kept returning as he travelled home on the southbound Englewood Express El, "I don't want to be bothered with this. This guy, Harold Washington, is crazy. What is wrong with this man? Here I am just a young Democrat. This ain't even the big stuff, and he's already got me working around the clock."

When Sam got home, he took a half-hour nap, showered, shaved, changed clothes and returned to the hotel where he witnessed a master lesson in politics.

Washington almost succeeded in pulling off a coup that afternoon. He had set up a deal with the Young Democrats from the 2nd, 3rd, 4th, and 20th Wards to support a white state president if they, in turn, would change the constitution of the Young Democrats' organization to allow the first vice president to automatically become chairman in the next term. This, of course, would ensure that Bill Harris would succeed Richard J. Elrod as chairman. When Harris reflected on Washington's master plan of 25 years ago, he had a broad smile on his face:

> Harold had pulled together a package that was going to put the first Black in the seat of the chair. We had counted heads and knew exactly who was going to support our resolution. We had the numbers. I will never forget when we read the resolution, Eddie Rosewell, who was taking the minutes, almost fell off of his chair because he knew passage of that resolution would block his opportunity of becoming the next chairman. Elrod, the chairman, immediately called for a recess. The chair prevailed, and so the recess was in order. From that point on they used every technique known to man to try to get us to kill our resolution. They even called their committeemen, who in turn called us in an effort to get us not to vote on that resolution. The credentials of our delegates were challenged. When they discovered that they could not turn us around, they adjourned the meeting. Although we had the majority in that room by head count, the chairman had the prerogative to adjourn the meeting because he simply called for a voice vote as opposed to a roll call. The 'ayes' had it, and the meeting was adjourned. Elrod supported Eddie Rosewell because Rosewell had supported him when he became chairman.

Sam Patch remembers Washington's emotional response to the ruse of the young white Democrats who couldn't stomach the thought of Harris as their county chairman only because he had the wrong paint job—he was Black.

This was the first time in his life that Sam had seen a Black man stand up in a public meeting and call prominent white folk racist. Washington shouted, "You don't play the game by the rules. When we get in the game, you change the rules."

Harold was pointing his finger at men who are now some of the biggest political names in this town. Patch recalls, "I was very nervous. I had never seen or witnessed anything like that. Here was a Black man in a white hotel pointing his finger and shaking his fist at white folk during a period when

A group of Young Democrats in a moment of joviality. Left to right are: attorney Harold Washington; Richard J. Elrod, chairman of the Cook County Young Democrats; Clifford Kelley; Bill Harris and John Stroger.

they were calling Blacks 'colored' to their faces and 'niggers' behind their backs." Before Harold Washington closed his nominating speech for Bill Harris, he told the group:

> I will never appear before the Cook County Young Democrats again. This is my last time. I've been in this organization for a long time. I've worked hard. We have paid our dues. We have come up through the ranks. We've done everything you've told us to do. Our ward, the 3rd Ward, is the number one ward, the top ward in the state. We have won national recognition. Now when it comes our turn, this man, Bill Harris, who has served so diligently, is not acceptable.

Patch recalls that Harold's speech was very emotional:

> You will not change the rules when it's our turn. You will accept us for our worth. Now, if you don't vote for Bill Harris this time, don't look for me to come back anymore.

Although Harold Washington never attended another Cook County Young Democrats' meeting, he continued to monitor and teach the Young Democrats in his ward. He told the young Blacks that staying active in the Young Democratic organization was important. He explained that the Cook County organization was the training ground for white folk who were preparing to ascend the organizational ladder. Before Washington came on the scene, Blacks had treated the youth group as a social club. He turned that social club around and made it a training ground for political action.

Bill Harris followed Washington's advice and stayed in with the Young Democrats because he was determined to become the chairman of their county organization. Harris voiced his strategy:

State Sen. Charles Chew Jr., the first Black independent Democrat to beat the Daley machine in an aldermanic race.

I went to Eddie Rosewell, the current treasurer of Cook County, and told him if he would support me for chairman in the 1964 election that I would in turn, support him. Eddie agreed. We spent 1963 pulling everybody in line. If I had not been elected chairman in 1964, it would have been an embarrassment, not only to me but to the total party if the members had selected somebody else. There was no way they could bypass me without embarrassing themselves totally. And they knew I would walk, and that I wasn't controlled by the party because I didn't have a political job.

There was no way they could come to me and make a switch by saying that they would give me something better if I waited a couple more years. I was in a position where they pretty much had to accept me. I have to give Harold Washington credit for engineering this election because he was the one that was giving us the cues and guidelines. We all spent many, many hours in his law office after we left the Cook County Young Democrats' meetings figuring out strategies for putting together a package that would make it possible for a Black to become chairman of the Cook County Young Democrats. I served two terms and was succeeded by Alex Seith.

By 1962, Mayor Daley began to suffer from the same paranoia that had inflicted Metcalfe, a phobia about the latent power of the young Black democratic organization. Daley, the wise one, sent down word that he wanted the

Young Democrats to disband. In the spring of 1963, the mayor witnessed the reality of a Black independent political movement when Charles Chew ran against a white machine candidate in the 17th Ward and was elected alderman. The once-invincible wall of the Daley machine had been cracked.

Chew's election came a year after Washington had withdrawn from formally participating in the activities of the Young Democrats. However, he still acted as an advisor to the group behind the scenes. His low-profile activities pleased Metcalfe, but the alderman seized the opportunity to send Washington to Springfield to replace State Rep. Kenneth Wilson, who had been elected to a seat on the Cook County Board. Metcalfe felt that Springfield would put a comfortable distance between him and Washington, the man he viewed as a potential rival. With Washington away from Chicago, Metcalfe would have ample opportunity to lasso and co-opt the Young Democrats organization. And he did.

State Representative Harold Washington, a freshman member of the House, standing in front of the Illinois State Capitol in the spring of 1965. A statue of Abraham Lincoln looms in the background.

CHAPTER

6

Harold's Elected to the Illinois House (1965–1976)

On Jan. 6, 1965, Harold Washington was sworn in as a legislator in the Illinois House of Representatives in Springfield, Ill. Washington and 176 other Democratic candidates for House seats had a free ride to Springfield on President Johnson's bandwagon in 1964 because the Illinois legislators had failed to reapportion themselves. Lyndon Baines Johnson carried the entire Democratic ticket in Illinois in his presidential landslide.

In 1964, the federal court had ordered candidates for all 177 seats in the Illinois state house to run at-large. The '64 election was called the "Bed Sheet" election because the ballot was so long. Adlai Stevenson III, grandson of a vice president and son of the former Illinois governor who was the Democratic presidential candidate in 1952, led the state Democratic ticket. Washington came in 40th in a field of 177 candidates. The Democrats won 117 seats in the House of Representatives and the Republican ticket, which was headed by Earl Eisenhower, brother of the former president, captured 60 seats. Washington's seat mate in that assembly was Stevenson, another freshman in the "class of '65."

In the 1960s, it was customary for all of the Democratic members of the House and the Senate to receive a daily paper for which they had not subscribed. The paper was called an "idiot sheet" by some of the independent members of those bodies because it listed the state House and Senate bills scheduled for consideration that day and indicated how the respective party officials should vote on each bill. A legislator who was not from a strong independent political base such as the 13th or 24th Legislative Districts and failed to follow the "idiot sheet" to the letter, more than likely would not be reslated to run in the next election. (The 24th included the liberal 5th Ward in Hyde Park, which was the political home base of Sen. Richard Newhouse and State Reps. Robert Mann and Abner Mikva.)

Harold Washington's 3rd Ward, by no means liberal, was historically a part of Mayor Richard J. Daley's plantation. Harold's ideals of being an independent, nurtured at Roosevelt College, were dashed early in his legislative career. But, Harold did not fit the mold of a typical Daley political cotton picker, and found ways to bend and twist the plantation boss' rules. Years later, Mayor Washington, reflecting on his early days in the Illinois House, said:

> Adlai Stevenson was more independent than I or anybody else down in Springfield. He came in at the very top of a ticket with 176 candidates trailing him on the "orange ballot" of 1964, whereas I came in number 40, which was not bad considering it was the first time I had run for public office. I had no name recognition and even more miraculous was the fact that it was an at-large statewide election.

Adlai Stevenson recalls:

> Well, Harold Washington was a maverick, but not totally, because he was also dependent on the Democratic organization for support. I frequently saw the agony and tension in his face as he wrestled with the notions of what he wanted to do and what the Chicago machine wanted him to do. Harold turned to me one day and said, 'I'm very envious of you because of your total independence.' His observations helped me to understand the difficulty others were facing. It also made me realize Harold Washington was somebody who was going to work for the people and do everything within whatever the limits were to represent his own conscience. Nothing that Harold has done since those early days has come as a surprise to me.

Washington's stands in the Illinois House, and later in the state Senate, were no surprise to Congressman Gus Savage, for they had been friends since their college days. Congressman Savage stated:

> Washington was a freshman in the House when his committeeman and alderman, Ralph Metcalfe, along with Mayor Richard J. Daley, conspired to get Dr. Martin Luther King to leave town. Harold's stomach must have churned at the sight of that kind of activity because he is a principled guy and a well-read intellectual.
>
> Harold's heart also bled when his committeeman Ralph Metcalfe initially joined Daley in supporting (Edward) Hanrahan after the (Fred) Hampton-(Mark) Clark murders. Harold was against that kind of skullduggery because, in my opinion, in his heart he has always been with the people. Harold was independent by inclination and he knew the kinds of things which the Democratic machine was doing were wrong.

Adlai E. Stevenson III, former state representative, Illinois state treasurer, U.S. senator and a candidate for governor in both 1982 and 1986. He is the son of an Illinois governor and grandson of a vice president of the United States.

Gus Savage, U.S. representative of the 2nd Congressional District, and a classmate of Harold Washington at Roosevelt University.

He had been personally wronged by the way the machine had treated his father. And he, too, had been held back because any white boy with Washington's qualifications for operating in the political arena would have been high on the political ladder by the time Washington put his foot in the state house for the first time. On the other hand, he was afraid to become an all out independent because he felt he could not win an election without the support of the Third Ward Organization.

Black members of the 77th Illinois General Assembly. In the front row (left to right): Sen. Fred E. Smith, State Reps. Corneal Davis, Richard Newhouse, Kenneth Hall and Cecil Partee. Second row (left to right): State Representatives Richard A. Carter, Robert L. Thompson, James A. McClendon and Lewis A. H. Caldwell. Third row (left to right): State Representatives Elwood Graham, Otis G. Collins and Genoa S. Washington. Fourth row (left to right): State Representatives James Y. Carter, Harold Washington and James C. Taylor. Missing from the photo session were Senator Charles Chew Jr. and State Representatives Raymond W. Ewell, Isaac Sims and Eugene M. Barnes.

In 1969, Washington, Lewis Caldwell, Ray Ewell and Calvin Smith organized a Black caucus in the House of Representatives. The Chicago Democratic machine was definitely opposed to Black folk getting together for anything other than to dance. Congressman William L. Dawson was one of Daley's best dancers and he called the tunes that kept the other Blacks in step doing the hucklebuck. Lewis Caldwell put it bluntly, "Two-thirds of the Blacks in the House and the Senate failed to join the caucus because they feared losing their patronage jobs at City Hall."

In spite of the Democratic machine's opposition, Harold led the charge for a Black caucus in the House. He was definitely a legislative maverick in Springfield and one of Daley's best political soldiers in Chicago. He never confused the two roles.

It was also in 1969, near the end of Washington's second two-year term, that he ran afoul of Mayor Daley by digging into Chicago police affairs. Renault

Robinson was head of the Afro-American Patrolman's League. Daley considered Washington's alliance with Robinson on a bill for a Police Review Board to be the height of political subordination. The mayor relayed that message to Alderman Ralph Metcalfe in very strong language.

> Ralph Metcalfe, in turn, went to Harold Washington and said, "The Mayor wants me to dump you."
>
> Washington asked, "Why?"
>
> Metcalfe retorted, "You know why. You are messing around with the Police Department."
>
> Washington recoiled, "What do you mean? I'm cleaning the mother up. What did you tell him?"
>
> Ralph replied, "I told him that if he wanted to dump you, he would have to do it himself. I wasn't going to do it."
>
> Washington bristled, "You're inviting him to my behind, man. You should have told Daley to get lost and that I was your man."
>
> Ralph retorted, "I did the best I could."
>
> "Hell, you left me out there," Washington rebounded.
>
> After a brief pause in the conversation, Washington turned to Metcalfe and bellowed, "I will call Daley!"
>
> Ralph rose from his chair and said, "You can't call Daley; he won't talk to you."
>
> With a quizzical look on his face, Washington asked, "How do you know?"
>
> Ralph responded, "I know he won't. You should understand that elementary psychology, Harold. The boss won't talk to anybody other than another boss."
>
> Washington fired back, "You got your white man, and I got mine."

After the conversation with Metcalfe, Washington called Jack Touhy, speaker of the House, and said, "Jack, Daley has asked Ralph Metcalfe to dump me."

Touhy responded, "Hell, I told you to leave that goddamn police stuff alone. You just won't learn. I will take care of it."

That single call to Touhy ended the first in a series of dump-Harold Washington episodes. Ralph Metcalfe did not understand why Daley's thunder and lighting subsided, and later asked Washington, "What happened?"

Harold replied, "I don't know."

However, Harold did know he owed a debt to Jack Touhy.

Friends like Touhy, Cecil Partee and Metcalfe were often busy bailing Harold out of political trouble because Washington continued to fight for Black causes. Harold, the major advocate for Black rights in the House of Representatives, never learned how to be a complete "Uncle Tom" in the usual 20 easy lessons.

On May 11, 1971, when Vice President Spiro Agnew addressed the Illinois General Assembly, Harold Washington succeeded in getting 10 of the 20 Black members of the Illinois legislature to join him in a boycott against

Jack Touhy, speaker of the Illinois House of Representatives, and a man who fully appreciated the legislative talents of Harold Washington.

Agnew. Harold declared the vice president was, "anti-Black, anti-student, anti-peace, and anti-poor. He's like the Klu Klux Klan, he's anti-everything."

In spite of Washington's "Peck's bad boy" behavior in Springfield, he was an integral part of Richard J. Daley's plantation machine when in Chicago. Harold ran his precinct in the 3rd Ward like a czar and was one of the brightest and the best in the Democratic organization. He survived as a maverick in Springfield because many of his political peers respected him as a person and liked his political style and integrity. More importantly, his sponsor, Metcalfe, kept a protective arm around him because Harold was the nerve center for many of Ralph's programs. In addition, Washington was an excellent legislator who served the party well in that capacity. On 11 occasions, his colleagues voted Washington one of the top 10 Illinois state legislators. Moreover, the precinct captains in Metcalfe's 3rd Ward organization loved him.

Harold Washington summed up his relationship with Metcalfe and the Third Ward:

> Metcalfe and I were never close. It wasn't his fault. Ralph tried to effect a friendship but we were just two different kinds of people. I was his main recruiter. I brought a lot of people into the organization. However, I always told them the same thing. I said this man Metcalfe is a good role model for a while. I said he is thoroughly disciplined. He has good work habits, he's precise, he's strong-willed, but don't

> hang around too long. He will screw up your mind. Although we had our personal differences, I was a loyal member of his organization.

Washington's loyalty was certainly demonstrated in 1971 when Alderman Metcalfe was elected to Congress and his aldermanic successor was chosen. It was at the time of the succession that the 3rd Ward Organization started eroding. Washington described the scenario as follows:

> I don't know why Ralph supported Tyrone Kenner. I will never know. I didn't want the job. I was in the state legislature then. Anyway, irrespective of why he did it, it hurt his organization. There had been a lot of guys in the organization who could have been aldermen. For example, Gaylord Lott or Charles Freeman. Oh, you can forget Charles Freeman because he certainly wasn't going to move back into the 3rd Ward.
>
> My preference was Sam Patch. A lot of people in the 3rd Ward liked Sam. I didn't like aldermanic work. Moreover, Sam was a loyal member of the organization.
>
> Ralph faked me out. I will never forgive him. I was chairman of the executive committee and I had to go to Springfield for something. It wasn't something I couldn't come back for. Anyway, I went to Springfield and I told Helen Powell (Ralph's secretary), 'If anything breaks, call me, particularly when they get down to selecting Ralph's successor.'
>
> A rush meeting was called by Ralph Metcalfe before I reached Springfield and I never received a call from Ms. Powell. Kenner was voted in. I was blue.
>
> I knew Kenner. He had never been a member of our organization. Didn't nobody know him. It crippled our organization. Everybody got to grumbling, but you know how political organizations are. You grumble but you don't do anything. I was pretty upset. I remonstrated with Ms. Powell.
>
> There was a little chill between Ralph and me. He just simply abused the good officers of the organization and told them that he wanted Kenner. Had I been there, I would have said no and we would have argued. He would have won and that would have been the end of it. He didn't do that. He didn't give me a chance to argue. He just hit and run.
>
> Ralph later asked me to support Kenner and I said, 'I am not going to do that. I'm going to fight it and I'm not going along with your program.' As a matter of fact, I went out and helped Sam Patch raise money and also helped him organize some community support. However, I told Sam, 'I'll do anything for you but I'm going to shut you out of my precinct because that is my job.' Sam got 14 votes in my precinct and Kenner got approximately 300.

Although Washington was in total disagreement with Metcalfe's selection of Kenner, he delivered his precinct almost 100 percent for the organization. In addition to being loyal to Metcalfe, Harold harbored hopes of Ralph becoming the champion for Black people:

I always looked upon Ralph as the guy who could break the back of the machine and straighten it up. In other words, I thought he should have been more assertive. I felt that Ralph could have made history in those days and he was the guy to do it.

I didn't know it, but deep down, I was getting ready to get out of the machine. I just wasn't happy with it. I didn't like the system. I didn't like the way we were pushed around. I didn't like a lot of things. I just wasn't satisfied.

When I began to resent what was being put down, I looked upon myself as one of the 'Toms.' I didn't have any policymaking position in the Democratic party. My influence, such as it was, was designed for the 3rd Ward and the Cook County Young Democrats and things like that. But I was not a part of the system. I just couldn't live with it anymore.

Ralph, I guess in retrospect, was the avenue through which I could express my resentment against a system which I felt was unfair. When he decided that he wasn't interested in breaking the system, and he had every right to do so, I resented it.

There was an interesting side note to Ralph's selection of Kenner. Kenner was the first to defect. He went over to Daley. Daley got the message to bankroll Kenner and they set up a totally new organization and transferred all the patronage from Metcalfe to Kenner. A transfer of power from Metcalfe to Kenner simply represents another illegal transition of power in the 3rd Ward. There was never a legal transition of power in the 3rd Ward up until I became mayor. It's interesting that in 1947, (Christopher C.) Wimbush co-opted Sneed. In 1952, Metcalfe co-opted Wimbush. In 1972, Kenner co-opted Metcalfe.

Chicago politics generally, and 3rd Ward politics in particular, would not allow Washington to be too reckless with his political career. On occasion, he straddled the fence or simply got lost when he could not conscientiously support a Chicago machine-sponsored bill. On three bills that the Independent Voters of Illinois considered critical, he simply acknowledged his presence in the House and did not vote yea or nay.

The three bills were: no fault divorce, a bill that was sponsored by Catholics who opposed divorce in any form; the restrictions of abortion rights, another Catholic-supported issue; and the protection of rape victims in trials. These are examples of some instances when Washington could not vote against the machine, but could not vote for the bill. The decisions not to vote against the Daley establishment lowered Washington's rating as a legislator in the eyes of the Independent Voters of Illinois in the following years:

1967	rank	3
1969	rank	9
1971	rank	13
1973	rank	33
1975	rank	42

Not taking a position on some bills was tantamount to twisting in the winds for the liberal-minded Harold Washington. Overall, his voting record was a long way up from those legislators he used to refer to as being at the bottom of the barrel on civil liberties and civil rights issues. Washington was not a legislative mechanic by no means. He was considered by his colleagues to be one of the most creative of the breed.

In 1965, Harold was in the forefront of a political fight to reform consumer credit and won. In 1969, he introduced a bill to make Dr. Martin Luther King Jr.'s birthday a holiday. It passed in both the House and the Senate but was vetoed by Gov. Richard Ogilvie. He submitted two other bills over a period of four years to memorialize Dr. King's birthday. The second, which passed the House and Senate and was signed by the governor, simply made King's birthday a commemorative day when the Illinois public schools would give recognition to his accomplishments. Rep. Washington explained the importance of the bill after it was passed:

> This legislation accomplished two things: it honors a great American, and it attempts in a small way to fill a gap in our school curriculum which has given little recognition to Black Americans. Recognition of Dr. King by the children of Illinois represents a great public honor and the continuation of his role as a symbol of morality, dignity, and integrity. For the Black community, this new holiday provides a means of creating a sense of pride and dignity and honor in the Black children that is so necessary for every child.

The saga of the King birthday bill is best told by its chief sponsor. State Rep. Harold Washington said:

> The first year we filed a state-wide King holiday bill, I was unable to get it passed because there was a tremendous resistance to that form of recognition to Dr. King at that time. I therefore amended the bill and provided for a commemorative holiday for Dr. King to be celebrated by all school children in the state through appropriate ceremonies on Dr. King's birthday. It was the only such commemorative holiday in the country.
>
> With the help of such people as Harold Charles, Farragut High School teacher and head of Operation Breadbasket's teacher division, and Sam Patch, we were instrumental in getting the state superintendent of public instruction and Dr. James Redmond (superintendent of Chicago Public Schools), to send out directives to every school in the state together with a proclamation setting up guidelines for the commemoration of Dr. King in all public schools. To that limited extent, the commemorative holiday law must be considered a successful innovation. It did not satisfy Black folk's legitimate demands for recognition of Dr. King.
>
> Nor were we satisfied with a commemorative holiday. And so, in 1971, I again filed bills for a state wide holiday in memory of Dr. King. At that time, I incurred no resistance in the House nor did Sena-

tor Partee in the Senate. Legislative attitudes had changed. Unfortunately, Governor Ogilvie, pursuant to some extremely bad advice, refused to sign the bill into law. He amended it to provide that Illinois would celebrate Dr. King's birthday only if it became a national holiday. I refused to accept Ogilvie's amendment because the southern-dominated Congress, as well as many northern bigots, are not about to make Dr. King's birthday a national holiday. Do you know that Abraham Lincoln's birthday is not yet a national holiday? And you know why!

At first, I could not understand why Ogilvie could commit such a blunder. Then the answer occurred to me. We had not taken time to alert the brothers to zero in on Ogilvie.

Nevertheless, I was incensed with Ogilvie's position and made no bones about it when he ran for re-election in 1972. Since he was defeated by only 75,000, I'd like to think that his refusal to sign the King holiday bill was instrumental in helping to bring about his defeat.

We then come to the present King holiday bill, maneuvered through the House and Senate, through the Washington-Partee effort, to Governor Dan Walker's desk. I did not think he would make the same the mistake as Governor Ogilvie. However, I decided to muster as much public sentiment for a King state holiday as possible, to involve all who wished to be involved.

Three weeks prior to the bill reaching the governor's desk, my staff circulated petitions throughout Chicago in hopes of acquiring 50,000 signatures on the petition urging Gov. Walker to sign the King holiday bill into law. The response was terrific, and with the cooperation of such organizations as Operation PUSH, Kennedy-King College, approximately 300 ministers and business establishments, the bill was signed by the governor on Sept. 17, 1973.

In the final analysis, controversial legislation is not passed solely due to the efforts of even the most skilled legislators; it is passed and signed only when there is respect for and fear of those who stand behind the elected officials-you, the people.

The third bill to have Dr. King's birthday declared a legal holiday in Illinois got full passage with the assistance of State Sen. Cecil A. Partee. When it was signed into law Sept. 17, 1973, by Governor Daniel Walker, Illinois became the first of the 50 states to officially declare King's birthday a legal holiday. As chief sponsor of the legislation, Harold Washington had written a page in civil rights history.

In 1973, the year that Dr. King's birthday was declared a legal holiday in Illinois, Rep. Lewis A.H. Caldwell (D-24) was inspired to place the name of Rep. Washington (D-26) in nomination for the office of speaker of the House of Representatives. Caldwell said, "Harold Washington, during his four terms in the House, has emerged as an articulate, constructive spokesman for progressive legislation." In justifying his proposal, Caldwell argued that:

Gov. Daniel Walker, signing the Dr. Martin Luther King bill on Sept. 17, 1973, while State Representative Harold Washington, who sponsored the bill, observes.

> At this junction in history, the Illinois House needs a leader of strength, dedication, knowledge and compassion. Washington has demonstrated a deep-seated appreciation for the Democratic process and can direct those affairs without fear or favor.
>
> During his legislative career, Washington has been in the forefront to uplift the quality of life for all people. Equal opportunity, protection for witnesses in criminal prosecutions, voting rights for youth and equal opportunity for all sexes. This was characterized as his legislative input. He also has advocated decent housing and meaningful education, consumer protection and greater employment opportunities.
>
> It is now time to elevate to the highest policy-making position in the Illinois House a person from the state's largest minority group. In my opinion, Washington possesses all the necessary qualifications to be speaker.

Harold Washington's taste for legislative reform ran the gamut from the Fair Employment Practices Act to providing protection for witnesses in criminal prosecution, from opportunities for small minority business contractors to reform of the Currency Exchange Act, from the passage of a state Human Rights Act to the enactment of a bill to save Provident Hospital, one of Chicago's oldest Black institutions, with a $15 million grant.

Cecil Partee handled most of Washington's bills when they came to the Senate. "Many of Harold's bills had something to do with affirmative action. The Senate was deaf on those kinds of bills unless they were shepherded

State Representative Lewis A. H. Caldwell, a member of the Black Caucus, nominated Harold Washington for speaker of the House in 1973.

through by someone with political savvy and who could make the case," Sen. Partee said. In most instances, Partee was the man who made the case.

In 1985, Chicago City Treasurer Cecil Partee, in a retrospective mood, commented:

> Harold was an excellent legislator, very dogged and determined all the time. Many of the things he wanted were considered controversial by the political establishment. For example, when Harold Washington and some others organized a Black caucus, I did not join because I did not think it would be kosher for me to do that, being the leader of the entire Senate and segregating myself into a Black caucus. But be that as it may, there was no doubt in my mind about Harold Washington's ability to lead in causes in which he believed.

Mayor Harold Washington, while sitting in his living room with a glint in his eyes and a broad smile on his face in 1985, explained Partee's involvement:

> Having Sen. Partee handle my bills was the best thing going. For one, we were both from the 26th Legislative District. Secondly, he was the majority leader in the Senate, and he subsequently became the president of that body. By the same token, I handled most of his bills in the House-not all of them because some had to be handled by the House leadership.

Harold Washington is remembered by both friends and foes in the Illinois House of Representatives as a hard worker and as a person with an unabrasive demeanor. He is also remembered as a legislator who, in the heat of

Attorney Cecil A. Partee, former president of the Illinois State Senate and currently Chicago city treasurer, shepherded most of Harold Washington's bills through the Senate.

debate, maintained the aplomb of a seasoned diplomat. He never permitted himself to get into screaming and wrestling matches on the floor of the House. He usually put on kid gloves when he found it necessary to knock heads because he never wanted to leave his protagonist with a headache to remember him by. Like his father Roy, Harold could be as hard as steel or as soft as butter, depending upon the occasion.

Representative Harold Washington debating before the Illinois House of Representatives against a bill that would ban picketing on public streets.

CHAPTER

7

1976: Harold Graduates from the Illinois House to the State Senate

By 1976, Harold Washington bore a multitude of political scars that were camouflaged by his infectious smile and laid-back, all-is-well-with-the-world attitude. Behind his pleasant disposition there was a man with a no-nonsense commitment to a fairness that was alien to the Chicago-style politics. His duplicitous role as a Democratic machine hack in Chicago and a political independent on most issues in Springfield took a mental and physical toll.

On legislation involving civil rights and civil liberties, Harold voted independently. He was in the forefront in the fight for the equal rights amendment, a bill to strengthen FEPC, consumer advocate bills and legislation for public aid recipients. Although these bills were not considered a threat to Chicago Mayor Richard J. Daley, the dyed-in-the-wool Democrats would not vote for them until they got the signal from the fifth floor in Chicago's City Hall.

Daley demanded that the Chicago delegation play by the machine rules and march lock step through the legislative labyrinth. Washington was expected to vote according to the daily idiot sheet on such issues as no-fault divorce and abortion, which were opposed by the Catholic-dominated machine; the establishment of a statewide probation system, which would have eliminated the juice that flowed to the pocketbooks of city and county officials; exemption for some public officials from incriminating disclosures; and on a ban on picketing on public streets. Harold objected vociferously to the latter bill as a violation of civil liberties and an attempt to eliminate street demonstrations such as those organized around the activities of Dr. Martin Luther King Jr. in Chicago in the 1960s.

Washington's conscience would not permit him to vote for the anti-demonstration bill, yet with his political umbilical cord tied to the Daley political machine, he could not vote against it. This dilemma caused him to take what Ralph Metcalfe described as "one of Harold's famous walks out of the statehouse doors to get lost before the roll was called."

Congressman Washington was troubled by the compromising roles he had to play to stay in Daley's political arena, and was disgusted with himself because he was neither fish nor fowl. In 1974, he saw an opportunity to break out of the political prison by encouraging his mentor, Rep. Ralph Metcalfe, into a mayoral contest against the last of the big-city plantation bosses, Richard J. Daley. Harold envisioned that the time had come for the Black community to fracture the chains that bound them to the outhouse of the plantation. He also felt that Metcalfe should seize the moment to lead the grandchildren and great-grandchildren of former slaves out of political bondage.

With a great deal of perseverance, Washington managed to push Metcalfe to the plantation boundary. However, when Ralph looked back over his shoulder at the guts of the ghetto, all he saw were a few troops with empty rifles, very little money to enlist mercenaries and no hope of winning the battle. Metcalfe hastily retreated to the safety of his position as congressman in Illinois' First District, the district Harold Washington viewed as America's largest post-antebellum reservation.

Harold was deeply hurt by Ralph's retreat. The Committee for a Black Mayor, chaired by attorney James Montgomery, president of the Cook County Bar Association, viewed Harold Washington a prime mayoral candidate, but Washington deferred the honor to Metcalfe in a statement before the committee on Sept. 14, 1974:

> I am greatly honored and highly appreciative of the opportunity to meet with you this morning. I consider your invitation to meet with you in order to consider me as a candidate for mayor of the city of Chicago, under the sponsorship of the Black community one of the crowning achievements of my career. There is no way in which I can adequately thank you individually and collectively. I am aware of the fact that I ran well in the name-recognition survey you conducted, and I would like to believe that those votes were earned. I would like to think that those votes came as a result of my work and productivity in the General Assembly in Springfield, not from the electronic and print media. I would like to think that the support of the people came from their knowledge and belief that I have been a servant of the people.

In July of this year, I read a column entitled "Daley Machine Black Target," in which syndicated columnist Victor Riesel wrote about the Committee for a Black Mayor. And although Riesel is not one of my favorite journalists, he did quote Mr. Charles Hayes as saying '. . . we're rousing the Black sleeping giant. After all, we are one of the two basic supports of the Illinois Democratic Party . . .' I agree with Mr. Hayes that the Black voter in Chicago represents the potential political power to turn this city around, in fact turn this state around.

Again, I commend you all for your foresightedness in forming this group, taking the survey and interviewing those individuals who you believe have the basic qualifications for becoming the first Black mayor of our city. You are to be congratulated.

I am known in many circles as an independent machine politician. Frankly, I take a great deal of pride in that title because it explains how a Black person can be within the party structure and still be a man who represents the interests of Black people. Some years ago, the Chicago League of Negro Voters, in a pamphlet called *Freedom Now,* described this phenomenon as 'intraparty independence.' Their postulate was that a Black person within a political party could be in a better position to deliver than an 'independent' as long as the party politician concerned himself with the needs of his community. In spite of the regular party line, he could be more effective than someone outside of the organization. This has been the role I have attempted to play during my years of public service.

I would venture to say that the most effective candidate to oppose Mayor Daley in the upcoming race is a man who can attract support from those Black voters who respond to the leadership of persons who are not primarily politicians. In other words, the candidate must appeal to the regular organization people as well as the independent voters, the Black voter, the white, and the Latino, the old and the young, and both sexes.

Another factor that I hope we can agree on is that name recognition is an extremely important item. Many of the bush league, instant-replay political analysts who were yesterday's front room revolutionaries have criticized this committee's progress to me. I always asked them what have you done for the group. If you can't help them, leave them alone. Black folk don't need arm chair quarterbacks. Many of these people say it is too late to put together a campaign for a Black mayor. Under ordinary circumstances, I might agree. But when the candidate has good name recognition among the entire community and when he can inspire confidence and trust because of a proven record that will bring financial support, I say it is not too late if this committee is serious.

Let me quote Riesel again: 'Political realists predict Hayes' committee won't dent the Daley machine. But how much can the committee shake the entrenched labor-Daley establishment, as Hayes puts it?'

I would like to beg your indulgence for a few more minutes because I am trying to make myself clear as possible. This is the reason I wrote this statement, because if something was lost to you doing this brief meeting, I hope you will pick this document up again and peruse it.

I am a person who fits most of your criteria, and I am one of the leaders in the survey, so I am going to take some liberties I hope will be taken by you in good faith.

Until a few days ago, I was wrestling with the idea of seeking the high office of mayor of Chicago because I felt that I represented to a large degree the concepts mentioned above. In other words, I am able to draw votes from the regular voters as well as the independents. I have good name recognition, I meet most of the committee's criteria, and my record of public service is as good, and in some cases better, than any other person being considered.

After discussing the pros and the cons with some of my political advisors, we arrived at a decision that the man who fits the bill better than I do is Congressman Ralph H. Metcalfe. He has an illustrious record of public service. He can draw support from the regular voter and the independent voter. He can get support from the white, Latino and Black communities. He fits the criteria of this committee. It is my considered opinion that Congressman Ralph Metcalfe is your best candidate.

Let me repeat that I consider myself a servant of this committee, and I would be hard-pressed to say no to a legitimate draft. But we are all interested in promoting the empowerment of Blacks in this city and throughout the nation. Based on that premise, I say let's go with our best-Ralph Metcalfe.

In view of my support of Congressman Metcalfe, I do not think that any consideration of me as a prospective candidate for mayor of the city of Chicago is necessary, but I will wait upon the will of this group.

I will also strongly support any candidate selected by this group because I respect its judgement. If I may beg your indulgence, I would like to refer to the Riesel article a last time: 'This isn't militant Black power, clenched-fist street horseplay . . . This is sophisticated power-block politics.' I buy it. If you have any questions, I would be glad to answer them.

Less than two months after Metcalfe declined to run under the banner of the Committee for a Black Mayor, he endorsed Alderman William S. Singer for the Feb. 25, 1976 Democratic mayoral primary. Metcalfe said, "I have broken with Daley and his regular Democrats because, despite their promises over the past 20 years, we Blacks in Chicago have remained the nation's most segregated and have suffered all the resulting plagues of systematic discrimination."

Metcalfe added:

I am endorsing 43rd Ward Alderman Bill Singer, a white, over the only Black candidate in the Democratic mayor's race, State Sen. Richard Newhouse, because I do not support Newhouse's position on several is-

> sues. I can't conceive of a man running this city who doesn't support the ERA. I considered Richard Newhouse a friend but would not support him just because he is Black. On the other hand, I believe Singer can win this uphill battle against Daley with my help in the Black community. His record is clear. He has always cast his votes in the City Council for human rights and civil reform.

Daley quickly dumped Ralph him from the regular Democratic ticket and threw his support behind Erwin France for the congressional seat. Metcalfe, in turn, joined the enemy camp of Gov. Dan Walker. The mayor characteristically attempted to appease the Black community by selecting Cecil Partee to run against William Scott, the Illinois attorney general. On the surface it appeared that Daley was moving Partee up. In fact, he was moving him out of the statehouse because there was no way Partee could beat the popular Bill Scott, the Republican's highest vote-getter in the history of the state.

Since Washington and Partee were both from the 26th district, Harold saw the mayor's move as an opportunity for him to move up to the state Senate, but making that move was not a simple matter. Washington was despised by Mayor Daley, "the anointer," because of his quasi-independence and the frequent bouts he engaged in, which were in contraposition to the Daley regulars in the Illinois legislature.

Mayor Daley never forgave Harold Washington for his open defiance in 1975 when he ran a symbolic race for Illinois House Speaker against the mayor's man, political veteran Clyde Choate of Anna. The balance of power was so evenly divided between the Cook County Democrats and the downstaters that a single vote could tie up the House of Representatives' ability to organize itself for long periods of time. Washington had only two votes, his own and Lewis A.H. Caldwell's, but he held out for 92 ballots before swinging his thin balance of power to the little-known William Redmond, the independents' candidate from Bensonville.

Redmond rewarded Washington with the chairmanship of the Civil Judiciary Committee. The thwarted Daley was hellbent on punishing Washington for his audacious behavior. The mayor's refusal to give any consideration to Washington as Partee's successor spurred Harold to outmaneuver the old fox by persuading the United Auto Workers Union to support him in a run for the state Senate. The UAW officials went directly to Daley. They threatened that if Daley didn't support Washington, who had a superior labor record in the house, they would have no choice but to support Harold on a Metcalfe-Walker ticket. Daley hated Walker and Metcalfe more than he detested Harold, but he was too proud and arrogant to acquiesce.

Finally, Sen. Partee interceded on Harold's behalf. "The mayor was not enamored of Harold," said Partee. "In fact, he wanted anybody but him. But I insisted. Harold was a competent, articulate and concerned legislator. And I felt like I should be followed by someone who would do a good job."

Daley knew that he owed a basket full of favors to Partee, the powerful

William A. Redmond, Bensenville, Ill., became speaker of the House when Harold Washington swung his votes to him in defiance of Mayor Daley's orders to vote for the political veteran from Anna, Illinois, Clyde Coate. Redmond subsequently rewarded Washington with the chairmanship of the Civil Judiciary Committee.

20th Ward committeeman, so he granted Partee's request. Harold ran for the Illinois state senate in the March 16, 1976 primary against Alderwoman Anna Langford, and won by approximately 2,000 votes. Therefore, Washington, who was not opposed in the November general election, got a free ride.

In analyzing her defeat, Langford said she was "cheated by the Democratic machine. Washington called himself an organization liberal but whatever he was, he's not now. He's heavily indebted to the machine to the point where I doubt he can really do much on his own.

"They spent a lot of money to beat me," Langford said. "I have been very strongly anti-Daley. I have been very critical of the organization and they don't like that."

Unlike Anna Langford, Sen. Cecil Partee was not angry about losing the Illinois Attorney General race to Bill Scott. But he was "miffed," he said, because he was not appointed to fill the State Treasurer's position vacated by Alan Dixon.

At a press conference, Partee contended that he had sacrificed an almost certain re-election to the legislature, where he had been the senate president, to make an unsuccessful race for Illinois attorney general. He believed he should have been given more consideration by the party leaders for the treasury post. Partee also indicated at the press conference that he would be available to run for Chicago mayor.

Illinois Treasurer Alan J. Dixon, elected Secretary of State in November 1975, had the option of resigning before Republican Governor-elect James Thompson took office or waiting until the last minute before the inauguration to vacate and letting Thompson name his successor. Dixon took the latter course and Thompson appointed Donald R. Smith, a DuPage County Republican and chief fiscal officer in the treasurer's office under Dixon, to finish the two years left on the unexpired term.

In the author's opinion, Partee's empathy with Harold Washington, despite their differences, was based upon their common Black experience under a Democratic party that has historically been unfair to minorities. How else can one explain how a man who had served the party as faithfully as Cecil Partee could be bypassed as state treasurer for the benefit of a Republican?

Four members of the Black Caucus discuss strategy on the floor of the Illinois state Senate: (left to right) Senators Richard Newhouse, Harold Washington, Kenneth Hall and Earlean Collins.

CHAPTER

8

The Opening Volley of the People's Movement in the Battle for City Hall

Richard J. Daley died Dec. 20, 1976. He had been mayor of Chicago for 21 years. Within hours after Daley's death, racism in its rawest form was unmasked through the vicious behavior of some white majority members in the Chicago City Council.

Alderman Wilson Frost, president pro tem of the City Council, thought that the conventional constitution procedure would have automatically elevated him to the position of acting mayor. On the evening that Daley died, Frost announced that he was the acting mayor of Chicago. He was the first Black to claim that post. William R. Quinlan, the city corporation counsel, disputed Frost's contention and said there was no specific statute outlining the order of succession. The City Council must elect an acting mayor from its membership, he ruled.

Alderman Frost rebutted:

> I am the mayor of Chicago because of the way the law is structured in Illinois. All municipal bodies must have continuity. When Mayor Daley died, I was the only person who had the power to call a meeting. And as the president pro tem, I am the only person who can preside over that meeting. Therefore, I am, in fact, the mayor until the City Council holds its first meeting to elect one of its members as interim mayor.

After Mayor Daley recovered from a stroke two years ago, he called me into his office and said, 'If I had died, you would be here now,' meaning that I would be sitting in the mayor's chair.

Daley's political old guards symbolically spit in the face of the Black community when they directed members of the Chicago Police Department to forcefully turn Frost away from the door of the mayoral suite at City Hall when he presented himself as the acting mayor. The party hacks did not want the Black alderman to even entertain the notion that he was the chief official of the City By the Lake.

The Black community was furious over the treatment Frost received at the hands of the City Hall storm troopers. Political activist Gus Savage[1] fueled the flame of the Black political movement by insisting that the time was ripe for a Black mayor of Chicago. Savage said to Wilson Frost:

> You have the right credentials, and there's a momentum in the Black community to support your candidacy. If you give me permission and your word that you will stand up to the end, I'll go out and mobilize the entire Black community in your behalf. You won't have to lift a finger or spend a dime.
>
> Frost is said to have agreed.

Savage also recalls:

> On Wednesday evening, December 22, the people who crowded into the Roberts Motel's 500 Room were a mixture of regulars and independents. They did not believe that Frost was going to come until I brought him through the back door. Frost did not want to come through the front door because there were a large number of reporters out there, and he didn't want to answer any questions.
>
> On Thursday morning, State Sen. Harold Washington (D-26), State Sen.-elect Earlean Collins (D-21) and I went to Alderman Edward Vrdolyak's office and attempted to persuade him to support Wilson Frost. The meeting erupted into a shouting match with Vrdolyak screaming, 'You are not going to come and threaten me in my office!'
>
> On Monday, December 27, at 11 a.m., Harry Golden, of the *Chicago Sun-Times,* called me at home from the press room at City Hall. 'What's your rationale for Frost not running for mayor?' he asked.
>
> I replied, 'That's not what he said at a public meeting we held at Roberts Motel last Wednesday.'
>
> Bob Lucas was at my house when Golden called. We immediately organized a delegation that included Renault Robinson of the Afro-American Patrolman's League; Tommy Briscoe of the Coalition of Black Trade Unionists; and Ed Smith and Danny Davis, of the Westside Coalition for Unity. We went directly to Frost's office at City Hall, where we confronted him.
>
> I said, 'I heard that you have decided not to run for mayor. If that is

[1]U.S. Congressman 2nd District of Illinois, elected in 1980, whose term ends in 1990.

the case, you're going to embarrass us because we have organized to have the City Hall chambers packed tomorrow.'

Frost replied, 'You got me wrong, Gus.'

I retorted, 'Remember, all I asked you to do man is to stand up.'

Frost snapped back, 'That's right. And I intend to stick with my promise.'

Shortly after one o'clock that day, Rep. Metcalfe met with Alderman Frost. Metcalfe told reporters when he came out of the meeting that Frost had not agreed to a compromise. The white lawyers who were present when Metcalfe spoke to the reporters said that Frost had reached an accord. Frost's lawyer, Jerome Torshen, said Frost had shaken hands on a deal. Reverend Jesse L. Jackson, founder of Operation PUSH, visited Frost later that Monday afternoon with another delegation of Blacks and later told reporters, "There's no deal. Frost just told me he had never agreed to a deal."

"If it's true, you couldn't even print my reaction," State Rep. Jesse Madison (D-21) told a reporter following a jam-packed meeting held in a meeting hall at Daniel Hale Williams University, 5247 W. Madison St. "But I don't believe it's true."

In fact, an agreement had been reached the day before in a 7 1/2-hour closed-door session involving members of the late mayor's palace guards. The meeting took place between two casts of characters in separate offices who bargained by telephone for the choice leadership positions in the post-Daley era. At the City Hall, 129 N. LaSalle, were Corporation Counsel Quinlan, patronage chief Thomas R. Donovan, Aldermen Fred B. Roti (1st) and Michael Bilandic (11th), who was the council's finance committee chairman. In the law offices of Alderman Edward M. Burke (14th) down the street at 39 S. LaSalle, were Burke, Aldermen Wilson Frost, Edward R. Vrdolyak (10th), Vito Marzullo (25th), Terry M. Gabinski (41st) and two of Frost's lawyers.

After the political air cleared in mid-evening one smoky Sunday, everybody seemed set for a smooth transition at the upcoming Tuesday's council meeting: Bilandic would get the acting mayor's job with the understanding that he would not be a contender in the special mayoral race; Frost would take the chairmanship of finance; Vrdolyak would temporarily submerge his ambitions for a higher post and become the president pro tem of the council, which had been Frost's post. The Polish block of 13 was appeased by the promise of selecting their senior member, Casimir Laskowski (35th), for the post of vice mayor in the reorganization of the City Council. It was also assumed that the newly created office of vice mayor would eliminate any future succession problems.

By 6 p.m. Monday, rumors of a Frost deal were thicker than a London fog. In response to a reporter's questions, Reverend Jackson expressed the consensus of the Black community:

> We are not concerned with a back-room deal. For the Black community, there are three options. One is to accept the humiliation of being

Former State Representative Jesse Madison, the current executive vice president of the Chicago Park District was one of the early leaders from the West Side in the movement for a Black mayor.

Former Alderman Wilson Frost, the current commissioner of the Board of Tax Appeals is the man who should have succeeded Daley when he passed in Dec. 21, 1976. Frost was denied the late mayor's seat for only one reason. He is Black.

dealt out. The second is for a group of people to have a back-room meeting and accept something that is less than we deserve. Third is for us to line up our friends across racial lines in the council meeting tomorrow and to emerge victorious. It appears that the constituency of Alderman Wilson Frost and the Democratic party are on a collision course.

Contrary to what Wilson Frost had told Metcalfe, Jackson and Savage in his offices on the second floor of City Hall that Monday, there was activity on the fifth floor that indicated a deal had been made. The policemen who had been stationed at the double doors of the mayor's suite on Christmas Eve had been removed, and the doors were unlocked and ajar. People working in the foyer of the late mayor's office appeared to be relaxed and no longer tense or agitated.

When the City Council convened the next day, Frost refused to stand up, and the deal that was negotiated on Sunday was put in place despite the threats by leaders of the Black community to revolt from the Democratic party. Alderman Michael Bilandic was elected acting mayor by the City Council by a lopsided vote of 45-2. Two of the four independent minority bloc aldermen, Martin Oberman (43rd) and Dick Simpson (44th) voted against the resolution. Bilandic abstained. The 50-member council had two vacancies at the time.

Two policemen, one white and one Black, were assigned to watch Gus Savage during the council meeting and to arrest him if he attempted to start a demonstration. The Black officer confided to Savage that he was ashamed of his assignment.

After the council meeting, Frost said, "Why should I be the one to take the suicidal leap?" Vernon Jarrett, political analyst, noted in his column in the *Chicago Tribune* on Dec. 29, 1976, "What a sad reflection on the entire spectrum of Black leadership that a black man would consider such a harmless move 'suicidal' in Chicago in 1976."

Frost gave these reasons for not committing political suicide on the floor of the City Council:

> I could not muster more than 19 votes out of 48 and I needed 25 votes to be elected acting mayor. Therefore, I worked out an accord to accept the chairmanship of the finance committee, which is the most powerful committee in the City Council. On the other hand, I could have gone to the council floor fighting like a lot of people wanted me to do, but I would not have come out with any benefit other than knowing that I gave some people a good feeling.

Leaders of Black community groups reacted quickly by holding a mass meeting on Tuesday, December 28, at 7 p.m., in the Community Progressive Church, 56 E. 48th St. Gus Savage, one of the meeting's organizers, expressed his dismay:

> I am deeply disappointed that Alderman Wilson Frost refused to stand for election this morning in the city council for the office of acting mayor of Chicago. In his refusal to stand, he completely violated a solemn and specific pledge he made to a delegation of leaders who are present here tonight and who met with him Monday. We asked specifically, twice, would he stand Tuesday for election by the City Council for the post of acting mayor, regardless of pressures of the office or lack of sufficient support to win. Twice, he replied yes!
>
> We were mobilized, particularly to oppose efforts to deny Frost the post because of his race. In general, we stand for the principle that political authority must be fairly shared by all minorities who make up Chicago's population, or these minorities will not be able to equally fulfill their responsibilities of citizenship.
>
> The principle we support goes beyond the person we supported. Frost's failure to stand up this morning did not end our cause; rather, it represented merely the end of our beginning. If the politicians would deny the most qualified person the post of acting mayor because he happened to be Black, we propose that the people elect a qualified Black as permanent mayor. This is the only effective way to reverse this racist decision. We ask Chicago to be fair.

Savage's emotional report to the people was interrupted more than 10 times by sounds of stomping feet and loud applause. Savage continued:

> The first alderman to stand up for racism in the council this morning was one whose far Southeast Side constituencies are at least half Black. 'Fast Eddie' Vrdolyak, of the 10th Ward, placed in nomination Michael Bilandic, of the 11th Ward, which includes the late Mayor Daley's Bridgeport residence.
>
> Two of the aldermen who spoke for Bilandic's nomination were Black: Bennie Stewart, of the far South Side 21st Ward and Eloise Barden, of the 16th Ward, which includes Englewood.
>
> White Alderman Ross Lathrop, of the Hyde Park 5th Ward, and Dick Simpson, of the North Side 44th Ward, sought to support Frost, but Roman Pucinski successfully objected on a point of order. Pucinski noted that Frost had not filed with the city clerk a written statement of consent to candidacy as required by the rules adopted by the council Tuesday to govern this election. Frost, presiding as president pro temporary, verified that he had not consented to standing for acting mayor.
>
> Following that scenario, all aldermen (excluding white independents Simpson and Marty Oberman, of the Near North Side 43rd Ward), voted for Bilandic. The 13 Black aldermen even held a press conference before the council meeting to indicate they would not support Frost.
>
> It was wrong for Alderman Wilson Frost to permit prominent Blacks and some whites to mobilize public sentiment for him as acting mayor. He appeared at a rally we organized for that purpose, at Roberts Motel Wednesday evening of last week, and inspired the audience with his apparent commitment to seeking the post.

> Frost is not the main culprit. However, he should have stood, although he would not have won. The bitter and aging culprit is racism.
>
> Racism brings to mind a question that was raised by a young white woman reporter earlier today. She asked me how I felt about Frost. I replied, 'Why don't you ask me how I feel about Vrdolyak, Stewart, Marzullo, Laskowski, Natarus and Cohen, who lead the fight against Frost running?' They, more than Frost, represent the main problem of racism.
>
> I am distressed but not deterred. We can overcome by June at the special election expected to be announced by the council next Thursday. Let's let today's disappointment become a springboard for justice. Racism seriously aggravates the ills of our city-it harms us all, whites as well as Blacks and Latinos. Be fair, Chicago!

All of the people in that jam-packed auditorium-politicians, businessmen and civic leaders-jumped to their feet at the conclusion of Savage's statement and gave him a six-minute ovation.

Following Gus Savage's report, State Sen. Harold Washington introduced a resolution to elect Chicago's first Black mayor in the 1977 special mayoral election. The motion to adopt the resolution was seconded by trade union official Tommy Briscoe.

Specifically, the resolution called for the grassroot organization to: 1) select a search committee that would identify one or more qualified candidates; 2) present the candidates to the group on Jan. 13, 1977, the date of the next public meeting; 3) organize a citizen's committee to raise funds and 4) mobilize to turn out the vote, particularly in the Black wards, to elect a Black mayor.

Washington continued, "The resolution is a major move to set in motion a new direction for Chicago's minority population." Ralph Metcalfe urged Black unity: "a goal that has long passed us. We have paid our dues and now it's collection time."

Jesse Jackson called the resolution "a six-month date with destiny. Nobody will save us from us for us but us. Therefore, the singular goal of the Black community should be to elect a Black mayor." Like many other Black leaders, Reverend Jackson contended that Alderman Frost was denied his rightful position as acting mayor because of his race. "He should have challenged the council's racism," Jackson said. He described Frost's decision not to run for acting mayor as "a measure of embarrassment" for the Black community. "We should have lost the vote without losing our respect," Jackson contended.

Following the mass meeting, State Rep. Jesse Madison and Renault Robinson, along with a group of prominent business persons, were charged with finding one or more candidates for mayor and presenting them at the January meeting.

In less than a week, the Committee for a Black Mayor came up with the names of Cecil Partee, Richard Newhouse and Renault Robinson. Most surprising of the three was Robinson, because he had never entered a political campaign. Yet Robinson had earned more respect at the grassroots level of the black community than perhaps any other leader in Chicago because of his nine-year struggle against racial discrimination in the Chicago Police Department.

On the night of January 2, the Committee for a Black Mayor barely avoided self destruction when the group voted 12-13 to open membership to several angry persons, who had originally been excluded. Renault Robinson cast the deciding vote for the new committee members.

Robinson, the committee chairman, suffered a great deal of pressure from prominent Black leaders who called the added committee members "possible troublemakers" and felt the size of the selection committee would prove unmanageable. Robinson resigned. The resignation of the chairman put the broad-based, 80-member committee out of business.

A nine-member selection committee was formed. Charles Hayes (chairman), Reverend Jesse Jackson, Barnetta Howell Barrett, Gus Savage, Addie Wyatt, Dempsey J. Travis, Reverend Maceo D. Pembroke, Dr. James Buckner and Nancy Jefferson comprised the group.

Among those who pressed for this smaller, "more manageable" committee were businessmen John H. Johnson, George Johnson, Al Johnson, Alvin Boutte, plus Ralph Metcalfe and Edwin (Bill) Berry. These leaders favored a smaller committee because they felt a larger body would lead to confusion, dissension and hurt feelings.

On Jan. 12, 1977, the members of the selection committee received the following telegram:

> On Saturday, January 15, from 3 to 8 p.m. at Roberts Motel, 301 E. 63rd St., in Rooms 119 and 120, our committee will meet to interview possible candidates for mayor. Your presence is urgently needed because we must complete our report on that date. Notices have been sent to all remaining prospective candidates on our list. If you have any suggestions as to additions to the list, please notify them to be present between the hours of 3 and 8 p.m. on Saturday, January 15, 1977.
>
> Charles Hayes and Al Boutte

The mayoral possibilities to be called for interviews were: Warren Bacon, Alvin Boutte, Roland Burris, Leon Davis, Erwin France, Wilson Frost, Jesse Jackson, Louise Quarles Lawson, Jesse Madison, E. Duke McNeil, Congressman Ralph Metcalfe, James Montgomery, Richard Newhouse, Cecil Partee, Renault Robinson, George Sims, Thomas N. Todd, Dempsey Travis, Robert Tucker, Harold Washington, Addie Wyatt.

The committee received another letter that day:

> To: All members of the Committee for a Black Mayor
>
> Dear Member:
>
> Our group is reconvening at 4 p.m. on Monday, January 17, at Johnson Publishing Company, 820 S. Michigan Ave., to hear a report from

the committee which was given the responsibility to seek the name of a suitable candidate that we could support for mayor of the city of Chicago.

Please set aside two hours of your precious time to be in attendance at this meeting.

Sincerely yours,
Charles Hayes
Co-Chairperson

All but three of the Black mayoral prospects removed themselves from consideration. Those to be considered were Harold Washington, Richard Newhouse and attorney E. Duke McNeil. Washington, the top choice of the low-profile search committee, was also selected by a high-profile West Side committee headed by Tommy Briscoe and State Rep. Jesse Madison. The selection of Harold Washington as the mayoral candidate was unanimous.

The following mailgram was received by each member of the Committee for a Black Mayor and other community leaders on Jan. 20:

We ask you to join us in standing with our candidate for mayor this Friday, January 21, at 7 p.m. in the Progressive Community Church, 56 E. 48th Street. Your participation in this historic occasion is essential to the progress of our community and the city. We look forward to locking arms on the platform with you Friday night.

Alvin J. Boutte and Charles Hayes

Ralph Metcalfe dropped a bombshell on the crusade for a Black mayor five hours before the Friday night meeting. He told the *Chicago Sun-Times*, "I have indicated to my associates on the committee that I cannot support Harold Washington. We need a candidate who will advance the interest of Black people and who will be a good mayor for all the city of Chicago." Metcalfe also said he had "a bill of particulars" against Washington. He suggested that Harold's confrontation with the Internal Revenue Service and a subsequent brief term in prison should disqualify Washington as a candidate.

At the meeting that evening when Gus Savage, co-chairman with Metcalfe of the Black Leaders Steering Committee, read Metcalfe's comments, the crowd booed when Metcalfe's name was mentioned. Many in the audience had supported Ralph in his bouts with the regular Democratic organization and felt betrayed and confused by Metcalfe's behavior.

Labor leader Hayes attempted to pacify the people, assuring them that Metcalfe had not deserted them. "Ralph is recognized as the top black political leader," Hayes admonished.

Harold Washington, the committee's choice for mayor, removed his name from consideration that night before a very disappointed group of people who had come to celebrate his candidacy. Obviously stunned by Metcalfe's opposition, Washington made no reference to the congressman in his speech. Instead, he said that the Black business leaders had failed to come through with necessary funding.

Savage declined to make any further comments about Metcalfe's remarks and declared philosophically, "We are discouraged but no less determined." It was Tommy Briscoe, general chairman of the 5,000-member Chicago local of the American Postal Workers Union, who responded:

> Either Ralph has lost his mind or he's a goddamn fool. He's laying the ground work for the damn machine to make another overture to him. If Metcalfe does not back the Black candidate this time, then he will not be elected again. We will defeat him.
>
> The same people who rallied to him and carried him past the Democratic party last year are now backing Washington. We tried to make a statesman out of Ralph. We tried to make him a symbol for Black people. But we aren't creating a monster. We can drop him like a hot potato.

On the day that Metcalfe publicly repudiated Harold Washington, Edward Vrdolyak sent up a hot air balloon for the mayoral candidacy of Acting Mayor Michael Bilandic. In an address to the Chicago City Club, Alderman Vrdolyak said that the late Mayor Daley told him several times that he wanted Bilandic as his successor. "I have never said this in public before, but as I remember it, the last time he said something like, 'Mike would be a good man for the city of Chicago after I'm gone.' "

Vrdolyak was one of the Daley loyalists who engineered the negotiations that had given Bilandic the acting mayoral post. "Mike Bilandic at that time said that he would not run, and he has not altered his position yet," Vrdolyak said. "However, I would hope he will change his mind." He further asserted that Bilandic was the best choice for mayor because, "his idea of a good time is doing research, and he knows the nuts and bolts of the business of running a government."

On Sunday, January 30, attorney Robert Tucker threw his hat in the ring to run against Bilandic. He announced, "I am a candidate for the office of mayor of the city of Chicago. I promise to bring a new and enlightened leadership."

Tucker is always well-dressed, poised, urbane and articulate. Bob is the only man the author knows who graduated from Tennessee State University and Northwestern University Law School in Chicago, Ill., and sounds like he was breast fed at the university at Oxford. Tucker fielded questions from the reporters in the manner that Hank Aaron, the home run champion, might have faced a DuSable High School pitcher. In replying to a question about his experience to be mayor, Tucker replied, "As a teacher, lawyer and former assistant regional director of the Department of Housing and Urban Development, I handled a budget of more than $400 million a year. The elements of government are by no means foreign to me." When queried about the source of funds for his campaign, Tucker replied, "If 100,000 (of the people of Chicago) respond to my call with a single contribution of $10, it will afford me the opportunity to present myself before my people."

Robert Tucker's mayoral campaign barely got off the ground. Exactly one week after he announced, an article in the Feb. 6, 1977, *Chicago Tribune* reported that the federal government was seeking an accounting of a $300,000 loan to Tucker and some other businessmen. The money was to promote a plan conceived by the attorney involving the purchase of real estate. Tucker claimed that the *Tribune* report was misleading, but withdrew from the mayoral race shortly after the story appeared.

Following the attorney's withdrawal, the following letter was mailed to members of the Committee for a Black Mayor:

> February 25, 1977
>
> Dear Committee member:
>
> You are herein notified that after our selection committee projected the name of attorney Robert Tucker as our candidate for the office of mayor of the city of Chicago and he subsequently withdrew from the race, this ended the life of our committee.
>
> This will make it unmistakably clear and avoid any possible misunderstanding. Anyone who was a part of our group is free to support whoever they desire for the office of mayor. My tenure as chairperson of the group obviously ended with the dissolution of the committee.
>
> With sincere best wishes, I am very truly yours,
>
> Charles Hayes
> International Vice President
> Director of District #2
> Director of Organizing

Senator Harold Washington crisscrossed the city many times in his mayoral 1977 campaign against Acting Mayor Michael Bilandic. In the above picture, the senator is shown being interviewed by Hugh Hill of Channel 7 on the left, and several other print and radio news reporters.

CHAPTER

9

1977: The Year Harold Washington Threw His Hat into the Mayoral Ring

In late January of 1977, State Senator Harold Washington's split with the regular Democratic organization had come full circle. He was angry at the way members of the Chicago City Council had treated Wilson Frost and he was embarrassed because Frost did not have the testicles to stand up with the Black community. Moreover, he was deeply wounded by Metcalfe's public denunciation of him in the January 21st edition of the *Chicago Sun-Times.* While bearing those crosses, Harold decided to burn some bridges between himself and the Chicago Democratic machine.

Harold punctuated his discontent with the regular organization by joining forces in the General Assembly with a group of independent state senators known as the "Crazy Eight." Included was Sen. Dawn Clark Netsch, his Northwestern Law School classmate. The objective of the coalition was to derail the election of Thomas C. Hynes, a Chicago machine candidate, as senate president. It was Washington's contention that the members of the Illinois senate's Black caucus should have the right to select their own leader. His determination was a dramatic departure from Illinois tradition, which mandated that Black political leaders would be selected by white public officials. In this case, Hynes had announced that he would name Sen. Charles Chew (D-Chicago) as leader of the Black Caucus.

Washington's choice for the leadership position in the Black caucus was Kenneth Hall from East St. Louis, Ill. He reasoned that if Blacks could not select their own man, then the rainbow coalition would throw up every parliamentary roadblock imaginable to prevent them from electing Thomas Hynes. The opposition to Hynes was not personal; it was based on the belief that he had been hand-picked by George Dunne, the newly elected Cook County Democratic chairman, and Sen. Richard M. Daley, the son of the late Chicago mayor. The reformers held against electing Hynes for five weeks. After a 17-hour marathon of negotiations in Springfield, Washington pulled out of the race for president on the 186th ballot. The Washington group had won the senate rule changes they sought and Kenneth Hall of East St. Louis, Ill., was named assistant majority leader in the senate.

After the victory in Springfield, a splinter group of political activists who had been members of the original organization to elect a Black mayor drafted Harold Washington to run against Acting Mayor Michael Bilandic in the special mayoral election. Congressman Gus Savage, an early advocate of Black political power, had supported Robert Tucker for mayor after Washington withdrew. However, just before the deadline to file the mayoral petitions, Savage had a premonition that Tucker was going to drop out of the race. To cover all bases, he, Renault Robinson, Tommy Briscoe, Sid Ordower and Slim Coleman had circulated petitions and obtained 6,500 names for Washington's candidacy before Tucker finally withdrew. Since this was accomplished without Washington's permission or knowledge, their next step was to convince Harold to become a candidate for mayor of Chicago.

Mayor Harold Washington recalled:

> Gus Savage and Sid Ordower came by my house and told me that they had gotten 6,500 names without my agreement.
>
> Frankly, they didn't have any place to go. So Gus said, 'Look Harold. I will guarantee you that we will do all the work that has to be done. We will raise the necessary money. It won't cost you a dime. All you have to do is continue to breathe and agree to be our candidate.'
>
> I realized several things: 1) Somebody had to do it because the political apparatus in the Black community was out of hand. 2) I didn't have anything to lose. 3) I was going to continue to have trouble with the machine because they didn't want me down in Springfield. They hadn't at that time fully made up their mind to take me on yet, but I realized that I was at a transition point in my life: Either go up or go down. What did I have to lose?
>
> Gus Savage and those fellows that I mentioned put the whole thing together. I didn't have to do anything. My first act in the 1977 campaign was to go down to a campaign office that Gus Savage had rented, at 6 E. Randolph, which was just above the Walgreen drugstore on the northeast corner of State and Randolph. Gus even had cardboard window signs printed with my name on them lying on the floor, and a battery of telephones had already been installed. Gus must have got a real good peek at my hold card.

> After spending a brief time in the new headquarters, I walked with Savage and a small delegation over to City Hall, had a brief press conference and filed my petitions.

In less than 24 hours after Sen. Washington filed for the mayoral race, the Afro-American Patrolman's League dispatched Frank Lee, a member of the group, to Washington's Englewood office to discuss security. Frank Lee recalls:

> I told the senator that I was part of a small group of Chicago policemen who had agreed to protect him during his mayoral campaign on a volunteer basis on our off days.
>
> Washington looked at me with a very solemn expression on his face and asked, 'What do I need security for?'
>
> I replied, 'It might get kind of tough when you begin your campaign against the establishment.'
>
> Washington retorted, 'I have been doing tough things all of my life. If they are going to do something to me like shoot me, cut me or kidnap me, your presence would simply mean they would do it to both of us.'

Washington had a logical rebuttal for everything that Frank Lee said. Frank eventually called the Afro-American Patrolman's office at 71st and Jeffrey and told both Renault Robinson, the executive director, and Howard Saffold, the president, that the senator did not want any security. Renault asked to speak to the senator and they talked briefly. Lee then left Washington's office.

Back at the league headquarters, a group of the policemen decided they were going to give Washington protection even though the candidate did not want it. Some members of the league began to show up and just sort of hang around wherever the senator would make a public appearance. Initially, the presence of the security group kind of irritated Washington, but he eventually told Frank Lee, "Well, since you are determined to follow me around, you might as well do something useful like hold my coat while I make a speech or something."

Howard Saffold, a member of the team of volunteers who protected Washington, said:

> We could not have a Black man running around by himself seriously talking about being mayor of the city of Chicago. The establishment might pay some dude to hit him upside of the head just to discourage him. We felt that it was our obligation to make certain that something like this does not happen. We also wanted to be part of a campaign for a serious Black mayoral candidate, whether he had a chance or not.

The volunteers from the patrolman's league eventually became campaign workers. They decorated an old camper with Washington For Mayor banners and paraded the candidate through the streets of Chicago's South, West and Near North neighborhoods whenever he came in from Springfield.

A few of the members of the Afro-American Patrolmen's League who volunteered to give Senator Harold Washington protective security during his 1977 mayoral campaign. Front row (left to right): Officer Howard Saffold; Renault Robinson, executive director of the league; and Senator Harold Washington.

In a reflective mood about the '77 campaign, Washington said:

Behind the mayoral campaign, I knew that in 1978 the machine was coming after me with everything including the kitchen sink, and I would have to fight them all. And at the same time, I had to stay in the Senate. So, the 1977 mayoral campaign offered me an opportunity to establish myself in the First District and build.

For example, Bob Shaw, who lived in the 9th, wanted to be alderman. He handled the 9th Ward for my mayoral campaign. We took the 9th. Niles Sherman wanted to be the alderman in 21st Ward. We took the 21st Ward. Monica Faith Stewart, who incidentally was running for an open aldermanic spot in the 8th Ward, and we took that part of the 8th which was Black. Danny Davis over on the West Side wanted to be an alderman. We didn't take the ward but we got 2,000 votes, which was unheard of. Alderman David Rhodes of the 24th Ward was trying to save himself from the Bilandic administration because they were after him. We didn't take the 24th, but we got 2,500 votes. Gus Savage wanted to be congressman in the Second District, and I campaigned more in the Second District than I did in the rest of the city combined, putting that together. We got 11 percent of the vote and carried five wards. We carried the 5th, 6th, 8th, 21st and 9th. We almost carried the 17th. We ran well in all of the South Side Black wards. And did well on the west side. But nobody really looked at it. It was revolutionary. It really showed what could been done if you get out there and worked, even if you lost.

The bad taste from the political frosting that had been layered on the Black community by the establishment was one of several reasons that Sen. Harold Washington ran for mayor in 1977, although he knew he had no chance of winning.

On the other hand, Washington recognized that resentment against the Democratic machine was manifesting itself in a people's movement in at least six South Side wards. He also sensed that the pent-up hostility against Daley needed a political exit to avoid an explosion. He was determined to provide a positive escape valve by proving that Black folk could lose and still not end up on the debit side of the ballot box. The cadre of bright, politically-oriented young women and men who emerged from his 1977 campaign became a potent force in Washington's 1980 congressional race and in his 1983 mayoral victory.

A few days after losing the April 19 mayoral primary to Bilandic, Harold held a press conference. He told a small group of Black journalists, "I am going to do that which maybe I should have done 10 or 12 years ago. I'm going to stay outside of that damn Democratic organization and give them hell."

Harold Washington punctuated his commitment on May 31, 1977. He walked erectly and calmly into Acting Mayor Michael Bilandic's conference room, which is adjacent to the mayor's office on the fifth floor in City Hall, where some 20 media representatives were waiting for the mayor to hold a press conference.

Harold went directly to the rostrum and proceeded to read a three-page statement which, in part, denounced both Mayor Bilandic and his Republican opponent Alderman Dennis H. Block. He called Bilandic, "a third-rate boss Daley." And he further said, "Block insulted the Black community by seconding the nomination of Bilandic in the December 28 election. Mr. Block proved he was not a serious opponent of the machine by participating in that charade."

Midway through his recitation, Police Sgt. Ernest Burgin, who was in charge of the reception desk in the mayor's outer office, stepped up to the lectern and turned off the microphone system that relayed sound to the TV and radio technicians.

Washington ignored the police sergeant and blithely continued reading from his prepared notes. He said, "He'd like to be able to support the Democratic nominee, but Bilandic appears to share all of the late mayor's weaknesses and blind spots while bringing to his work as our city's chief executive little of Daley's skill as a balancer of conflicting needs and interests."

Washington had earlier been critical of his good friend Cecil Partee, the gentleman who had interceded for him with Richard J. Daley a year earlier and had persuaded the mayor to slate Harold for the senate seat that Partee vacated. Washington felt he had been betrayed by Partee because Partee supported Bilandic during the primary mayoral campaign. So, he told some reporters that, "Senator Partee is the biggest Uncle Tom on God's green earth."

Partee wasn't terribly upset at Washington calling him an Uncle Tom. He said:

> Washington has to do some things, at times, to make his people feel good. I worked for him to get my Senate seat because I didn't think it was fair of the organization to try to get rid of a Black independent and let the white independents survive. If they were going to try to get rid of all the independents, I might have been supportive.

On the other hand, when State Rep. James C. Taylor read Washington's criticism of Partee in the newspaper, he smiled like a fox who had been turned loose in the chicken house. He figured he could finally attack Washington without risking Partee's wrath. Taylor hated Washington with a passion that paralleled J. Edgar Hoover's eminity toward Dr. Martin Luther King Jr. "Bull Jive" Taylor saw Harold as a sniffly, elitist, educated punk. To him, Harold was the intellectual son of a lawyer and grandson of a minister and the antithesis of Taylor's unlettered rural Arkansas background. Taylor's long-brewing antipathy for Harold had led him to attempt to double-cross Washington nine years earlier in the 1968 election. Bennett Johnson, Harold Washington's close friend and political ally, describes the event:

> It was a spring-like election day in the February primary of 1968. Harold and I were sitting in his office at 6301 S. Wentworth Ave. discussing political strategy. I told Harold that in my opinion, we would be OK in Committeeman Partee's 20th Ward and in Metcalfe's 3rd Ward, but we had better watch our backs in Committeeman Jim Taylor's 16th Ward.
>
> Washington assured me that everything was OK in the 16th Ward because he had talked to Mayor Daley and Daley had said that everything was alright. At this point, we decided to take an automobile ride and survey the various polling stations in the 16th Ward. At our very first stop, by coincidence, we ran into James Taylor and William Shaw, who were standing in front of the polling place. Washington got out of the car and chatted with them both for about 15 minutes.
>
> In the interim, I spied a precinct captain passing out political literature about 200 feet from the polling place. I got out of the car, walked down the block, introduced myself and asked him how things were going. He said, 'OK.'
>
> 'That's great,' I replied. I then said, 'Let me see your palm card.'
>
> He gave me a palm card and it read three votes for James Taylor. Taylor had instructed his people to cast a bullet vote (three) for him and bypass his other two Democratic running mates.

State Representative James Taylor is credited with putting forth his very best efforts to end Harold Washington's political career when Washington ran for re-election to the Illinois state senate in 1978.

Clarence McClain was the only subject that State Representative James Taylor and Senator Harold Washington had in common. McClain once served as administrative assistant to both Taylor and Washington, in that order.

> When I returned to the car, I showed the palm card to Harold and he almost had a seizure. From that point forward, Harold's and Jim's mutual hatred was as much personal as it was political.
>
> Taylor, as the ward committeeman, had such a lock on the area that Harold had to set up his own ragtag political army. This group included me, Charles Freeman, Sam Patch and Jan Roland, along with some others.

Washington called Committeeman Taylor, "One of the worse lowbrow politicians I have ever dealt with in my entire political life."

The only thing the two men had in common was that they both had employed a man by the name of Clarence McClain.

After being introduced to Washington by Judge Charles A. Freeman, McClain quit his job as an administrative assistant to James Taylor in early 1970 and joined the Washington troops. It was McClain who gave Harold the insight for breaking Taylor's lock over Washington's constituents in the 16th Ward. Washington was steadfast in his gratitude for McClain's assistance.

Harold gave Clarence high marks for service rendered when Washington served in both the Illinois legislature and in the U.S. Congress, and for the first couple of years that he was mayor of Chicago. McClain's talents can best be evaluated through the eyes of Herman Gilbert, who was the assistant administrator of the Illinois Bureau of Employment Security and McClain's supervisor. Gilbert said:

> McClain is a very bright guy. Although his formal education ended after one year at Tilden Tech High School, he was better read and a better administrator than most people working for the state with master's degrees. He got three letters of commendation from high-ranking officials of the Internal Association of Personnel and Employment Security, the Illinois chapter. He also got an award as one of the 10 outstanding employees in the state of Illinois. McClain was definitely an excellent administrator.
>
> McClain's responsibilities included the purchase of supplies and equipment for the entire Illinois Bureau of Employment Security. The bureau had some 195 employment offices across the state and 5,000 employees.
>
> To handle this many offices and people with the credibility and skill of Clarence McClain, you would have to be very bright.

McClain's briefings on the 16th Ward were of little help to Washington when Rep. Taylor, who controlled 700 patronage jobs for his 16th Ward, ran an unknown precinct captain, Clarence Barry, for Harold's Senate seat in 1978. The Democratic machine joined Taylor, the most powerful Black committeeman in Chicago, in his efforts to bury Sen. Washington's political career. The intensity of their efforts was awesome.

Rep. Taylor, in concert with Sen. Frank D. Savickas (D-27) of Marquette Park, along with Alderman Tyrone Kenner (D-3), backed Clarence C. Barry against Harold Washington in his bid for re-election to the state senate. They also filed petitions for Sabrina and Denise, two young Black women with the surname of Washington in an effort to confuse the voters into pulling the lever for the wrong Washington. To further their conspiracy, they tore down all of Washington's election billboards throughout the 26th district and posted more than 1,000 anti-Washington cardboard bulletins on lamp posts throughout the various precincts.

The 26th District covers 148 precincts in five South Side wards: 22 in Metcalfe's and Kenner's 3rd; 17 in the 15th, controlled by state Sen. Frank B. Savickas; 43 in Taylor's 16th Ward; 21 in Alderman William Shannon's 17th; and 45 in Partee's 20th.

The overwhelming desire to defeat Washington can best be measured by the amount of money that was spent in that senatorial campaign. Beat-the-hell-out-of-Harold money poured from anonymous sources into the 16th Ward headquarters like rain on a spring afternoon. The primary source that would benefit from Harold's defeat was the regular Democratic organization.

Washington said:

> The Democratic machine came after me with everything but the atomic bomb. We managed to win by only 212 votes that year. They must have spent $150,000 in the 26th District, an unheard of amount of dollars for a senatorial district campaign. I couldn't have survived in the race had it not been for Cecil Partee (20th) and William Shannon (17th) coming to my rescue.
>
> (Jane Byrne beat the machine the following year with a mayoral campaign fund of $75,000.)

Partee delivered for Washington against Barry by 5-1. And Shannon carried for Washington by a margin of 3-1. A little-known factor behind Partee's fight to save Washington's senate seat was a behind-the-scenes struggle between Partee and Taylor to be the most powerful committeeman in the 26th legislative district. Washington's victory undoubtedly made Partee the winner in the contest.

Another factor that enabled Harold Washington to survive the political onslaught was the discovery by David Canter, a confidant, that one of the two Washington women running for the senate under the Taylor banner had filed her consent to run on the wrong form. Her petition was for the Illinois House of Representatives rather than for the state Senate. She was challenged and her petition was thrown out. It is conceivable that had the second woman with the surname of Washington stayed in the race, she could have picked up much of the 212 vote margin that Washington received and the course of Black political empowerment Chicago would have taken a detour.

A happy and emotional constituent embraces Congressman-elect Harold Washington in his campaign headquarters at 640 E. 79th Street, upon learning that Washington was the overwhelming victor in a campaign against three other candidates in the March 18, 1980 primary. Looking on (at far left) with childish admiration is Bennett Johnson III, presently 18 and a sophomore at Harvard University. Also, directly behind Washington wearing a dark coat, is former State Representative Robert Mann. Second from the right (wearing a white cloth headpiece) is Lois Evans, a lady who served as secretary to both the late Roy Washington Sr., and to Harold. Directly behind Lois, to her right, is Paula Thomas.

CHAPTER

10

Harold Goes to Washington

Illinois Sen. Harold Washington de feated incumbent Bennett Stewart in the race for Democratic candidate for U.S. Representative from the 1st Congressional District. In the primary held March 18, 1980, the final count gave Washington ran a 2-1 margin over Loop City College instructor Ralph Metcalfe Jr., who came in second. Stewart, the Democratic committeeman of the 21st Ward, came in third and Cook County Commissioner John H. Stroger Jr., the 8th Ward committeeman, placed last.

Following his primary victory, Washington said:

> This campaign didn't start when we filed our petitions. This campaign started Oct. 16, 1978, at Liberty Baptist Church when former Mayor Michael A. Bilandic and patronage chief Tom Donovan pressed down our throats Alderman Bennett Stewart, a gentleman we did not want. We are not going to be controlled by anybody outside of the First Congressional District.

In retrospect, Harold's congressional campaign looks like a cakewalk. In reality, it was not a dance but a very tough journey. Washington announced his candidacy at Operation PUSH Saturday, May 26, 1979, choosing an early entry because he was leery of competing against Metcalfe, who bore the name of a his legendary father, a Black folk hero. Harold had no money when he announced, and no funds were raised for the congressional race from May to December of 1979. It was just before the Christmas holidays, when Harold and Sid Ordower started looking seriously for a campaign headquarters, that the campaign sprang to life.

Gus Savage had suggested a Black Muslim-owned building at 640 E. 79th St. as a possible location. They inspected the facilities that formerly had been a Muslim-operated clothing store and commenced negotiations with the real estate agent without a red cent in their pockets. The management company was asking $1,500 per month rental. They told the agent that they could not afford that amount. The real estate agent, in turn, asked Harold and Sid what was their budget. They said they could pay $500 a month, with three months in advance. The agent said, "Make it a $2,000 advance and you've got a deal." Harold and Sid looked at each other for a moment and without exchanging words, Sid then said to the agent, "I will bring you the money right after the first of the year." He was counting on an old connection for borrowing the $2,000.

On Jan. 2, 1980, Sid and Harold returned with the money. On January 13, they held an open house in the spacious storefront located on the northeast corner of 79th and Champlain Ave. The event attracted approximately 400 people. Five thousand dollars was contributed during the open house and Harold Washington began to seriously campaign for the congressional seat.

The independent political image that state Sen. Washington forged in the 1977 mayoral campaign pushed him over the top in the 1980 congressional primary, establishing him as a political savior in the eyes of many Black voters. Style was a major factor in his success. Harold campaigned as strenuously when he had no opposition as he did when he was opposed. He moved through the laundry mats and pool halls on Saturdays, and visited from four to six churches every Sunday. In his joy of campaigning, he swept the South and West Sides of Chicago like a warm summer breeze. No corner where potential voters could be found was too dark to escape Harold Washington's attention.

I asked Washington during one of his campaign stops why he worked so hard. He replied, "Public service is my life. It's like eating Cracker Jacks or shooting pool. It is a fascinating game and I am proud to be one of the players, Dempsey. I am one man who uses the political game for the good of the people."

Indeed, Sen. Washington was the principal author of most of the "people bills" that were introduced during his tenure in the Illinois Legislature. He implanted real teeth into the mouth of the state's Fair Employment Practices Commission. He upgraded the Illinois Code of Corrections. He placed a protective blanket around witnesses to crimes. He obtained special aid for small businesses, and he extended both arms to help poor and elderly consumers. Washington personally steered these and many other people bills through committee and saw them passed into law.

Rose Jennings, former director of marketing for Playboy Magazine, said, "Harold was the supreme marketer. He knew exactly how to market himself and the legislation in which he had an interest. He instinctively had it. He was the best of a breed."

The prologue of Harold's odyssey to the U.S. Congress began on Oct. 9, 1978. U.S. Rep. Ralph Metcalfe, the 1936 Olympic gold medal winner and former alderman and committeeman of the 3rd Ward, was found dead of an apparent heart attack in his third floor apartment at 4530 S. Michigan Ave. that morning.

Before the funeral arrangements for Metcalfe could be made, the local Democrats were falling over each other to meet the mandatory eight-day deadline for his successor's name to be placed on the November 7 general election ballot. Bennett Stewart, Cecil Partee and Joseph Bertrand were the names most frequently mentioned, though Stewart had been designated as Metcalfe's successor in a clandestine meeting held in City Hall by Mayor Michael Bilandic's patronage chief, Thomas Donovan.

On Monday, Oct. 16, 1978, more than 2,000 registered voters of the First Congressional District crowded into the Liberty Baptist Church at 4849 S. King Drive to participate in the ward committeemen's selection of Metcalfe's successor. Samuel Ackerman, the First District state central committeeman who chaired the meeting, planned to allow nine individuals other than the committeemen to address the restless observers. The regular Democratic committeemen quickly shut off participation after the first speaker, Gus Savage, representing Black newspaper publishers, shouted, "Above all, don't select Bennett Stewart."

When Stewart's name was put into nomination, more than half the crowd loudly protested. Many left the meeting shouting, "We won't vote . . . vote socialist." Seven of the 10 ward committeemen voted for Stewart over County Board Commissioner John Stroger and Loop City College Professor Timuel Black. Stroger received two votes, his own and one cast by Joseph Bertrand; Tim Black's sole vote came from Alan Dobry, an independent committeeman from the 5th Ward.

The hostility among some of the committeemen and members of the audience was thick enough to cut with a knife. Dobry was trying to put a motion before the ward committeemen to postpone the election when Alderman Tyrone Kenner, a former Chicago policeman who had been elected committeeman earlier that day by the 3rd Ward precinct captains, attempted to jerk the microphone out of Dobry's hands. Tim Black describes the Kenner-Dobry scene as being so crude and rough that he left the building.

Harold Washington, a member of the 3rd Ward regular Democratic organization, quietly watched the political spectacle, and reflected on that evening some five years later:

> In 1980, it was very natural for me to run against Bennett Stewart for Congress. We had taken all kinds of polls in 1979. The polls showed in a solid four-man race I would get 50 percent of the votes. In none of the polls did it go up or go down; it stayed at 50 percent. And that's the way it came out. I got 50 percent, and the other candidates split the balance almost evenly.

Washington commented on the new political freedom movement during a speech in August 1980.

> I want to lay to rest rumors that the Chicago Democratic machine is dead. There appear to be many misconceptions about the machine no longer being in full use in terms of its control of the patronage system and the electoral apparatus.
>
> Chicago's Democratic machine has been disrupted, but it is far from dead. Beware of premature notices of its passing. We politicians know, and the pundits often forget, that the Democratic machine is a hardy and resilient beast.
>
> Progressives and political independents will be caught off-guard and crushed if they are fooled by the latest round of eulogies. The commentators who herald the machine's fall will be forced to retreat to the feeble, false, face-saving cries of 'upset' or 'political miracle,' which they so often use to mask their ignorance.
>
> All Chicago will suffer through four, eight or 12 more years of political despotism, cronyism and blatant racial and economic discrimination if we go to sleep with the notion that the machine is dead.
>
> Chicago's revitalized political freedom movement can win only if it avoids the twin traps of despair and overconfidence. Those who would make Chicago a city that works for all its people must recognize both the roots of machine power and the independent movement's own potential strengths.
>
> That movement should understand that my Congressional primary election victory and the simultaneous wins of such Black independents as Gus Savage, Robert Shaw, Danny Davis, Niles Sherman, Arthur Turner, Earlean Collins and Carol Moseley Braun-were no upsets. They were the logical, predictable result of a long-brewing, still-deepening Black political revolt. But that movement must equally understand that the machine still possesses the patronage power and the political influence it needs to turn our victories into defeat.
>
> The two bulwarks of machine control, the patronage system and regular Democratic control of the electoral apparatus, stand virtually intact. Through the county clerk's office, the Circuit Court judges, and the Board of Elections, all largely machine-controlled, the Democratic machine decides how elections will be run and won.
>
> Through the ward committeemen and their precinct captains, it picks most of the election judges, usually including those nominally labeled Republican, and then its tentacles grip every Chicago polling place.
>
> The bottom line is that the Democratic machine and it operatives control the counting and casting of ballots, rule on the validity of all nominating petitions, certify the results of election, decide who is a legal voter, and determine when election fraud is committed.

At this point in the speech, Harold was pounding his huge hands on the lectern. The menacing expression on his face rivaled that on Muhammad Ali as he prepared a knockout blow for one of his opponents. Harold's facial features mirrored the four seasons: One moment his brow was furrowed and his look was threatening; minutes later, his large, oval-shaped face would break into a grin and his eyes would light up like a kid opening Christmas presents. He continued:

> It is true that some of the most blatant election day abuses have been limited or eliminated in recent years. But fraud still runs rampant, particularly in poor communities like mine. In close races, vote thieves can still reverse the final outcome.
>
> The term 'patronage,' like its close cousin, 'paternalism,' comes from the Latin 'pater,' meaning 'father.' For most Chicagoans, the word patronage conjures up images of jobs dispensed by the local political father, the Democratic ward committeeman. This practice gives the ward bosses a power no individual should have-total control over the lives of thousands of men and women. The ward bosses exact a price which no citizen of a democracy should be forced to pay, and that is the fact that patronage workers must set aside their personal political values and forget the needs of their communities to work for machine candidates who are often unqualified, incompetent or completely unresponsive to constituents.
>
> People forget that the jobs are only a small part of the patronage system. The big patronage and the most corrupting aspect of Chicago's political system is the use of government contracts to the tune of hundreds of millions of dollars each year, to buy campaign contributions and political support from business.
>
> There are the printing contracts, insurance policies, brokerage fees, bank deposits, building maintenance contracts, and countless other government outlays, all corrupted to buy support for Chicago's ruling clique.
>
> Every citizen pays for the patronage system in poor city services and poorly constructed facilities. We pay for it when city government puts big business and downtown interests before the needs of average citizens. But my community, Black Chicago, suffers most deeply.
>
> Downtown bosses force Black patronage workers to campaign for politicians who work against Black interests and they deprive Black Chicago of its fair share of city jobs. They hand Black businesses only the smallest crumbs from the thick government contract pies. I once believed that the patronage system should be reformed so that my community would receive its fair share, but I now understand that patronage can't be doled out fairly. Equity demands that we dismantle the entire patronage structure, grant present and future city workers full political freedom, and take affirmative action to distribute jobs and contracts fairly to minority people and businesses.
>
> The Northside ward boss Paddy Bauler said in his day that the Chicago machine 'ain't ready for reform.' Ready or not, the machine is today confronted by a new force, which is the growing political confidence and maturity of Black Chicago. White Chicagoans often forget that my community is the bearer of our city's oldest and strongest political reform movement.

The origin of Chicago's Black political freedom movement can be traced to 1955, when independent Sidney Jones ousted a white machine incumbent to become 6th Ward alderman.

In 1959, the Chicago League of Negro Voters put together an interracial slate headed by Lemuel E. Bentley, who received 60,000 votes for city clerk as the first Black to seek citywide office. Former 5th Ward Alderman Leon Despres, who for 20 years was known as the dean of City Council independents, credited his 1959 re-election victory to the work of the league.

In 1963, Southside Black voters elected an independent to the City Council, and they've elected two or more to every City Council since.

In 1972, Black votes tossed out Cook County State's Attorney Ed Hanrahan while Jesse Madison cracked the machine's grip on the West Side by winning election to the state legislature.

In 1976, Blacks united to save Ralph Metcalfe from (Mayor Richard) Daley's wrath. In 1975 and 1977, Richard Newhouse's mayoral campaign and my own began the difficult struggle to elect a Black mayor. This struggle, I hope, we will see through to success in 1983.

In order to win the mayoral election in 1983, the Chicago political freedom movement must renew and refine its sense of purpose. We must remember that replacing white despots with Black or brown despots is not reform. We must remember that replacing a tyrannical machine with a more benevolent model is not reform. We must remember that clean government is important but not sufficient. We Chicagoans must work together to make ours a city in which every individual can find economic equity and can live and work with dignity.

These goals can be achieved only by a broad coalition of Blacks, Latinos and liberal whites coming together as equal partners who respect each others' particular needs and unique strengths.

Both justice and political common sense demand that it be what I call a 'right-side-up' coalition, a coalition led by Blacks. Black Chicagoans have the skills, the experience, the proven leaders and the deep experience of oppression which prepare people to fight for change. Black people are ready to rise up. Polls conducted for me in the Southside's 1st Congressional District show that more than 90 percent of those eligible would vote for a Black mayoral candidate in 1983.

For the sake of our entire city, I hope that white independents will join Blacks in a right-side-up alliance. If they don't, you can be sure that the machine's masters of ethnic politics will push forward some Black willing to front for white interests. We must not let the Democratic machine steal our best hope for political freedom in Chicago.

That speech did not endear Washington to the white political machine or the Black submachine. It propelled him into a mudwrestling with State Rep. James C. Taylor, Mayor Jane Byrne's hand-picked Black political leader. They clashed in the fall of 1980 over Gov. James Thompson's bill to consolidate three state civil rights agencies into a Department of Human Rights.

Washington won that match, but lost the bill sponsored to empower an election in which Chicago voters could remove Mayor Jane Byrne from office.

After his overwhelming victory over Republican George Williams in the general election on Tuesday, Nov. 4, 1980, Washington moved quickly to shore up his Illinois stronghold. But, the onerous political shadows of Jane Byrne and James C. Taylor refused to evaporate, hovering over Harold as he toiled in the District of Columbia. Mayor Byrne was determined to maneuver Taylor into a position where he could succeed Washington as state senator from the 26th legislative district.

On Sunday, Dec. 28, 1980, Harold Washington held a press conference and warned Mayor Byrne against continued interference in the selection of his replacement as state senator. He told the press assembled at Chicago's Conrad Hilton Hotel:

> Mayor Byrne is exercising undue influence in selection of a successor, which should be made by the five ward committeemen and the people in the district.
>
> The committeemen are Alderman Tyrone T. Kenner (3rd), Alderman Tyrone L. McFolling (17th), Cecil Partee (20th), Frank Savickas (15th) and James C. Taylor (16th).
>
> Taylor, a state representative, asked Byrne for support and she then urged the committeeman to support him. Taylor has no accountability or concern for the community. Taylor's negative votes on such matters as legislation against redlining, currency exchange reforms and the Cook County Hospital make him unacceptable.
>
> I urge the mayor to respect the Democratic processes and not repeat the mistakes of her predecessor, who dictated the successor of the late Ralph Metcalfe.
>
> It was Mayor Michael A. Bilandic's selection of Bennett M. Stewart to run for Metcalfe's unexpired term that angered independent voters and made it possible for me to win the seat in the November general election.

Washington was so aroused by Byrne's interference on Taylor's behalf that he refused to resign from the Illinois Senate unless state Rep. Ethel Skyles Alexander (20th Ward) was made his successor. He declared that, "Skyles would carry on in the progressive and independent tradition of that district." Cecil Partee joined Washington in the unsuccessful attempt to block Taylor in favor of Skyles.

During the squabble in Chicago over who should fill Washington's state senate seat, Gov. James Thompson and the GOP forces in Springfield seized the opportunity to elect a Republican president of the senate. With Sen. Charles Chew ill in a Chicago hospital and Harold Washington absent to attend a rally commemorating Dr. Martin Luther King Jr.'s birthday at Operation PUSH headquarters, the Thompson contingents circumvented the 30-29 majority the Democratic senators held that year in the legislative session.

On Monday, Jan. 26, 1981. Washington issued a statement:

> I had no intention of being in Springfield on the birthday of Dr. Martin Luther King Jr., and I made this fact widely known. For Black people and other people of goodwill, Dr. King's birthday is a holy day. West Side State Sen. Earlean Collins even protested the propriety of the Legislature being in session on the birthday of Dr. King, pointing out that it does not convene on Columbus Day, Washington's birthday or on Jewish holidays.

He added:

> I sat among 300 or so citizens celebrating this century's greatest leader at Operation PUSH with my resignation statement in my hand dated January 8, effective January 5. Partee is a witness to the fact that I had my resignation statement with me at the commemoration service of the slain leader.
>
> None of my actions violated either state or federal law. They were designed solely in response to the wishes of the 26th District residents.

On Feb. 9, 1981, the Democratic-dominated Illinois Supreme Court threw out the selection of the Republican senate president and ordered Gov. Thompson to hold a new election. That action validated Democrat Philip Rock as president of the senate. State Rep. Taylor (D-26), Mayor Byrne's $70,000-a-year deputy chief of staff, was sworn in to fill the vacated Senate seat.

Harold Washington had been sworn into the 97th Congress of the United States a month earlier. On a cold Jan. 5, 1981, a Chicago-style inauguration was held for the new congressman that could best be described as the Poor Peoples' Inaugural. Harold had invited his foot soldiers to the capitol, and they were a heady mixture of young, old and middle-aged men and women. The majority were women who had stood out on the blustery Chicago streets passing out political leaflets and working the precincts. They came to Washington, D.C., to witness three Black congressmen from Chicago-Cardiss Collins, Gus Savage and Washington-being sworn in at the same time. No other city in the nation could claim that political distinction.

At least 200 of Harold's people made the historic trip to the capital. A few arrived by plane, others by car, but most of them came by bus. The cost of the round trip bus ride was arranged by Charles Hayes, who was the international vice president of the United Food and Commercial Workers' Union, and has subsequently become the congressman of Illinois' First Congressional District.

The delegation traveled smoothly until the bus driven by Charles A. Wilson, owner of the C.W. Limousine Service, ran into a heavy snowstorm and hit a patch of ice as it exited from the Pennsylvania Turnpike. Roy Washington, Harold's oldest brother, describes sliding off the road and down a hill in a four-wheel bus as a "discomforting and frightening experience." No one was seriously injured, though one woman required minor medical attention.

Congressmen Savage and Washington were among the anxious people waiting in the lobby of the Skyline Inn in the District of Columbia for the arrival of those who had been involved in the bus mishap. During their vigil, Gus frequently kidded his old college buddy because Washington could not afford to bring his people to the capitol by plane and put them up at a first-class hotel, as Savage had done for his troops.

Harold's people could not afford to come to Washington by plane, boat or train or go out to a first- or second-class restaurant or any other kind of eatery in Washington. They were Harold's people and he loved them and they loved him. He kept a courtesy room open around the clock and had it stocked with cold cuts, cheese, bread and wine. Thus, there was no need for Harold's folks to journey to a greasy spoon.

The hotel room was always crowded and the victory celebration prevailed until the swearing-in ceremony. Then, the room was stilled as the celebrants listened intently over a loud speaker at the ceremony where their leaders raised their right hands and swore to uphold the constitution. Harold's people understood that Harold would never forsake them even while he was reaching for the stars.

U.S. Representative Harold Washington of the 1st Congressional District.

The election of three Black congressmen in Chicago, Illinois, is guaranteed until 1992 as a result of the 1980 District Court ruling on reapportionment. The lower court's ruling was ratified by the U.S. Supreme Court.

U.S. Representative Gus Savage of the 2nd Congressional District.

U.S. Representative Cardiss Collins of the 7th Congressional District.

CHAPTER

11

Three Black Congressmen in Chicago Were Two Too Many

In November 1980, Black Chicagoans achieved fair representation in the U.S. Congress for the first time in more than 100 years. That was the good news.

The bad news was that the 1980 census showed that Chicago had lost 400,000 in population between 1970 and 1980. Hence, Illinois would be forced to reduce its Congressional representation by two in the next election, which would be held in 1982. Before Gus Savage and Harold Washington could be sworn in, they were haunted by the "Lifo" practice of "Last in, first out."

Savage quickly reacted to the Lifo theory as it was being applied to politics:

> The last-in, first-out concept is the political translation of a longtime racist practice of 'Last hired, first fired.'
>
> Chicago's population dwindled 23 percent between 1970 and 1980; whites left the city at a time when the Black population had increased 6.8 percent.
>
> Under no circumstances will Blacks and Latinos give up their political gains because white folk picked up their bags and ran to the suburbs. We cannot be well-advised to pull ourselves up by our bootstraps when sources threaten to take away our boots.

Black leaders generally and Black elected officials specifically perceived a "back of the bus" mentality among the Illinois state lawmakers. Their plan was to reduce the Illinois delegation in the U.S. House of Representatives to 22 districts from 24 districts, each representing 519,000. Black Chicagoans had every reason to fear that their two new independent congressmen would be the fall guys.

Sen. Earlene Collins (D-Oak Park, Ill.) said, "I think Savage and Washington are vulnerable, and it will be my responsibility to make sure we don't lose any representation."

Congressman Harold Washington and the Rev. Jesse Jackson, head of Chicago's Operation PUSH, prepared to work through the Congress and the courts to prevent racial gerrymandering.

"We're going to fight like the dickens to retain three Black seats for Chicago," Washington declared.

"Black representation is in the eye of the hurricane," said Jackson. "We will have alternative maps to present and we are prepared to go to the streets and to court. We will not sit idly by."

State Rep. Jesse White (D-Chicago) said:

> Savage, who is not part of the Chicago Democratic organization, probably will lose in 1982 if the lines of his district are shifted farther west into predominantly white neighborhoods.
>
> Whites vote more religiously than Blacks, and a white candidate, especially one from the regular Chicago organization, stands a good chance of winning.

Washington had served with distinction on the Illinois Senate Judiciary Committee. In the midst of the remap tug-of-war in Illinois, the freshman congressman was appointed to the powerful House Judiciary Committee. Washington asserted:

> In this era of tax on basic human civil rights and civil liberties, the work of the Judiciary Committee is critically important. I pledge to block the right-wing attack on our basic human rights and to advance the case of justice.
>
> Already, conservatives have served notice that they want to destroy the voting rights act, limit the enforcement of civil rights and affirmative action laws and enact a host of other regressive legislation.
>
> They must be stopped. I will work with like-minded committee members to stop them.

Back in Chicago, the Political Action Conference of Illinois (PACI) proposed a redistricting map designed to prevent Chicago from losing any Black U.S. representative.

The PACI map proposed to retain the seats in the 1st, 2nd and 7th Congressional Districts represented respectively by Washington, Savage and Collins. The PACI contended that Black congressmen should be retained because Chicago's population decline was caused by a loss of white residents, not by a decrease in the number of Black residents.

Washington supported the PACI proposal:

> It is not favoritism but fairness. If Blacks are half the city's population, representative government dictates that our Black citizens are entitled to half the six remaining congressional seats when the remapping is completed. Nowhere has the Supreme Court decreed that the last in Congress should be the first out.

In 1970, the 2nd Congressional District was gerrymandered to keep a burgeoning Black population from acquiring a seat. That injustice was rectified in 1980 with the election of Augustus Savage in a district that is 70 percent Black. Again, Blacks earned that seat.

In the name of our most cherished and democratic ideals, legislative leaders should approach the task of recarving congressional districts in Illinois with the fine-tuned precision of a surgeon and a mind set committed to fairness.

Al Johnson, a Chicago Cadillac dealer who was president of PACI, attempted to open the communication lines among Chicago's Black U.S. congressmen. He encouraged Bill Berry, vice president of Johnson Products and former executive director of the Chicago Urban League, to set up a luncheon for the three legislators and any of their staff they cared to invite. Only two appeared: Gus Savage and Harold Washington.

Harold spoke to the group first, made suggestions about the PACI map and indicated that the proposal could be justified in court. Buttressed by his experiences as a lawyer and as a legislator, he felt confident that PACI could mount an effective campaign to maintain three Black congressmen.

Al Johnson said:

Gus Savage indicated he was not enthusiastic about the map at all. He wanted to draw his own map and said he did not need us. He further indicated that we were not qualified to draw a map and that it was something that politicians should do.

I don't think there were any lines of communication between Congressman Savage and Congressman Washington at the time. This was my feeling and the feeling of my group.

According to Herman Gilbert, Savage's administrative aide:

It was the remap that caused Gus and Harold to have serious disagreements. Gus accused Harold of joining forces with Al Johnson, Bill Berry, Jim Compton and all that crowd to reorganize the district so it would be more favorable to Harold.

Harold said that wasn't the case, that Gus had as much right to be a member of PACI as he did. As a matter of fact, the remap issue became so hot within the Black political camp that Jesse Jackson had to call a special meeting and appoint Robert Starks, of Northeastern University's Center for Innercity Studies, to be the referee.

Dr. Starks supported the PACI redistricting proposal in an appearance before a reapportionment conference in Champaign, Ill.:

There is an extremely nasty situation developing in regard to Chicago's growing minorities.

Incumbent white legislators may try to establish new districts in a way that would thwart minority effort to elect Chicago's first Black mayor in 1983.

Chicago's white officials, including Mayor Jane Byrne, will try to redraw district maps to squelch the voice of the city's growing Black and Hispanic populations.

> Running new district lines through strong Black and Hispanic neighborhoods will make it harder for the two groups to build enough clout to elect a Black mayor.
>
> The Democratic machine does not want a high number of minorities to vote because it will weaken its power in City Hall.
>
> Mayor Richard J. Daley was a master at gerrymandering. His 11th Ward is one of the best pieces of art I have ever seen. It was drawn to exclude Blacks.
>
> Since the death of the late Mayor Daley, an identifiable motivation is developing in the Black community and I feel, as other Blacks, that a Black can be mayor in 1983.
>
> The whites are hoping that Blacks won't know the implications of redistricting this year, and that Black political leaders won't get out the vote and register.
>
> Civil rights activist Jesse Jackson and U.S. Rep. Harold Washington (D-Ill.) are likely Black candidates against Byrne for the mayoral office seat in 1983.

Congressman Savage was not listening to Dr. Starks. Gus was unhappy with the Independent Voters of Illinois-Independent Precinct Organization, who were also proposing a redistricting map. He felt that the IVI-IPO map would change his district into the longest bowling alley in the world-112 blocks long-and force him to run against a lifelong friend, Harold Washington.

Savage discussed the IVI-IPO map:

> There is a question of morality here. They are trying to express a personality preference. The IVI has endorsed Congressman Washington. I have no quarrel with that. Washington is my friend.
>
> I am concerned with the fairness when a group deliberately changes my boundaries to include 120,000 whites, 60,000 more than are now in my district. The question of numbers doesn't bother me. The type of whites does bother me.

A spokesman for the Independent Voters of Illinois replied:

> We drew the map lines down into the South suburbs to include Dixmoor, Harvey, Phoenix, Markham, East Hazelcrest and a small portion of the predominantly white area of Homewood. If this map is selected, Savage will have 400,000 to 120,000 whites. Does that sound racist? There is no way a Black can lose in a district that is 78 percent Black.

The reapportionment map pitted Savage and Washington against each other in a struggle for survival. Harold, a seasoned legislator who knew his way around both the Illinois House and the Senate, held the upper hand. Gus was equally bright, but his political artillery depended heavily on his excellent debating skills and his knowledge of Western and Eastern philosophies. These attributes alone did not constitute the heavy payload required to win a political battle with Harold Washington.

In contrast to Savage's confrontational stance, Washington's smooth style captured the approval of Black and white independent voters, and laid the basic strategy for a court battle. Savage entered the remap fray as an anti-machine candidate, but received considerable support from Mayor Jane Byrne and her cohort, state Sen. James Taylor, Harold Washington's arch enemy. Gus also had the support of independents such as Alderman Robert Shaw (9th) and Alderman Niles Sherman (21st).

To undergird his position on reapportionment, Washington assigned Sam Patch, his friend and staff member, to work with the IVI-IPO in drawing up a map based on retention of the three Black congressional districts. Patch was also instrumental in helping draw the map for the Political Action Conference of Illinois.

Congressman Savage had some legitimate concerns in that the IVI-IPO and PACI had been pro-Washington and neutral on Savage in the previous primary. Both groups heightened the tension between the two legislators by proposing redistricting plans that transferred big chunks of Savage's political terrain to Washington's district. On Monday, May 11, 1981, Savage labeled the activity of Washington supporters as "racist."

Charles Hayes, currently U.S. Representative of the 1st Congressional District, retorted, "He's nuts."

The author's position on the sad schism that separated my friends in the Congress has not changed: It was power politics, not racism, as charged by Savage, that fueled the fight to save the three Black congressional districts. In fact, it was the consensus of the groups that if someone had to lose, it would not be Washington.

Reminiscing about Washington's maneuvers during the remap struggle, Congressman Savage recently observed:

> Harold was the best politician, while I tried to be the best philosopher. There is a difference. Politicians and philosophers have different limitations. And I respect that.
>
> Washington is the greatest, which was evidenced by the way he distinguished himself time after time in the Illinois General Assembly and in the halls of the U.S. Congress. Most of the politicians I have met were not as literate as Harold. Harold read vociferously. He was extremely knowledgeable, far more knowledgeable than most.
>
> Harold, unquestionably, was committed to the welfare of Blacks, not so much because they were Black, but because he saw this as a way of healing the divisions in our society that would make it possible for people to move forward. I'm convinced of that. So that made him the best of the breed.
>
> Harold had another dimension. He had probably more practical experience and street knowledge of the real world of politics than anybody out there in the field. So you put all those things together and you've got an unusual, almost political, Renaissance man. And that was the man that I was in the ring with during the remap bout.
>
> I recognized that I was exchanging blows with the Joe Louis of politics. However, I wasn't frightened because I never saw myself as a politician in the sense of being in competition with Harold. Neither did I

see myself as limited or circumscribed by any possibility or particular circumstance.

Savage's comments about Harold Washington were not an overstatement. In June of 1981, Washington accomplished an unprecedented political coup when he persuaded 14 Republican state legislators to agree to a plan that would assure friendly districts for the three Black congressmen, as well as for the Republicans, in the forthcoming election. To assure success, Washington persuaded four Black independent Democrats to vote with the Republicans on the reapportionment plan. The proposal barely made it through the House on Tuesday, June 23, 1981. Reps. Monica Faith Stewart and Arthur Turner, two Washington supporters who argued the PACI position before the Republican leaders, deserve a great deal of credit for the passage of the PACI-GOP reapportionment plan.

The Washington strategy was to guarantee that if the GOP map did not reach the governor's desk, it would at least get top consideration in federal court. He built his case on a ruling handed down a decade earlier when the U.S. District Court stepped in to take over the responsibilities of another stymied Legislature.

The Washington-Republican strategy was basically simple. The 14 white Illinois Republican legislators entered into an agreement with four Black Democratic legislators to draw congressional maps for two members of their team and the three Black Chicago congressmen at the expense of white incumbents Edward J. Derwinski (4th District) and Robert McClory (13th District).

As a former Illinois Senator, Washington had anticipated that the Senate would not approve the compromise. A three-judge panel in the U.S. District Court, composed of one Democrat and two Republicans—one a Nixon appointee—heard the case.

Former Democratic Secretary of State Michael Howlett and former Republican Gov. Richard B. Ogilvie presented a "coalition map" that would have eliminated two Black congressional districts. The court found their proposal unacceptable. Ogilvie let it be known that he considered it most important to eliminate two Black congressional seats in order to elect two white establishment stalwarts. However, when he realized that the court was not going along with his rationale, he had the coalition map hastily revised to create three Black districts.

Under the revised map, Washington's new district would have stretched into Gage Park, Marquette Park and a portion of Evergreen and West Beverly, a district that was 57 percent Black. The Black community, including the *Chicago Defender,* almost went into shock when Congressman Savage endorsed the Ogilvie-revised map. The revision was a blatant attempt by the Jane Byrne-Edward Vrdolyak Democratic machine to deprive Harold Washington of his Congressional office.

Harold never forgave Gus for his disloyalty, and later refused to endorse Tommy Savage, Gus' son, in subsequent races for alderman and state representative.

Harold's bitterness toward Gus was so great that in the winter of 1982, he did not want to be in the same public hall with him. On Jan. 30, 1982, the streets were piled high with snow. Congressman Washington's advance man called me to ascertain the time that Congressman Savage was scheduled to appear at an autographing party unveiling *An Autobiography of Black Chicago,* which would be held at Chicago State University. I told him that Gus was expected at 1 p.m. Harold's advance man responded, "We'll be there at 12 o'clock." Harold and his people arrived at noon sharp, took pictures with the author and left 15 minutes before the Savage entourage was due.

In many ways, Gus and Harold were cut from the same cloth. Mentally fast and articulate, they shared the traits of being tough, unforgiving and vindictive. For example, Gus has never forgiven State Rep. Robert Shaw for running against him in the 1984 election. Savage has said to the writer, "I am not going to make peace with anybody who runs against me one time."

Over and above the remap conflict, Harold and Gus had to deal with an ego-inspired territorial dispute. Soon after they were elected to Congress, Gus declared, "I am not going to appear on television with Harold Washington because I am not one of the Gold Dust twins." On the other hand, Harold did not subscribe to a Mutt-and-Jeff routine. He felt that his legislative experience entitled him to the leadership role. Savage demurred.

Harold's legislative experience proved invaluable. The Howlett-Ogilvie remap that Gus Savage had supported failed. A Washington-endorsed map with PACI principles grafted to it finally passed the court with a 2-1 majority, an implicit admission by the Nixon-appointed judge that the Democratic map was the sensible and practical solution. The Federal District Court ruling was subsequently ratified by the U.S. Supreme Court. The three-judge federal court approved reapportionment that insured the election of three Chicago Black congressmen for the next decade.

Harold Washington hailed the court's opinion as a hallmark victory for the Black community:

> We all owe a great deal to Political Action Conference of Illinois for initiating the drive to retain three Black districts and for rallying the entire community behind the principle. For the first time, a Black organization drew a reapportionment map that was computer-verified and met all the Supreme Court requirements in every respect.
>
> The PACI map drafting and planning caused the Democratic and Republican parties to incorporate the concept of three Black districts in their respective maps, and influenced all three judges to state that dilution of the Black vote was unacceptable. Therefore, I say again, that without PACI we would not have three Black districts in the map that was finally adopted by the U.S. District Court.

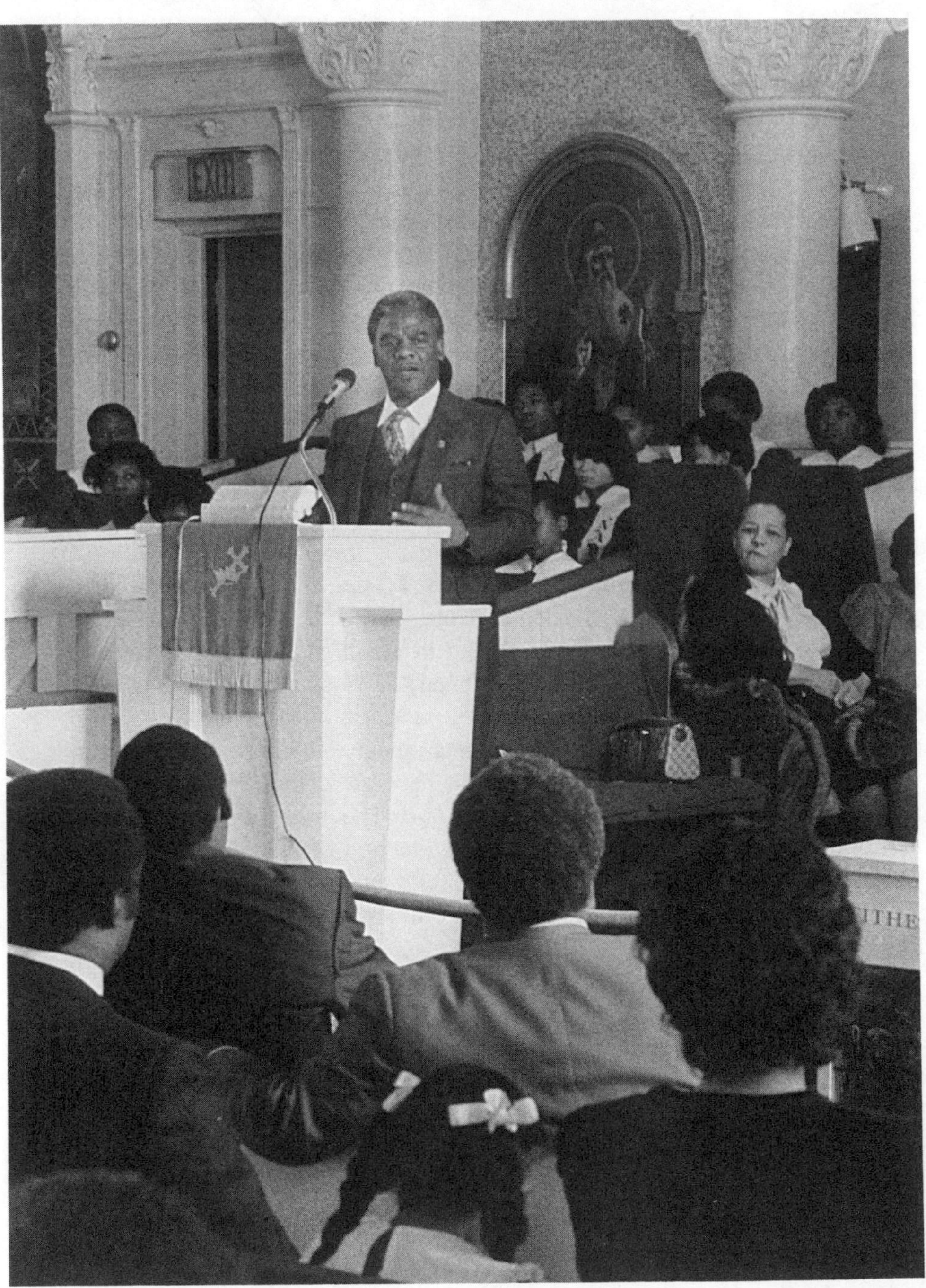

Congressman Harold Washington made more than 400 appearances before community organizations and churches, and on radio and television shows, during his first year in Congress. Above, he is shown addressing one of six scheduled church services on a typical Sunday.

CHAPTER 12

Harold's Second Trip to the House on Capitol Hill

Since members of the U.S. House of Representatives stand for election every two years, Harold Washington had not sat in his congressional chair long enough to get it warm before it was time for him to file petitions to run for a second term. The brevity of Harold's service in the House did not displease his Nemesis, Chicago Mayor Jane Byrne, or her deputy, state Sen. James Taylor. Neither intended for Harold to stay in Congress long enough to find his way to the latrine.

Jane and Jim had worked frantically to block Washington's ascendancy to the House and labored indefatigably during his first 12 months in Congress to find a viable candidate to replace him. Candidates on the mayor's list to challenge Washington were Gerald Bullock, Lenora Cartwright, Chicago Commissioner of Human Services, Alderman Tim Evans and state Sen. Richard Newhouse. As an added incentive, members of the Byrne machine let it be known that a basket of cabbage-size campaign dollars would be available for Harold Washington's challenger.

Washington knew he was on the Democratic organization's short list of one as the man to defeat, and he was running scared. Forewarned that both the white and Black wolves of the political machine were out to get him, Harold hit the ground campaigning for re-election within a few days after he was sworn into Congress.

Touching every strand in the fabric of his political constituency was a Harold Washington hallmark. Every weekend, beginning with Friday evening, Jan. 10, 1981, he returned to Chicago and held meetings with various constituents. At noon each Saturday, you could find Harold in the north hall of the United Packinghouse Workers headquarters, 4859 S. Wabash, providing soul lunches for 75 to 100 supporters and briefings them on what had taken place in Washington during the past week.

Around mid-Saturday afternoon, Washington would go to the North Side to Slim Coleman's territory, known as the Heart of the Uptown Area, and make speeches on countless issues of interest to Appalachian whites, American Indians and other disadvantaged minorities. Although Uptown was not in the First Congressional District, the Uptown coalition, under the leadership of Coleman and Helen Schiller, had supported Harold when he ran for mayor in 1977. He never forgot their priceless loyalty.

Washington also frequently addressed peace rallies and hand gun control groups on the Near North lakefront along the Gold Coast, where he had a small but affluent Jewish constituency and support from other "lakefront liberals."

Harold met regularly with leading clergymen of the First Congressional District in accountability sessions where they exchanged ideas on matters of concern to the clergy and their parishioners. The Rev. Stephen J. Thurston, pastor of New Convenant Missionary Baptist Church, 740 E. 77th St., was the convener of the multiracial ministerial group who represented every faith, denomination and neighborhood in the 14 wards of Washington's district. Men and women of the cloth from outside of the district—and occasionally from outside the state—were attracted to the meetings.

Congressman Washington made more than 400 appearances before community organizations, churches, and on radio and television shows during his first 10 months in Congress. To my surprise, he admitted that he enjoyed every minute of it. On some weekends, he addressed as many as six to nine meetings on critical issues confronted by Chicagoans of every economic and social stripe. Washington frequently told his constituents:

> Accountability requires community response and dialogue between a congressman and his community. The 1st Congressional District is one of the most vocal in the country. When I walk the streets of my district each weekend, people tell me about their problems and also vent their anger about the Reagan administration.

Harold Washington was circling the wagons, aware that aliens were snipping at his heels and howling hot rhetoric in his ears. The activity in his 1st Congressional District headquarters, 7801 S. Cottage Grove, reflected his stewardship. During his first 300 days as congressman in 1981, 11,408 people communicated with his office by phone. About 5,000 individuals visited the office requesting service of some sort. More than 3,000 people attended 100 public meetings chaired by Washington and held in the community room of the headquarters building. The congressman explained:

This office belongs to all the people of the district. It has been organized as a service, information and community action center to meet the people's needs. I want to make sure that I'm always accessible to every constituent who has something to say on the issues that I will vote on in Congress.

In order to distance himself from potential challengers for his congressional seat, Harold Washington filed re-election petitions in Springfield, Ill., on the earliest possible date, which was Monday, Dec. 28, 1981. Those petitions held the signatures of 25,000 voters, more than 10 times the number needed to qualify. A surplus of signatures on the petitions of a politician who is running scared is called wolf tickets. The candidate is saying, "If you get too close to me, I will do more than growl, I will bite you."

The majority of voters in the 14 wards of the 1st District had been organized by the Citizens Committee for Harold Washington, and the petitions were gathered by leaders of Political Action Conference of Illinois (PACI), Chicago Black United Communities (CBUC), Independent Voters of Illinois-Independent Precinct Organization (IVI-IPO) and by some friends of Harold who were members of the regular Democratic organization. The junior Congressman observed:

The sheer number of signatures indicates the community-based support for my re-election. Every petition I carried to Springfield represented a vote of confidence in my campaign for re-election and an endorsement of my efforts to return to Congress and continue to fight for jobs, justice and freedom.

Though I believe I have accomplished much in the last 11 months, much more remains to be accomplished.

I turn again to the voters for a renewed commitment to the independent progressive thrust we have charted for this district.

I want to continue the fight in the Congress and in the community against the dangerous, troubling assaults on our liberties.

I am angered by the rampant assaults on domestic justice, civil liberties and world peace launched by the Reagan administration and its allies in Congress.

I am angered by the needless suffering inflicted on our community by inflation, by cutbacks in human survival programs, and by elimination of jobs and training programs in our community. I am further angered by the slashing of federal programs for stimulation of Black business.

I want to return to Congress to fight against a totally unprincipled Reagan and his minions who have set out to undermine the living standards of the Black community. They have deliberately created unemployment on a scale that can never be tolerated in a civilized society and for which there is only one remedy—fight back and fight back until the battle is won.

I want to return to Congress to fight the disease of Reagonomics, which is sweeping the country and threatening to devastate the working people of Illinois and kill the city of Chicago.

I want to return to silence the drumbeats of war. To solve problems at home, we must stop squandering hundreds of billions of dollars on war programs, the neutron bomb and other massive weapon systems.

I want to stop the secret shipments of hazardous nuclear waste on the busy highways where you and your family travel.

I want to continue the fight with my fellow Black and progressive congressmen against the 'new right, Republican solutions.' Their 'solution' to environmental problems is to gut the Clean Air Act and rape our coastline with indiscriminate off-shore drilling. Their 'solution' is to end job training programs, putting hundreds of thousands of mostly minority youth out of factories and offices onto the streets. Their 'solution' is arrest without warrant, detention without trial, hanging in the prison cells and other crimes against humanity, which are all too common in our community.

I want to fight the system that makes the basic decisions affecting your life, your future and perhaps even your survival behind the closed boardroom doors on LaSalle Street, in City Hall and the White House.

The system is the problem. Its top and bottom line is racism. It perverts our political processes. It sustains and manipulates. It subjects us to the incredible dangers of nuclear power and the growing risk of nuclear war. It squanders our natural resources, pollutes our environment and jeopardizes our livelihood with inflation and deliberate unemployment. It levies crushing taxes on the poor and fig-leaf taxes on the rich.

But we need not sit silently by and let the tide of Reaganism overwhelm us. We can and we must fight back.

There is proof that Reagan can be stopped. We must stop him before it's too late.

The first line of defense is in the Congress. It is in the Congress that the battle line is most active. And it is in the Congress that we will have our first chance to defeat him.

In the next year—unless you and I can prevent it—Reagan will continue to pick and pinch our pockets.

If we do not win, our country can look forward to more slashing of Social Security benefits, the further gutting of environmental laws, the escalation of the nuclear arms race, the crippling of programs to educate the unemployed and the further incursion of the Moral Majority doctrine into our lives.

It's up to you and me to stop this attack on us.

Together, we can meet the crucial challenges ahead. Together we can achieve justice at every level of government. Together we can help turn our country around toward jobs, justice and peace.

Harold's clarion calls for the voters to join him in the fight against Reaganomics and for Black empowerment galvanized the people of the district. The formidable organizations behind the drive that generated the signatories on 25,000 petitions sent an unmistakable message to the regular Democrats.

The reaction of the Democratic organization's reslating committee was described by David Canter, a Washington campaign coordinator, as the strangest behavior he had ever seen. He said he never thought that he would live to see the day that members of the regular Democratic organization would actually embrace an independent Democrat like Harold Washington. At the reslating meeting held in the McCormick Inn, there was no opposition to Congressman Washington's bid for a second term. Even Jim Taylor endorsed him, a signal that Mayor Byrne had dropped her opposition to Washington's re-election in preparation for her own 1983 mayoral bid.

Although Mayor Byrne and her supporters gave U.S. Rep. Harold Washington a free ride in the March '82 primary, he did not stop fighting or become any less critical. During a speech at a civil rights conference held on March 27, 1982 at the Church of the Good Shepherd, 5700 S. Prairie Ave., Washington frequently assumed the stance of a boxer, thrusting his huge fist forward to punctuate major points:

> The Reagan administration, armed with blueprints written by conservative 'think tanks,' is trying to strip us of every gain we have made over the last 30 years, particularly in the field of civil rights.
>
> There is a broad gap in the field of civil rights. There are no civil rights laws, no civil liberties and almost no guarantees of economic opportunities that have been left untouched by the Reagan administration.
>
> It should be obvious by now that individuals and organizations who thought they could exert moderating influence have no impact on the policies of the administration.
>
> Time after time, on issues like extension of the voting rights act and of the tax status of discriminatory schools, the administration has refused to accept moderate positions even where those positions were clearly shared by the overwhelming majority of the Congress and the American people. It should also be clear that this is not politics as we have traditionally known it to be.
>
> We have to accept the fact at this moment that the presidency has been captured by the radical right. Our job now is to arm ourselves with the facts and revitalize our coalitions and to alert people everywhere to what is going on.
>
> Nowhere is the Reagan administration's strategy more clear than in its attempts to disregard Title VI and Title IX of the 1964 Civil Rights Act, Sec. 504, and the Rehabilitation Act of 1973.
>
> The point is, until Reagan took over the White House and his appointees took over the justice department, nobody thought there was any question as to whether or not the federal government would grant tax exemption. The law itself is very simple. It permits no discrimination by those that receive federal grants and aid.
>
> By executive order signed by President Jimmy Carter in 1980, the Justice Department is responsible for coordinating the interpretation of each standard by all of the other federal agencies. The Reagan administration has abused that authority. It has given indications that it intends

> a wholesale review, and is doing so by proposing block grants to transfer that responsibility to the states.
>
> This approach would end federal leadership in promoting equal opportunity, jeopardize the federal civil rights portion and leave it up to the individual states to decide whether to incorporate and how to interpret non-discriminatory requirements such as those under Sec. 6.

The fine-tuning of Washington's innate political talents during his 16 years in the Illinois Legislature enabled him to unravel federal gobbledygook in a language comprehensible to his constituency. Fellow legislators and representatives from the American Civil Liberties Union, NAACP, National Urban League and other similar organizations pressured him to accept a heavy workload throughout his two years and four months in Congress.

Washington jumped at opportunities to serve on the Education and Labor Committee, the Government Operations Committee and the prestigious Judiciary Committee. The rules of the House had to be changed to enable him to accept the Judiciary Committee assignment, which was his third appointment. Though the increased workload caused him to vote by proxy in some committees and miss other votes, Washington made special efforts to be present when important votes came to the floor.

The indefatigable congressman accepted several subcommittee assignments. He served on the Elementary and Secondary Vocational Education, Employment, Safety and Health subcommittees within the Education and Labor Committee. In the Government Operations Committee, he worked on the Manpower and Housing Subcommittee. He devoted a great deal of his attention to the Civil and Constitutional Rights Subcommittees within the Judiciary Committee.

His workload was further increased with his appointment to the position of secretary of the Congressional Black Caucus.

Washington's popularity and skills in the halls of Congress did not go unnoticed by Chicago's Black and Hispanic population. When prospective Black mayoral candidates were discussed in the spring of 1982, Harold's name was at the top of every list.

On Sunday, May 23, 1982, Washington said on the WBBM-AM radio program "At Issue":

> I am sure that I or some other politically potent Black would enter the mayoral race, and that a Black candidate would reshape Chicago politics. Such a candidate would bring a record Black voter registration and would raise the chances of Blacks running in the aldermanic election coinciding with the mayoral primary in February 1983.
>
> Byrne is mediocre as mayor. She is forever embroiled in crass, everyday, mundane politics. Private polls show Chicago Blacks are totally disenchanted with Byrne.

State Sen. Charles Chew Jr. (D-Chicago) differed with Washington, convinced that Blacks' only realistic choice in the 1983 mayoral race would be between Mayor Byrne and State's Attorney Richard M. Daley.

While not openly endorsing either white candidate, Chew said, "My community doesn't feel Byrne has done a job worthy of support. Daley has done a good job in his office."

Sen. Chew dampened efforts to field a Black candidate when he said, "There is no viable organization that can come up with an acceptable Black candidate and enough money to support him. Many Blacks are qualified to run, but the time is not right."

In reference to Rep. Washington, Chew said, "I think he would do well in the Black community, but he doesn't have a following in the white community. Moreover, I don't sense a movement for a Black mayoral candidate."

In answer to the rhetorical question of what Black candidate could raise a million dollars to run for mayor, Chew replied, "I don't think there is one."

THE PEOPLES COALITION TO BOYCOTT CHICAGO FEST

URGE YOU TO

BOYCOTT CHICAGO FEST! aug. 4 - 14

Why A Boycott?

BECAUSE MAYOR BYRNE HAS REPEATEDLY INSULTED THE BLACK COMMUNITY BY:

- Putting three (3) whites on the CHA Board in charge of 150,000 residents who sought more Black representation;
- Giving orders for and condoning outrageous acts of Police Brutality, especially against those who assembled at City Hall over the CHA issue. WE MUST NEVER FORGET THE BARRICADES!
- Removing Blacks from key positions on the Chicago School Board, in the Police Department & Fire Department, in CTA, in CHA and replacing them with whites;
- Packing the City Council chambers with city workers - in contempt of Black efforts to address grievances and politicize serious issues ... and in violation of Open Meetings Acts.

DON'T BUY A TICKET! DON'T ACCEPT A FREE TICKET!

DON'T COME NEAR FEST AREA!

FIND OUT MORE ABOUT THIS MOVEMENT BY CALLING THESE NUMBERS FOR INFORMATION:

373-3366 (PUSH) • 548-2000 (CBUC) • 268-7500 (BUF/CHI) • 337-0218(TRANQUILIT

'FED UP WITH MESS? BOYCOTT THE FEST'

*Our Struggle for human dignity goes far beyond a few days of entertainment!

The boycott of Mayor Jane Byrne's Chicago Fest was one of the linchpins of the 1982 voter registration campaign.

CHAPTER

13

Washington: The People's Choice to Run for Mayor

U.S. Rep. Harold Washington was the Black community's favorite to run for mayor of Chicago in the 1983 election. This was determined by a citywide survey conducted by the Chicago Black United Communities (CBUC) between May 1 and June 15, 1982.

Lu Palmer, founder of CBUC, was one of the 10 individuals on the survey list. On July 7, 1982, he contacted the other nine and asked them if there were any circumstances or conditions under which they would not run for mayor. The persons he called were Roland Burris, Margaret Burroughs, Manford Byrd, Lenora Cartwright, Alderman Danny K. Davis (29th), Jesse Jackson, Alderman Anna Langford (16th), Renault Robinson and Harold Washington. Palmer recalls:

> Both Manford Byrd and Renault Robinson indicated they had no interest in running. Margaret Burroughs also said she wasn't interested; Lenora Cartwright said the same, and I withdrew my name. So, we ultimately ended up with just six people. Our keynote speaker at the plebiscite meeting, which was at the Bethel AME Church on July 26, was Congressman Harold Washington. And, of course, he was the runaway winner in votes, like 10 to one.
>
> Harold's speech disturbed me because he kept harping on the theme that it is the 'plan and not the man.' I looked at some of the other organizers of the meeting and frowned. I did not know what he was talking about when he said that, because he was our man and we wanted him to run.

> Directly after the meeting, we went to the congressman to see what factors would have to be in place for him to make the run. Harold replied, 'There has to be war chest of at least $250,000 to $500,000, and you have got to prove that you can get at least 50,000 new people registered.'

At one of his regular Saturday afternoon meetings, two days before the July 26 meeting, Washington said that his decision to run for mayor hinged greatly on Black voter registration leading up to the February 1983 primary. "As a practical politician, I would seek to build a coalition of Black and white campaign workers throughout the city. The issue would not be anti-race but anti-greed and anti-corruption," he declared.

Two weeks later, Lu Palmer, Tim Black, Zenobia Black, Connie Howard, Oscar Worrill and Nate Clay organized a group called People's Movement for Voter Registration. It was launched with a mass meeting at the Bethel AME Church in mid-August 1982. The keynote speaker was Harold Washington.

In the interim, Slim Coleman, a white Harvard-educated Texan who was the leader of The Heart of Uptown Coalition, and Nancy Jefferson, a civil rights veteran and executive director of The Midwest Community Council, along with a coalition of community organizations called POWER (People Organized for Welfare and Employment Rights) launched a citywide voter registration campaign.

POWER entered the voter registration movement through the back door because the group was formed in June 1982 to fight Illinois Gov. James Thompson's reduction in the poor people's general assistance grants to $144 from $162. The coalition received no respect from state legislators for their efforts because most people on general assistance were not registered voters. So, Jefferson and Coleman came up with the bright idea that they could get the attention of public officials if the 110,000 plus grant recipients were registered voters. Coleman describes the rationale for pursuing the voter registration route for relief recipients:

> We believed that if we got all our welfare people registered that elected officials would listen better. Moreover, we had a captive audience because we knew exactly where each one of these people would come every month to sign their general assistance checks. However, first we had to file a lawsuit to get the Election Commission's permission to register aid recipients at the various Public Aid offices. Then, we had to negotiate with the Board of Election Commissioners to place registrars at the sites since they initially would not deputize our people as registrars.
>
> The commissioners were stubborn, so I went to Joe Novak, who was running the campaign for Adlai Stevenson, and said, 'Look, we can register a lot of voters for your campaign if you can get the Board of Election Commissioners to cooperate.' Novak went to Edward Vrdolyak, and Vrdolyak got the commissioners to cooperate and agree to furnish

two voter registrars outside of each public aid office providing we could furnish vans that would remain at every site all day.

We did not have any money, so we got the radio people to give us some public service time to make our plea. Vans poured in from all over the city. We went back to Novak and told him we needed some money to keep the campaign going. He got Alfred G. Ronan (14th District), a state representative and North Side committeeman, to give us $5,000. In the last two weeks in August, and the first two weeks in September, we registered 47,000 people. When Al Ronan learned about the success of our efforts, he said, 'The hell with Stevenson. Those votes could be used to elect Harold Washington the next mayor of Chicago.'

The voter registration campaign smoldered up to mid-July 1982, when Mayor Jane Byrne fanned the flames with the appointment of three controversial whites to the Chicago Housing Authority Board and locked out members of the Black community from the City Council hearings. Byrne's actions raised Black temperatures above the boiling point. Early Sunday morning, July 24, 1982, a woman who identified herself as a Gary, Indiana, resident called into Derrick Hill's *Sunday Morning Live* talk show on radio station WBMX (102.7 FM). "If Mayor Jane Byrne can lock us out of City Hall, why can't we boycott her upcoming Chicago Fest?" she asked.

The Reverend Jesse Jackson, who was the next speaker on the radio program, was asked his opinion of a boycott. "It was an excellent idea," he replied. On July 31, at the regular Operation PUSH meeting, Reverend Jackson burned his Chicago Fest tickets in the presence of 2,000 supporters and declared:

> We will begin boycotting Chicago Fest down at Navy Pier this Wednesday morning, August 3, at 10. This boycott is a religious rebellion. We must put dignity over dollars and emancipation over entertainment. It is better to boycott with dignity than to sing and dance in shame. We are not bound by Chicago plantation politics. We must aggressively and militantly use our dollars and our votes. We will win, not because we are the majority, but because we are the margin of profit. We will win because of Black volume. . . . They can't do without us. We are necessary. The Black dollar is the margin of failure or salvation. We are a wild card, not a discard. This is not a Black-only Chicago Fest boycott.

Standing on the podium with Reverend Jackson that Saturday morning to demonstrate their support of the boycott were aldermen Lawrence Bloom (5th), Ivan M. Rittenberg (40th), and Martin J. Oberman (43th), and a representative of the Independent Voters of Illinois (IVI). Also supporting the boycott were aldermen Danny K. Davis (29th), Allan Streeter (17th), and Niles Sherman (21st); Alderwoman Marian Humes (8th); Illinois Representatives Larry Bullock (D-22) and Carol Mosley Braun (D-24); state Senator Richard Newhouse (D-24); Cook County Board Commissioner John Stroger;

Congressman Harold Washington (D-1); and Congressman Gus Savage (D-2). Alderman Clifford Kelley (20th) said he would be leading the way.

A worker on the Byrne political plantation, who asked not to be identified, told Chinta Strausberg, a *Chicago Daily Defender* political reporter, "I have never before seen one issue (the mayor's recent confirmation of the three controversial white CHA board members) unify the Black community in my life. It is the most beautiful thing I have ever seen. I am surprised."

Stevie Wonder, Motown superstar, was scheduled to perform at Chicago Fest on August 7, but cancelled his engagement after learning of the festival boycott. Stevie was the first of the main attractions to bow out of his fest contract.

Reverend Jackson denounced the white news media for saying that singer Aretha Franklin, known as the Queen of Soul, wanted to perform in Stevie Wonder's place. "Aretha said to me, 'How can I sing *Respect* and do this to my brother? I never said I would replace Stevie,' " Jackson blasted. "This is just another tool to divide the Black community, but it won't work. Instead, it's bringing us closer together."

Roger Simon, a *Chicago Sun-Times* columnist, wrote:

> Jesse Jackson's planned boycott of Chicago Fest has already succeeded. Not because Stevie Wonder, probably the most popular Black performer in America, has cancelled his appearance. Not because Jackson believes that large numbers of people will stay away. And not because he expects Black vendors to pull out. He has succeeded because his goal was to engulf in controversy Jane Byrne's most popular event, to tarnish her image as a kindly provider of bread and circuses, and to turn up the heat on her summer. It has even led him to hint he may run for mayor in 1983.

Jackson responded:

> I will not rule it out. I will not reject it with some public statement. I am eligible. I am qualified. I could gain a significant following, which I deserve.
>
> There are not just Blacks, but Hispanics and whites and members of labor movements who would all vote for a credible Black candidate. If I run, I would be a factor to be reckoned with. The polls show that.
>
> Chicago has become a coronation site for Jane Byrne's queenship. Now, with this boycott, we are letting people know that those who choose to blatantly disrespect Black persons must face the consequences.
>
> Jane Byrne is not my magnificent obsession. I don't want any anti-Byrne mania. She can organize that herself. In fact, she's the best organizer of that in the city.
>
> I don't think she can be elected without the Black vote. So her actions are baffling. She assumes that Blacks will not vote for her and she has written them off, or that we are so docile and stupid we will vote for her no matter what she does.

The success of the fest boycott escalated the enthusiasm for voter registration. The fumes of barbecue at the ChicagoFest were supplanted by the smell of an impending voter registration victory.

On a clear, bright Tuesday morning shortly after the fest, Renault Robinson was driving north on the Dan Ryan Expressway, thinking about the Chicago Fest victory and its potential for a very successful voter registration campaign. Someone announced on the radio that Edward Gardner, chairman of the board of Soft Sheen Products Inc., and one of American's most successful businessmen, had made a substantial contribution to some struggling charitable organization. Robinson immediately picked up his telephone, dialed information and got Mr. Gardner's telephone number. He recalls:

> Without giving it a second thought, I called Mr. Gardner's company cold. I had never met Mr. Gardner, neither had I ever heard his name mentioned until I heard that radio announcement. However, I was able to get through to him immediately. I told him that I would like to see him.
>
> He said, 'Come on.' I got off the northbound expressway and got back on the southbound and went directly to his office at 1000 E. 87th St.
>
> I told Mr. Gardner about my connection with the Afro-American Patrolmen's League and some other activities in which I had been involved. I also told him that we wanted to do something about the voter registration campaign right now.
>
> Mr. Gardner asked, 'What difference will it make?'
>
> I told him I thought it would make a significant difference in that there was a good possibility that we could put a Black mayor in City Hall next year, one who would respond to the needs of all the citizens of Chicago.
>
> Mr. Gardner seemed to be very, very interested in what I was saying. As a matter of fact, he called his son Gary and his daughter Terri in to meet me and he also introduced me to his wife Bettiann. And we all talked some more about the possibilities of a Black mayor and the need to get a maximum number of people registered. I also told him that we had to have a media campaign and message that was more dynamic than our current street efforts, which, in my opinion, were not going to make it.
>
> I indicated that I thought that Black people had to be educated politically. We discussed a media campaign a bit more and before I left Mr. Gardner put me in touch with some of the media people in his organization and gave me a check for $5,000. This was the first significant sum that I had received for the voter registration campaign.

Renault Robinson was the first person to approach Mr. Gardner about participating in the voter registration campaign. Gardner shares vivid recollections of that day:

> I asked Renault how we could bring about a change in the political life and enable Blacks to be more representative in the City Council, have

more voice and get their share of contracts and of business and so forth.

Robinson replied, 'Ed, you can't bring about any change unless we get more Black people to register and vote. That's the problem. We can talk until we're blue in the face, but if they don't register, then you are not going to have the numbers to effect any kind of political change in the city where people can see that jobs are equally shared with all sectors of the city.'

I turned to my son Gary, who is the president of the company, and said, 'It's near the end of our advertising period, which is September and October. Why don't we allocate a certain amount of our advertising dollars and time to voter registration between now and October 5?' My son and I both agreed that that was a good idea. So we decided that we'd turn it over to Brainstorm, which is our in-house advertising agency headed by my daughter Terri.

Terri's Brainstorm people came up with some fantastic, creative ideas to make voter registration a significant part of Black Americans' lives here in the city of Chicago. Their idea was, 'Come Alive October 5.' Their slogan was a voter registration rallying call that caught on.

We at Soft Sheen became so wrapped up in the campaign that went spent our company's advertising dollars on the voter registration campaign. We even increased the number of dollars we put in the campaign. One of my sons said, 'Well, look daddy, we want to be sure we don't say this is being brought to you by Soft Sheen Products Company.' And we never did. On the 60-second commercials, nothing was ever said about Soft Sheen at all. Finally, Marty Faye, the WBEE (1570 AM) radio disc jockey, said, 'Damn, I'm going to tell the people who's behind all this.' And that's the only time it ever got out that Soft Sheen was paying for those 60-second commercials.

The big boys downtown were in a quandary about who was paying for all of those 'Come Alive October 5' commercials. We weren't concerned, because by the time Marty Faye went public, our program was in high gear. This campaign was not for any specific politician. It was primarily to improve the quality of life for Black Chicagoans because our strength, growth and dollar capabilities is derived from the Black Americans. If successful Black businesses don't take steps to use their dollars in a constructive way to move Black Americans forward, then we cannot blame the major white companies who say we are not doing anything.

Keep in mind that for every spot Soft Sheen Products ran on the radio, the radio people gave us a spot. And that was just beautiful. We purchased thousands of spots on the major radio stations, and they ran an equal number. And I'd say between print advertising, posters, window streamers and T-shirts, buttons and so forth, we spent over $350,000 on the voter registration campaign. And I am saying every dollar I think was well-spent. It was not only exciting to Chicago, it has excited the Black communities across the nation to realize the power and the strength within Black America.

After we got the advertising and promotional part of the voter registration program off the ground, the Soft Sheen community service people invited various community groups such as the Urban League and Operation PUSH to meetings at our 87th Street office. Initially we had a meeting at the Reverend Jesse Jackson's home to make sure that they were with us in the voter registration drive. The Soft Sheen people had formulated a program and procedure that was orchestrated strictly by the creative people at our company.

During our meeting with the Rev. Jackson, he inferred that he wanted our voter registration meetings held at Operation PUSH headquarters and become a part of Operation PUSH. I told him that 'Come Alive October 5' was a brainchild of the creative people at Soft Sheen and that the meetings were going to be held at the Soft Sheen Products headquarters, at 1000 E. 87th St.

It was our opinion that we could get more city organizations to meet on neutral ground and become united. As a matter of fact, we got organizations working together that had never worked together before. We had more than 30 organizations that met regularly at Soft Sheen and formulated citywide programs.

Many of the organizations—the Citizens Committee, CBUC, Operation PUSH, People Organized for Welfare Rights (POWER), the Chicago Urban League, People's Movement and others—had already started serious plans for massive voter registration to support a Black mayor. Out of the meetings at Soft Sheen, it was determined that:
a) There were 300,000 unregistered Black voters in Chicago;
b) The objective was to register 100,000 new Black voters in time for the mayoral primary and c) Soft Sheen's advertising and marketing department would prepare a marketing plan for a massive voter registration effort, which would be implemented following approval by the assembled body.

The assembled body, recognizing the need to work together, formed a coalition known as Voice of The Ethnic Communities. By working as a unit under the umbrella of VOTE Communities, concerned citizens, grassroots organizations and businesses were able to pull together and draw from each other.

The goal of VOTE Communities was to expand the number of registered voters within Chicago before the November 2 general election.

The deadline for voters to be registered to vote in the election was October 5. Specifically, VOTE Community's goal was to register 100,000 new minority voters on or before Oct. 5, 1982, another 100,000 by January 25 for the mayoral primary on Feb. 22, 1983, and an additional 100,000 by March 14, 1983, for the April 12, 1983 mayoral election.

October 5 was established as 'Precinct Registration Day.' This meant that regular voter registration sites would operate through Sept. 25, 1982, and then on October 5 (one day only) 3,000 additional registration sites would open throughout the city. This date was designed as the target around which all our efforts would revolve. Organizational members included the Afro-American Patrolman's League, the Black Illinois Legislative Lobby, Ethnic Communications Outlet, Chicago Urban League, the First Congressional District, Soft Sheen Products Inc., People's Action Coalition, Inc. (PACI), People's Movement, the Woodlawn Organization, Leon's Bar-B-Que, Operation PUSH, Salter and Cater Advertising, Central Advisory Council-Chicago Housing Authority and the CAA Black Secondary Educators.

Soft Sheen's rapid growth was due largely to the effectiveness of the company's marketing and advertising strategies. My son Gary believed that those same concepts and strategies could be applied to marketing a Black mayoral candidate.

I think that our success in having all of these groups working together resulted from the fact that this was the first time that they had a strong financial business organization as a supportive rallying point. They appeared to be proud to come out to Soft Sheen headquarters and meet and express themselves and not feel threatened. They also knew that they were under the umbrella of a major financial source that would help them do what they wanted to do. Remember, most of these community organizations are perpetually strapped for dollars. Dollars were not their problem in this voter registration crusade because we had the dollars to fit their needs.

The role that Operation PUSH and the other organizations played in making the voter registration campaign an unqualified success was significant. However, I am still of the opinion that had we not been independent of the PUSH operation, we would not have had the uniqueness and the freshness of what happened at Soft Sheen. Our company was considered neutral territory by all the groups that participated in the campaign.

Some of the Black churches were instrumental in getting people to register in the 'Come Alive October 5' campaign. Father George Clements, pastor of the Holy Angels Church, made a dramatic move that caught the attention of the national media when he proclaimed, "I do not want any child attending classes at Holy Angels School whose parents are not registered to vote. And those parents who refuse to present their registration cards can simply take their child and go someplace else."

Although Father Clements received a lot of criticism from the general public and the media for making that demand, he would not be deterred. He took his proclamation a step higher and said, "Dr. Martin Luther King and others died for people to have the right to register and vote. I am not going to let those deaths be in vain. Therefore, I do not want anyone to hold membership in the Holy Angels Church who does not have a voter registration card."

Pastor Joseph Wells of Mount Pisgah Baptist Church, 4622 S. Dr. Martin Luther King Drive, announced that the church would no longer distribute free food to any person who could not present a registration card. In the meanwhile, Rev. Jesse Jackson called a meeting of more than 100 ministers at the Operation PUSH headquarters to discuss the voter registration campaign. The clergy men left the meeting agreeing to conduct a crusade for voter registration in their respective churches. They were joined by some Black doctors and lawyers who got on the band wagon and announced that they would not accept any patients or clients, except on an emergency basis, that did not have a registration card. The voter registration campaign had indeed taken hold from the depths of the grassroots to the peak of the mountaintops.

The voter registration campaign exceeded the expectations of even the most optimistic Black leaders. Although only 70,000 people had registered during July and August 1982, 135,000 "came alive" on Tuesday, October 5 and registered to vote. Forty-two thousand of those registered in the July-August period were placed on the rolls by POWER at Public Aid and unemployment offices. Another 35,000 persons had registered between January and July that year, making a grand total of 230,000 new registrants.

More people registered in the first nine months and five days of 1982 than had registered in the nine-year history of the Community Voters Registration Outreach Program that had been sponsored by the Board of Election Commissioners. According to the election officials, at least twice as many Blacks as whites registered in '82. The Black community was definitely on a political roll.

The 42nd and the 3rd Wards, which have the highest concentration of CHA housing in Chicago, were among the top five wards in voter registration on October 5. Their high turnout is indicative of the involvement of grassroots organizations who were concerned about survival issues such as welfare, housing and education.

In mid-October, Congressman Harold Washington, in a speech at a banquet sponsored by the Concerned Young Adults (CYA) said, "The recent massive voter registration effort had created an almost certainty that there would be a Black mayoral candidate in 1983 who would force a full discussion of the issues for a change in this city."

In less than 30 days after the "Come Alive October 5" registration victory, Congressman Harold Washington was re-elected for a second term. He won by the largest plurality of any congressman in the United States, according to the Joint Center for Political Studies. In addition, he received the largest number of votes that were ever cast in the 1st Congressional District. On November 1, the eve of his latest victory, Rep. Harold Washington predicted a Black would challenge Mayor Byrne and said that on November 10, he would announce whether he wanted to be that challenger.

But petitions were already circulating to put Harold on the ballot for the Feb. 22, 1983, mayoral primary. David S. Canter, chairman of the Hyde Park-Kenwood chapter of the Independent Voters of Illinois-Independent Precinct Voters of Illinois-Independent Precinct Organization, said the petitions were not authorized by the congressman. "It's a draft," said Canter. "We're attempting to force Washington to run."

On Wednesday morning, November 10, 1982, Congressman Harold Washington announced from a small podium at the Hyde Park Hilton Hotel that he would run for mayor. Left to right: unidentified security person; Washington's fiancee, Mary Ella Smith; the Congressman; Lu Palmer (head partially shown near white drapes); and Renault Robinson, chairman of the Afro-American Patrolmen's League.

CHAPTER 14

Washington Reluctantly Jumps into the Mayoral Race

Renault Robinson, a Washington disciple and a member of the board of the Chicago Housing Authority, was exuberant after the November 2 landslide re-election of Harold Washington to the U.S. House of Representatives. "We have proven that Washington has a lot of voting strength. Now, all we have to do is harness it and make it work," he bellowed. Making it work meant assembling a substantial financial war chest to comply with Washington's prerequisites.

Renault thought the Congressman would run for mayor of Chicago, but the decision had not been announced. On the other hand, a top Washington aide, who requested anonymity, said that Harold had not made any preparations for organizing or financing a mayoral campaign. So, acting as a committee of one, Robinson made the rounds of Black businesses in an effort to raise funds. Renault figured that the campaign needed at least $100,000 as a starter, $50,000 to set up shop and another $50,000 in cash for seed money. The amount was minuscule in comparison with that of "Calamity Jane," the incumbent mayor, who had a political war chest of $10 million dollars.

Robinson, in his search for funds, initially turned to Al Boutte, chairman of the board of Independence Bank. After Robinson laid out his plans and his hopes, Boutte asked, "Do you really think we can win?"

Robinson retorted, "The numbers are there. It's up to us to do the work and make it happen. It ain't going to happen automatically. But the potential is there."

Boutte queried, "How much money do you need?"

Renault replied, "I have estimated that we need between $750,000 and $1 million to make it a credible campaign."

Al Boutte leaned back in his plush swivel arm chair, put his right hand under his chin and looked out of the window toward the east in the direction of 80th and Cottage Grove. Several minutes passed before he said, "Okay, I'll tell you what. I will try to commit my bank to raise $50,000. See if you can get Seaway National Bank to match it."

Robinson immediately arranged a meeting with Ernest Collins, chairman of the Seaway National Bank, along with Al Johnson and Jacoby Dickens, who were directors of the bank. They accepted Independence Bank's challenge. With those oral commitments, Robinson returned to Washington and reported his progress. Harold congratulated Renault for his efforts, then softly stated, "You know we can't go with promises. We've got to have the money."

With the bank commitments under his arm, Robinson began receiving monies from a variety of sources. Although the total was not as much as they had wanted, it was enough for Washington to direct Robinson to set up a private luncheon for Tuesday, Nov. 9, at the Hyde Park Hilton Hotel. Among the 40 guests invited were Al Johnson, George Johnson, John H. Johnson, Edward Gardner, Bill Berry, Lu Palmer, Jesse Jackson, James Compton, Alvin Boutte, George Jones, Timuel Black, David Canter, state Rep. Robert E. Mann (D-Chicago), attorneys Thomas N. Todd and E. Duke McNeil, and about 25 other movers and shakers.

Harold Washington told those who attended the meeting, which was closed to the press, that he would bow to public pressure and wage a vigorous campaign. "To be blunt," Washington admitted, "I don't want to run for mayor. I like the Congress. I have been trying to find someone else to run, but unless that person appears within 24 hours, I will announce that I will run for mayor."

Two days before the November 9 meeting, Lu Palmer had invited 62 political activists to convene at the Roberts Motel to discuss options in the event Harold Washington did not declare. Palmer had been bugging Harold on a non-stop basis to jump into the mayoral waters, but Harold, being the private and independent person that he was, always ran according to his own timetable. Lu felt that Harold should step out front because CBUC and other civil rights organizations had promised the people that they would have a major Black candidate in the 1983 mayoral race. If Harold didn't run, they'd look like fools, Lu felt. And if Harold did run, they needed time to kick off the campaign.

Palmer had sent Aldermen Allan Streeter, Danny Davis and Ed Smith to talk to Harold before the November 7 meeting, but Harold had not given them a clue. Lu found this frustrating and said, "We never know which way this guy is going to go, and we're only a few days away from November 10. Therefore, we're going to have to come out of this mini-summit meeting with some sort of resolution."

There were several factions represented at the meeting called by Palmer. Alderman Davis represented one faction, Nancy Jefferson another, Lu Palmer a third and Anna Langford a fourth. Anna was angry because she had declared in mid-October that she was willing to run for mayor. "I feel like a fool," she said. "I said I would run, and nobody paid me any attention. I went and printed up all kinds of stuff and spent money. And now here you are begging Harold, and he won't run. It doesn't make any sense. Let's get another candidate."

Alderman Clifford Kelley was singing the anti-Harold Washington chorus louder and stronger than Anna Langford. As the meeting grew steamier, Palmer asked Tim Black, the college professor and political activist, to leave because he had not been invited.

Renault Robinson sat quietly in the midst of all this bickering, knowing that an announcement of Washington's intent to run was imminent. As Robinson sat there, he was fearful that someone would show up at the meeting with a early edition of the Nov. 8 *Chicago Tribune.* The paper's front-page article, written by Monroe Anderson, read:

Washington In Mayor Race

> Bowing to a groundswell of public pressure and finding encouragement in the record number of Blacks who registered and then voted in last week's election, U.S. Rep. Harold Washington (D-Ill.) will announce Wednesday that he is entering the Chicago mayoral sweepstakes, the *Tribune* has learned.
>
> Washington, an independent Democrat whose name has been mentioned frequently as a "unity" candidate in a bid to elect the city's first Black mayor, will hold a news conference Wednesday morning to announce officially his entry into the February 22 Democratic primary, sources said.
>
> Washington's campaign will be directed by Renault Robinson, a Jane Byrne-appointed CHA board member and executive director of the Afro-American Patrolmen's League, the *Tribune* has learned.
>
> 'Blacks have got the numbers. The only job we've got to do is convince Black people that a Black man can be the mayor of Chicago. We got a substantial war chest to mount the educational campaign,' Renault Robinson said.
>
> Renault Robinson further made the observation that there were more than 600,000 registered Black voters in Chicago. And that since the average primary turnout has been 850,000 voters, if 80 percent of the registered Blacks vote for Washington in February, he could easily win the race with Mayor Jane Byrne and State's Attorney Richard M. Daley splitting the white vote. Daley announced his candidacy last week.

> 'All of the other Black elected officials will support him in making the race. We see it as a legitimate shot, and we're going to make it. Washington was legitimately drafted by the Black community. He is the most logical candidate we got,' Robinson uttered.

On the evening before Congressman Washington was to announce his candidacy for mayor, Lu Palmer received two telephone calls. One caller asked him to be present at the Hyde Park Hilton for the Washington announcement, the other was from the advertising agency for the radio sponsors of *Lu's Notebook.* The second caller requested that Palmer present himself at their North Michigan Avenue offices the next morning, November 10, which was when Washington was to announce.

At the agency office the next morning, after two minutes of exchanging niceties, Palmer was told by the public relations officer for the sponsor that he would no longer represent them on the radio. In other words, he was fired.

Lu said, "Why are you knocking me off of the air?"

The sponsor's representative replied, "Your show has become too partisan."

Lu demanded: "What do you mean too partisan? I talk about Democrats. I talk about Republicans. I talk about communism. I talk about all parties."

The sponsor's man replied, "Yes, Lu! But what it boils down to is your work with CBUC and your relationship to Harold Washington. We don't care if you support Mayor Byrne or (Cook County State's Attorney) Richard M. Daley. We bought a news commentary show, but quite often your show has been a platform for partisan political support. It undermines the advertising effectiveness of the program."

Within moments after leaving the meeting with his former sponsors, Lu Palmer proceeded to call his wife Jorga and Harold Washington to tell them what had happened. Lu indicated in his conversation with Washington that he didn't want to discuss it in any detail on the phone because he knew that the Congressman was rushing to the Hyde Park Hilton press conference.

When Palmer reached the hotel some 20 minutes later, cars were bumper to bumper on the Outer Drive, and a crowd had gathered in front of the hotel. The room in which the press conference was being held was already jammed tighter than sardines are packed in a can with people from all ethnic groups. Palmer managed to muscle his way through the crowd and joined his wife Jorga and Jesse Jackson on the front row, where the three of them shared two seats. Standing beside Washington on the small podium was his fiancee, Mary Ella Smith. on the wall, directly behind Washington and Ms. Smith, was a huge picture of the Congressman with the inscription: Washington for Chicago! '83.

The emotionally charged press conference started with a prayer by the Reverend John Porter of Christ United Methodist Church: "Lord, we thank you, for the man, the moment and the movement have come together."

Congressman Washington delivered the announcement of his candidacy with his customary gusto:

Chicago is a divided city. Chicago is a city where citizens are treated unequally and unfairly. Chicago is a city in decline. Each year for the last decade, we have lost 11,500 jobs, 3,500 housing units and nearly 36,000 people.

Since 1955, women, Latinos, Blacks, youth and progressive whites have been left out of the Chicago government. Since 1979, the business, labor and intellectual communities have been allowed but token involvement in Chicago government.

Sadly, we have learned what happens when there is no governmental stability–and when the few rule over us. The results are that more people don't have jobs, more are out of food, out of their homes and out of hope.

Our businesses are failing at the highest rate since the Depression, in part from high interest rates, and the only answer the city government provides is fat consultant contracts for a few politically connected firms and jobs for a few patronage workers.

We have a school system which does not educate, in which students continue to lag far behind the rest of the country in tests of reading and math ability.

At this point, the new mayoral candidate was interrupted by activist Marion Stamps, who shouted, "Harold, you are like the Second Coming."

Somebody else across the room yelled, "Tell 'em, Mister Mayor!"

And then, of course, there were those who were chanting, "We Shall See In '83."

After the applause and shouts subsided, Washington continued:

We have a continuing crime problem in the city. Despite a drop in crime statistics, it's still not safe to walk the streets or run a business. Even at home, Chicagoans are robbed, mugged and beaten.

We no longer have dependable housing in this city. There has been an epidemic of abandoned buildings and rents have skyrocketed. Subsidized housing is no longer being built. And, with interest rates as they are, no one can afford to buy their own home anymore.

Finally, 'the city that works' doesn't work anymore. City services cost more than in any other city in America, and yet they just aren't there–sewers are in disrepair, streets are marred with giant pot holes. We have one of the highest infant mortality rates in the country, and traffic appears to be permanently snarled.

We have these terrible problems in Chicago, partly because leadership has not striven for unity and pointed boldly to the new directions. Instead, it has perpetuated outdated politics and pie-in-the-sky financing.

I have compassion for the terrible plight of our people and a vision for its future: I honestly believe that of those candidates mentioned, only I can rebuild Chicago by rallying Chicagoans to create a city in which every individual will receive his or her full measure of dignity. In the future, I see a Chicago of compassion; a city where no one has to live with rats, where the sick can be cured and where no one is overtaxed on property and burdened with other hidden taxes.

All the other candidates who have declared and who will be running for mayor would perpetuate politics as usual. Those candidates will continue the shell game of city financing at a time of crisis.

I would prefer not to run. But, there is a sense of urgency which moves me. Chicago can only be rebuilt if all the people of Chicago and her leaders work together. I was born, raised and educated in this city, and I have served it on three levels of government. I love representing Chicago in Washington, where we need courageous voices to speak out and act against (President Ronald) Reagan and Reaganomics. But I can't watch the city of Chicago be destroyed by petty politics and bad government.

I have heard the earnest pleas of thousands of people to enter the race. Therefore, I declare that I am a candidate for mayor of Chicago. Not to do so would be a mockery of my longstanding dedication to public service.

Again, Washington was interrupted by applause, stamping feet, shouts of joy and tears of happiness. After about five minutes, he continued:

I see a Chicago that runs well, in which services are provided as a right, not as a political favor.

I see a Chicago of educational excellence and equality of treatment in which all children can learn to function in this ever-more-complex society, in which jobs and contracts are dispensed fairly to those that want and qualify for them, and in which justice rains down like water.

I see a Chicago in which the neighborhoods are once again the center of our city, in which businesses boom and provide neighborhood jobs, in which neighbors join together to help govern their neighborhood and their city.

Some may say this is visionary—I say *they* lack vision.

Already, a new day is dawning. The unprecedented voter registration and voter turnout in Chicago in last week is evidence of this. The people of Chicago who have been neglected by the political bosses have announced their willingness to become involved, to unify and to act. I invite them to join my campaign. If I'm to be mayor, it would be as the spokesperson of this new movement—not the mayor of just a political faction, but mayor of all Chicago. We devoutly search for unity.

As mayor of this city, I would open the doors of City Hall. I would dig into that untapped reservoir of talented whites, Latinos, women and Blacks and unleash that ability for the benefit of this city.

Fairness will be our standard. On my first day in office, I will sign a freedom of information order to open the secret files of City Hall to inspection by all citizens. We seek *accountability.* As mayor, I shall gather the best talent of the city to tackle the record of problems I have outlined. We shall strive for excellence.

Thousands of Chicagoans have beseeched me to undertake this task. Their faith is not misplaced.

When the last word dripped from Washington's lips, the crowd chanted, "We Shall See In '83." People were rejoicing and congratulating one another. The only solemn face in the crowd was that of Lu Palmer, who was standing in the northwest corner of the room with his head slightly bowed. Lu had become the first political casualty in Chicago's crusade for a Black mayor.

The reaction to Harold's declaration to run for mayor was typified by Charles Hayes, international vice president and director of United Food and Commercial Workers (AFL-CIO and CLC). "Washington's announcement was long overdue, and with Harold Washington, we have a candidate that can win and serve all of the people," he declared.

Rev. Al Sampson, pastor of Fernwood United Methodist Church, said, "This is a great time. Some Blacks have died for this moment."

Alderman Danny Davis said, "The enthusiasm is beyond anything I've witnessed in the city . . . in fact, in my entire life. It is a rebirth. Anytime you have a room full of middle-class Black folks and you can't get them to be quiet, that tells you something."

"Washington had to run. He was chosen by the community," said Dorothy Tillman, a disciple of Dr. Martin Luther King and community activist who was a candidate for alderman in the 3rd Ward.

Alderman Eugene Sawyer (6th) and Alan Dobry of the 5th in Hyde Park, publicly declared their support of Washington two days before Harold officially announced. Sawyer said his constituents were clamoring for a Black mayoral candidate, and that he must comply.

Alderman Clifford Kelley said, "If a Black committeeman does support the machine, it will be tantamount to buying a deck chair on the Titanic. The Byrne administration is going down."

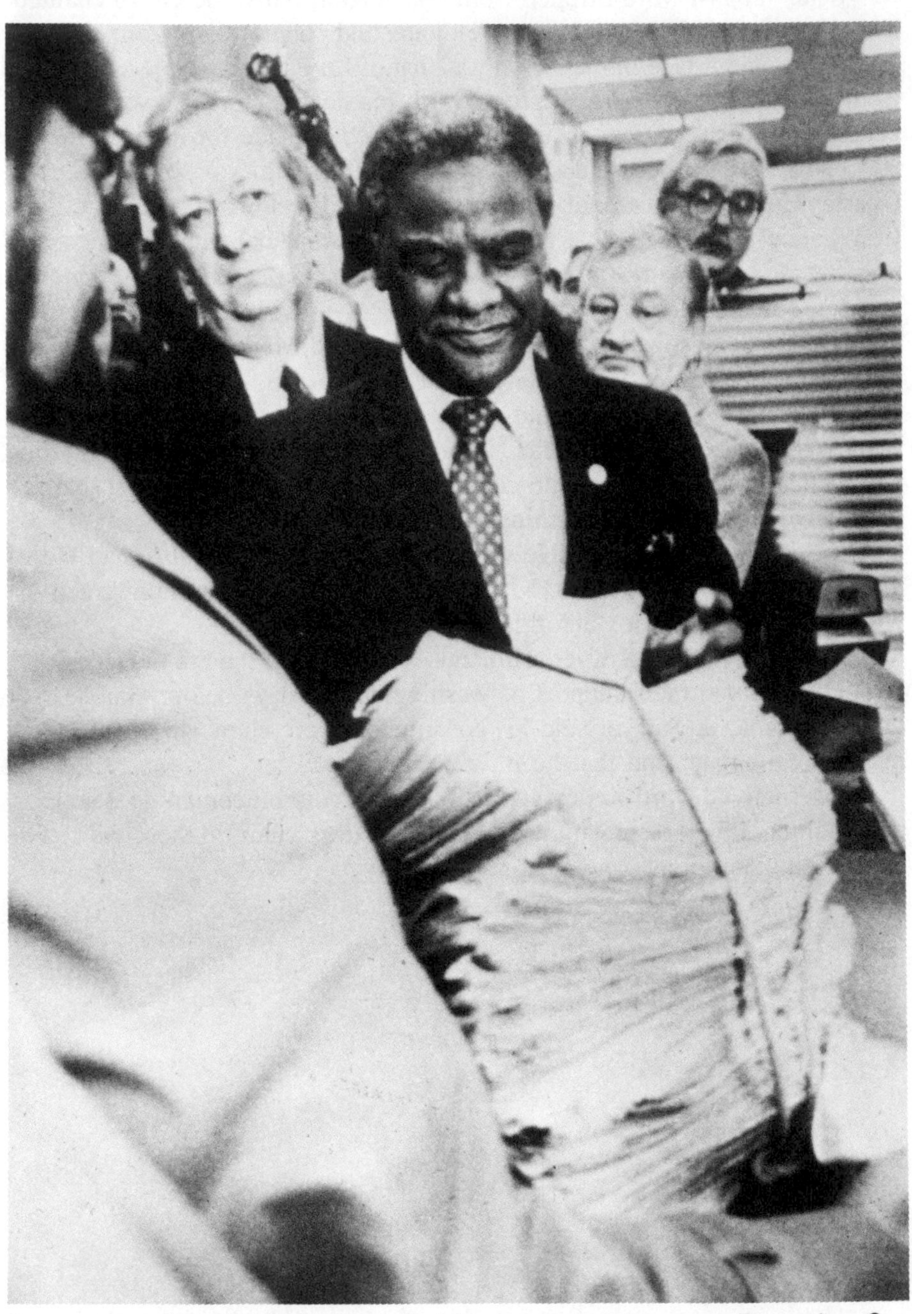

Congressman Harold Washington filed his mayoral petitions on December 6, 1982, with the city clerk. Directly behind Washington on his right is former State Representative Robert Mann.

CHAPTER

15

A Crusade Without a Slogan

But Jesus said unto them, They need not depart; give ye them to eat.

And they say unto him, We have here but five loaves, and two fishes.

He said, Bring them hither to me.

And he commanded the multitude to sit down on the grass, and took the five loaves, and the two fishes, and looking up to heaven, he blessed, and brake, and gave the loaves to his disciples, and the disciples to the multitude.

And they did all eat, and were filled: and they took up of the fragments that remained twelve baskets full.

And they that had eaten were about five thousand men, beside women and children.

Matthew 14:16-21

The sentiment of many Chicago residents, not limited to the Black community, was that Harold Washington's declaration to run for mayor on Nov. 10, 1982 was God-inspired. The thought of a Black man becoming the mayor of a municipality often labeled as "the most racist city in America" was tantamount to believing that Moses could have become a pharaoh in ancient Egypt. Harold Washington and his band of disciples, strong believers in the Gospel of Saint Matthew, were confident that they could overcome the political oppression of Chicago's pharaohs.

On Monday, Dec. 6, 1982, after Congressman Washington filed a stack of nominating petitions that was taller than 10 large Bibles with the City Clerk's office, he announced:

> We have just filed the nominating petitions for our candidacy in the Democratic primary.
>
> This campaign is built on the premise that the citizens from every part of Chicago want and deserve fairness, excellence and accountability in city government.
>
> Together we can move forward into the future with new vision and a new mutual respect among the fellowship of men and women throughout this great city.

Harold Washington was not the cause but the conduit for a people's movement that had not even adopted a campaign slogan.

The Washington mayoral campaign was initially held together by the glue of faith. There was neither money in a political war chest nor bank credit to enable it to rent office space for the volunteers who were anxious to move a political mountain.

Renault Robinson volunteered the use of the Afro-American Patrolmen's League's offices, which were located at 7801 S. Cottage Grove, in the same building as Washington's congressional office. Robinson temporarily suspended all operations of the league and had extra phones installed for the campaign volunteers in the name of the league because the $100,000 in commitments that had been promised for Washington's political war chest were still unfulfilled promises.

Not a single piece of literature existed that said, "Vote for Harold Washington as Mayor," except that which appeared in the *All Chicago City News,* the bimonthly newspaper of which Slim Coleman was editor and chief. "Washington for Mayor" stationery had not been printed because no printer would extend credit. Helen Schiller designed the blue and white "Harold Washington For Chicago" campaign buttons and the first 10,000 were paid for by an anonymous donor.

To get things rolling, Congressman Washington had to pay for the initial campaign literature out of his own pockets. The workers in his political trenches couldn't get a quorum of the Washington for Mayor committee to approve any campaign literature. The committee members did not intend to be obstructive; they were simply too embarrassed to confront the fact that there was no money in the campaign cupboard.

Funds to build the political organization did not began to trickle in until about mid-December 1982. Approximately $30,000 of the $100,000 of the initial commitment had been honored and instantly spent. The monies enabled the committee for the mayoral campaign to search for larger and more adequate campaign offices. On Sunday, Jan. 9, 1983, Washington announced the opening of six campaign sites at these locations: 109 N. Dearborn (5th floor), 22 E. Van Buren (4th floor), 215 S. Cicero, 4859 S. Wabash, the Fernwood United Methodist Church at 10057 S. Wallace and 2507 W. Fullerton.

The congressman gave short dedication speeches at each of the new offices that Sunday. As he toured the offices, he repeated the theme that the people of Chicago could not afford Jane Byrne as mayor. He also said that the opening of the six campaign offices around the city stood as proof that he had put together "one of the most awesome independent organizations ever to set forth on this earth." Washington told the audience at his Wabash office not to let anyone tell them that the campaign "was not structurally well directed." He told them that he was critical of the news coverage of his campaign, and said he was "sick and tired of being called the Black candidate. They don't talk about Jane Byrne as the white candidate. I don't even want to be called intelligent. That's a put-down. It's manifestly obvious I am intelligent," Harold said to loud applause.

He continued, "Nor is it necessary to constantly refer to me as articulate. Why don't they just come out and say that I know what I'm talking about? Richard M. Daley believes he should be mayor simply because his father was. But I don't think we have the divine right of kings in this country."

Odell Hicks Jr., a certified public accountant, was the campaign treasurer and co-chairman, with Walter Clark, of the finance committee. He recalls that the organization's finances were hand-to-mouth because the big boys downtown did not think that Congressman Washington had a ghost of a chance of winning the Democratic mayoral primary. Hicks states:

> The early financial integrity of the organization was heavily dependent upon the weekend fund-raising parties given in homes across the city by various "Washington for Mayor" volunteers. Some weekends, there would be as many as 20 fundraisers. The members of the finance committee would always arrange to have someone from the committee present at each party to bring the money directly back to the campaign headquarters. On a Friday afternoon, the organization would usually be broke. However, by the time Monday morning rolled around, we might have as much as $15,000 or $20,000 in the treasury. We were averaging approximately $1,000 per fundraiser. In some instances, we'd get a check as small as $1. On the other hand, we'd might get one for $500 or even $1,000. It was truly a people's movement. There's no other way I can describe it.

As a matter of fact, the late Bill Berry, who came aboard Washington's political freight train in early December with the blessings of George Johnson of Johnson Products, was somewhat distraught. The "big-shot" white folk downtown with whom he was associated at the Chicago United and some others who had worked with him on the board of the Chicago Urban League turned deaf ears when he asked for them money to support a campaign for a Black mayoral candidate. Many of Bill's white friends did not even give him the common courtesy of returning his calls. Bill Berry was so hurt about being rejected that he told his story to a reporter at the *Chicago Sun-Times*.

Washington had relied on Bill's ties to the white establishment to lure campaign funds and support, but Berry's hundreds of phone calls yielded little. The tradition in the city of Chicago is for the business community to hedge

Some members of the ''Harold Washington for Mayor'' Finance Committee. Seated left to right: the late Garland Grice, unidentified member, John Dobbs Jr., Jacoby Dickens, chairman of the board of the Seaway National Bank, unidentified member, the late Bill Berry, the coordinator of the ''Washington for Mayor'' campaign. Standing left to right: attorney Thomas Coffey, attorney Robin Charleston, Earl Hord, president of the Independence Bank, Clarence Jenkin, Donald C. Walker, publisher and editor of *Dollars and Sense* Magazine, Walter Clark, vice chairman of First Federal of Chicago and also co-chairman of the ''Washington For Mayor'' Finance Committee, the Reverend Jesse Cotton, attorney Garland Watt, Odell Hicks Jr., co-chairman, the late Ernest Bush Sr., president of Bush Construction Co., John Swain, president of Swain Drugs, the Reverend Al Sampson, Mrs. Jolyn Robichaux, president of the Baldwin Ice Cream Co. and an unidentified member.

their bets with any serious mayoral candidate by giving each candidate some money. But not even the most liberal among them were willing to place a bet on Washington to win.

"The largest individual white pre-primary victory contributors were former Cook County Hospital administrator Dr. Quinton Young, author Studs Terkel and U.S. Sen. Alan Cranston of California," according to the mayoral campaign fundraiser Jay Doherty. Sen. Cranston was the only white politician of national standing to endorse Harold Washington. Former Vice President Walter Mondale supported Richard M. Daley while Sen. Ted Kennedy supported Jane Byrne in the mayoral primary.

Local white support was also scarcer than hen's teeth: only State Rep. Barbara Flynn Currie, 5th Ward Alderman Lawrence S. Bloom and former 44th Ward Alderman Dick Simpson supported Washington in the primary. The only media endorsements of Washington's candidacy came from *Chicago*

Defender, Chicago Journal, All Chicago City News, Dollars and Sense magazine and radio station WBBM (78 AM).

The amount of monies raised to finance the Washington mayoral campaign was so minuscule that Richard Daley and Mayor Byrne dismissed Washington's movement as an effort that would disappear like the smile of a Cheshire cat.

The first big public rally for Washington's mayoral campaign was sponsored by the Women for Washington Committee. Nancy Jefferson, Reverend Willie "Little Warrior" Barrow, Mildred Bush, Addie Wyatt and Rebecca Sive-Tomashefsky spearheaded that group. A rally held at the Hilton Hotel on Dec. 20, 1982, was attended by more than 300 women, only eight of whom were white.

Rebecca Sive-Tomashefsky recalls:

> We set a goal that night of $100,000. Rev. Willie Barrow went to Mr. Edward Gardner and asked him to give us some assistance. Mr. Gardner offered us a building near his Soft Sheen plant on East 87th Street, and he installed approximately 30 or 40 phones that we could use in our campaign in soliciting other women and other individuals who would be interested in working in the Washington campaign. He also furnished Peggy Montez as the staff person for the Women for Washington campaign committee.

In the meantime, the Kenwood-Oakwood Community Organization, Midwest Council, Operation PUSH, the Heart of the Uptown Coalition, Fernwood Methodist Church and dozens of other grassroots institutions converted their headquarters into "Washington for Mayor" satellite offices. It was this kind of brush-fire independent action that made Congressman Washington's mayoral movement a crusade rather than a campaign. Congressman Washington spoke at six to eight Black churches throughout the city of Chicago every Sunday. Even more significant was the fact that he had maintained that kind of itinerary for the five years between his first mayoral campaign in 1977 to his second campaign in December 1982.

Out at the Soft Sheen campaign offices, the Women for Washington Committee made plans for their January 16 rally at the Liberty Baptist Church. Nancy Jefferson, who was the co-chairperson with Rebecca Sive-Tomashefsky, explains:

> Our goal was to recruit 10,000 women volunteers. The strategy was to get every woman who had been present at the Hilton rally to bring 10 to the Liberty rally. The press had ignored our December rally because they did not think that we had anything going. However, the print and electronic media showed up in full force at the Liberty Baptist Church rally because by that time they probably sensed that we were for real. What they found at 4:30 that Sunday afternoon was a large church that was packed to its rafters with thousands of women standing around the walls, in the lobby, some outside on the street because they could not get in. All these women had one common goal, and that was to elect

> Harold Washington mayor of the city of Chicago. Although there was no room in the temple, when Congressman Washington arrived the waters parted as he walked down the center aisle towards the dais. The Barrett sisters jumped up and started singing "I'm Looking for a Miracle," and the walls of Liberty Baptist Church shook like the walls of Jericho.

On Jan. 12, 1983, four days before that Women for Washington's rally, 150 Black ministers met at the Hyde Park Hilton Hotel to endorse the candidacy of State's Attorney Richard M. Daley. This meeting was held despite the fact that Dr. Robert Starks and Reverend Al Sampson led 20 members of the Task Force for Black Empowerment in a picket line outside of the hotel and chanted, "Plantation politics must end" as the pro-Daley ministers entered the hotel.

Daley received a standing ovation from the Black ministers. After the applause subsided, he told the group, "To me, each and every one of you have stood by your conviction. I need your help because this is a long and difficult election. We are up against a $10 million (Byrne) campaign fund." Daley did not mention Washington's name because he did not consider him a contestant.

Dr. Starks asked Daley, "Have you spoken out against police brutality? Have you spoken out against abuses of Blacks in your community?"

Daley replied, "We have," and then proceeded to change the subject.

Rev. Sampson, pastor of the Fernwood Methodist Church, said he believed that "Black ministers must support U.S. Rep. Harold Washington in the February 22 Democratic mayoral primary." He added, "What has Byrne done to buy her way into the Black churches? What has Daley contributed to politic himself into Black churches?"

Some ministers who attended the Daley rally asked *Chicago Defender* reporter Chinta Strausberg not to identify them; others didn't care who knew their beliefs about why Chicago was not ready for a Black mayor. Rev. O.D. White, pastor of the Spirit of Love Baptist Church, at 6035 S. Ashland, said:

> If Harold Washington is elected, the city would go down the tubes . . . like Gary. We know what happened to Cleveland, Gary and Detroit. When Mayor Hatcher was elected, the white officials took all the money to Merrillville, Indiana. Gary is now a ghost town. Maybe with the name of Daley, this will not happen to Chicago. However, we're not banking on his name. He can motivate the businesses to produce the jobs.

Rev. E.J. Jones, pastor of the First Unity Baptist Church, 5129 S. Indiana, and an aldermanic candidate for the 3rd Ward, announced his support at the meeting for Daley and said he hoped his parishioners would follow his suggestion. Jones said he should be able to support whomever he pleased.

> But I am not hung up on Black. I'll look at the man. And with Daley, I like what I see. He's the right man for this time.
>
> I know there will be a lot of friends lost in this election, but I'll

stand by my convictions. My choice of mayoral candidacy puts me in a bind . . . running for alderman in an all-Black ward and supporting a white mayoral candidate. But I have to do what I think is right.

It is my spiritual insight and my better judgment that guided me to this decision. I am not an Uncle Tom, but I believe that homework should be done. We moved into this 'Harold Washington for Mayor' too rapidly. I guess we got excited with the extra few thousand registered voters.

Dr. Conrad Worrill, press secretary for the Task Force for Black Political Empowerment, retorted:

They said Blacks needed more time in 1977 (when Washington ran for mayor.) I think his (Jones) remarks are ludicrous and insane. Is he saying that if Washington is elected mayor, the Sears Tower and Prudential will leave because a Black man is mayor?

We are not attacking the Black church as an institution. We want spiritual reciprocity. We want Richard M. Daley and Jane Byrne to invite Father George Clements to churches in Bridgeport and in the white 42nd Ward. We want an open-door policy. Our position is that these Black preachers cannot eat in Bridgeport without being physically attacked. Daley would never invite them to dinner in his home in Bridgeport, and yet these same preachers have allowed Daley to come into their pulpits. Many Black churches have always been an appendage or parasite to the Democratic party in this town. I have always felt that that was a theological error. If God is who he says he is, then He ought to take care of you rather than the Democratic party. You never heard of Moses running with pharaoh and eating at pharaoh's table.

Two other South Side ministers openly endorsed Jane Byrne, one believing Harold Washington couldn't win and the other because he had done Byrne a personal injustice four years before.

Father Paul Smith, 52, principal of the Holy Angels School for the past 13 years, said that he was endorsing Mayor Byrne because she had done a credible job. Smith added:

Washington is an eloquent speaker and an excellent congressman who should be gunning for (Charles) Percy's seat. Harold Washington is the most outstanding, most articulate politician we have, and I believe Washington would serve himself and the Black community better by remaining in Washington, D.C. My support of Mayor Byrne is in no way disparaging to him.

But I feel that a person should not run for office unless he is certain he will win, and I don't think he can. I don't think we should send our finest candidates down the drain.

Father Smith said his endorsement of Byrne "as a private citizen" was not connected in any way with Holy Angels Church, which was pastored by Father George Clements, a long-time civil rights activist.

The Reverend Joseph Wells, pastor of Mount Pisgah Baptist Church, 4622

S. King Drive, said he was also supporting Byrne after he turned down her request to speak at his church during her 1979 campaign. He explained, "I turned thumbs down on her, I criticized her and I did not know her. I did the lady a wrong."

Rev. Wells said that when he was working with the African relief fund he decided to see Mayor Jane Byrne and ask her for a donation to the program. He said, "Byrne came through to the tune of $5,000."

"If she was that gracious," Wells added, "This time I owe her because she cared enough to help those Black babies in Africa. I have no problems with people picketing my church. They are misguided. . . . These things happen because we have no base, and before you can elect a Black mayor, you have to get a base."

The Rev. Jesse W. Cotton, pastor of the Greater Institutional African Methodist Episcopal Church, was very disturbed when he read that 150 Black ministers had endorsed Daley, and another large group of Black ministers had come out for Byrne, and yet no group of Black clergy had endorsed Congressman Harold Washington. Therefore, Rev. Cotton convened a group of ministers from various denominations comprising Gessel Berry Jr., A.I. Dunlap, Harry Gibson, Gregory Ingram, John W. Jackson, B. Herbert Martin, Al Sampson, Jeremiah Wright and Claude Wyatt. The ministers drafted a statement to support Harold Washington that was given to Rev. Jeremiah Wright to polish and refine. The Rev. Cotton said:

> We made it known among the clergy that we were not interested in anyone who wanted to simply say 'I support Harold Washington' without putting his or her signature on the line in a full page ad endorsing the congressman for mayor. I realize that this was a hard pill to swallow for some of our members because they were already being hassled by Jane Byrne's City Hall. I believe Jeremiah Wright was one of them and Claude Wyatt was another who was attempting to build a new church on Stony Island and was left with a hole in the ground for some years because of his civil rights activity. Plus there was another minister in our group whose name escapes me now who was trying to get a simple permit to do some work in his church, which he never was able to get.

In spite of the political threats, harassments and hassles, 250 ministers signed the "Washington for Mayor" statement that appeared in the *Chicago Defender* and also in the *Westside Journal*. The ad read:

> THE BLACK CHURCH SUPPORTS
> HAROLD WASHINGTON FOR MAYOR
>
> The Black church, which stands firmly in the tradition of Dr. Martin Luther King, Jr. (and not that splinter group which backs the 'Daley Regime' who opposed Dr. King) . . .
>
> The Black church, which stands firmly in the Afro-Christian tradition of Richard Allen, George Liele, Henry Highland Garnett, and Henry McNeal Turner—a tradition of liberation and self-determination

(and not that other splinter group which rolls over and plays dead in the face of insult after insult to the Black community from the 'Byrne Regime') . . .

The Black church which stands on the shoulders of those African slaves who sang 'Before I'd be a slave, I'd be buried in my grave; and go home to my God and be free!' . . .

Unashamedly Black and unapologetically Christian, we—the undersigned 250 Black ministers of the Chicago metropolitan area—put our full personal support behind Congressman Washington in his mayoral bid, and we urge our congregations to do the same.

The following denominations supported Harold Washington's candidacy:

United Methodist Church, African Methodist Episcopal Church, African Methodist Episcopal Zion Church, United Church of Christ, The Lutheran Church, The Presbyterian Church, Reformed Church, Advent Christian Church, Community Church, Christian Reformed Church, Catholic Church, Baptist Church, Church of God and the Christian Methodist Episcopal Church.

We urge you—especially in this month of Black Liberation—to do the same. On February 22nd strike a punch for freedom. Vote for Harold Washington for Mayor of Chicago and Let us march on . . .

TIL VICTORY IS WON!

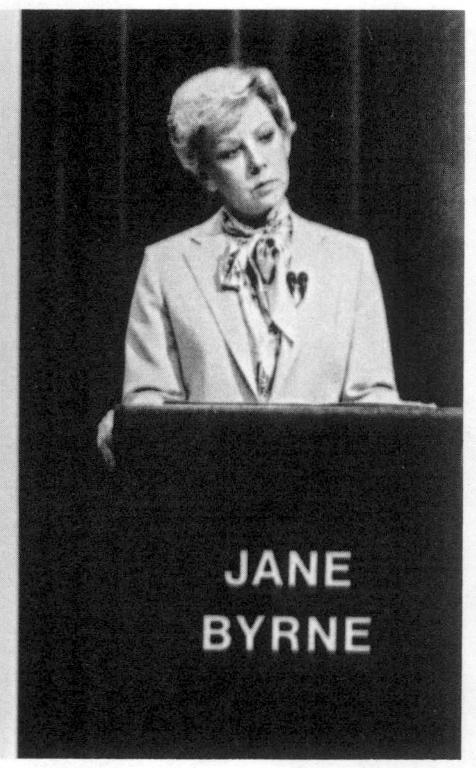

The Chicago mayoral candidates, 1983.

CHAPTER

16

The Debates That Turned the Tides for Harold

Mayor Jane Byrne's offer to debate Richard Daley and Harold Washington was one offer that Washington literally could not afford to refuse. The January 1983 debates proved to be the turning points in Congressman Washington's anemically funded mayoral campaign. Unlike the other two candidates, Washington needed the television exposure he could not afford to buy. Moreover, outside of political circles, he was not well-known, except in the Black community.

Byrne, the incumbent, made the unprecedented offer to debate because she felt she could beat both candidates with her scythe-sharp intelligence and her killer instincts. There was no doubt in her mind of whether she could beat Daley in a debate. But Washington was an unknown quantity in this context. Initially, Daley declined Byrne's offer. Whereas Harold Washington reacted like the sly old "Brer Rabbit" who asked not to be thrown in the briar patch.

The tenor of Washington's debates gave Black folk strong hopes for his candidacy:

> There are some who believe that I should avoid the race issue, but I will not avoid it because it permeates our entire city and has devastating implications. . . . I'm running to end Jane Byrne's four-year effort to further institutionalize racial discrimination in this great city.

The congressman's statement was a reaction to remarks Byrne had made three days earlier to a group of DePaul University students. The mayor had itemized her record of minority appointments, including their names and credentials, and mentioned that the person 'happened to be Black.' In speaking of Commissioner of Human Services Lenora Cartwright, Mayor Byrne said: "She happens to be Black, but she's good." When she came to Elmer Beard Jr., the Chicago Housing Authority executive director, she noted that he also "happened to be Black, but also happens to be good." The audience gasped at both of these references in total disbelief that the mayor of Chicago would imply that it was unusual to be Black and qualified. Her remarks incensed Blacks in general and Harold specifically.

Washington's ability to respond to insensitive remarks in the debates made people who did not know him begin to see him differently and accept him as a serious mayoral candidate. The congressman said, "Until the debates, I was practically unknown outside of my community. The debates represented the only way for me to project myself as experienced and knowledgeable. It was my role to project a proper image, and I think I did."

Alderman Marian Humes (8th) said that many of the white aldermen who had watched the debates acknowledged that Harold Washington was the best of the three candidates. They also admitted that their constituents were actually frightened by Congressman Washington's competence and intelligence.

Vernon Jarrett made the following observations in his Jan. 23, 1983, *Chicago Tribune* column.

> U.S. Rep. Harold Washington registered one of the big gains during the first debate last week between the Democratic candidates for mayor of Chicago. It enhanced his support among Black people who already supported him.
>
> Washington made a fine impression among Blacks throughout the city, including some of those who were beholden to Mayor Jane Byrne and State's Attorney Richard M. Daley. Regardless of how Washington impressed other voters, the 1st District congressman looked 'mighty good' to blacks in all sections of Chicago. His composure, display of knowledge, superior verbal skills and general stage presence evoked an understandable pride on the South and West sides.
>
> I've listened closely to comments from individuals from all levels of Chicago's Black social and economic life for many hours since the debate. As of Thursday afternoon, I had not met a single Black person who did not feel that Washington came across 'much better' than Byrne or Daley.
>
> One of the first individuals to praise Washington 'off the record' was one of the high-profile Black regular Democrats who is openly campaigning for Daley.
>
> 'There's no doubt about it, Harold was better than the others,' he said as he left the auditorium of the First National Bank, where the debate was held.

'Every Black who tries to sell other blacks on supporting anybody but Harold will have to do a lot of explaining–if he can.'

Another 'neutral' (usually meaning an individual obligated to Byrne or Daley) said the following about the debates: 'Probably the greatest impact of Washington's television appeal will be felt in the Black churches, particularly those who have pastors who support Byrne or Daley.

The more Washington is seen and heard by large audiences, the greater the gain in respect for his knowledge and forensic skills learned over many years in politics.'

'What I like about the brother is that he didn't have to think so hard to come up with the right answers,' said a Black city employee. 'You could tell that he had been thinking about this city for a long time. The brother is smart with guts. I bet his I.Q. is higher than those other two.'

While Harold Washington was making debating points on the stage at the First National Bank theater, his security people were catching hell off-stage. Howard Saffold, the congressman's security coordinator, reported:

> Those white police officers were not taking us seriously during the first month of the mayoral campaign. The night of the first debate it came to a head. Dominick Frigo, the police officer in charge of special events for Mayor Byrne, decided that the Black police officers with Congressman Harold Washington could not have access to the back-stage area and the immediate front stage area.
>
> Dominick Frigo told me to bring U.S. Rep. Washington in the back door through the First National Bank garage and usher him directly into his dressing room backstage. They assigned the congressman to the dressing room that was the furthest from the stage and assigned him car space in the most remote corner of the First National Bank's underground garage.

These incidents caused Saffold and Frigo to lock horns. Out of that confrontation there came an understanding that the Black officers were there for the same purpose as the white officers, to protect their respective candidates. Their agreement resulted in sublimation of some of the overt hostility between Black and white officers and heightened the enthusiasm among the Afro-American Patrolmen's League security volunteers.

The general excitement that was generated during the mayoral debates spilled over into the February 6 "Washington for Mayor" rally, which was held at the cavernous University of Illinois Pavilion at Racine and Harrison. More than 12,000 high-spirited citizens braved Chicago's "hawkish" weather that Sunday afternoon. The sponsors of the event had feared that the rally would be a failure because low temperatures and a heavy snow were forecast, but no one had measured the political temperature of the people's movement. At this point in the campaign, nothing could prevent them from coming out to support their beloved Harold. Many persons arrived hours before the event was to begin at 4 p.m.

Unlike Mayor Richard J. Daley's Democratic rallies of the '50s and '60s, the people's session at the pavilion had the flavor of a religious revival. Rev. Henry O. Hardy, pastor of Cosmopolitan Church at 52nd and Wabash, intoned a rhythmic invocation. The musical beat was furnished by the Barrett Sisters and Curtis Mayfield rather than by the Shannon Rovers. When Congressman Harold Washington entered the pavilion, he received a six-minute standing ovation as thousands of balloons floated down from the rafters, and people chanted, "Harold! Harold! Harold!"

In addition to Congressman Washington, many elected officials were present from all over the United States: U.S. Rep. Ronald Dellums from California, U.S. Sen. Alan Cranston (D-Calif.), U.S. Rep. Gus Savage (D-Ill.), Jesse Jackson, former New York mayoral candidate Herman Badillo and U.S. Rep. Mervyn M. Dymally (D-N.Y.). Congressman John Conyers Jr. (D-Mich.) pledged that the appearance of the Black congressmen was not just cosmetic and declared, "As many of us who can will be here every day we can from now until February 22."

Father George Clements, pastor of Holy Angels Church, praised the national leaders for coming to Chicago to assist Washington's election bid. Slim Coleman told the festive audience that "When you're poor in Chicago, you know what you can afford. And you know you can't afford Jane Byrne for another four years."

State Sen. Richard Newhouse said, "A Washington victory will be a boost to putting many of the unemployed persons here tonight back to work." Newhouse was indicating an end to Byrne's patronage formula, which excluded many Blacks from city employment.

So many speakers and dignitaries were on the dais that Congressman Washington did not get an opportunity to address his followers until the third hour of the program. However, as always, he had a lot to say, and he said it well. The congressman began his address by announcing that Byrne was turning the Board of Education and the Chicago Housing Authority into a racial battleground. He added, "I pledge to you that I will take the Chicago Public schools out of politics and put them back into the business of educating our children." Then he said he had made one other pledge, but before he could finish his sentence, the crowd anticipated his words and broke into a chant, "Fire Brzeczek! Fire Brzeczek! Fire Brzeczek!"

(Police Superintendent Fred J. Brzeczek campaigned for Mayor Jane Byrne and warned that the streets would not be safe if Washington were elected. "I guarantee that it (the police department) will be a circus," Brzeczek said. Washington's subsequent appointment of Fred Rice as superintendent proved Brzeczek 200 percent wrong.)

Odell Hicks, the treasurer of the Harold Washington For Mayor campaign, made the following observations about the pavilion rally:

> I don't think anybody outside of the Black community thought that the campaign was serious until the Illinois pavilion rally. Even the sponsors

of the event thought that if we could raise enough money to simply pay for the rally expenses including printing tickets, circulars and rent, we would have done well. As a matter of fact, all we wanted to do was to break even and not end up in the hole. Fourteen thousand (dollars) was our break-even point.

My fear of not breaking even went out of the window when I saw that huge crowd. Particularly, after Rev. Jesse Jackson started his fund-raising ritual. The Reverend Jackson started calling on people to come down to the front of the auditorium who wanted to give $100 and so forth. And of course, as he developed the plea for funds, he continued to lower the dollar amount of the requested contribution. We had two large barrels at the foot of the podium where people could deposit their money. In addition, we had large collection buckets that were being passed up and down the aisles for those who couldn't come to the front or who didn't desire to come to the front.

About 7:30, I left the stage to go under the bleachers to see how the money counters were doing. To my surprise, there were dollar bills everywhere, like that picture I saw in the *Sun-Times* where dollars where scattered all over the floor in the CTA office out on 78th Street. We started sorting and counting money about 8 p.m. and we did not finish until after midnight. We counted in excess of $40,000 in $1 and $5 contributions. I will never forget how nervous I was that night carrying two mail bags full of money with no police protection around in the trunk of my car. I certainly felt relieved when I was able to deposit the funds at the Independence Bank the next morning.

As the campaign became more visible and more viable, the hatemongers began to beat their drums louder and more consistently, prompting the Reverend Jesse Jackson to make the following remarks to the Steering Committee of the Harold Washington for Mayor Campaign:

The enemies of Black emancipation will be unrelenting in attacks upon the candidates and people identified with the candidates the closer we get to February 22. I am convinced that volunteers must operate with the fervor of a crusade and not merely succumb to the mechanisms of a campaign. The will to be free can be neither bought with a big campaign chest nor sold. It was the fervor of the people that allowed Martin Luther King Jr. to overthrow the southern military occupation forces without a standing army and allowed Jane Byrne to overthrow Bilandic with a $75,000 budget.

The spirit of a crusade is children writing term papers, churches putting out bumper stickers with 'God Bless Harold Washington,' and various forms of freedom-code words and hand shakes.

The thunderous motion of the ground swell among Black voters will attract a significant number of whites who will not permit themselves to commit suicide by identifying with losers. The greater the unity among Black voters, the more attractive a Black candidate will be to the financial and judicial vested interests of the city, the state and the nation.

The week following the Washington for Mayor rally at the university, the voter interest in the Washington campaign gave us a strong indication that victory was in sight. The South and the West sides of Chicago broke out with an epidemic of "blue and white measles" as more and more people wore blue and white campaign buttons that read, "Washington For Chicago." For some people, one button was not enough-they decorated their caps, jackets and overcoats with Washington buttons. The author will never forget a seedily dressed Black gentleman who was passing out literature for Mayor Byrne on the northeast corner of 79th and Stony Island Ave., in front of one of her Southside satellite offices. The gentleman stopped me on that corner and handed him a piece of the Byrne literature and said, "I bet you don't know who I'm going to vote for."

I replied, "Mayor Byrne."

He looked at me with a very hurt expression and threw back his overcoat to display 10 Harold Washington blue and white buttons pinned to his jacket lapels, five on each side. This gentleman may have been an extremist. The blue and white epidemic finally reached a point where people were actually stealing the buttons off of other people's garments in order to be identified with the people's movement.

Zenobia Black, wife of Loop College Professor Timuel Black, was shocked when someone broke her car window and stole 1,000 "Harold Washington For Chicago" buttons. She issued a plea for their return saying, "They are really hot items. Everyone's not bad, but if you see somebody out there selling Harold Washington buttons—they are not for sale."

The blue and white button mania was spreading down Lake Shore Drive where the Black penthouse crowd was beginning to open up their wallets. Al Johnson, the Cadillac dealer, gave a fund-raising party for Congressman Washington on February 18, four days before the primary, in the penthouse of his North Lake Shore Drive condominium. Johnson invited approximately 60 people and they contributed $60,000 to the Washington fund that night. His party was the most successful private fundraiser given by an individual prior to Washington winning the primary. John H. Johnson, of Johnson Publishing Co., gave $10,000, and an additional $28,000 following the primary. Edward Gardner added $50,000 to the $350,000 he had spent earlier. He also set up a satellite office on 47th Street three weeks before the primary, with a battery of telephones and volunteers to encourage the new registrants to come out and vote in the primary on Feb. 22, 1983.

The weekend before the primary, the political pharaohs of Chicago declared full-scale war by letting all of their bigotry hang out. Eddie Vrdolyak, the Cook County Democratic party chairman, addressed a Northwest side rally and said very frankly:

> A vote for Daley is a vote for Washington. It's a two-person race. It would be the worse day in the history of Chicago if your candidate, the

> only viable candidate, was not elected. It's a racial thing. Don't kid yourself. I am calling on you to save your city, to save your precinct. We are fighting to keep the city the way it is.

Mayor Byrne picked up on the theme and went to the Southwest side, which was Daley territory, and said Daley was through and that the choice was either Byrne or Washington. It was the mayor's intention to strike fear in the hearts of the Gage Parkers with the thought that a Black man would be the mayor of Chicago. The racism displayed by both Byrne and Vrdolyak made George Wallace of Alabama look like a pious Sunday School teacher.

On Tuesday, Feb. 22, the rhetoric ceased, and the voting began. However, the southbound Dan Ryan El trains stopped running without any explanation. The voter turnout during the day in the Black wards had been excellent, but at about 5 o'clock, just as people were getting off from work and rushing back home to vote, they were stranded in the Loop. Thousands of Blacks could not return to their neighborhoods in time to cast their ballots. How many votes were lost, why the lights went out and why the trains stopped running may never be known. Until this day, no one has given a satisfactory explanation.

By 7 o'clock primary election night, thousands of Washington supporters had invaded the McCormick Inn. The hotel lobby was jammed with people wall-to-wall and the elevators from the upper floors were packed by the time they reached the lobby. People had to walk up to the fourth and fifth floors in order to get an elevator that would take them to the upper floors of the hotel.

Outside the hotel, cars were parked bumper to bumper, double-parked on the Outer Drive and on the ramps exiting and entering the Drive. The closest legal parking spaces on the street or vacant lots were six to eight blocks from the McCormick Inn. A view of the parking scene from the mayor's suite on the penthouse floor of the hotel reminded the author of a quilt patched by his grandmother with 1,000 bits and pieces of scraps of material of various colors. Like small scraps of cloth, cars were parked at inconceivable angles. The only description for the parking was chaotic.

Celebrants stood hip to hip and stomach to back, with no breathing room in between, in the main ballroom on the second floor, where Sid Ordower was the master of ceremonies.

The Rev. Jesse Jackson, who was accused by many who saw him on television that night of trying to take the limelight from Harold Washington, describes what happened in the Grand Ballroom. The author and many others who were there support Jackson's description of the event:

> In the first place, the place was too small, just an explosion. It was predictable. I came to McCormick Inn. I brought my son Yusef with me because I was going to leave for Dayton early the next morning. Harold was supposed to come down at 7 o'clock, then 8, then 9. Sid Ordower, who had been buying time trying to keep the people in order, introduced Lerone Bennett Jr., who in turn, introduced some other

people in an effort to try to keep some sort of order in the crowd. Then about 10 minutes later, Lerone Bennett and I were trying to get out of the crowd. And as I reached the door, Sid Ordower said, 'Ladies and gentlemen, here is Jesse Jackson.' People started screaming, 'Jesse! Jesse! Jesse!' So I went back to the front of the stage. I could see people falling out and fainting from the pressure of the bodies and the extremely high temperature caused by such a large hunk of humanity crammed into such small space. We discovered that there was an ice cube maker in the back of the stage. We sent for Dr. Andy Thomas and some nurses to set up a first-aid station on the floor. And as people fell out, we brought them through the crowd and put ice packs on their heads in the makeshift medical station back stage.

Meantime, it's 10 o'clock, then it's 11 o'clock, then it's 12 o'clock and Harold's still upstairs. People are still coming in, and everybody is asking when is Harold coming. Dr. Conrad Worrill was trying to get an elevator to go up to the penthouse floor to bring Harold down, but as you know, the elevators were jammed. In the meantime, I'm still standing up there doing everything from singing *We Shall Overcome* to telling jokes in an effort to buy time. I did not realize that the entire episode was being shown live on television. Blacks were celebrating; whites were upset because they lost. People who lose get upset. Somebody said Walter Jacobson, in one of his rare insightful moments, said, 'You know, part of the problem is us.'

And somebody said, 'What do you mean?'

He said, 'Look at us. Six white men sitting up here doing a group analysis about Black people.'

Our friends felt good about what was happening for Harold Washington. Our enemies used it as a takeoff point. A Black had won, and not the Black of their choice. I just became a convenient diversion. That's what happened.

Ordower announced at 12:40 a.m. that Jane Byrne had gone to bed. There was a loud "boo" from the audience. They were disappointed that she had retired without conceding. Ordower said, "Knowing that we are dealing with snakes, Harold Washington wants to know what the exact vote is. We are asking you, pleading with you, to be patient."

A parade of campaign officials continued to march across the podium to proclaim that victory was on the way. "No more Byrne! No more Byrne! No more Vrdolyak!," shouted a member of the crowd. "Ten million dollars down the drain, and with $1 million we made it," another Washington supporter yelled, referring to the $10 million that Byrne had collected and spent in her campaign to derail the Harold Washington movement.

Early Wednesday, shortly after 2 a.m., 98 percent of the votes had been counted. The unofficial returns gave Congressman Harold Washington 410,780 to Mayor Jane Byrne's 380,840. State's Attorney Richard M. Daley trailed with 339,227 votes. For those who did not believe what they heard, the Reverend

Jesse Jackson and George O'Hare jubilantly held up a large sheet of paper with the latest political score. Shortly thereafter, the first Black Democratic nominee for mayor of Chicago appeared on the stage of McCormick Inn's Picasso Ballroom before an excited and joyous throng.

Harold Washington said in a very hoarse voice, "I proudly and humbly accept on behalf of the people of the city of Chicago, the Democratic nomination for mayor of Chicago. Less than three months ago, we started out with no money, nothing more than a dream." The crowd cheered and applauded as several people standing the near podium shouted, "Dr. King's dream lives."

After the cheering subsided, Washington continued. "By your vote, the Democratic party has been returned to the people. We shall have an open and fair government in which all people of all colors, races and creeds are treated fairly, equally and equitably." The crowd continued cheering as Washington inched his way off of the podium.

The majority of the crowd was Black, reflecting the base upon which Washington had won. But a number of whites and Hispanics were also present for the final countdown, a reflection of the coalition that the congressman had formed. A large sign across one wall in the ballroom echoed the congressman's philosophy: "We have the voting power to heal this city and turn it around toward justice for all Chicagoans."

Sid Ordower pulled down the curtains for the evening, shouting to the audience, "We still have another election, Tuesday, April 12. Don't forget now! We have a general election to win!"

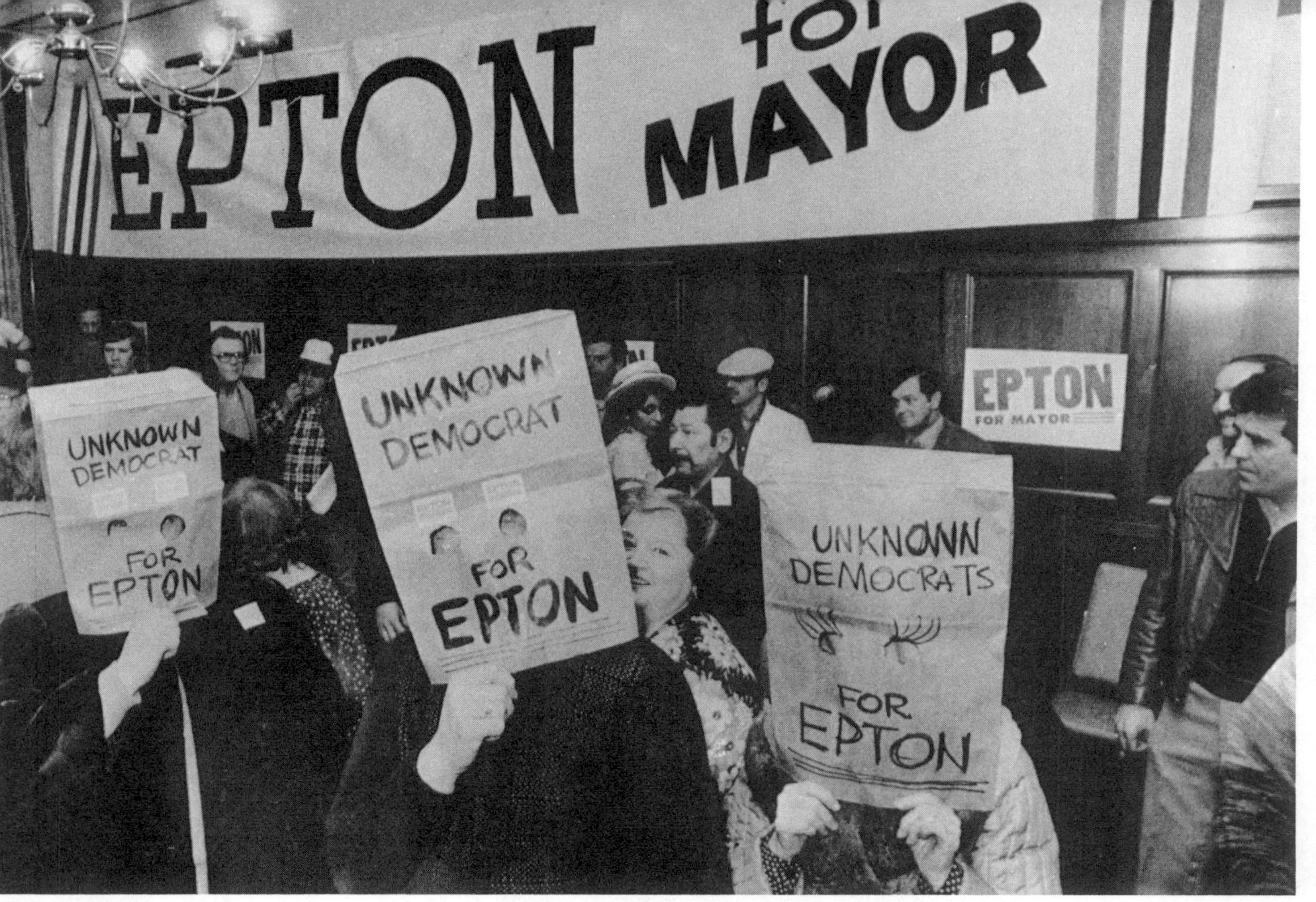

Democratic turncoats in the 1983 mayoral campaign.

CHAPTER
17

The Double-Cross at the Polls

Traditionally, the winner of the Democratic mayoral primary is supported by the Democratic party in the general election. In the 1983 Chicago race, that practice was quickly buried when Congressman Harold Washington, a Black, became the party's winner and nominee.

Immediately after the defeat of Mayor Jane Byrne and State's Attorney Richard M. Daley in the Democratic primary, many white Chicago Democrats defected to support Republican Bernard O. Epton. Their crossover was the consequence of color. Bernie Epton had been anointed Chicago's white hope. His whiteness transcended the fact that he was Jewish and, in the eyes of some ethnics, hated almost as much as Blacks were abhorred.

Washington's surprise victory and the defeat of the party's white saviors escalated racial divisiveness. The white rage, sans physical violence, that flared toward Blacks paralleled the emotions that enveloped Chicago at the time when jet-black Jack Johnson defeated snow-white Tommy Burns for the world heavyweight boxing championship on Dec. 26, 1908. The victories in both instances punctured the balloon of white superiority.

The reality of a Caucasian toppled from the number one position in the Chicago political arena caused many whites to become frightened enough to imagine other disasters: the Sears Tower was going to fall into the Chicago River; the Amoco (Standard Oil) building was going to crumble into Lake Michigan. Whites from both parties were wet-in-the-pants scared. You could see panic on the faces of many of those who were bold enough to make eye contact. On the day after Washington's primary victory, several white folks turned their heads or looked over or through me as our paths crossed. The voices of some of the whites who were forced to speak to me because of some commercial circumstance took on the tenor of a death rattle. My experiences were mild compared with those of some of my friends.

Some Democrat turncoats thought that they had heard the final call, and were spooked by imagined Black ghosts for days after Washington's victory. Just seven days after the primary upset, some of the white citizens who attended an Epton mayoral rally at 3252 S. Halsted St. wore paper bags over their heads, as though they were attempting to hide from the boogey man. The paper bags proclaimed that they were "Unknown Democrats for Epton." A woman at the rally said, "We are called racist and he (Washington) has cultural pride." Another 11th Ward resident, James Murphy, holding an Epton for Mayor poster, blurted, "I never have seen this many Republicans in the late Mayor Richard J. Daley's Bridgeport before. I know the good mayor must be whirling in his grave."

The views of the majority of Bridgeport's 11th Ward residents were shared by Alderman Aloysious A. Majerczyk (12th), the first elected official to bolt the Democratic party and endorse Epton for mayor. Majerczyk said, "The people in my ward prefer Epton because they are Polish, Lithuanian, Eastern European and German. My constituents are giving me a message of racial pride."

The Harold Washington triumph caused the majority of the white committeemen to sit on their hands while deciding what they were going to do. Alderman Ralph H. Axelrod (46th), echoed popular sentiment when he said, "We are in a state of shock. We have never experienced anything like this before and we're waiting for somebody to make a move."

A move was made by four prominent businessmen who offered $1 million and a city job to Ed Warren, the Socialist Workers candidate for mayor. They wanted an unnamed high-profile white candidate to take Warren's slot on the ballot in the general election against Harold Washington. Warren rejected the offer, which he denounced as "racist."

The offer to Warren had been made in shadows of several Democratic leaders scheming on how they might get one of their own on the general election ballot to defeat Washington, the Black, Hispanic and liberal hope. Aldermen Richard Clewis (45th) and Ivan Rittenberg (40th) took the option of crossing party lines and joining Majerczyk (12th) on the Epton team. In a Tribune article dated March 6, 1983, Edward Burke, the 14th Ward alderman and committeeman, said, "There are alternatives."

Mayor Jane Byrne thought she was the real alternative and laid plans to seek re-election as a write-in candidate in the April 12 general election. The prospect of a Byrne candidacy lowered the volume of talk among white committeemen about a concerted effort to support Epton. Her decision was made despite the advice of Edward R. Vrdolyak, Edmund Kelly and William Griffin, the guiding lights of her unsuccessful primary campaign.

Byrne felt that her re-entry into the mayoral general election might persuade Bernard Epton to relent and take a walk. Epton, a proud standup man, made it clear that he had no intention of stepping down in spite of the fact that members of the Byrne camp met with national Republican leaders to explore such a possibility.

Harold Washington, the independent Democratic candidate, was astounded by Byrne's decision to run as a write-in candidate. "Byrne would rather destroy Chicago and the Democratic party than abide by the will of the people," Washington thundered. "She is willing to do anything in order to pay off her campaign debts. Such conduct simply cannot be tolerated," he roared.

Ed Gardner, president of Soft Sheen Products Inc., and an early financial backer of the successful Black voter registration drive, called Byrne's action "an insult to the white community and to white voters. It is also an insult to the Black community and shows a lack of respect for the Black community.

"I believe voters will turn out en masse," Gardner said. "We must remain intelligent citizens. The power is in the vote."

George Johnson, president of Johnson Products, said:

> Byrne's move is harmfully divisive. I was shocked and stunned. It's the action of a poor loser. It will no doubt further polarize the city along racial lines.
>
> She appears to think she's the only one who can run this city. I would hope that the move by Byrne would mean more Black votes.
>
> It can't possibly hurt Washington. Her move will make Blacks work that much harder to get him elected. I believe voter turnout will be twice what it was for the primary.

Alderman Robert Shaw (9th), a Black ward committeeman who backed Byrne in the primary but switched to Washington in the general election, said the mayor's reported plan was "ludicrous. Getting write-in votes is harder than plucking hen's teeth," he said. "She can't win and she'd look silly and racist trying."

Cook County Board President George Dunne took a stand opposite to the majority of white Democratic committeemen who were wringing their hands and lamenting that the primary had produced a Black nominee. "The party had better get used to the idea. Washington may be the first in a series of Black Chicago mayors," he said. "The Chicago organization should put aside intramural differences and get behind Washington's candidacy."

George Dunne was out of step with the old Democratic machine that had placed him in office, and was marching to the beat of a righteous drummer. Following behind Dunne in support of Washington were Cook County Sheriff Richard J. Elrod, Circuit Court Clerk Morgan M. Finley, Treasurer Edward J. Rosewell, Sanitary District President Nicholas Melas, Cook County Democratic party chairman Edward R. Vrdolyak, State's Attorney Richard M. Daley, and Illinois House Speaker Michael J. Madigan (13th).

But, the Daley and Vrdolyak endorsements were duplicitous; precinct captains in both of their wards were already beating the get-out-the-vote drums very loudly for Epton. Moreover, a *Chicago Tribune* reporter overheard Vrdolyak set the stage for a racist campaign prior to Washington's primary victory. Vrdolyak reportedly told a group of Northwest Side precinct captains that the election had become "a racial thing" and exhorted the captains to save their neighborhoods by rolling up a big vote against Washington. The county Democratic chairman subsequently rejected Washington's unity luncheon invitation.

"Fast Eddie" Vrdolyak was the phantom cheerleader for Edmund Kelly, committeeman of the 47th Ward, park district superintendent and the leader of the Democrats for Epton on the Northwest Side. Vrdolyak's token support of the Democratic mayoral nominee was consistent. He had supported Republican nominee Richard Nixon over George McGovern in the 1972 presidential election. His donation of funds to the political war chest of a scrub team in the 26th Ward who was openly campaigning for Epton was not a new turn of events.

Eighteen days after the primary, Vrdolyak sent up another anti-Washington flare by urgently advising the 46th Ward precinct captains to reject an independent aldermanic candidate endorsed by Washington on March 13, 1983. Vrdolyak argued that the regular Democrats would need "every vote we can get" to control the Chicago City Council under the next mayor. This suggestion of council control by "Fast Eddie" was a prelude to the "council wars" that prevailed during the first 3 1/2 years of the Washington administration. The constant battle between the mayor's reform forces and the Democratic machine stalwarts prompted the *Wall Street Journal* to label Chicago "Beirut on the Lake."

Vrdolyak was physically absent from a March 14 strategy session led by his ally, Edmund Kelly, when at least 10 North and Northwest Side Democratic ward committeemen met in the 47th Ward headquarters at 1951 W. Lawrence to discuss whether to reject Harold Washington openly or secretly. Other committeemen attending the meeting were Howard Carroll (50th), Michael Brady (47th), William Banks (36th), Anthony Laurino (39th), Martin Tuchow (48th), Thomas Cullerton (38th), John Geocaris (40th) and John Merlo (44th).

The issue was not whether they were for Bernard Epton and against Harold Washington. They were all for Epton. The question was whether it would help or hurt Epton for the committeemen to publicly support him. They feared the potential of an open endorsement of Epton could create a backlash that would stir more Blacks and white liberals into supporting Washington. And it did.

Kelly was running scared because he had more to lose than any of his fellow committeemen under a Washington administration. Washington had charged throughout his campaign that the park district had systematically deprived the Black neighborhoods of equal services, and stated that he intended to put the park district under directions of the City Council. Such a move would shift control of the 3,000 park district employees to the City Hall and erode the base of Kelly's political power.

On March 24, 1983, 29 days after Harold Washington won the Democratic primary, the Chicago Democratic Central Committee Organization gave Washington a lukewarm endorsement. More than half of the committeemen were not even present to do that. Ten committeemen, most of them from predominantly white areas of the Northwest and Southwest sides, skipped the meeting and 12 others sent representatives in their places. The Black committeemen were in attendance 100 percent and were led by Alderman Wilson Frost (34th), who proposed Washington's endorsement, and urged party leaders to fall in line behind the city's first Black mayoral nominee.

John Stroger, Cook County Board commissioner and 8th Ward Committeeman, angrily lectured his white colleagues for failing to close ranks behind Washington.

> I am very hurt and ashamed to say that I have been a friend of some of you . . . and now you won't stand up for a man who has the ability and has been nominated.
>
> I fail to understand your behavior in the light of the fact that Blacks have faithfully supported white Democratic nominees in the past.

Alderman Roman Pucinski (41st), on a WIND-AM radio broadcast, explained his absence from the endorsement meeting by saying, "I had other things to do." He insisted his problem with Washington was not racial. "He (Washington) wants me to provide him with a guillotine with which to cut off my political head," he said. "And I don't intend to do that. He has publicly said he's going to disavow the Democratic organization."

Alderman Niles Sherman (21st), a committeeman and Washington supporter, was also a guest on the WIND radio show. He told Pucinski, "If Washington were white, you'd be sitting here with a horn blowing it for Gabriel to come in."

In a radio interview on behalf of Bernard Epton, Illinois Gov. James Thompson, who was U.S. Attorney when Washington was charged with a failure to file income taxes for four years, said he believed at the time that "Washington's 40-day sentence was inappropriate because it was too light."

"So far as we could determine, Mr. Washington had not filed for 19 years," said Thompson. "In fact, we found no evidence that he had ever filed returns, based on a look at the Internal Revenue records."

Washington had anticipated such allegations, and had aired his tax conviction before a Rotary Club luncheon in January 1983 during the early days of the primary. At that time, Washington showed three charts that disclosed his failure to file federal income tax returns for the years 1964, 1965, 1967 and 1969.

"Everyone has skeletons," Washington told the Rotarians. "The only difference is that you may look at mine. This is not to say that I am proud of this, but I don't want to carry around a neon sign advertising it. I want to lay to rest rumors that I have been charged with fraud, that I have been disbarred and other untruths."

According to official tax records, Washington's gross income in 1964 was $8,899.92. Taxes withheld were $1,221.08 and taxes owed were $35.53. In 1965, his gross income was $15,370.83. Taxes withheld were $2,054.64 and taxes owed were $32.94. In 1967, he grossed $18,000. Taxes withheld were $2,452 and $0 taxes owed. In 1969, his gross income was $24,000. Taxes withheld were $3,262 and $439.58 taxes were owed, thus making the total tax amount for the years in question $508.05.

The IRS-invoked sentence was 40 days of imprisonment, three years' probation and a fine of $1,036.68.

Washington's lawyer, Elbert W. Washington, felt that the prosecution of his client was politically motivated. It appears that Honorable J. Sam Perry, judge of the Senior Court of the United States District Court, Northern District of Illinois, East Division, supported Elbert Washington's implication in his statement from the bench on March 27, 1972, at 2 p.m. in the presence of:

Hon. James Thompson, United States Attorney,
(currently governor of Illinois)
represented by
Attorney Howard Hoffman,
appearing on behalf of the plaintiff

and

Harold Washington
represented by
Attorney Elbert W. Washington,
appearing on behalf of the defendant.

On behalf of the defendant, Judge Perry said:

I just want the record clear that this is not a fraudulent case. This man is not charged with defrauding the government and filing false returns. It is a misdemeanor in each of the four years. It is not a felony . . .

So this case is not the case of fraudulent taxes. This is not the case where a man has paid no taxes at all. He simply refused to file his return for these particular years . . .

Mr. Washington, incidentally, the reports (*sic*) I get here is he is an excellent legislator, he has a high standing in this community and is well liked . . .

So far as I know, a number of Democrats have been indicted within the last year or two and I have yet to see a person affiliated with the *Republican party* who has been indicted for any of these charges . . .

> Moses had 40 days when he refused to obey the laws that were handed down to him by the Almighty; and the Almighty sent him out 40 days to meditate in the wilderness. We don't have any wilderness to send you to, but I think you need 40 days' meditation on this matter. You are not a vicious person. You are just refusing to do what is required, namely file returns, and that is the action that I feel is proper.

The information contained in the U.S. District Court Case #71 CR 292, United States of America, *Plaintiff vs. Harold Washington* and the judge's comments, to my knowledge, have never been printed in the establishment media.

Bernard O. Epton, the Republican mayoral candidate, and his wife, Audrey.

The meanness of the mayoral campaign between Bernard Epton and Harold Washington is reflected in the faces of the Epton supporters who greeted Vice President Walter Mondale and Washington with racial jeers when they visited the St. Pascal Church on Palm Sunday, March 27, 1983.

CHAPTER

18

Running and Winning the Final Mile Against the Chicago Machine

Harold Washington's final mile in the general mayoral race was loaded with political booby traps that were set to destroy him before he reached the ultimate seat of power on the fifth floor of Chicago's City Hall.

Bernard O. Epton, the Republican mayoral candidate, and his forces–emboldened with new Democratic turncoats–utilized every propaganda scheme conceivable to prevent the Black gladiator from winning the crown that had adorned the head of Richard J. Daley of Chicago for 21 years.

The race among Democrats Jane Byrne, Richard M. Daley and Harold Washington to qualify for the right to run the final mile in the general election was comparatively free of booby traps. Neither Byrne nor Daley attacked Washington personally because each was hopeful of attracting Black voters. In contrast, Epton, the Republican challenger in the general election, believed that he could break through the loyalty knot that tied most Blacks together politically. He made that assumption because he had served on the board of directors of several Black institutions, and had been chairman of the board at the Jane Dent Home for Colored People. The millionaire lawyer had been a substantial contributor to many civil rights causes, and felt he had paid enough dues to make a frontal attack on Washington without retribution.

Moreover, Epton had affected a friendship with Washington during the 16 years that they had served in the Illinois House of Representatives. So, Epton and James Fletcher, his general campaign manager, along with John

Deardourff, his media consultant, decided that they would use any negative information that they had in their portfolios to put some meat on the bones of any skeletons that were floating around in Harold Washington's closet. Specifically, they decided to make a case on Washington's jail term in 1972 for failure to file federal income tax returns, the suspension of his license to practice law in 1970 for not performing work for which clients had paid him, and Washington's failure to disclose that five legal actions were on record against him when he petitioned the Illinois Supreme Court to regain his law license in 1975.

Harold Washington had aired all of his previous legal problems when he ran for mayor in 1977, and had displayed the same laundry list early in the 1983 campaign before the print and electronic media. Those disclosures were not sufficient for Epton and his advisors. The Republicans were determined not to let Washington bury his past. They viewed Washington's past legal and tax problems as his Achilles' heel, their golden opportunity to enable whites to vote Republican without suffering any guilt about their underlying racial motives. For the benefit of those who might miss the subtleties of the message, they produced a mock campaign button bearing Washington's official prison mug shot, number and all.

Washington counterattacked his opponent with a barrage of accusations. He publicized medical records that indicated Epton had been hospitalized several times for mental illness and charged that the campaign slogan, "Epton Before It's Too Late," was not a non-too-subtle appeal to racist fears. Congressman Washington called Epton's media consultant, John Deardourff, "one of the slimiest, funkiest, lowlife, scurrilous individuals who ever crawled out from under a rock."

Bernie Epton's people were not daunted by Washington's hot rhetoric and continued to bombard the media with new angles about Washington's past. They kept the congressman busy explaining his past to deter him from securing his future. Epton continually employed sarcasm to plant seeds of doubt about Harold's character. During a debate when Washington promised to promote affirmative action at City Hall, Epton quipped, "I'm glad the congressman is going to follow the law. It would be refreshing."

The Republican seized every opportunity to twist the American flag around himself and project his image as a war hero, while depicting Congressman Washington as a tax fraud, a shady lawyer and an ex-convict. Many of Epton's television spots included a pitch aimed at countering any guilt Democrats might feel about voting Republican. One of his TV commercials quoted the late President John F. Kennedy: "Sometimes party loyalty asks too much. Surely, this is such a time."

Rhyming to the beat of popular music standards was another Epton campaign ploy. For example, the melody of "Bye, Bye Blackbird" was played to the following lyrics: "It's not a case of black or white. We need someone who will do things right. Bye, bye, blackbird. Your record, Bernie, shows you are tough. And as for us, we have been pushed enough. Bye, bye, blackbird."

There was nothing subtle about this ditty, and the message was well-received by white folks looking for a reason to jettison the Black Democratic nominee. A television news poll showed Washington's 28-point lead over Epton suddenly crumbling to 15 points as a result of Epton's effective propaganda campaign.

Bernie Epton's venomous campaign style was unrelenting. During the final days of the race, it seemed that the only political voice in town belonged to Epton, Chicago's "last white hope." Life-long Democrats packed Epton's political rallies, cheered his coded racist remarks and applauded his presence. In spite of all of the media coverage, the white Republican complained bitterly that his Black Democratic opponent had been treated gingerly by the media and received far more coverage than he had. Epton said he would request time logs from every television and radio station in Chicago, turn them over to the federal government, and ask for a determination under the Fairness Doctrine of whether he had been slighted.

"We have been monitoring Washington's media coverage," Epton said. "And if they (the media) consider this (fairness) in equal time to my candidacy, then they should go back to Russia and learn how to do it properly."

When Congressman Washington was asked to comment on that statement, he replied:

> If Epton wants more coverage, instead of working two hours a day, he should work 14 hours a day like I do.
>
> It's going to be a tough, tough election. You know why. You know what they're saying out there. But we are not going to let them polarize this city.
>
> Every time a Black person gets closer to the Holy Grail, they move it back.

On Palm Sunday, March 27, Harold Washington, accompanied by former Vice President Walter Mondale visited St. Pascal's Church, on Chicago's Northwest side, at the invitation of Father Francis Ciezaldo. There they found that the Holy Grail was being pushed farther back by the Epton demonstrators shouting, "Go home!" "Tax cheater!" "Carpetbagger!" "Epton!" "Epton!" "Epton!" The door that Mondale and Washington had to enter to get inside the church was freshly sprayed with the words, "Nigger, Nigger die!"

The shouts and jeering of Epton's angry placard-waving supporters outside of the church was so disruptive that Washington and Mondale left the sanctuary shortly after they had been seated. The police had to form a cordon to protect Mondale and Washington from the several hundred sneering and screaming whites who stood in front of the church.

Washington's media people used film footage of the Palm Sunday incident in a TV commercial that contrasted children reciting the pledge of alle-

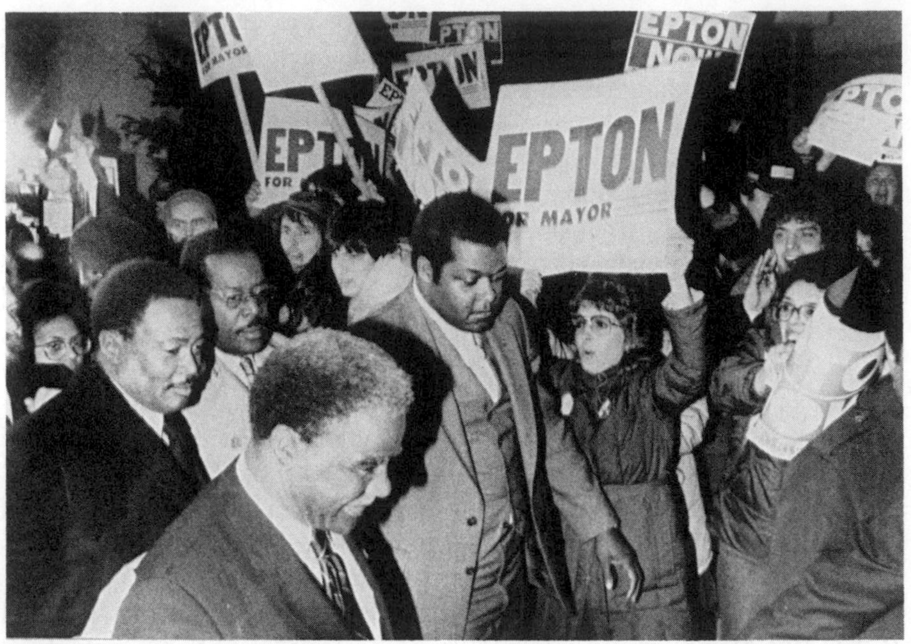

Democratic mayoral candidate Harold Washington is surrounded by plain-clothes policemen and policewomen as he is being escorted away from the hostile crowd at St. Pascal Church.

giance to the flag with the contorted faces of the anti-Washington pickets blocking the entrance of St. Pascal's church.

The ghastliness of that Palm Sunday received national headlines. *Newsweek* did a four-page cover story on "Chicago's Ugly Election" and *People Magazine* carried a picture of a jeering mob and the headline "Hatred Walks The Street." *Esquire Magazine* warned that, "The campaign is disastrous for Chicago in terms of its own immediate future and certainly in terms of its national image. The image is taking. And the unfortunate thing is that part of the image is true." The *Boston Globe* said, "Obviously, there are people who are hyping the racial aspect of this campaign, but it can't be minimized. It is the overriding issue. Racial polarization tends to give the city a black eye that maybe is not fully deserved. But at the same time, there's a great deal of truth in it."

On the day after Palm Sunday, the bold reality of racism in the City by the Lake enveloped Congressman Claude Pepper, the 80-year-old Floridian who came to Chicago to campaign on behalf of Harold Washington, his congressional colleague. Congressman Pepper was treated very rudely when he addressed a group of senior citizens in the same section of the city from which Mondale and Washington had to make a hasty retreat the day before. The very mention of Harold Washington's name evoked catcalls, boos and jeers.

On Easter Sunday, April 3, 1983, Harold Washington is confronted with another jeering crowd of Eptonites as he leaves the Albanian Orthodox Church at 2701 North Narragansett.

"This is America," Congressman Pepper shouted to the pack of gray wolves. "It isn't the color of a man's skin . . . it's his character and the spirit he possesses that determines excellence. I wouldn't be here if I didn't believe that Harold Washington would be a good mayor for every man, woman and child in this city."

Congressman Pepper's pleas fell unheeded. The Northwest side seniors were the roots of the antipathy for Washington or any other Black who threatened the status quo. On Easter Sunday, when Washington went to the Albanian Orthodox Church, 2701 N. Narragansett, to speak before a "Greek-American for Washington Rally," he was greeted by jeers from the children and grandchildren of adults who had taught them to hate. The youthful group gathered outside of the hall chanting, "Epton! Epton! Epton!" Congressman Washington's attempts to talk with the Epton groupies were shouted down.

The number of agitators grew outside of the church as Washington spoke inside, and it became necessary for the congressman's aides to call for reinforcement. The additional police officers were hard-pressed to hold back the jeering detractors while Washington smiled and blew kisses at them as he exited from the church. The Easter crowd was smaller and a bit less menacing than the one that had disrupted Washington's Palm Sunday visit at St. Pascal's Church one week earlier.

In the eight days before the April 12th general election, the mayoral race was shaping into a photo finish. In an effort to push Epton over the finish line ahead of Washington, Police Supt. Richard Brzeczek announced his resignation on Tuesday, April 5, exactly one week before the big day. Brzeczek, who had campaigned for Byrne in the primary, once warned the citizens of Chicago that the streets would not be safe under a Washington administration. The faint of heart were being led to believe that Chicago would become a 20th century Wild West Dodge City under a Black mayor. White police officers, among whom Epton had a great deal of support, expressed regret and anger at Brzeczek's departure. Black officers considered his resignation as a step forward.

Epton used the police issue to rally more white support, and Brzeczek's actions simply moved it to the front burner. Danny Davis, a Washington supporter, said, "Brzeczek's action is an underhanded attempt to help Epton. The police superintendent is hoping to stir up whites even more by saying, 'Washington's about to win, therefore I'm going.' "

With the police department getting into the act, only guerrilla theater was missing from the mayoral race. William Zimmerman, media consultant for Harold Washington, provided that when he crashed a screening of television advertisements for Republican Epton and bellowed, "John Deardourff is a disgrace in the profession we both practice." The reporters gaped as he continued, "The Epton misinformation effort was one of the most racist campaigns since George Wallace ran for president in 1968."

Zimmerman's description of the Epton campaign was an understatement: the following day propaganda flyers flooded the city, and Washington surrendered his usual cool facade to rage.

The flyer described Washington as a child molester. Harold stunned a lakefront audience at Mundelein College when he waved the flyer over his head and shouted, "Here I am running a campaign in which little children all over my community are ecstatic. . .telling their mothers to vote for me. Why am I the victim of this scurrilous, incessant low-life kind of attack?. . .Well, I've had enough."

Contending that his character and manhood were at stake, Washington launched into a five-minute attack against what he said were other "lies" about his taxes and bill payments.

> I say to you, Mr. Epton, if you want this job so badly that you will destroy character . . . if the taste of power is so much in your veins . . . if that's the kind of man you are . . . and these are the kinds of dogs of racism and scurrilism you are going to unleash, I say to you Mr. Epton I will fight you day and night.

The audience, most of whom were white people from the 48th and 49th Wards, cheered wildly at Washington's remarks, repeatedly interrupting him with chants of "We Want Harold."

In the opinion of some political pundits, Harold Washington won his margin of victory during the last few days before the election when he put on his boxing gloves and came out in the middle of the ring fighting like Mike Tyson.

Shortly before midnight on April 12, 1983, Cook County Democratic Chairman Edward R. Vrdolyak predicted a victory for Harold Washington of only 35,000 out of a record turnout of slightly more than 1.3 million. Vrdolyak said, "No one expected this kind of turnout." At the same time, a glum Epton rushed past reporters at the Palmer House and said, "This is certainly not conceding. But Washington got a surprising number of votes in the Black area, more than enough to take over the lead I had." Minutes later, Gov. Thompson left Epton's headquarters with a grim look. "There are some new numbers," Thompson said, explaining that they "are Harold's."

Washington and his fiancee, Mary Ella Smith, left a North Michigan Avenue hotel about 12:45 a.m., where they had been watching the election returns with some friends. They stopped by the Imperial Suite in the Hilton Hotel and Towers to greet about 100 of his supporters who had gathered there at a victory party sponsored by Al Johnson. From the Hilton, a caravan of cars followed the mayor-elect to Donnelley Hall at 23rd and King Drive, where he arrived at approximately 1:30 a.m. to be greeted by 15,000 supporters hoarse from screaming "Harold! Harold!" whenever television sets flashed returns showing that Washington was in the lead. Now, with 96.4 percent of the city's 2,914 precincts counted, Washington had 640,738 votes, or 51.5 percent of the vote. Epton had 599,144, or 48.2 percent of the vote. The Socialist Workers candidate, Ed Warren, had 3,613.

The throng who had been waiting all evening chanted, "Harold! Harold!" when they spotted Washington moving toward the podium with his arms raised in victory. After the welcome had subsided, the mayor-elect said:

> Tonight, we are here to celebrate a resounding victory. We have fought a good fight. We have finished our course, and we have kept the faith. We fought it with a mostly unseasoned phalanx who had mostly never been involved in political campaigns before.
>
> This has truly been a pilgrimage. Our government will be moving forward, as well, including more people and more kinds of people than any government in the history of Chicago. Today, Chicago has seen the bright daybreak for this city and for perhaps the entire country. The whole nation is watching, and Chicago has sent a powerful message. Oh yeah!
>
> They are watching, they are watching out of the crucible of this city's most trying election, carried on in the tide of the most massive voter turnout in Chicago's history.
>
> Blacks, whites, Hispanics, Jews, gentiles, Protestants and Catholics have joined hands to form a new Democratic coalition and to begin in this place a new Democratic movement. The talents and dreams of our citizens and neighborhoods will nourish our government the way tribu-

taries feed into the moving river of mankind. We have kept the faith in ourselves as decent, caring people who gather together as part of something greater than themselves.

We never stopped believing that we were a part of something, something good and something that has never happened before. We intend to revitalize and to rebuild this city, to open the doors and be certain that its babies are healthy and its old people are fed and well-housed.

We intend that our city will grow again and bring prosperity to all of its citizens.

We have been victorious, but I am mindful that there were many other friends and neighbors who were not a part of our campaign. But that's alright. It's alright.

We will never get them all. That's why we have a democracy, because there are many opinions in a city as diverse and multiethnic as the city of Chicago.

To those who supported me, I offer my deepest thanks. I will initiate your reforms, but challenge you. I challenge each and every one of you to rededicate your efforts to heal the divisions that have plagued us.

Each of us must reach out and open our arms. Together we will overcome our problems and restore Chicago to its proper position as one of the most dynamic cities in all the world.

To those of you, wherever you are, who opposed this election, I assure you I understand your needs and your desires. I know I can rely on you for your assistance and cooperation.

Chicago is one city. We must work as one people for our common good and our goals. Our politics are strong and vigorous and are on the verge of revibrant growth and development here. I want to reach out my hand in friendship and fellowship to every living soul in this city. The healing that we seek—the healing we are winning—is economic and social and more. And it includes justice and love, not just ourselves as individuals alone, but for all, all, all in this city.

Our most important concern at this moment is unity. Tomorrow, we'll begin with a prayer breakfast. It will be a symbol that our gathering together includes all Chicago. I intend to lead a prayer for our continued unity and great success as a great city.

I can't tell you how happy I am. History—history was made tonight. And this history has been coming on the horizon, it's been talked about in our streets and homes, but there's nothing like victory to make an old track man like me glad he dared to enter this race.

A great adventure has begun right here. I am proud to be a part of that great adventure. I am so humble by the fact that you have seen fit to give me the responsibility to lead that adventure.

And, as I said before, I did nothing during the course of that campaign that would make it difficult to govern this city with fairness and justice to all.

And so to all of you here who worked so hard for this day, and to all of you out there who worked so hard for this day but are not here, and

> to all of you over this country who wished us well, sent us your honor, sent us some of your children to work with us, prayed for us and worked for us. God bless you all, and thank you from the bottom of my heart.

Earlier that evening, the Reverend Jesse L. Jackson had saluted about 800 college students bussed in from seven colleges to help turn out the vote for Harold Washington. "You are Harold Washington's unpaid army, his silent force," Jackson told the young people at the Operation PUSH headquarters at 930 E. 50th St.

The reaction to Washington's victory, even among his supporters, was varied. One woman struck a sour note when she murmured, "There are not enough (white people) who hate us enough to turn this Democratic stronghold over to the Republicans."

With tears in his eyes, Father George Clements, pastor of Holy Angels Church, stated, "Never in my wildest dreams did I feel I would live to see the day my city would elect a Black mayor. I am gratified for those fair-minded white people who voted for Harold Washington, because they proved that we do have a city where there can be love and brotherhood."

Despite the light, intermittent showers and chilly night air, an elderly woman murmured, "I may be sick in the bed with a cold tomorrow, but this miracle is what I've been waiting for all my life. I am not about to let the weather keep me from witnessing it."

The Honorable Charles E. Freeman, judge of the Circuit Court of Cook County, swears in Harold Washington as Chicago's 42nd mayor. Cardinal Joseph L. Bernadine looks on.

CHAPTER

19

The Inauguration

On April 28, 1983, the day before the inauguration of Harold Washington as mayor of Chicago, the 50 members of the City Council were already engaging in a conflict that plagued his first term in office. They became locked in a struggle to determine whether the Washington loyalists, under the leadership of Alderman Wilson Frost (34th), or the Democratic machine forces, led by Alderman Edward Vrdolyak (10th), had the votes to organize the council and shape the new mayor's ability to govern. The Vrdolyak supporters claimed 29 solid votes were lined up on their side of the chamber. Their count included all of the white aldermen except Lawrence Bloom (5th), Burton Natarus (42nd), Martin J. Oberman (43rd), Marion K. Volini (48th) and David D. Orr (49th).

Harold Washington was not yet involved in the City Council fray, and spent the day before his inauguration sequestered in his 5th floor campaign suite in the Monadnock Building, 53 W. Jackson, talking to friends and aides. He broke the midday by lunching on a sandwich and a soft drink, while taking telephone calls at his second-hand desk.

The anteroom and a partitioned main room outside of Washington's private office were packed with people seeking interviews for jobs with the city, while others in the waiting rooms were attempting to secure tickets or press passes to the inauguration.

Historically, the inauguration ceremonies had been held in the City Council chamber and restricted to immediate relatives and a few close friends because of the limited seating. Harold, the people's candidate, broke tradition and enlarged the event to accommodate 4,000 guests, including VIPs and his entire family.

Washington selected the Navy Pier as his inaugural site because it represented a symbolic victory for minorities. The pier was the place where

Rev. Jesse Jackson launched his successful Chicago Fest boycott against Mayor Jane Byrne in the summer of '82. The success of the boycott was Exhibit A of the rise of Black political clout in Chicago.

Harold Washington's inaugural day began like most of his days-early. He rolled out of his bed at 4:15 a.m. on Friday, April 29, 1983, to dress and prepare to go to the NBC local affiliate, the WMAQ television station, located in the Merchandise Mart, where he was to be interviewed on the nationally televised "Today" show.

When the mayor-elect left apartment number 27 on the 2nd floor of the Hampton House at 5300 S. Shore Drive shortly after 6 a.m., he was seen by fewer than a dozen persons, including his press aide and five security agents, before he stepped into his midnight-blue Oldsmobile with the red and white congressional license plates, and was driven off to the telecast. His car was tailed by an unmarked, privately owned car carrying four of his security people. It took the two-car motorcade approximately 20 minutes to reach the television station. He arrived at the NBC studio seven minutes before he was to go on the air, and spent the short time before the telecast reading some notes and smoking a cigarette.

Following the televised interview, Stewart Dan, the WMAQ producer, invited Washington and his aides to a scrambled eggs and bacon breakfast in the NBC commissary. When Stewart announced that he was picking up the tab, Washington turned and shouted with gusto, "Eat heartily men."

The "Today" show interview was the only pre-inauguration event on the mayor-elect's Friday schedule. He went directly from the breakfast at NBC to his sparsely furnished one-bedroom apartment. He catnapped, engaged in some small talk and joked with several of his security people until noon, when he went into his bedroom and changed from a light gray suit to a darker gray pinstripe suit.

While Harold Washington was making himself pretty for the people, his aides delivered to the front door of the Hampton House the sleek stretch black Cadillac limousine that his predecessor, Jane Byrne, used during her four years on the throne. Although Harold had said during the campaign he was not going to use the limo because it was too ostentatious, he later decided that it seemed appropriate for the inauguration. When Washington stepped out of his apartment building, he paused and gave the limo a quick, overall glance as one of his security men opened the rear door of the car for his entry. Just before setting foot in the Cadillac limousine, he turned and looked at some of his neighbors who had gathered on the sidewalk, flashed his infectious smile, winked and said, "I am going to work."

Instead of going directly to the inauguration site at Navy Pier, Washington stopped briefly at the Conrad Hilton Hotel and went up to the 10th floor to suite 1000 to pick up his relatives and friends. They included his fiancee, Mary Ella Smith; his four sisters; his half brother, Ramon Price; and an older brother, Roy Washington Jr. Also among the select few in the suite were John

Cheefus, his boyhood friend; Margaret Burroughs, a former teacher at DuSable High School and founder and executive director of the DuSable Museum of African American History; and Vernon Jarrett, the *Chicago Tribune* columnist.

Washington disappeared into one of the bedrooms for a last-minute rehearsal of his inaugural address. He stayed there until his aide, Bill Walls, knocked on the door and reminded him it was time to go. Washington told Walls that he had timed the speech to make sure it would not last more than 15 minutes, preferably 12.

As the mayor-elect left the hotel suite, he was greeted at the 10th floor elevator lobby by approximately 50 young adults and teenagers who cheered and applauded. The crowd who greeted Chicago's first Black mayor that afternoon was white. Harold turned to his fiancee, Mary Ella, with a broad smile on his face and said, "This is a good start."

Washington waved goodbye to the young people as he stepped into an elevator and rode to the mezzanine of the hotel, where he got off and walked down the wide, regal center staircase to avoid a throng of people his security said had gathered around the bank of elevators in the main floor lobby.

"We've got to be on time," Harold said with a wide grin, "because if we are late, you know what they will be saying."

An escort of five police motorcycles and three squad cars helped insure that he arrive at his inauguration in proper time. Eight minutes after leaving the hotel, he was greeted by fire boats that had gathered along side Navy Pier to pay homage. An honor guard of police officers and firefighters in full-dress uniforms lined the path from his car to a VIP holding room next to the stage, and across the back of the huge semicircular auditorium.

Two and one-half hours before the mayor-elect arrived at Navy Pier, many of his invited guests had begun to descend on the nearly mile-long structure built in 1916, a year before America entered World War I. Although the sky was partly cloudy, smiles brightened the pier with human sunshine. Strangers cheerfully greeted one another: "We did it this time." "I never thought I would see this day." "I am so proud of Harold." Their gleeful words matched the spring in their steps and the sparkle in their eyes as they approached the auditorium. The joy reflected in the faces of those people would have led a Martian to believe that something very special was about to happen in Chicago that day.

The beautiful dresses that draped the bodies of ladies of every hue, along with men who were groomed to the button, further brightened the atmosphere of an auditorium that was half the size of a football field. Couples and individuals glided to their seats to the strains of "Oh Happy Day," which was being played by Morris Ellis and his orchestra. Although the guests with the red-white tickets were seated in the front of the auditorium, and those with solid white tickets were seated in the back of the hall or in the balcony, they all had one thing in common. They were Harold Washington's people.

By 1:45 p.m., the auditorium was packed to its steel lattice work arches and people were beginning to get antsy with anticipation. Celebrities such as Louis Gossett Jr., Coretta Scott King, Dick Gregory, Rev. Ralph Abernathy and many others occupied the attention of some of the people watchers.

But there was no substitute for "Harold."

At 2 p.m. sharp, the honor guards, consisting of approximately 100 parade-dressed uniformed policemen and firemen in white gloves, began lining both sides of the center aisle of the auditorium. At 2:08 sharp, the orchestra struck up the "Colonel Bogey March" and the honor guards snapped to attention. Mayor Jane Byrne rose from her seat and led the 4,000 guests in the rotunda in a standing ovation as Harold Washington and his fiancee led members of his family, plus his security guards, in a march down the center corridor. Each member of the honor guard saluted as mayor elect reached his station. Vernon Jarrett, the *Chicago Tribune* columnist, was at the tail of the march, carrying a microphone and a large tape recorder chronicling the historic event.

Bedlam reigned in the auditorium for at least five minutes as the emotional crowd expressed their feelings about their leader. Harold acknowledged their greetings, his head oscillating from the left to the right as he waved and smiled while marching down the aisle. Dignitaries filled the three-tiered dais on a stage that was decorated with 50 large bouquets of giant white roses.

After the applause for Washington subsided, Mayor Jane Byrne performed her last official act by calling the assembly to order. A swift roll call of the City Council was made by City Clerk Walter J. Kozubowski, who declared that there was a quorum of aldermen present.

Following the roll call, Cardinal Joseph L. Bernadine, Archbishop of Chicago, delivered the invocation. He made a special reference to Jean Baptiste DuSable, the Black man credited as the first non-Indian settler of Chicago, and noted that the inaugural was being held within walking distance of the first settlement in Chicago. The cardinal also made a special plea for unity and pointed to the beauty of the diverse group who had supported the efforts of the new mayor. In closing, he urged the city's officials to keep alive the spirit of the 19th century city planner Daniel Burnham, who expressed the philosophy that one should "Make no little plans."

Members of the Chicago Police Department posted the colors after the cardinal's invocation. The Chicago Children's Choir, in their bright red blazers, led the assemblage in singing several verses of the national anthem.

His Grace Bishop Lakovos, of the Greek Orthodox Diocese of Chicago, delivered a prayer for unity and peace, which was followed by the Chicago Children's Choir singing Spanish, "Jesu Christo, Hombre Y Dios," by Antonio Kabezon. The choir then led the audience in singing three stanzas of "Lift Ev'ry Voice and Sing," the Negro National Anthem composed by James Weldon Johnson. The anthem brought expressions of wonderment on the faces of the whites in attendance who were not familiar with the song. As the anthem was being played, Walter Jacobson was heard blurting to Harry Porterfield, the co-anchor on Channel 2, that he had never heard "Lift Ev'ry Voice and Sing" before.

The planners of the inauguration recognized that prayer and hard work played major roles in Harold Washington's election, so another prayer for guidance was delivered by Rabbi Harold P. Smith, president of the Chicago Board of Rabbis.

The inauguration moved smoothly as the oath of office was administered to the Honorable Walter J. Kozubowski as city clerk and the Honorable Cecil A. Partee as city treasurer. The Honorable Daniel P. Ward, justice of the Illinois Supreme Court, administered the oaths.

The arts were represented by two of Mayor-elect Harold Washington's favorite writers. Pulitzer Prize winner Gwendolyn Brooks, the Poet Laureate of Illinois, delivered a powerful reading of her poem, "Chicago, the I Will City." The poem was in commemoration of the 150th birthday of the city of Chicago. She was followed to the lectern by another Pulitzer Prize winner, author Studs Terkel, who was attired in a blue blazer, pink shirt, red tie and red socks. He read Carl Sandburg's "The People, Yes!," a paean to the Windy City, with great flare.

Terkel was followed by a spirited rendition of Aaron Copeland's composition, "Fanfare for the Common Man," from the Morris Ellis Orchestra.

The moment that we had all been waiting for finally came at 2:52 p.m. The Honorable Charles E. Freeman, judge of the Circuit Court of Cook County, summoned Harold Washington to the podium. Eyes teared and some people quaked in their shoes. A few persons in the audience actually held up their right hand, as if they were being sworn into office, when Judge Freeman intoned: "Raise your right hand and repeat after me: I, Harold Washington, due swear to uphold. . . ."

A silence followed Washington's recitations of the vows. Then, after a few seconds, pandemonium broke loose as his supporters realized that Harold Washington had been installed as the 42nd mayor of Chicago.

The new mayor paused briefly to allow the jubilant crowd a chance to release their emotions before beginning his speech:

> This is a very serious vow I've just taken before God and man, to do everything in my power to protect this city and every person who lives in it.
>
> I do not take this duty lightly. I was up late last night thinking about this moment—it went through my head hundreds of times-and the words I was reading put me in a reflective and somber mood.
>
> On my right hand was the Bible, which is a very good book for a new mayor to pay attention to. In front of me was a report on the city's finances, which my transition team had prepared, and it did not contain very good news. To my left there was no book, because the one I wanted most doesn't exist. It's the one that I wish had been written by

After taking the oath of office, Mayor Harold Washington is congratulated with a kiss by his fiancee, Chicago schoolteacher Mary Ella Smith. Looking on are Cook County Clerk Walter J. Kozubowski and Judge Charles E. Freeman. Pictured in the background are Alderman Wilson Frost, second from the left, and Gwendolyn Brooks, Illinois' Poet Laureate, on the right.

my tribesman, Jean Baptiste DuSable, who settled Chicago over 200 years ago.

What I wish he had written was a book about how to be mayor of a vast city like ours, a repository of wisdom to be handed down from mayor to mayor for all these years. After reading the report about the actual state of the city's finances, I wanted some good, solid, sound advice.

Then I realized that how to solve the problems facing us will have to be decided by you and me, because every mayor begins anew and there is no blueprint these municipalities must follow.

So I made a list of some of the things you told me during the election campaign, and I found out that you had given me some good advice.

The first thing you told me is to do no harm. You told me that the guiding principle of government is to do the greatest good. Your instructions, which I heard from neighborhood after neighborhood, said to be patient and fair, be candid and, in short, to keep on telling the truth.

(Applause)

So, without malice and living up to my mandate to tell the truth, the first act of my administration is to tell you what we have inherited. I must tell you the truth about city finances. As I said, I have no good news. The immediate fiscal problems Chicago faces are enormous and complicated.

Our school system is not $100 million short next year, as we believed during the mayoral campaign. We now find that the income may be $200 million less than the expenditures of that vast bureaucracy.

My transition team advises me that the city government is also in far worse financial condition than we thought. The city's general fund has a potential shortfall this year of as much as $150 million.

To further complicate the matter, in the waning days of the outgoing administration, hundreds of new city jobs were passed out and hundreds of other jobs reassigned. I say this with malice toward none, but simply to keep the record straight.

The city's transportation system faces a $200 million deficit and no internal solution is on the horizon.

All during the campaign I knew that the city had financial problems and I talked about it repeatedly, incessantly. A majority of the voters believed me and embarked on what can only be described as a great movement of revitalization and reform.

My election was the result of the greatest grassroots effort in the history of the city of Chicago. It may have been equaled somewhere in this country, but I know not where.

My election was made possible by thousands and thousands of people who demanded that the burdens of mismanagement, unfairness and inequity be lifted so that the city might be saved.

(Applause)

One of the ideas that held us all together said that neighborhood involvement has to replace the ancient, decrepit and creaking machine. City government, for once in our lifetime, must be equitable and fair. The people of Chicago asked for more responsibility and more representation at every city level.

It's a good thing that philosophy prevailed, because otherwise I'm not sure the city could solve the financial crisis at hand.

Reluctantly, I must tell you that because of circumstances thrust upon us, each and every one of us, we must immediately cut back on how much money the city spends.

Monday, I will issue an order to freeze all city hiring and raises in order to reduce city expenses by millions of dollars. We will have no choice but to release several hundred new city employees who were added because of political considerations.

The audience rose to its feet and cheered and applauded loudly.

With malice toward none, but only in the interest of clarity and truth, we will continue.

Beginning Monday, executive salaries will be cut. Some members of my cabinet will be required to take salaries considerably less than their counterparts are making now. Holdover chiefs will be ordered to take salary cuts as well.

Unnecessary city programs must end, and the fat removed from all departments until they are sinew and bone. So that there is no confusion, these cuts will begin in the mayor's office.

But these measures are not enough to make up the enormous deficits we have inherited. Like other cities across the state, we simply cannot provide adequate public service without additional sources of revenue. During the election I said that there was no alternative to higher state income taxes.

Chicago is not an island unto itself. Other municipalities and municipal and state officials have joined us in the fight for more tax support. We must have new sources of income soon, and I have joined the governor of this great state in his quest for additional sources of income.

In the months ahead, we are going to be instituting some new fiscal methods and controls and I shall certainly keep you informed—if necessary, on a day-to-day basis—as to our progress.

But when it finally comes down to basic issues, I'm only going to be successful if you are involved. The neighborhoods and the people who reside in them are going to have to play an active, creative role in this administration. I am asking you now to join that team.

In the late hours last night, while contemplating the enormity of the challenge we face together, I remembered the great words of President John Fitzgerald Kennedy at his inaugural address in 1961, and I quote: 'Ask not what your country can do for you,' he said. 'Ask what you can do for your country.'

In that same spirit, today I am asking all of you-particularly those of you who have taken the oath with me today-to respond to a great challenge: help me institute reform and bring about renewal of this city while there is still time. Business as usual will not be accepted by the people of this city. Business as usual will not be accepted by any part of this city. Business as usual will not be accepted by this chief executive of this great city.

The only greater challenge in our history was 110 years ago when Mayor Joseph Medill looked over a city burned to the ground and called for an enormous outpouring of civic spirit and resources to make the city new.

I'm asking the people in the neighborhoods to take a direct role in the planning, development and city housekeeping so that our city becomes a finer place to live.

I'm calling for more leadership and more personal involvement in what goes on. We know the strength of grassroots leadership because our election was based on it. We want this powerful infrastructure to grow because the success of tomorrow's city depends on it, and the world and this country look for examples.

The city's books will be open to the public because we don't have a chance to institute fiscal reform unless we all know the hard facts. I believe in the process of collective bargaining when all the numbers are on the table and the city and its unions sit down and hammer out an agreement together. The only contracts that ever work are the ones that are essentially fair.

Having said all this, I want you to know that the situation is serious, but not desperate. I am optimistic about our future. I'm optimistic, not just because I have a positive view of life, but because there is so much about this city that promises achievement.

(Applause)

We are a multiethnic, multiracial, multilanguage city and that is a source of stability and strength.

(Applause)

Our minorities are ambitious, and that is a sign of a prosperous city on the move. Racial fears and divisiveness have hurt us in the past. But I believe that is a situation that will and must be overcome.

(Applause)

Our schools must be improved. They're going to get a lot better because we're calling on students, teachers and administrators to study longer and achieve more.

(Applause)

I'm going to set a personal example for what we all have to do by working harder and longer than you've ever seen a mayor work before.

(Applause)

Most of our problems can be solved. Some of them will take brains, and some of them will take patience, but all of them will have to be wrestled with like an alligator in the swamp.

(Laughter)

But there is a fine new spirit that seems to be taking root. I call it the spirit of renewal. It's like spring coming here after a long winter, this renewal. It refreshes us and gives us new faith that we can go on.

Last night I saw the dark problems and today I see the bright promise of where we stand. Chicago has all of the resources necessary for prosperity. We are at the crossroads of America-a vital transportation, economic and business center. We are the heartland.

We have a clear vision of what our people can become, and that vision goes beyond mere economic wealth, although that is part of our hopes and expectations.

In our ethnic and racial diversity, we are all brothers and sisters in a quest for greatness. Our creativity and energy are unequalled by any city anywhere in the world. We will not rest until the renewal of our city is done.

Today, I want to tell you how proud I am to be your mayor. There have been 41 mayors before me and when I was growing up in the city and attending its public schools I never dreamed the flame would be passed my way. (Applause, laughter and cheers.) But it has.

It makes me humble, but it also makes me glad and emboldened. I hope some day to be remembered by history as the mayor who cared about people and who was above all fair, (extended applause) a mayor who helped to heal our wounds, who stood the watch while the city and its people answered the greatest challenge in more than a century—and who saw that city renewed.

My good friends and neighbors, the oath of office that I have taken today before God binds us all together. I cannot be successful without you. But with you, we cannot fail.

I can reach out my hand, and ask for your help. With the same adventurous spirit of Jean Baptiste DuSable when he founded Chicago, we are going to do some great deeds here together.

In the beginning, there was the Word. Throughout this campaign, you have given me the word. The campaign is over. Let's go to work!

Most of the people in the audience could hardly restrain themselves from applauding or shouting "Right on!" throughout Harold's speech. In contrast, there were others in the auditorium who sat tight-lipped, displaying little or no reaction to his remarks. However, the tide of the afternoon raised 4,000 people to their feet in a thunderous shower of applause for Mayor Harold Washington at the conclusion of his inaugural address.

The Reverend Jesse Cotton, of the Greater Institutional A.M.E. Church, asked everyone to join hands with their neighbors as he gave the benediction. Alderman Wilson Frost then made a motion to recess.

Harold Washington immediately stepped to the podium and performed his first official act as mayor by saying, "You heard the motion. All in favor, signify by saying 'Aye.' " The audience responded "Aye" in unison. There was no opposition. "It is so ordered," he declared.

Many of us figuratively danced out of the auditorium to the beat of "Oh Happy Day," reprised with gusto by the Morris Ellis orchestra. "I feel very good. It's been a good day," Washington said as he walked toward the Navy Pier holding room, where he greeted some of his closest friends and associates. Following 20 minutes of handshaking and back patting, the new mayor left, in the company of police escorts, for a short ride to the Hilton Hotel. There, he hosted a party for 50, which included his relatives and a few friends, in the Imperial Room on the penthouse floor.

Long after the mayor left the site of the inaugural ceremony, many of his guests lingered to enjoy the champagne and wine reception that had been prepared for them in the rotunda. Streams of good wishes and political talk surged among the guests with the rapidity of Niagara Falls. Conversations flowed more profusely between each swallow of that expensive strawberry-garnished champagne.

Among the comments at the reception:

Vernon Jarrett captured the essence of the mayor's speech when he said, "That speech evinced the personality of a man trying to enjoy his moment in history while pondering the challenge of a 'house divided,' which he had inherited from decades of cynical machine politics."

"You got to tell it like it is," said Walter H. Clark, executive vice president of First Federal Savings and Loan Association of Chicago, and the financial co-chairman of the Washington campaign. "You can't lie to the people, then come back the next day with a different story."

William Lee, president of the Chicago Federation of Labor, praised the mayor's speech. "I thought he did very well with it. We're looking forward to a good administration," he said.

Alderman Lawrence Bloom (5th) said the address was "a little more combative than I had expected. But clearly, well-received, judging by the applause from the crowd."

"I think this is the best speech he's ever given," said Alderman Danny Davis (29th). "He laid out the situation as he found it, and he told us things were going to run differently now. He was great."

"He came off like Atilla the Hun," Thomas Cullerton (38th) said. "That's not going to help him win aldermen over."

"The address was tough," echoed Alderman Roman Pucinski, who wondered whether Washington's promise to end patronage would hurt his chances of getting a majority on the City Council.

Alderman William O. Lipinski (23rd) said he thought it was a "hard speech" that could do more harm than good.

"That was a unifying speech?" asked Alderman Bernard Stone (50th), a member of the Vrdolyak bloc. "I think we are all unified now. Maybe not the way he wanted, though."

Alderman Edward Vrdolyak (10th), leader of the ''29.''

CHAPTER

20

The "Vrdolyak 29" vs. the "Washington 21"

The Chicago City Council chamber was the battleground for lengthy skirmishes between the "Vrdolyak 29" and the "Washington 21." In this tale of two political teams, one side comprised 28 whites and one Hispanic and the other was made up of 16 Blacks and five whites plus Mayor Harold Washington. Members of both council teams claimed to be political reformers, though a few of the "29" admitted that "reform" in the traditional sense was contrary to their philosophy. The philosophical differences and the ethnic makeup of the two constituencies doomed them to push and pull in opposite directions for approximately 1,314 days.

Mayor Washington's team won the pre-season matches on a reform platform that promised to dismantle the corrupt political machine that had run Chicago for 50 years. The new Black quarterback renewed his vow to stomp on the grave of bossism.

On the other side was Alderman Edward "Fast Eddie" Vrdolyak (10th), chairman of the Cook County Democratic party, quarterback for the "29" and chief enforcer for previous Chicago machine bosses. A dynamic individual with a street fighter's instincts, Vrdolyak was determined that he would not be buried politically by the new mayor. Under the Washington regime, "Fast Eddie" assumed the posture of a reformer who would out-reform the reformers, calling political signals that confirmed him as an instant advocate of the separation of powers between the city council and the mayor's office. Vrdolyak also proclaimed the importance of an active city council as opposed to Chicago's customary legislative rubber stamp, and called for fiscal responsibility and budget controls. Although those political concepts were cradled in the mind of the 10th Ward alderman, he did not publicly espouse them until the "Washington 21" took center stage in the political arena.

Vrdolyak used the 48 hours following the Washington inauguration to ensure his team of "29" a good field position in the new administration. He gave his squad a rousing pep talk and signed them to a duration contract while parceling out bonuses in the form of committee chairmanships and other posts of authority.

When Harold Washington's team walked onto the playing field on Monday, May 2, 1983, the mayor immediately noted that his "21" had been out-gunned. The Vrdolyak "29" had moved the ball to the one yard line and had the numbers and the power to reach their legislative goal in one play. Mayor Washington, who was a quick study, recognized that he was in a no-win position and stalked off the field only seconds after he had walked on, with his entire team in close pursuit. The audience in the chambers howled in shock.

Vrdolyak, the council's president pro tem, and his crew of 28 assumed full control of the turf the moment that Mayor Washington and his team of 21 left the playing field. The Vrdolyak squad, by a roll call of 29-0, enacted new game rules that increased the number of committee chairmen to 29 from 20. They also strengthened the power and position of all the players on the team. The spectators, most of whom were Black, stood and roared their disapproval of the quick maneuvering of the "29" bloc.

"We didn't elect you mayor," they shouted, pointing their fingers at Vrdolyak. "We want Harold." In the interim, the police and the sergeant at arms were busy trying to restore order.

"I love it, I love it," gloated Alderman Vrdolyak as he paced back and forth in the pit of the city chambers like a caged lion on the field of triumph.

It was a "blood bath," said Alderman David D. Orr (49th), a member of the Washington team. The Vrdolyak "29" had pulled off a political coup against Mayor Washington and his "21" without hitting the line or throwing a pass.

"It was a mockery," said Alderman Eugene Sawyer (6th), who had been offered the position of mayor pro tem in the reorganization scheme by the "29." He initially rejected the post but subsequently accepted it after a huddle with Black and white members of the Washington team.

"We had eight Black chairmen of committees before this game. And now, we only have three. Is that representative government?" queried Sawyer.

Beneath the stand, Dorothy Tillman, a civil rights activist and a Washington cheerleader, accosted Alderman Richard F. Mell (33rd) and said, "That was racist, what you did out there. You would never have done that to a white mayor."

Mell replied, "What is racist? Is racism when the mayor says he wants all the white chairmen out? He wanted to get rid of Vrdolyak, Edward M. Burke (14th) and Fred B. Roti (1st). Why didn't Wilson Frost (34th) have to go?"

"They will negotiate," said newly elected Alderman William Beavers, a

Washington supporter. "You can't count the votes if you don't have them. You adjourn until you get them. This is just like a football game: when you're losing, you take time out and regroup."

From his fifth floor sky box overlooking the political field, Washington said, "The rump session held after the game was called was illegal and actions taken at that session have no standing whatsoever."

Vrdolyak retorted, "Twenty-nine votes out of 50 is a rump session? We had the majority. We followed the law to the letter."

Mayor Washington, in rebuttal, said:

> Those aldermen have long been opposed to reform in city government and have been going forward at breakneck speed in an effort to hold on to an inordinate portion of their former power with no regard to necessary prudence. It appears that some members of the council are apparently experiencing a nervous reaction to the process of reform and the new spirit of democracy, which the voters have mandated.
>
> Vrdolyak's action was tantamount to breaking this city apart, a blunderous attempt to embarrass this administration.

Vrdolyak scoffed, "I have never, ever seen a mayor turn and run. The problem here is mathematical-29 is more than 21."

The scrimmaging between the Vrdolyak and Washington forces for control of the City Council lasted almost as long as the Civil War. The parliamentary haggling and name calling between the "29" and "21" was so mean-spirited and hostile that "council wars," a sobriquet coined by Chicago comedian Aaron Freeman, was picked up by the national media.

The racial tension exacerbated by the "council wars" resulted in the assignment of around-the-clock bodyguards to several council leaders. At one point, Alderman Vrdolyak had 11 Chicago policemen protecting him. Both Vrdolyak and Burke found it advisable to wear bullet-proof vests after receiving numerous threats on their lives.

In an effort to allow the city to cool down and avoid a bloodletting, the council reorganization issue was thrown to a Circuit Court judge who would act as referee and also call the play. On Monday, May 16, 1983, lawyers representing both teams appeared before Circuit Judge James C. Murray, who ruled that the Vrdolyak "29" had every right to name the new City Council leaders and that Mayor Washington had no power to veto the action. Prior to voicing the ruling, Judge Murray noted that the case before him "would defy the imagination of the writers of two of the best English political satires, 'Alice In Wonderland' and 'Gulliver's Travels.' "

Washington said that he found some good in the decision, since it reaffirmed the authority and perogative of the mayor to utilize the executive veto. Washington insisted that he did not intend to use the veto frequently but implied it might come up as he "relentlessly pursued broad government reforms."

The mayor also raised the issue of race, which was not dealt with in the

Alderman Edward Vrdolyak extends a hand to one of his young white supporters wearing a "29" on his chest while Blacks in the background jeer and give the alderman a "thumbs down."

suit. "Still unaddressed," he said, "is the apparent intentional exclusion of Black aldermen from the meeting where the disputed council reorganization plan was discussed and conceived."

There was some confusion in the decision handed down by Judge Murray in that he ruled that the Vrdolyak committees were legal but did not designate which committees should function while the case was being appealed. Both sides interpreted his silence on committee functions as favoring their position. Lawyers for Mayor Washington and his loyalists took their case to the Illinois Appellate Court at noon on May 17, 1984, and, immediately after filing the appeal, asked the Illinois Supreme Court to take over the case on an emergency basis.

On Wednesday, June 27, the Illinois Supreme Court upheld the position of the "29," and Mayor Washington promised to file a civil rights lawsuit in the federal courts.

Later in the day, after the Illinois Supreme Court decision, the mayor had some second thoughts. He told a press conference that he would not stand in the way of the transition. He said he expected Wilson Frost (34th), who had been the finance chairman and leader of the 21 Washington loyalists, to comply with the order of the court by yielding his office to Edward M. Burke (14th).

The mayor also said he "looked forward to negotiations, this time in good faith, to resolve the impasse," and reiterated that the Vrdolyak group "excluded Blacks from meetings in which leadership was discussed. They nearly shut out Blacks from leadership jobs, thus violating civil rights laws."

Washington further contended, "With party officials campaigning against the Democratic (mayoral) nominee based on race, and race alone, and with white members of the council being herded together in secret meetings to conspire to strip the Blacks and whites who supported the mayor of key positions . . .this is the impasse which must be resolved."

Vrdolyak and his lieutenants were quick to deny Washington's charges. "It is unfortunate," Vrdolyak said, "that when people of different races disagree, the losing side sometimes says it's because of race. It's not so. It never was."

Burke called a civil rights appeal "ill-advised." He said that "if any conspiracy exists, I think it is in (Washington's) mind. From the very beginning, he sought to exclude certain people (from leadership) by conspiring with Wilson Frost and others."

Roman C. Pucinski (41st) said, "You can only rattle those racist bones so often."

A Washington ally, Danny K. Davis (29th), called for new peace talks. "In spite of the court decision, the City Council remains deadlocked and stalemated," he said. "The '21' cannot pass legislation. The '29' can pass legislation, but cannot override the mayor's veto, which requires 34 votes."

Thus, the "29" effectively put legislative handcuffs on the newly elected Black mayor within one-half hour after he gaveled his first City Council meeting to order. Washington's opponents sought to symbolically place him in leg irons because they did not intend for him to ever run for mayor again. They concentrated on attempts to make Washington appear inept as he tried end runs around the stalemates.

Alderman Burke filed a suit to have Washington removed from office because the mayor's aide had failed to file a financial statement, after it had been signed by the mayor, by the deadline. The corporation counsel, James D. Montgomery, called Burke's move "just another attempt to embarrass the mayor."

The reorganization of the council by the "29" was the hub of the handcuff and leg-iron strategy that virtually left the mayor powerless to control the flow of ordinances considered by the council or to make appointments to certain important committees.

As of Aug. 17, 1984, 15 months after Washington's inauguration, the Vrdolyak team had successfully blocked 49 of the mayor's appointments to various committees and commissions.

In reflecting on the negative reactions of the "29" toward his appointees, the mayor said:

The delays were obstruction tactics designed to deliberately frustrate my government. It is a crime and a shame. I have done everything a mayor can do. What did they want me to do, cry? There's an element in the city that is hellbent on obstructing the flow of government.

Alderman Dorothy Tillman called the roll of the "29" and blasted them individually for delaying the confirmations of the nominees. She said, "They are holding them hostage."

A list of the some of the appointees who were "held hostage" as of August 17, 1984, were: Harold Washington, appointed public building commissioner 9/28/83; Mark Jones, Robert M. Anne, Arnette Hubbard, Lillian Delgado for the cable commission, appointed 12/16/83. Warren Bacon, personnel board, 12/22/83, and Quinton Young, president of the Board of Health, 12/22/83.

Also, Carmelo Rodriquez, Dorothy McConner, Dr. Cannutte Russell, for the library board, 2/2/84. Garland Guice, Chicago Regional Port District, 3/30/84. William R. Spicer, purchasing agent, 3/30/84. Dr. Margaret Burroughs, Walter A. Netsch, Chicago Park District, 3/30/84. Tommy Briscoe, Dr. Shirley Buttrick, Ronald Girzywinski, Carman Riveria Martinez, Rev. Albert Sampson and Rev. Jeremiah Wright, appointed to the educational school board of trustees, 4/13/84.

Frank W. Gardner and Joyce E. Moran, Board of Education, 4/25/84. Walter Clark, Marshall Holleb, Laurina Esperaza McNeilly, Leon Finney and Edward Myerson, appointed to the Chicago Housing Planning Commission, 4/24/84. There were an additional 22 hostages in the "29 lockup" as of April 30, 1984.

Council Finance Chairman Edward Burke publicly declared war on Mayor Washington and vowed to reject all mayoral appointments and proposals.

Washington retorted:

I will not submit to blackmail. I have to live up to my responsibility as the city's chief executive officer. The council initiated this fight. They grafted on three ordinances a proviso that limited the mayor's contractual spending to $50,000. Contracts exceeding that amount would require council approval.

By the council holding up contracts, businessmen may be enticed to give up inordinate sums in campaign contributions. He (the contractor) would almost be open to blackmail.

"Hostage taking" was not limited to healthy, civic-minded individuals who usually served pro bono. It extended to the very young and old, to the sick, and disabled, and to those who cared for the afflicted.

Pat Barnett, chief negotiator for the nurses, said, "We are appalled that the contract has still not moved out of the finance committee. These nurses, who will have waited two years for pay increases, are being held hostage in the council wars.

Alderman Burke responded with his customary arrogance, "Stalling appointments is fully and completely within (the council's) perogative. It is one of the few tools that the legislative body has to express its displeasure with the executive."

Burke's disdain and hatred for Washington was manifest in November of 1984, when the number of Washington-backed "hostages" totaled 86. As of Nov. 25, 1985, exactly two years to the day before he died, the appointee who had waited the longest for formal council approval was none other than the mayor himself. Washington had submitted his own name for the mayor's traditional spot on the public building commission on Sept. 28, 1983.

After 31 months in office, Mayor Washington still did not have control of key civic boards because the City Council simply refused to confirm his nominees to serve on 20 boards, which ranged from the Chicago Housing Authority to the Cultural Affairs Advisory Board. Thus, Washington was unable to put his stamp on parks or planning, and his proposal for dealing with problems in mass transit were stymied.

Working under such handicaps was business as usual for the tough-minded mayor with the Teflon stomach. The "29" were baffled by the enthusiasm with which he regularly dove into situations that would have run most men and women up a wall. As he moved through the council frays with the speed of a marathon runner, Harold seemed to be energized by the legislative leg irons.

Part of the mayor's glee was derived from the fact that he understood the mindset of most of the members of the "29." When he spoke about them outside of the council chambers, he frequently laughed and said, "It just burns them up and hurts them to the quick to have to walk into the chambers and say, 'Mr. Mayor' to a Black man. I recognize the council as a legislative body. And Richard J. Daley recognized the council also. However, Daley said, 'Pull that barge. Lift that bale.' "

Since Mayor Washington displayed no signs of weakness while pulling that political barge or lifting that "hostage" bale, his detractors sought to split the "21."

On Jan. 30, 1985, James "Skip" Burrell secretly taped a conversation he had with Mayor Washington in the mayor's Hyde Park apartment. Burrell was one of eight candidates running against Alderman Dorothy Tillman (3rd), who was appointed by the mayor to replace Tyrone Kenner, who had been convicted of a felony. Also present was Sam Patch, the head of the Political Action Conference of Illinois (PACI).The purpose of the meeting was to encourage "Skip" Burrell to drop out of the aldermanic race in the 3rd Ward. The secret tape made that day was turned over to the *Chicago Tribune* by an aide to Alderman Vrdolyak in February, at the height of a special election campaign in the 3rd ward.

John Kass, a writer for the *Chicago Tribune*, approached Dorothy Tillman at a precinct meeting in the home of Rufus Walton, with a copy of a tran-

Holding hands in a unity salute at Operation PUSH are (left to right): the Rev. Willie Barrow, Alderman Dorothy Tillman, Mayor Harold Washington and Rev. Ed Reddick.

script from the tape of the meeting between Burrell and Washington. The Tribune photographer present at the confrontation must have used four rolls of film while attempting to capture an angry expression on the face of Dorothy Tillman as she heard Kass recount all of the unpleasant things that Mayor Washington had said to Burrell about her.

Tillman made the following statement about that occasion:

> Coming from the movement, and understanding white people, I knew that he wanted some pictorial and editorial reaction to put in the *Chicago Tribune*. I was calm. I said to him, 'I don't believe what you're saying about Mayor Harold Washington.' John Kass then showed me this long strip that had been translated from a so-called alleged tape. I said, 'Well, you can do anything with a transcript. Let me hear the tape.'
>
> John Kass promised to let me hear the tape. I said, 'Until I hear the tape, I won't talk to you. When I hear the tape, then I will answer your questions.'
>
> As of this date, July 2, 1988, which is more than three years after the incident, I have not heard the tape. I will not give John Kass an interview. I will not respond to any of his questions anywhere or anytime. If Kass says something to me, I say, 'You know you haven't brought me the tape yet.' So there's no other discussion.
>
> A lot of people thought it was heroic the way I handled the taping episode. I think it was very simple; that is, the Black community is too

> fragile to have Dorothy Tillman and Harold Washington fighting. I am opposed to airing any intrafamily differences in the press. Therefore, I met with Mayor Washington and discussed the tape and we came out of his office with a united front.
>
> Dr. Martin Luther King taught me in the movement that white folks have always worked overtime in dividing Black people for their own welfare and with no regard for ours.

Following the politically damaging expose by the *Chicago Tribune*, Edward Vrdolyak assumed a very low profile for the next two months or so. However, at the annual Democratic county dinner on May 30, 1985, he gave a strident speech attacking the left wing of the Democratic party, which was led by Mayor Harold Washington. That speech signaled that Vrdolyak was prepared to vilify the mayor at the drop of a microphone. Occupying the mayor's suite had become "Fast Eddie's" obsession for 1987.

Vrdolyak understood that to wrest the mayor's chair from Washington in 1987, he must split the Black vote and court the city's two swing blocs: the Hispanics and the white independents on the Near North Side.

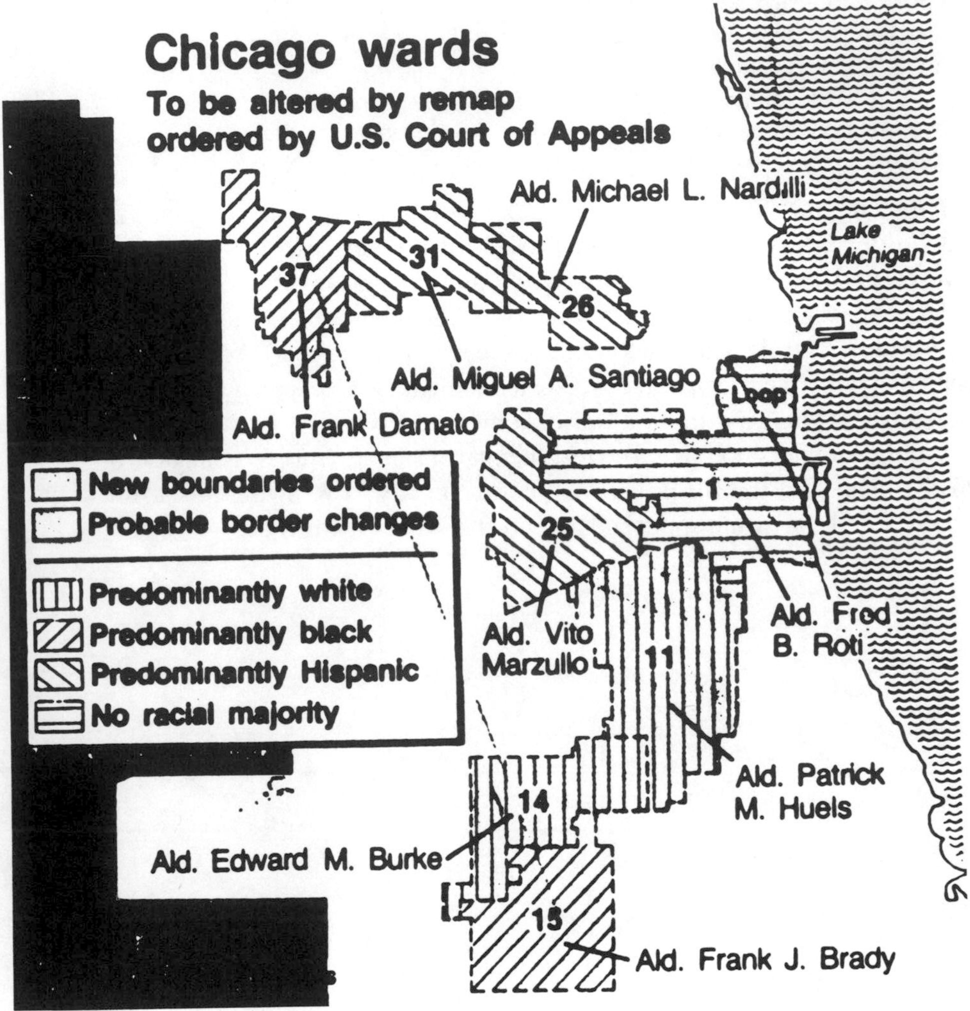

The Chicago ward map above, which was ordered by the U.S. Court of Appeals in 1985, has an interesting history. In 1970, Thomas P. Keane, Mayor Richard J. Daley's floor leader, designed a map that reduced to 17 the 19 predominantly Black wards by extending the 15th and 37th Wards and more whites within their boundaries. In 1980, Keane fashioned another map for Mayor Jane Byrne that "impotized" the Hispanic voting power by dispersing Hispanics into several adjoining white wards. In the summer of 1982, a suit was filed in the federal court by Blacks and Hispanics to correct the inequities.

CHAPTER

21

Remap: The Road to Political Liberation

The holding of hostages by the "Vrdolyak 29" fanned the flames of discontent higher among the politically disenfranchised who realized that the redrawing of Chicago's political ward maps was the only solution to achieving the parity mandated by Section 2 of the 1965 Voting Rights Act and of the 14th Amendment. The Nov. 13, 1981, remap approved by the Chicago City Council, which flagrantly and illegally diluted the voting strength of both Blacks and Hispanics, framed the struggle for political power between the "29" and the "21."

On June 30, 1982, a coalition of Black groups filed suit in federal court to strike down the inequities of the November 1981 remap, alleging racial discrimination. A similar suit was filed on behalf of the city's Hispanics on July 16, 1982. The U.S. Justice Department joined in the legal action on Sept. 15, 1982, charging that the new map did indeed discriminate against Blacks and Hispanics.

In December 1982, U.S. District Judge Thomas R. McMillen ordered the city of Chicago to draw a map to accommodate four additional wards, two wards with Black majorities and two with Hispanic majorities. Two days later, the judge approved a new city map that incorporated the changes he had ordered.

Although Judge McMillen's decisions bolstered minority voting rights, it did not alter the reality that the regular Democratic party, under the leadership of Edward R. Vrdolyak, controlled the City Council.

The "Vrdolyak 29" sought to halt any movement that threatened their control of the council, and voted to appeal the court order for new ward boundaries.

Mayor Washington vetoed the appeal, and the veto was challenged. The mayor devised other strategies to thwart the council; the "29" continued to block his efforts. The council wars continued to roar like a forest fire, reddening the political skies over Chicago as the nation watched.

On May 17, 1984, the 7th U.S. Court of Appeals partially reversed Judge McMillan's decision, ruling that Black majorities in three wards should be increased to at least 65 percent, and that Hispanics should be expanded to a 70 percent majority in four wards. It ruled that McMillan did not go far enough in assuring minority representation in that the U.S. Department of Justice had set 65 as the minimum percentage needed to assure minorities "a realistic opportunity to elect a representative of their choice."

William Harte, attorney for the "29," said the Justice Department guideline "was never anything written in stone, and I would advise the council to appeal the decision."

The "29's" hope of keeping a council majority was based on the Harte appeal. Recent history was not on their side, however. The federal courts had ordered the integration of the Chicago fire and police departments, in addition to banning patronage hiring and firing, and curbing the segregation practiced by the Chicago Housing Authority. It was not unrealistic to assume that the federal courts might pave the way for Chicago's first Black mayor to have a majority in a legislative chamber that has been the white man's domain since the election of the Windy City's first mayor 147 years ago.

The formula for achieving voting parity for Blacks and Hispanics was arrived at by adding 5 percent to a simple majority because minority populations are younger, another 5 percent because minorities have a lower voting registration among eligible voters, a third 5 percent because of the generally lower voter turnout, and an extra 5 percent for the benefit of the Hispanics.

In addition to the local remap changes, the 7th U.S. Court of Appeals ruled that the Black percentages in the 7th, 15th and 37th Wards would be increased to at least 65 percent and further mandated that two wards on the Near Northwest Side, 26th and 23rd, should include at least 70 percent Hispanics. All but one of the wards slated for changes had been represented by the "Vrdolyak 29."

The court ordered the redrawing of boundaries to restore Black and Hispanic majorities in at least five wards, ruling that the ward boundaries had been altered by the City Council in 1981 to favor re-election of entrenched white aldermen and Democratic committeemen.

As of May 20, 1984, there were 15 Blacks and one Hispanic among the 49 sitting aldermen, despite the fact that Blacks and Hispanics make up 55 percent of the city's 50 wards.

With eyes on both the election calendar and the census data, the mayor's political enemies rallied to maintain the status quo until the 1987 mayoral election. Thus, they explored every legal avenue to block any special election based on the new ward map.

Mayor Washington and members of his team were convinced that enforcement of the appeals court decision would lead to additional Black and Hispanic allies in the Chicago City Council and pressed for an early election under the proposed new ward map.

The reapportionment required that Blacks comprise at least 65 percent of the 37th and 15th Wards where white opponents of the mayor flourished under the 1981 map despite the wards' Black majorities. It also called for extensive redrawing of several other wards in which white aldermen represented a largely Hispanic population. In those wards, the court called for 70 percent majorities to give Hispanics a reasonable opportunity for victory.

"I would hope to expedite things as much as possible," said Judson Miner, one of the attorneys for the plaintiff, who called for a special election in the affected wards as early as spring of 1985.

A member of "Vrdolyak's 29" said:

> We don't want any election before '87 that would give Harold control of the council. The big thing is to knock him out in '87 and keep him in handcuffs and leg irons in the interim. If he wins in '87 again, it's all over. However, if we knock him out, we can handle the council no matter who is in the mayor's chair. Without control of the mayor's office or the council, we'll have no leverage.

A four-vote shift under the court's remap plan could result in a 25-25 deadlock, which could be broken by the presiding officer, the mayor.

In May, a letter signed by most of the "Washington 21," rejected Harte as their legal representative. The letter said, in part, "We do not believe your appeal is valid. It is ill-advised. And not representing the interest of all 50 aldermen." The letter asked that Harte "end all efforts to reverse" the court decision. Alderman Eugene Sawyer (6th), a mayoral ally, said the letter was hand-delivered on Wednesday, May 30.

On June 3, Mayor Washington praised his council allies for their stand. He said, "The minority bloc was absolutely right in saying that Harte, who customarily represents council majority leader Alderman Edward R. Burke and the rest of the '29,' doesn't represent the entire council in his bid to appeal the May 17 decision of the 7th Circuit Court of Appeals."

In an interview with Chinta Strausberg, reporter for the *Chicago Defender,* Alderman Burke, the council finance chairman, said Harte has been instructed to proceed with the appeal process, indicating that time was on the majority's side and that the "Vrdolyak 29" will dominate the City Council until at least 1991.

"It is not Burke's role to represent us in their efforts to try and block fair representation," said Sawyer. "We agree with the appeals court. We need to get on with holding the special election." Referring to Burke's prediction on city control, Sawyer added, "I don't know where he's getting his information."

In response to the letter from the "21," Harte said, "The Washington administration can't fire me. And even if it could, I would keep fighting the remapping on behalf of the City Council majority, for no fee, if necessary."

Alderman Vrdolyak responded: "It's too bad these people (Washington and his aides) are wasting time with machinations and interpretations that are totally erroneous and have no basis in truth or law." Piggybacking on that statement, Burke said, "Washington likes to cite statutes and ordinances, but when it comes to ethic statements, he conveniently ignores the law. There will be an appeal. It will be successful. If Washington wants to play hardball, he better get out his batting helmet," he added.

Attorney Harte ignored the letter from the "Washington 21" and appeared before the appeals court. In his argument, he used the 27th Ward as an example of why the ward boundaries were drawn as they were:

> The 27th Ward lost something like 20,000 to 25,000 in population in the last decade. So when you went to look at the redistricting, we found that 19 wards under the 1970 Census Tract had less than the 60,000 population, which would accommodate the 'one person, one vote' principle. What we did in these instances was to move the ward lines to cover that problem.

Harte further claimed:

> The alternate map developed by the plaintiff (they have three) favors Blacks instead of Hispanics. Indeed, Chicago is a segregated city with regard to Black and white. With Hispanics, there is dispersal. It is difficult to get a minority-controlled map; therefore, fracturing and manipulations are going to occur.

Alderman Martin P. Oberman (43rd), plaintiff in the Political Action Committee Inc. (PACI) appeal; Sam Patch, former administrative assistant to Washington when he served in Congress and also an unsuccessful candidate for the 3rd Ward aldermanic seat; and Marlene Carter and Bruce Crosby, along with their attorneys, were present when Harte made his appeal.

Several members of the majority bloc also attended, and one was overheard saying he did not understand why former Mayor Jane Byrne and the City Council majority were named as defendants, while Alderman Wilson Frost (34th), who played a significant role in the adoption of the initial map, was excluded. According to court records, Frost said, "An alderman could only propose changes on his or her ward configuration." At the time in 1981, Frost was the powerful chairman of the Finance Committee and the chairman of the subcommittee on redistricting for the City Council's Committee on Committees and Rules.

Alderman Burke, Frost's successor as council finance chairman, was the head cheerleader for those who vowed to appeal the court decision to discard the '81 ward map.

"I don't think we should spend another penny on this matter," said Alderman Sawyer. "I think the judge is correct in his decision. Should the '29' continue in its efforts to appeal the decision, we will fight them to the end."

Rep. Carol Moseley Braun declared:

> After the map is redrawn, the ramifications will be profound. And ward battles will ensue. I believe the majority bloc will attempt to stack the deck in these aldermanic elections by planting several Black and white candidates in the race in an effort to divide us.
>
> At the same time, they will desperately try to hold on to their organizational core. If we can win these elections, you may see the demise of the '29' and the people will gain control of the City Council. That is what they're afraid of.

Mayor Washington said, "It is a well-established law under the Voting Rights Act of 1965, whose extension I fought for as a congressman. You cannot deliberately dilute representation of minorities. It is unconstitutional, and the court is applying that principle. The matter should be resolved."

"Alderman Edward Burke has a policy of citing discrimination suits that have been ruled against the city," David Canter said. "He and Vrdolyak are practicing obstructionism at the cost of the taxpayers. The IVI-IPO is in favor of the court's decision, and we condemn Vrdolyak and Burke for their desire to return to the good old days."

On June 6, 1984, Mayor Harold Washington made his intentions known in a letter mailed to the 50 aldermen, including Alderman Edward Burke, and to attorney Harte. The letter was an official notice of Harte's dismissal, and verification that City Corporation Counsel James Montgomery was the sole representative of both the council and the administration on legal matters. The letter further instructed Montgomery not to appeal a May 17th order by the U.S. Court of Appeals that directed that the map of Chicago's 50 wards be withdrawn.

Washington's letter, in effect, short-circuited any possibility of an easy appeal by the "29" using taxpayer's dollars, and set the stage for a special election as early as 1985.

Harte was contacted by a *Chicago Tribune* reporter that Wednesday when Washington's letter was made public. Hired by the "Vrdolyak 29" following the 1982 challenge of the 1981 redistricting ordinance, Harte had received more than $200,000 in fees as special counsel to the City Council by June of 1984.

Harte told the reporter that he would follow through on his plan to petition for a rehearing on the remap case. "They knew it was due tomorrow," Harte said. "That's why they sought to fire me today." He maintained the city "has no legal basis" for his dismissal.

Alderman Roman C. Pucinski (41st), a majority bloc stalwart, accused Washington of attempting to "disenfranchise aldermen and their constituencies."

Corporation Counsel Montgomery countered, "Obviously, the entire litigation has political ramifications. But it is futile to stone wall the courts, when the decisions are right."

The bottom line of Mayor Washington's letter meant that any aldermen whose wards are affected by the remap must retain counsel at his own expense. There would be no more free rides for appeals.

At the June 10, 1984, rally commemorating slain Latin activist Rudy Lozano, Mayor Washington declared:

> The true litmus test of whether or not someone believes in Hispanic and Black representation is not if they buy ads in a newspaper or donate money, but if they believe you should represent yourself.
>
> There is no need to stall and wait until 1987 to remap the city's wards. The wards should be remapped now and a special election held in 1985.

On Sept. 11, a federal appeals panel rejected requests by the majority bloc aldermen to reconsider the redistricting. Majority bloc leaders promised further appeals that could tie up any ward reapportionment past the 1987 election. However, the attorneys for the minority groups that filed the original districting challenge predicted special elections for five wards as early as February 1985. Judson Miner, one of the attorneys for the Blacks and Hispanics, said, "No legal basis for appeal remains."

Mayor Washington said, "The court decree involves a remap of as many as eight wards. Obviously, this is a significant step by the federal courts to enforce the U.S. Voting Rights Act.

"This decision will bring an end to the discrimination which has resulted from ward maps in Chicago, particularly against Hispanic voters."

On Thursday, Oct. 19, the 29-member bloc, headed by Alderman Vrdolyak, asked Supreme Court Justice John Paul Stevens to stay the map designed to increase minority representation on the council.

The appeal accused the district and appeals courts of going beyond the federal law by not only giving minority voters an equal chance to elect representatives of their choice, but maximizing their strength in certain wards.

A spokesman for the mayor said, "They are trying to keep the current ward map, that a federal court has found discriminates against minorities, in effect at least until the next scheduled election in 1987."

On Monday, Oct. 22, Supreme Court Justice John Paul Stevens temporarily blocked any change in the way Chicago City Council members are elected.

Acting on an emergency request from the Vrdolyak contingents, Justice John Paul Stevens ordered that Chicago's 50 wards not be altered until the full Supreme Court considered the council's formal appeal. Stevens said the temporary injunction "will facilitate the orderly process of this litigation," by remaining in effect until the higher court decision.

Judge Stevens, who handled emergency matters for the court in Illinois, Indiana and Wisconsin, emphasized that he was not expressing any views on the outcome of the politically explosive case.

Joe Novak, spokesman for Vrdolyak, said sarcastically, "Isn't that sad news for the minority side in the council? You're talking about a six-month delay and a strong chance that they will hear the case. You can bet there will be no April special elections."

On June 3, 1985, the U.S. Supreme Court refused to consider an appeal of the appellate court ruling, setting the stage for redrawing boundaries in seven wards, and for special aldermanic elections in at least five Northwest and Southwest wards.

A new ward map giving Hispanics more political power was presented to a federal judge on Thursday, Oct. 31, 1985. Both factions in the City Council claimed credit for the map. Attorney Bridget Arimond, a counsel for the Black plaintiffs, said, "They want to appear as the good guys rather than the ones seen as depriving minorities of their right to vote."

Although Harte insisted that he was the author of the approved map, U.S. District Judge Charles Norgle ruled that Corporation Counsel Montgomery would be the legal representative for the city in future remapping hearings.

Mayor Washington's expectation that a special election based on the reapportionment could be held by the end of 1985 was squashed by Judge Norgle. When the judge set November 4 as the earliest date for hearings on how the map should be redrawn, it became unlikely than any special election could be held before 1986.

Mayor Harold Washington holds a miniature Mexican flag as he watches the Mexican Independence Day parade, 1986.

CHAPTER

22

The Court Ruled: The Black and Hispanic Map Is in and the White Map Is Out

The refusal of the U.S. Supreme Court in June of 1985 to hear the appeal of the redistricting case was a psychological victory for Mayor Harold Washington and the "21." However, the victory was strictly cerebral because there were no guarantees on how people in the four expanded Hispanic wards would vote in 1986. The question, "Whose side are they on?" hung in midair. The question was legitimate because the only sitting Latino in the City Council was Miguel Santiago (31st), one of the "Vrdolyak 29."

The primary issue before the 7th U.S. District Court was the remapping of five wards (the 15th, 37th, 25th, 26th and 31st). These wards were represented by buck privates aligned with Aldermen "Fast Eddie" Vrdolyak and Edward Burke. Mayor Washington's master plan was to capture these wards with Hispanics who, he hoped, would be loyal to him. He felt that with their aid he would win the special election once the boundaries were redrawn, tilting the balance of power in the City Council toward his side of the aisle.

James Montgomery, the corporation counsel, was optimistic that the special election would give Mayor Washington a council majority. Montgomery anticipated support from 19 Black wards, four Hispanic wards, and three to five lakefront wards under the new alignment. "It would change the picture tremendously. You would no longer have a 29-to-21 vote. Everything would be topsy-turvy and all the bottlenecks would disappear. We would have peace in this city of Chicago for the first time since former Mayor Jane M. Byrne got in bed with Vrdolyak."

Alderman Frank Damato (37th) disagreed:

> You can't tell a white person, 'You should stay here, but you will never have a chance for representatives of your color.' They will figure, 'To hell with you.' Whites will leave.
>
> I believe I'm the best man for the job. I am Italian. We were discriminated against. We advanced ourselves through education. People who say that the Black alderman would better represent this ward . . . are racist. I will fight anyone—white, Black, purple—who challenges me for my aldermanic seat.
>
> If I'm running the ward like a slave master or a plantation owner, why do I help several Blacks for every one white? I have taken over $20,000 out of my own pocket or my political fund in the last year to help Black residents pay for their groceries, their rent, their bus fare or to post bond to get their kids out of jail. Is that plantation politics? I'd like to see them go to some of the neighboring wards with Black aldermen to see what those people get.

Alderman Timothy Evans (4th), Mayor Washington's floor leader, did not share Damato's opinion about Black aldermen. He predicted that the special aldermanic elections would be held in conjunction with general elections in March 1986. "I keep hearing that our opponents will try and appeal to try and hold back the dam beyond 1987 (the mayoral election), but I don't think they will be able to do it."

If the mayor gained control of the City Council before the 1987 election, "We would have a whole new ball game," Evans said. "We could put the mayor's programs on track. They (the majority bloc) have tried to derail the mayor at every turn."

Alderman Burke countered Evans declaring that chances of a special aldermanic election before the scheduled 1987 mayoral election were "slim to none." He predicted that the matter will go back to the district courts where "the process will have to begin all over again."

Although the Vrdolyak/Burke bloc conceded privately that new ward boundaries were inevitable, they worked unrelentingly to stall the elections until they could regain the mayor's chair. The Vrdolyak forces had fought like tigers for three years to stave off the ward boundary adjustments while publicly minimizing the significance of the high court's action and insisting that they could not lose council control before the 1987 mayoral election.

Vrdolyak, the fox, realized that the court decision meant that he must find his way to the chicken coop in order to preserve his own political salvation. He began to romance the Hispanics, declaring that the regular Democratic organization would field several Hispanics for alderman in the special election. At the time "Fast Eddie" belatedly declared his love for Spanish-speaking Americans, there was a token Latino among the city's 50 aldermen. The other three potential Spanish-speaking wards were represented by Anglo Vrdolyakers.

Mayor Washington knew that he must win at least two additional Black wards and two Hispanic wards to ensure council control prior to the mayoral election.

Washington's choice among the potential Hispanic candidates for the 26th Ward was a young firebrand named Luis Gutierrez, an assistant superintendent in the city's Streets and Sanitation Department. Washington pledged his full support for Gutierrez and appeared at a fundraiser where some $6,000 was raised for Luis' campaign. The mayor also campaigned side by side with "Little Luis" on the streets and in the halls of the ward, where he repeatedly proclaimed that Luis Gutierrez was the man that he needed in the City Council. Luis' opponent in the ward was Alderman Michael Nardulli, an Italian American and a member of the "Vrdolyak 29."

Washington put his arms around Juan Velazquez for alderman in the 25th ward. Velazquez, a Washington appointee, had lost two previous elections, so he could not bring the freshness to his campaign that Gutierrez would bring to his race. A solid favorite of the mayor for alderman of the 22nd was Jesus Garcia, a top city aide in the Washington administration who had defeated Alderman Frank D. Stemberk for Democratic committeeman in 1984.

Luis Gutierrez, president of the 26th Ward Independent Political Organization, said that precinct workers are not only in the field but were working outside of the ward boundaries in anticipation of the redistricting. "We are ready to go. We don't fear taking them on," he bellowed. "We invite them to exercise democracy. We are ready to go tomorrow." He challenged the City Council to "exercise democracy" by allowing the redistricting to proceed.

By November 1985, four members of the "Vrdolyak 29" realized that their ward maps were beginning to disintegrate and began to scramble like rodents on a burning ship. Alderman Damato (37th), Stemberk (22nd), Frank J. Brady (15th) and Michael L. Nardulli (26th) sent save our souls (SOS) signals to Alderman Vrdolyak, begging him to use his clout as chairman of the Cook County Democratic Committee to slate them for seats on the county board.

The instincts of the "Vrdolyak 4" were on target. On Dec. 30, 1985, Judge Charles R. Norgle of the U.S. District Court ordered that a special election be held March 18, 1986. The wards included under the order were the 22nd, 25th, and 26th, which would have substantial Hispanic majorities under the redistricting. The 15th, 18th and 37th wards would have increased Black voting power, and the 31st would remain predominately Hispanic, though the Hispanic population was decreased slightly.

With the handwriting on the wall, Vrdolyak, Burke and their allies conveniently became born-again Christians. They filed documents in the federal court to support their new position in the remap battle. They contended that they had really been on the side of the Blacks and Hispanics in the remap fight all the time, although there was ample evidence that they had fought the minority plans tooth and nail for almost four years.

The "29's" court action was tantamount to rewriting the New Testament.

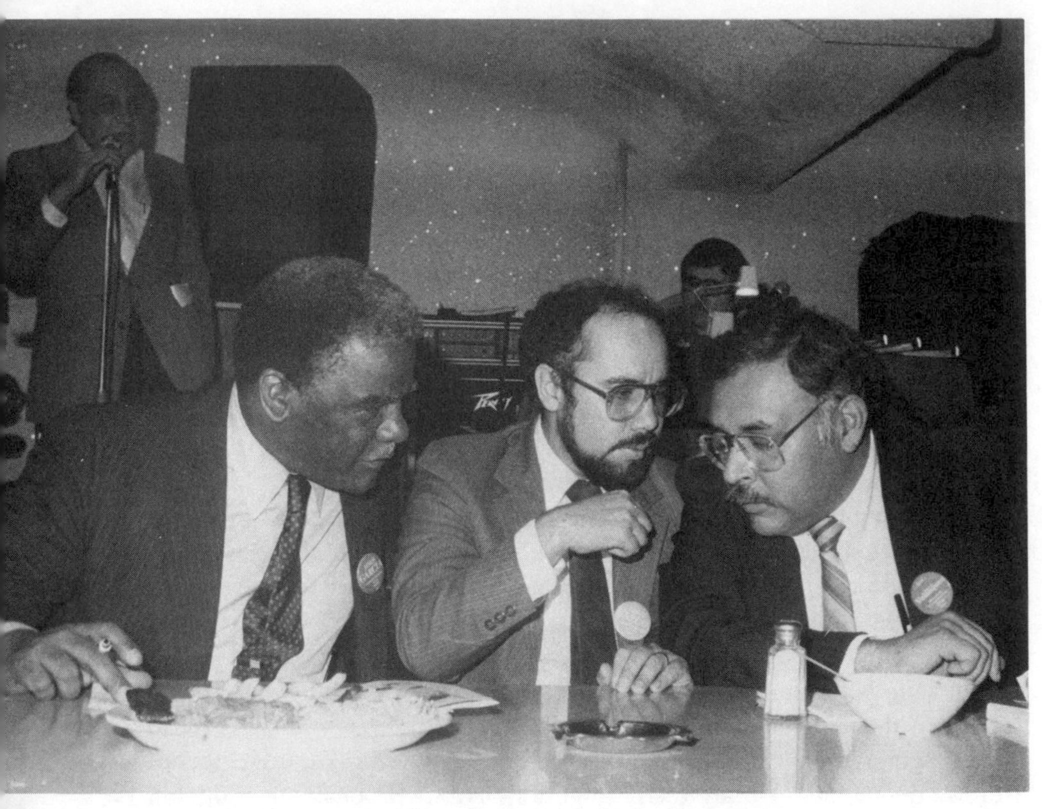

Discussing strategy for a political victory during a dinner rally are (left to right): Mayor Harold Washington, Miguel del Valle, candidate for state senator, and Juan Velazquez, aldermanic candidate in the 25th Ward. Standing at the microphone behind Washington is Civil Rights Activist Sid Ordower.

Judson Miner, lawyer for some of the plaintiffs, said, "It is simply offensive to my clients to suggest that Mr. Vrdolyak and Burke had been on their side."

Judge Norgle called the Vrdolyak cadre's arguments to switch "disingenuous."

The Vrdolyak switch and Judge Norgle's call for a special election collided with media headlines implicating the Washington administration and members of the "21" with political corruption.

On Dec. 26, 1985, four days before the judge declared the date for the special election, a front page story in the *Chicago Tribune* was headlined: "FBI Mole Gave Alderman Cash." The alderman named was Wallace Davis (27th), an ally of Mayor Washington. The following day, a *Tribune* headline screamed: "Swindler Sparked FBI Probe." The article began: "An FBI undercover investigation into Chicago government began in 1984." This was one year after Mayor Washington took office. A third news item, captioned "Aldermen, Contractor Feel Heat," appeared on Dec. 28: The first paragraph began: "At least five Chicago aldermen shopped for lawyers Friday, Dec. 27, and a federal grand jury was subpoenaing records of the New York firm connected with Michael Raymond, the convicted swindler who acted as an undercover agent in a FBI investigation of suspected corruption in the city government."

The front-page headline of the Dec. 29, 1985, *Chicago Tribune* barked: "FBI Mole's Credo: 'Let's Make A Deal.' " Four members of the "21" were named: Aldermen Perry Hutchinson (9th), Clifford Kelley (20th), Wallace Davis Jr. (27th) and William Beavers (7th). They reportedly had acknowledged that the FBI had questioned them about their relationships with Michael Raymond and Systematic Recovery Services Inc., the collection agency he represented.

Alderman Davis admitted that he took $1,500 from Raymond, who used the name Barnett during a meeting in Raymond's luxury apartment in Lake Point Towers. Davis described the money as a campaign contribution.

Alderman Marian Humes (8th) said she believed she was a target of the investigation, but refused to discuss it. All of the aldermen named were Black and allies of Washington.

On Dec. 30, 1985, the day Judge Norgle announced the special election, the front page of the *Chicago Tribune* headline read: "Businessman Links Informer to McClain." The story stated that McClain, a close friend of Mayor Washington, introduced Raymond to Black businessman Eugene Langston in July 1984.

On New Year's Eve, Dec. 31, 1985, the political corruption story slipped back to page 1, Sec. 2 of the Chicagoland section of the *Chicago Tribune.* The headline read: "McClain Must Go, Mayor Told. Aldermen Fear Backlash." The story stated that David Orr (49th) and Lawrence Bloom (5th) said that McClain's reputation as a power broker in the Washington administration was especially damaging for the mayor among liberal whites on the city's lakefront.

"The Clarence McClain issue is there on the lakefront," Bloom said. "From the mayor's point of view, it hurts him. The perception that McClain is a wheeler-dealer is inconsistent with the mayor's reform agenda. The lakefront, I think, doesn't appreciate that."

The corruption stories were played loud and clear almost until the eve of the special election on March 18, 1986. Mayor Washington did not believe it was a coincidence that the stream of negative press began to appear at a time when his chances looked good for gaining control of the Chicago City Council.

Washington addressed his concerns about the negative treatment the media was giving his administration and deplored the notion that votes might be stolen on election day from the Black and Hispanic people who had long been denied their proper place in city government. The mayor aired his grievances on these matters and others at a political rally held at the 139-year-old Quinn Chapel African Methodist Episcopal Church, 2401 S. Wabash, on March 10, 1986.

The mayor was greeted by more than 2,000 enthusiastic followers who cried, "We want Harold! We want Harold! We want Harold!" At last, the mayor stepped forward and said:

> You got him! For 17 more years.
>
> You know I shouldn't wipe my brow. Somebody might say I was crying. The only reason I want to be mayor for 17 years is because maybe they'll get used to my habits by then. They'll get it right.
>
> There is no simple way that I could even begin to give recognition to every group, every person, every soul, every prayer which went into this rally. I can't do it. And if I start doing it, I'll probably run short by 650-some-odd-thousand names. I want to thank Ed Gardner, not just for his lesson, his concern, exceptional words. I want to thank Ed Gardner for the contribution of a lifetime. I want to thank Dorothy Tillman for her spirit, vigor and the zealousness. I want to thank my pastor, Rev. Martin, for just being the spiritual leader he is. And I want to thank Rev. Ingram, pastor of Quinn, for just being a wonderful, wonderful citizen and a first-rate spiritual leader. And thank him for inviting us here tonight. I want to thank the business community, which is a cross section of this city. I want to thank the religious community. I want to thank the vast civic groups that have gotten together. I want to thank the young people. I want to thank the Hispanic community for educating its people.

The audience chanted: "Harold! Harold! Harold! Harold!" Washington continued:

> The communities all over this city are typified by Lawndale on the West Side. And I want to publicly thank Jim Chapman and the 44th ward because they probably won't show them on television. You can bet you life, Jim, when they select the speakers they want to show on television tonight, they are not going to select you, man. That's why I had to give a couple of minutes to prove to your wife where you were tonight. Can ol' Jim get a witness?
>
> I want to thank you all. This is time for some somber thought. This is time for some honest dialogue. It's time for some real serious reverberations and messages and overtones about this great American city. The institutions which have made this city great want to continue to make it great, but have somewhere along the line lost their way. They've been following false prophets. They've been looking for dirt when there was no dirt. And they have refused to find the dirt in front of their very eyes. The sad part about it is the crescendo reaches its zenith. . . .

Someone said, "Wait a minute!" Washington responded, "How about that?" He continued amid applause and laughter:

Present at this time are the 'Magnificent Seven.' The 'Magnificent Seven' are about to have their day in court on March 18th and tip the balance in the City Council. All at once we get this crescendo. I don't know where I can start tonight to really give you a picture, but let me start with the 'Magnificent Seven.'

There's chances that there is clearly an attempt to divide and conquer for the immediate purpose of defeating those seven 'magnificent' people who want to bring sanity to the City Council. Just to name them quickly: In the 15th Ward, Marlene Carter; in the 46th Ward you have Monica Faith Stewart; in the 22nd Ward you have Jesus Garcia; in the 25th Ward you have Juan Velazquez; in the 26th Ward you have Luie Gutierrez; in the 31st Ward you have Magdalia Collazo; and in the 37th Ward you have Percy Giles.

I gave you those names tonight and I'm certain that the other political figures here tonight can understand why we mentioned those names. Because that is the focal point of this attack and this crescendo that has hit us over the last few days. It's not by accident. It's by design. It's patterned. It's programmed. It's designed to destroy the base. And the base is here in the Black community, the Hispanic community, the white community. It's designed to show confusion, disruption and doubt simply because the day of reckoning is coming and they know that the "29" can no longer prevail.

It's just that simple. Sure, it's just that simple. In all those wards, those candidates mentioned must be elected. In all those wards, every voter in those wards will get a letter from us this week—every ward—with sample ballots laying out their names and others. And all those wards. Please, God forbid, you wouldn't vote on March 18th. Because a lot of money, a lot of toil and sweat has gone into providing that day. So that for the first time in the history of this city and for the first time in the history of this country, in any city, every substantial ethnic and nationality group will have a chance to vote commensurate with its strength and get representation in the City Council. And that's what this whole smear is all about.

The Janie Byrnes of the world and the Eddie Vrdolyaks of the world and Eddie Burkes of the world, etc., etc., etc., have systematically with malice and forethought denied Hispanic people in this city a right to sit in the City Council. And they have deprived many Blacks the same rights. And the day of reckoning is coming. And they want to do what nobody can do—try to hold back the clock—and they can't do that.

So if no other lesson goes out of here tonight, in these wards, 15, 18, 22, 25, 26, 31 and 37, make certain that you march to the polls and give us the kind of majority that we need. And give this city the kind of representation, rainbow, if you will, for the first time in Chicago. Rev. Ingram, no better pledge could be made in this here church than that this old edifice tonight brings freedom. It brings honesty. It brings the new City Council and gives hope.

How did we get to this place?

(Audience laughs)

There was a movement. I'm not the movement. I'm just a point, or a person in the movement. There was a movement which built up over a period of years. Became extremely discouraged with the kind of government that was given. Began to articulate and pocket the strength here and there and everywhere. A desire for change. And that movement would reach a crescendo, catapulting me into office with a mandate to reform this city. I was told in no uncertain terms that the matter must be resolved.

Institutional corruption. You asked me to get rid of it as best I can. You asked me to stay on that case. You asked me to call you if I needed you. You told me you would be with me. You said that you would see that the various institutions in this city would galvanize their support for us. You said that you would talk to the media. You said you would talk to the business people. You said you already had talked to the religious people. You said you would get the young people on the street corner of society to join you. You said you'd do all those things because you believed that this had to be done. We have not succeeded. We got a long way to go. The story has not yet been told. There has been a systematic attempt to keep the story from being told no matter what we do.

What is institutional corruption? Institutional corruption is simply, for example, the ability of a small group of people to year after year after year get the hundreds and hundreds of millions of dollars in contracts for a very few people in this city. A very few contractors. A very few professionals. That's what it's all about.

Corruption is the ability year after year after year to hire certain groups of people to the exclusion of others,be they women, be they Black, be they Hispanic. That's institutional corruption. Institution corruption is the conflict of interest which exists even today in the City Council, which we inherited, which permitted one alderman in the City Council to get almost every workman's compensation case involving policemen in the city day after day after day after day after day.

The people shouted: "Tell it! Tell it!" Washington went on:

And you'll never read a word about it in the press. Institutional corruption permits a major chairman of a City Council committee to sit in that committee and vote against the ordinance of the city and then go out and sue the city for not having an ordinance. That's what it is. Institutional corruption permits a powerful alderman to siphon off hundreds and hundreds and thousands of dollars to a member of his family practicing law who just got out of law school two days ago. Institutional corruption permits a powerful alderman to just take an alley belonging to the city and build his damn house on it. Institutional corruption permits this same alderman to look out over into O'Hare Field and say 'I see something I want' and the next day he's got a popcorn concession. Institutional corruption permits aldermen in the City Council to hire members of their family. Nepotism gone wild. And the press just says naughty, naughty, naughty, naughty. That's institutional corruption.

The audience shouted: "Put that on TV." Washington nodded his head in agreement and said:

> Put that on TV.
>
> Institutional corruption is a past mayor, without consent of counsel or any other pillar of law, loaning $20 million to a contractor with no means of paying it back. And nothing is said by anybody, including the press, for three years. And then the contractor winds up dead!
>
> Institutional corruption permits a past mayor to take millions upon millions of your dollars and give them to some fly-by-night hustler from Milwaukee, Wisconsin, who zooms through here, sort of like Chicago Fest, leaves here, files bankruptcy, owes everybody, including the city of Chicago, and you'll never see a damn thing about it in the papers.
>
> What manner of a city is it? What manner of a city is it? I come into office. One of the first things I do is sign an executive order. Freedom of Information. You all come, it's here. Year after year, the files are there. The archives are dusty. Look at them. If you want to see what Daley did, look. If you want to see what Bilandic did, look. If you want to see what Byrne did, look. Did they look?

Someone in the audience shouted: "Don't stop now, Harold!" Washington didn't:

> But you know what they can do? They can put five reporters out in front of City Hall to see what time I come to work everyday—and then lie about it!
>
> You know we're going to succeed. We're going to get rid of that institutional corruption. It's debilitating. It's depressing. It's insulting. It doesn't seem fit—a modern city of three million fine, sophisticated people to have that kind of thing there crawling around and disturbing us. We're going to get rid of it. And the more I get rid of it and the closer I come to getting rid of it, and the more I succeed the louder our predictions get and the more they keep sending someone down to see what time I come to work. You would have thought I passed the Freedom of Information Act just to look at me.
>
> What's wrong with this city? I am not about to say it's racism. I'm not going to say that.
>
> (Audience laughs)
>
> White folks would say I said it's because I'm a Baptist.
>
> (Audience laughs)
>
> Oh, I think the reason is that institutional corruption is so deeply ingrained into the bowels and the sinews and the muscle and the marrow of this city, it's going to take me at least 17 years to get it out of their system.

The audience screamed: "Go get it, Harold!" as Washington exploded:

> Individual corruption must go. We don't tolerate it. When we find criminality, we get rid of it. When we find conflicts of interest, we get

rid of it. When we find stupidity and lack of good judgment, we get rid of it. Everyday, suspensions, firings. Thirty-eight thousand employees, some of them got to be bad. Some of them got to be wrong. Some got to be stupid. And you have to deal with that. But you deal with it clinically, like a surgeon. You take out your knife and cut the cancer. You don't destroy your agenda. You don't day after day after day, etc., for 60 days talk about one simple situation. No!

Talk to me about Watergate? Watergate is the abuse of power. It's the abuse of process by government. It's the abuse of process by those who are protected by the color of government. And the only Watergate I see here is the insistence upon destroying through name calling, guilt by association, phoney logic, convoluted reasoning.

The question is why do they continue to do this to this city? Why? We have got to bring sanity here. Not anger, not insanity. We've got to hold all institutions accountable for what they do, including government. But we can't afford to harass any of them.

My day of reckoning will come when I face my Lord. I know I've lived the kind of life the Lord's going to say, 'Thou loyal servant, you've done the best you could.' But let me ask you this, What is he going to say to those who have used their power to abuse process, to destroy character through innuendos, and to out and out downright lie?

What are they going to say? You know what they're going to say: 'Give me a pass, O Lord.' I'll tell you this. Their forgiveness will have to come from the Lord. It will not come from me.

(Audience laughs)

Three years of character assassination. Three years of lying. Three years of spewed hatred, telling our ink, stink, pink, dink. Then they wonder about government. We're trying to collect money owed to this city. Millions and millions of dollars that previous administration just passed up. We said no. The money is owed and growing. We've got to pay our debts. We've got to pay our people who work here. We've got to buy our goods. We got to take care of our fire department. We need our money.

And so we put together as best we can under adverse circumstances—adverse circumstances being a City Council that keeps throwing sand into the gear. We tried to put together a collection process, and no one said it was absolutely perfect. No one said that. Did not suspect that there would be anything crooked about it. We put it together in all good faith. And what happened? One county officer jumped on a Black bank and assumed that there is something wrong because the Black bank was counting money. And the bank was working for almost nothing trying to do a public service. The state's attorney files a lawsuit, one of the craziest things I've seen. Who would assume he would be trying to stop the city from collecting its money? There were ways to handle it. He didn't do it right.

A TV commentator gets on the air and tells people don't pay your parking tickets. And you begin to wonder what's this all about. Is this a city we're running? Don't these various institutions which make up this city understand that the city cannot run without their cooperation? Don't they have the courage and the sense of responsibility not to say things like that? Have you no sense of responsibility at all? Or at least the state should have something to say like, 'Don't do that. Somebody may boycott you.'

The audience moaned in agreement: "We're going to do it, too." Washington said, "The current rumor going around town is that I'd like to resign." The audience bellowed: "Straighten them out, Harold." Washington continued:

> They say it's getting too hot in the kitchen. I'm going to tell you. It can't get so hot to make me leave it. I'm going to be there for 14, 17 more years. This is a good rally. We've brought together parties from all over the city who are concerned about their city and how it's made and run. Who want to make certain that government has a chance to function. Don't want to see it strike and truncated and cut back, interfered with, impediments thrown in its way.
>
> It's not a question of color. It's a question of decency, honesty and fairness to make this thing work. Everybody knows who the villains are in this play. There's no big deal about that. Everybody knows it. And we have to isolate those people like they have leprosy.
>
> We have a right to call for the various institutions, be they religious institutions that have done such a marvelous job to keep sanity in the city, or the business institution, in a broader sense. We want them to come in because we need their expertise, their dedication, their pooled capital and their ability to come up with answers to studies that the city cannot afford. We want the various community organizations to be mindful of the fact that we're trying to give them a better city. Not just by passing bond issues of $180 million that will take care of their sewers and their roads. But by making certain that we develop small businesses within their neighborhoods so that they can grow.
>
> And we also say to the media, you have a responsibility which is perhaps more transcendent than anyone else's, including the mayor's. You have the responsibility to search for thc truth and to tell the truth. We want you to live up to that responsibility because you are essential to the future of this city. We here in this audience know the power of the media. Many of the problems that we've suffered over the years have been swayed because the media would not see the light and bring it to the light. When you bring evil to the surface, obviously, clearly it will dry up like a raisin in the sun and fly away or melt away or whatever it does when it gets caught. That's your responsibility.
>
> And like other institutions, you've thrived on this great market here in Chicago. You've sold a lot of soap or whatever you sell in your paper and on your TV. You have a responsibility to tell the truth so that people can make serious decisions instead of having to come to rallies to get information about your city because it's not in print or on TV or radio. I want to wipe this sweat from my face but I'm afraid you'll say I'm crying.
>
> (Audience laughs)

Let's leave here with hope. Let's leave here with a new determination not anger. Zeal directed toward solutions in this city. This city is just crying, begging to be healed. It wants sanity to reign supreme. It doesn't want divisiveness. It wants people to come together. As I go through this entire city—north, south, east and west—and talk to people all over the city—Hispanics, Polish, Irish, Jewish, Ukrainian, Black, you name them, they all want this city healed. They want their mayor to be a good mayor. They want to help me be a good mayor. They want to give what they have to make this a better city. They want it all to come together. I can see it in their eyes. I can hear it in the voices of the women and the men as they come up to shake my hand. I can see the glee in the eyes of the young boys and girls—Blacks, whites, otherwise—as they walk up and say, 'Hello, Mr. Mayor. How are you doing?'

So don't let anybody give you the impression that this city is divided. It's not divided. People are sophisticated. They can see through the hate and the anger and the glumness. But they do want answers about their government. And they're entitled to answers about their government. And we, as a cadre here, must spread throughout this city and give them the information until such time as we can rely upon the fourth estate to do a more creditable job. I have great hope for that fourth estate because I am a person imbued, deeply imbued with a desire to have a better city.

We have an election coming up. Based upon what I've been hearing and discussing with my director of politics, Alderman Tim Evans, there's a lot of hanky-panky going on in those seven wards. A lot of it. People have been knocked off the rolls although they lived in the building. The canvassers have knocked many voters off in some of those seven wards who should not have been knocked off. The judges in many of those wards and precincts are stacked. Money is being thrown around like water in some of those places. Intimidation seems to be reigning supreme.

In the 22nd Ward, Jesus Garcia's workers are under siege. We're not going to sit idly by. The same federal law and the same federal judge who ruled that there should be an election, and the same federal congress who brought that law about are still there. We're not going to take it sitting down. We're going to get these election laws enforced no matter what the cost. We're are going through with this. We're going to call the U.S. attorney general and tell him to send federal marshals and observers to this city. We want federal marshals in here and observers observing those seven wards, and walk up and down those streets. And look into those precincts and check those computers. And see if there are any gangbangers out there. See who's loitering and see who's intimidating judges. And make certain that the police are doing their job—they probably will.

Let's look at the whole picture. We're asking them to come in here and make certain that Chicago doesn't turn into a Philippines. We'll have an honest election. If they won't honor our request, Alderman Evans, if they won't send federal observers in here, then I'll say do this—send Sen. Lugar here. He went over to the Philippines to make certain there were honest elections.

(Audience applauds)

Support me in this. Otherwise we will not have honest elections. You know it and I know it. Ask any independent who's fought in the vineyard. How many elections have been stolen? How many car windows have been broken? How many guns have been pulled? How many dollars have been spent? And let me tell you this. If they offer you money, I'm not going to tell you take it. But if you take it, go in and punish them and vote the other way.

The audience chanted: "Go on Harold. Go on," but he responded:

I'm going to end here. And the reason I want to end is because we've got about 2,000 TV monitors here tonight. Go home and see how much of this you see on the 10 o'clock news or read in tomorrow morning's paper!

(Audience laughs)

As the mayor left the dais, the audience rose like a tidal wave and gave him a thunderous round of applause, shouting, "Go, Harold, go! Go, Harold, go!"

Mayor Harold Washington marches with Committeeman Jesus Garcia in the annual Mexican Independence Day parade on the Near Southwest Side of Chicago, 1985.

CHAPTER

23

Scrapping the "29"

Mayor Harold Washington was beating the drums loudly for his Hispanic allies in the special aldermanic campaign of 1986. A Hispanic winner in at least two wards would be a linchpin for gaining control of the City Council. The buoyant Chicago mayor crisscrossed wards on the Near West Side like a whirlwind, encouraging campaign workers to get out the Hispanic vote. Washington bellowed to the precinct workers and pollwatchers at every stop, "Don't blow it. You know you are going to win, but act like you are 100 points behind. Your fate is in your hands."

The mayor feverishly pressed the flesh for Jesus Garcia in the 22nd Ward, Juan A. Velazquez in the 25th Ward, Luis V. Gutierrez in the 26th Ward and Migdalia Collazo in the 31st. The opposition, led by Alderman Edward "Fast Eddie" Vrdolyak (10th), used their big war chest to campaign equally as hard for Miguel A. Santiago in the 31st, Manuel A. Torres in the 26th, Juan M. Soliz in the 25th and Guadelupe Martinez in the 22nd.

Garcia, the committeeman who also served as Washington's deputy water commissioner, was considered the favorite to win against Martinez in the 22nd Ward. The 26th Ward was counted a tossup between Gutierrez and Torres.

Vrdolyak, former Mayor Jane Byrne and State's Attorney Richard M. Daley unconditionally supported Torres, their last Hispanic hope for retaining control of the City Council. On March 17, Byrne and Washington campaigned almost head-to-head for their respective aldermanic candidates in the 26th Ward, despite the tension created two days earlier when a reputed gang member allegedly fired a gun at Manuel Torres. Jane "The Fearless" Byrne, undaunted, set out to prove it by leading a band of 20 of Torres' supporters in a march past Gutierrez's Division Street headquarters on election eve.

Because of the potential for violence and the allegations of illegal tactics, Antoine R. Valukas, U.S. Attorney in Chicago, said, "We are putting more

U.S. attorneys and U.S. marshals on the streets this election day than we have for any other election in the city's history."

Despite the pre-election day nurturing, the Hispanic wards had an unexpectedly light turnout, alarming Washington's allies. A low voter turnout historically increased the chances of the regular Democratic organization candidate, who benefitted from the work of the more experienced precinct workers in getting out the vote.

To make bad matters worse, vote tallies were delayed. Cook County Circuit Judge Joseph Schneider ordered 43 percent of the polling places, about half of them in the seven special election wards, to stay open an additional two hours because they had failed to open on time. The judge's order set off a mad scramble for last-minute votes in the 26th Ward. Both Gutierrez and Torres sent their workers back to the precincts in what could best be described as a "turnout war."

Judge Schneider, at approximately 9:30 on election night, ordered hundreds of ballots from late voters impounded in three of the wards, one of which was the 26th, further delaying the vote count. The impounding order was the result of Vrdolyak's lawyers challenging all votes cast after the official poll closing time of 7 p.m.

Washington stormed that the Democratic machine was hellbent on winning at any cost. He charged that Vrdolyak's request to extend voting hours and his subsequent challenge of the votes in the 26th Ward precincts were made "just so someone could steal the election."

Alderman Vrdolyak ignored the mayor's allegations and said, "My position is that at 7 p.m., Torres had won the election, we think, by 300 votes. There should have not been any precincts open after 7 p.m. I don't know what the judge was doing. I don't think he knows what he was doing."

Although no official vote count was available, the titans of the council struggle—Mayor Washington and Alderman Vrdolyak—claimed victory for their respective 26th Ward candidates and each charged the other with vote fraud.

By March 19, 1986, the morning after the special election, the Washington forces had gained two seats, increasing their number in the City Council to 23. The winners on the Washington team were Jesus Garcia in the 22nd and Percy Giles in the 37th. Giles ran far enough ahead of his eight challengers to avoid a runoff election. In the 15th Ward, on the Southwest Side of Chicago, Marlene C. Carter, another candidate supported by Mayor Washington, barely edged out incumbent Frank J. Brady in a field of eight. Since neither candidate won a majority of the votes cast, a runoff between Carter and Brady was scheduled for April 29, 1986.

On March 21, Luis Gutierrez, the mayor's candidate, unofficially declared himself the winner of the special Democratic primary by 23 votes: "It is now clear that I have won and that I am the new alderman of the 26th Ward. And that this has happened despite massive vote fraud by my opponent."

Twenty-four hours later, after a search of election equipment revealed additional votes in two of the ward's precincts, Gutierrez's lead was reduced by three votes. A special search by the Chicago Board of Election Commissioners was ordered by Cook County Circuit Judge Robert J. Dempsey after ballots from another 26th Ward precinct turned up in the City Hall vault.

Torres, Gutierrez's opponent, received all three of the votes cast on ballots found in a transfer case in the 31st precinct. The official vote was finally set at 5,245 for Gutierrez and 5,225 for Torres.

On March 24, attorney Joseph Tighe, representing Torres, told Judge Eugene Wachewski that keeping the polls open late "inretrievably and fundamentally flawed and tainted the election. The election needs to be run over."

Following these charges, the Chicago Board of Elections found 10 more write-in votes, which further narrowed the margin of Gutierrez's victory. They ordered a special runoff election in the 26th Ward to be held on April 29th.

On Sunday afternoon, April 27, Luis Gutierrez was joined by Mayor Washington, a marching band and campaign workers in a last-ditch effort to get out the vote in the 26th Ward. They campaigned door to door past dusk. At a political party in the 2700 block on West Haddon St., the mayor thundered: "They stole the last one. We're going to get so damn many votes this time they won't be able to steal it from us."

He implored all residents of the 26th Ward to come out and vote on Tuesday, April 29:

> Latinos are coming into political fruition, and this is a steppingstone.
>
> Do not make the mistake that Blacks made in the 1930s. Don't be wedded to an operation which is based on a record that is opposed to you. Your future is in independent politics. Be sure your enemies don't control you.
>
> We made that mistake (referring to Blacks). We were a forgiving people. But while some people say we will not do it again, we went into political servitude for 40 years. I urge you not to fall into that bag.

Washington blasted State's Attorney Daley for endorsing Torres, saying, "He sullied and compromised his office by coming out and supporting Torres, knowing well he is the chief law enforcement officer in the city. There is no way he can be objective by doing this."

The mayor also chided the weekend presence in the 26th Ward of former mayor Byrne, City Council majority leader Vrdolyak, Alderman Roman C. Pucinski (44th) and Richard M. Daley.

The mayor was infuriated with Daley for his timing in announcing the indictment of seven men, most of them Latino, on vote fraud charges. He also objected to the presence of U.S. Immigration and Naturalization Service District Director A.B. Moyer at the press conference when Daley announced the indictment.

"The indictment was designed to intimidate voters. Otherwise, they make no sense at all," Washington huffed. "I think Daley was trying to send a mes-

Mayor Harold Washington leaps to victory over the ''Vrdolyak 29'' with the aid of the Hispanic vote. In the forefront, far right, is Luis Gutierrez, who won his race for alderman in the 26th Ward.

sage to the Gutierrez forces. We should come out and make it clear that the old way of playing games is over."

Although the election wasn't to be held until April 29, Ben Reyes, spokesman for Gutierrez, confirmed on the 26th that police were investigating the charges that opposition forces allegedly delivered a ballot box to an incorrect voting place in the 18th precinct of the 26th Ward, and that it had been opened.

Reyes said absentee ballots were sent to addresses where no houses or shanties had stood for years and added:

> We have to raise the integrity of the Board of Elections in all of this.
>
> The opposition is allegedly trying to confuse the voters by showing them how to use the old voting machines (with levers), then telling the Latinos they have already voted for the Tuesday election.
>
> It's going to be a dirty election, but we are ready for them.

Meanwhile, Board of Election Chairman Michael Lavelle had promised to have more than 500 officials monitoring the races in the 15th and 26th Wards. In the same breath, Lavelle admitted that 10 polling places had been moved, affecting up to 4,000 voters.

Tom Johnson, attorney for Luis Gutierrez, said, "Every absentee ballot will be challenged for authenticity." Johnson agreed that the machine-backed aldermanic candidate, Manuel Torres, may have a 750-vote edge due to a flurry of absentee ballot applications.

"There were 14 voters who come from households who have at least two people filing for absentee ballots, 61 from households having three or more persons applying for these ballots, and five members of one family also voting by this method."

Lawrence Kennon, attorney for 15th Ward aldermanic candidate Marlene Carter, said a similar pattern existed in that ward. "They, too, will be challenged on election today," Kennon said.

Dave Ocho, the 26th Ward election coordinator, confirmed reports that Alderman Vrdolyak had removed his workers from the Black precincts of the 26th Ward, abandoning their scheme of detouring Blacks into the Torres fold.

The political winds shifted ever so gently on election day April 29, 1986. The voters in Chicago's 15th and 26th Wards gave Mayor Harold Washington a belated 64th birthday present and a third mayoral anniversary gift. He captured a razor-thin control of the Chicago City Council with victories by his endorsed candidates in the two wards.

The new strength of Blacks and Hispanics flashed in bold relief onto the city's political arena. Marlene Carter defeated incumbent Alderman Brady by of 10,463 votes, or 65 percent of the total. Gutierrez defeated Cook County Board Commissioner Manuel Torres by a vote of 7,429, or 52 percent, to 6,549, or 47 percent. The shift of power recharged the atmosphere in which the city government conducted its business during the final year of Mayor Harold Washington's first term.

Speaking in the lobby of his apartment building after the polls had closed on election night, the mayor said the turning point in his administration was the ward remap ordered the year before by the U.S. District Court judge.

Now, having gained control of the council, Washington said his first priorities would be the confirmation of his appointments to commissions and other panels, adoption of an ethics code and passage of a city budget bearing his imprimatur.

"Their signals are clear," the mayor declared. "There has been a shift in the attitudes of a majority of the people of Chicago, and they (the Vrdolyak bloc members) have to live with them. The city's Democratic machine is dead."

Basil Talbot Jr., political editor for the *Chicago Sun-Times,* analyzed Mayor Washington's victories in the aldermanic races in his column of May 1, 1986, which was headlined: "The Mayor Spins Past Fast Eddie:"

> Alderman Edward Vrdolyak lost his old speed in Tuesday's runoff election while Mayor Washington reached his new stride. The mayor outran, outperformed, outpoliticked his roguish foe from the rusting 10th Ward. The mayor's perfect score in two aldermanic races put him in super shape for the 1987 mayoral marathon.
>
> The election of Luis Gutierrez to the 26th Ward and Marlene Carter to the 15th had lessons for all. Vrdolyak learned he can't sneak around in a limo with "EV" plates. When the car appeared at Torres' office, it was hard for Torres aide Keith Lesnick to keep a straight face while insisting Vrdolyak was neutral. . . .
>
> Vrdolyak also learned about Hispanic television. He discovered some down sides to allowing a challenger in a Puerto Rican election to participate in a debate on a Hispanic station and say he can't speak good Spanish.
>
> Vrdolyak can easily qualify for the dunce of the year award, except there are better candidates for the title.
>
> Ahead of him are committeemen, aldermen and public officials who followed Fast Eddie's lead despite his long string of electoral flops. Among the Vrdolyak lemmings were mayoral hopeful Jane Byrne, State's Attorney Richard M. Daley and Rep. Dan Rostenkowski, chairman of the House Ways and Means Committee. All of them endorsed Torres, while non-endorser Vrdolyak spoke for them on TV.
>
> Washington's big lesson was learning to play politics Chicago style. There were enough deputies in the ward to convene a cabinet meeting. They included wizards like Ben Reyes, the mastermind of Gutierrez's victory, and arrogant partisans like Paul Waterhouse, the mayor's Freedom of Information officer. In feathered hat and white running shoes, Alderman Dorothy Tillman (3rd) did more for Gutierrez than anyone did for Torres.

> The mayor also demonstrated his spell over Blacks and Hispanics. Breaking with the past, Washington turned out a larger vote in the run-off than in the March 18th election. Alderman Dick Mell (33rd), one of Vrdolyak's followers, had predicted the Black vote wouldn't pan out.
>
> The other plus for Washington was the voters' rejection of unfairness. State Rep. Al Ronan, another Mell protege, said voters rightly believe Gutierrez was forced into a runoff unfairly. . . .

With the council in a new 25-25 split, Washington was just itching to break the tie votes. He professed confidence that the old council can't get in the way. Talking with reporters over scrambled eggs and grits in the 8th Street Deli, 800 S. Michigan, Washington said that the triumph of his allies, Gutierrez and Carter, boded well for his re-election efforts in '87 and reinforced his belief that the trouble with the Democratic party is its chairman, Alderman Edward R. Vrdolyak.

"I don't think the victories in the 15th and 26th Wards will have any effect on the mayor's re-election chances," Vrdolyak retorted. "In fact, it does give more support where he can get some of the things passed that he couldn't get passed before, like tax increases. It may, in fact, damage him."

Contrary to any sour grapes spewed by "Fast Eddie," the mayor's bloc opened the first council meeting after the election sporting "25 + 1" buttons. Some of the mayor's supporters sitting in the gallery wore buttons that said: "Free our hostages: 67 + 1." The mayor himself was the 68th hostage.

The first meeting of the City Council after Harold Washington wrested a working majority for the "29" began at approximately 11:30 a.m. on May 9, 1986. The spectators gave the jovial mayor a standing ovation as he entered the council chambers for the City Council meeting with a broad, infectious smile on his face. The council proceedings were tranquil until an elderly man yelled from the gallery, "The people of Poland are starving. They need milk." As he was being escorted out of the chamber, he paused to yell: "Have a good day." That incident brought applause from the members of the City Council as well as from the spectators in the gallery.

After the slight disruption, the council appeared to be ready to move at full speed when the mayor's bloc discovered that their 25th vote, Alderman Burton F. Natarus, had not arrived. Mayor Washington dispatched Alderman Martin J. Oberman (43rd) to find Natarus. Burke, sensing an opportunity, moved to adjourn the meeting. Motions for a recess and for adjournment were entertained and debated until the missing alderman was found and brought into the chamber.

The arrival of Natarus elicited laughter and scattered applause from the audience and prompted Alderman Anna B. Langford, one of the mayor's supporters, to jump up and down, gleefully squealing, "Roll call, roll call."

"Do you want to proceed with the motion now?" Washington asked Burke with a grin almost as wide as the podium he was standing behind.

The first hostage nomination to come before the council that afternoon was Jacqueline Vaughn, president of the Chicago Teacher's Union, who had been appointed by the mayor to the board of the Chicago Transit Authority.

Before her nomination could be cleared, there were five roll call votes on procedural questions. The sixth roll call gave Washington his first 25-25 split, enabling him to break the tie. "The motion fails," he announced, not resisting a throaty chuckle. When Burke objected, Washington said, "We are not going to go around and around in a circle." The 29 aldermen who approved Vaughn's nomination included four from Vrdolyak's bloc: Fred B. Roti (1st), Juan M. Soliz (25th), Richard Mell (33rd) and Miguel A. Santiago (31st.)

Fred Roti was overheard grumbling to reporters standing nearby, "I will make up my mind anyway I want."

The other approved appointees were including their original dates for appointment were as follows: BUILDING BOARD OF APPEALS: Kenneth Groggs. CITY COLLEGE BOARD OF TRUSTEES: Ronald Gryzwinski. CULTURAL AFFAIRS ADVISORY BOARD: Amina Dickerson, Oscar Martinez. CHICAGO HOUSING AUTHORITY: Artensia Randolph. LIBRARY BOARD: James Fuerst. BOARD OF LOCAL IMPROVEMENTS: Timuel Black, Guadelupe Lozano, William Barr, Juanita Passmore and George Mgala. CHICAGO PARK DISTRICT: Margaret Burroughs. PERSONNEL BOARD: Warren Bacon and Addie Wyatt. CHICAGO PLAN COMMISSION: Edwin Myerson and Leon Finney Jr. CHICAGO REGIONAL PORT AUTHORITY: Johnny Smith. CTA BOARD: James I. Charlton and Walter Clark. RTA BOARD: Pastora San Juan Cafferty and Clark Burrus. URBAN RENEWAL BOARD: Joyce Wade. ZONING BOARD OF APPEALS: Lawrence Kennon and Michael Howell.

The City Council proceedings for approving the appointees had become too tranquil for Alderman Edward Burke. He jumped to his feet and said he would bring a lawsuit to challenge the procedures that were being followed and the circumstances under which Mayor Washington could break ties. At this point, Burke and Alderman Timothy C. Evans, the mayor's floor leader, began to spray each other with legal citations concerning Washington's authority to break ties and with insults.

"I suppose that Alderman Evans can tell us that horse manure tastes like chocolate ice cream, but that doesn't make it so," Burke speculated.

Evans quickly responded, "He's the one who knows how it tastes. I don't know anything about that."

"The score is one to one. Let us recess on that," Washington said, to the amusement of the folks who packed the chamber.

When the council meeting ended just a few minutes before 4 p.m., 25 of the mayor's nominees had been approved. Decisions on the other nominations were postponed until the next council meeting.

A beaming Mayor Washington said, "It tells me that reform politics are alive and well on the lakefront, and if that's true, I am in seventh heaven."

Anti-administration leaders Burke and Vrdolyak had been exposed as "obstructionists," he declared.

"It was a crass display in the arrogance of power and the inability to grow and mature. They voted negative on every single motion, on every single person, regardless of race, color or creed."

Burke, who would not relent to the reality that the mayor controlled the tying council vote, held a dialogue with the mayor in parliamentary shorthand.

Burke: "Same point of order."

Washington: "Same ruling."

Burke: "Same appeal."

Washington: "Same results."

This exchange between the two men was followed by the same laughter and same applause.

Appointments of the balance of the "hostages" was stalled on May 30, 1986, when Aldermen Marian Humes (8th) and Perry H. Hutchinson (9th) took a walk out of the council chambers without giving notice to Tim Evans, the mayor's floor leader. It was believed by many of the mayor's followers that their actions were with malice aforethought. The mayor's solid block of 25 had cracked within 23 days.

The absences of Humes and Hutchinson prevented the mayor from calling for the vote on the appointment of Walter Netsch, Rebecca Sive-Tomashefsky and Silvia Herrera to the board of the Chicago Park District. The approval of two of the three would have given the mayor a majority board, and speed his plans to oust the park district chief Edmund Kelly, a Vrdolyak/Burke ally.

During the Operation PUSH regular radio broadcast at 10 a.m. on Saturday, May 31, the Rev. Willie Barrow bellowed in her own unique fashion on the airways: "Where were they when the mayor needed them most? We want to know which side she (Humes) is on."

The Rev. Hycel B. Taylor, president of Operation PUSH, added, "Black people must learn never to walk out. Whatever their reasons, they cannot abandon their own, because it took a lot of hard work for the mayor to get control of that council."

On June 2, 1986, during a taping of WVON's (1450 AM) "Tell it to Ty" talk show, hosted by Ty Wansley, Alderman Humes and Cook County Commissioner John Stroger had a heated exchange.

Stroger accused Humes of "doublecrossing the 8th Ward and the mayor."

Humes called Stroger an "Uncle Tom Stepin Fetchit."

Stroger replied, "If that's so, I am a Stepin Fetchit because I selected her (Humes) over a lot of other good people to be the alderman."

Humes said she is being "castigated by a great big lie" and will "not back down."

On June 3, Keith Caldwell, an 8th Ward resident and Stroger supporter who subsequently defeated Humes in the April 1987 election, led a protest march outside of Humes' headquarters at 1227 E. 87th St. Humes invited the 30 marchers to come inside, sit down and discuss the problem. Soon after the demonstrators were seated, Humes and Caldwell engaged in a verbal wrestle match over who would control the impromptu session.

As Humes spoke, Caldwell tried to ask where she had been during the vote Friday. "What could be more important than a vote in the City Council?" The alderman yelled, "Sergeant-at-arms, remove this man."

No sergeant-at-arms was present and Caldwell continued to press the question. Humes finally replied, "Nothing is more important than a vote in the City Council—assuming that there was to be a vote in the City Council. I have supported every appointee. We haven't lost anything irretrievable as far as appointments are concerned."

The Reverend Jesse Louis Jackson also criticized Marian Humes at the Operation PUSH meeting on June 7, 1986, for blocking approval of the key mayoral park district nominees. He said, "We have been down for three years. All these rascals come by Operation PUSH looking for a big vote and don't show up at key council meetings."

"Don't come trying to put so much sugar around this mess, trying to make it taste sweet. Mess is nasty. I asked you to vote for me and you don't show up. Negro, you better explain yourself."

Alderman Perry Hutchinson explained why he walked out of the council meeting. "I had some chest pains Friday," Hutchinson said in a telephone call from the cardiac surveillance unit at Michael Reese Hospital and Medical Center. "I talked to the 20th Ward alderman, Cliff Kelly, who is my floor leader, and I left. I was not mad at anybody about anything."

Hutchinson said he checked into the Michael Reese Hospital on Saturday afternoon after receiving numerous threatening telephone calls as a result of the Operation PUSH radio broadcast. He said his ward office was also vandalized.

"This has just really upset me," he said. "My blood pressure just went up, getting all of these phone calls. I am supporting Harold Washington on all of his appointments. I am really sorry this happened."

The Vrdolyak-Burke bloc was scrapped June 6, 1986. In his long-awaited showdown with anti-administration forces, Mayor Washington invoked his controversial tie-breaking vote to slash the number of committees from 37 to 28, reward his allies with key chairmanships and also stack all of the important committees with his allies.

Vrdolyak lost his chairmanship when his committee was abolished. Burke, while allowed to stay on as the finance committee chairman, was stripped of his powers over the city budget. Alderman Hutchinson was whisked by ambulance to the City Council meeting to cast the tie-breaking vote that enabled Mayor Washington to capture the majority control of all City Council committees.

Washington, hearty and confident, replaced the rules written by his council enemies with new rules declaring that a mere majority would be required to change committee leadership and seize unbridled power over legislation.

A bitter and angry Vrdolyak stormed at Washington, "You're going to do what you want to do, whether the rules are there or the laws are there. You do the same things with bids. And you do the same things with taxes. It's madness. This is a sham of fairness and reform. The phony reformers are coming out of the closet."

"The majority shall prevail. No, it's a power grab. It's an adjustment of power," responded the mayor in a mellow tone.

When asked if he liked the 3 1/2 years of council wars, the mayor replied:

> No! I didn't like that. The battle was so futile. It was so useless and so unnecessary. That was a frustrating thing. I've been in public service all my life. And I have never seen people who were willing to take their city or their country or their government to the brink of disaster just because they could. They have amazed me. And it irritated me, obviously. People just don't do that.
>
> I've dealt with some hard-bargaining partisans in my life, but they all stop short of being destructive because they know if you start tearing up things, it's no good for anybody. But we've got some disspirited and distempered people, or did have, in the City Council, who just didn't care. Who really just didn't care. And their animosity toward me and what I stood for was so great, they'd rather see the city go down in flames rather than just make accommodations, which we tried to make day after day after day.
>
> The thing that disturbed me so much was that they had power to which their were not entitled. Because it was the same people who miscued and misconstructed the City Council. And the Supreme Court said they were wrong and that power was taken away and rightfully so. So it just goes to show you that even in a Democratic society, unless the institutions are working, unless the machinery is fair, mean-spirited people can get power that they are not entitled to and just disrupt everything.
>
> And so we have had 3 1/2 years, roughly, of abuse from people who had power which legally they were not entitled to. And that's the thing that disturbs me.

Vernon Jarrett, *Chicago Sun-Times* columnist, television talk show host on Face to Face, and a political commentator for ABC News (Chicago).

Vernon Jarrett, R. Eugene Pincham and Thomas N. Todd use their individual talents as drum majors for justice and fairness for these times and for years to come.

The Honorable R. Eugene Pincham, Illinois Appellate Court Judge for the First District.

Attorney Thomas Nathaniel Todd, a practicing lawyer, civil rights activist, former professor of law at Northwestern University Law School and a nationally-renowned orator.

CHAPTER

24

The 1987 Democratic Primary Donnybrook

The audacity of Mayor Harold Washington, a Black man, running for re-election as a Democrat rather than an independent in the 1987 primary created a hysterical free-for-all political atmosphere. Four white males and two females, one white and one Black, believed that they could defeat him in his bid to retain his office on the fifth floor.

Although the mayor had defeated Epton head on in 1983, his foes entertained the notion that Washington was afraid to go one-on-one against a white candidate. It was said in some quarters that Epton was Jewish, and beating him did not count. Thus, Alderman Richard Mell (33rd), a member of the "29," suggested that the rules for the mayoral race in Chicago should be changed to favor a non-partisan election, thus guaranteeing that Washington would be forced into a one-on-one race against a white candidate.

Rep. Dan Rostenkowski, D-Ill., shared Mell's feelings about a non-partisan mayoral election, a ploy that many believed would make it harder, if not impossible, for Mayor Washington to be re-elected. Members of the majority bloc put on a full-court press following the special aldermanic election, convincing 150,000 voters to sign petitions to place the question of a non-partisan election on the November 1986 ballot.

Washington's people circumvented that tactic by employing a seldom-used Illinois state law that dictates that only three referendums may be placed on a ballot in any single election and that the first three referendums filed would exclude any others. The mayor's partisans filed the initial three referendums and thereby precluded the question of a non-partisan election being voted on in the fall 1986 election.

This maneuver led Washington's opponents to believe that he feared running in a one-on-one election against a white candidate. They were mislead; the mayor relished a head-on confrontation against any candidate—white, blue or polka dot. However, he fought and resented the unrelenting efforts of white folks to change the rules in the middle of the game when it appeared that a Black had an outside chance to win.

Washington's chief opponent in the mayoral donnybrook—the presumed beneficiary of a non-partisan election—was former Mayor Jane Byrne, who entered the 1987 primary wearing the colors of the regular Democratic party. Alderman Edward R. Vrdolyak, a political heavy who was determined to beat Harold at any cost, switched from the solid colors of the Democratic party to the pale yellow stripes of the Illinois Solidarity Party. "Fast Eddie" opted not to enter the battle royal in the first round, and waited until Byrne and Washington had verbally beat each other onto the mat before he climbed into the ring after the primary. Sheila Jones, a fighter from the Lyndon H. LaRouche Jr., stable, was left in the ring to slug it out with Washington and Byrne.

Also weighing in for the primary was Cook County Assessor Thomas Hynes, who wore the Irish green trunks of his newly organized Chicago First party. It was Tom's intent to fight in the primary bout against Byrne in the event Harold Washington dropped out. Harold, who had said for months that he might skip the Feb. 24, 1987, primary and run as an independent, did not blink on the primary withdrawal date in late December. Recognizing the signal that Washington was prepared to confront Jane Byrne head on, Hynes withdrew from the frey. The county assessor vowed to return and fight in the general election against the survivor of the primary.

"I gather he wasn't ready to fight, so he had to pull out and get himself together," Washington said. "The Democratic primary is no place for people with no courage. He had to get out. He didn't belong there."

Vrdolyak was jubilant about Hynes' withdrawal, relishing a tough confrontation between "Fighting Jane" Byrne and Harold Washington.

"It's what we have wanted all along: Harold Washington one-on-one in the Democratic primary." Vrdolyak yelped as he admitted his delight about Hynes pulling out of the primary with a devilish smile on his face as he licked his lips as though preparing to devour a delicious steak.

Jane Byrne said:

> I have been working very hard to be the strongest alternative to the politics of Harold Washington and I think we are there.
>
> Now the candidates can concentrate on the issues rather than how many are in it, who's in it and where they are in it and when do they get out. Now, we will have a real campaign.

Bernard Epton, who narrowly lost to Mayor Washington in 1983, was knocked off the ballot because his petitions were between 200 to 400 signatures short of qualifying for the February 24 primary. His failure meant a free ride for Donald H. Haider, a Democrat turned Republican. Haider was looking forward to a bout with Jane Byrne.

No political waves were stirred by Bernard Epton's failure to qualify. It was the opinion of most of the political pundits that neither Epton nor Donald Haider had a ghost of a chance to win in the April 7 general election.

On the other hand, Jane Byrne looked stronger after the Richard M. Daley bloc joined her campaign. The first Daleyite to climb into Byrne's corner of the ring was Rep. William O. Lipinski (D-Ill.), the voice of Chicago ethnics in the 23rd Ward and the Southwest Side in general. He was followed by Tom Lyons, committeeman of the Northwest Side's 45th Ward. Following closely on their heels in climbing aboard a fast-moving Byrne bandwagon were three members of the Irish political mafia. Richard M. Daley's brother, State Rep. John P. Daley, Democratic committeeman of the 11th Ward; State Sen. Timothy F. Degnan; and Alderman Patrick M. Huels (11th).

It is a wonder that Mayor Harold Washington was not asphyxiated by all of the white ethnics piling on top of his head. Attorney Thomas N. Todd, the 350-pound, 6-foot-7inch Black giant, thought what he saw happening to Harold was unfair. In a speech he delivered to a capacity crowd at the Bethel AME Church, "Mr. TNT" roared:

> White people did not want a Black mayor in 1983, and they do not want a Black mayor now. White leadership is still trying to stop this Black mayor. White leadership did not want Harold Washington. White politicians did not want Harold Washington. Everywhere he turned they were against him.
>
> Why did they turn against him? Was it because he was not competent? It was not because he was not competent. Was it because he was not a good mayor? It was not because he was not a good mayor. They turned against him simply because he was a Black man. And Black people are hated in America.
>
> They tried this mayor every day in the newspaper, without indictments, without charges. They tried him every day. It was not Harold Washington. It was not corruption. They were trying to break the back of the Black movement. They wanted to break our backs. This we cannot permit to happen. I'm against all illegal acts. Oh, but I stand here without fear of contradiction and say to you that if every Black man, woman and child in America started to steal today and stole 24 hours a day forever, they could never catch up with white people who have stolen in America. Oh, I want you to understand that! It was not corruption.
>
> Yes, in the light of what I read about E.F. Hutton, I should not worry about a $50 check bouncing when E.F. Hutton is writing $100 million worth of bad checks each month. It was not corruption.

I say to you today, white media, white business people, white ethnics and what have you, like it or dislike it, accept it or reject it, Harold Washington is the mayor of the city of Chicago and will be for a long time. . . .

If Harold Washington had had as many white folks around him as Ronald Reagan or Jane Byrne, they would have called him a racist. Yet the movement that put him in office came from a Black base. I'm not going to apologize for that. Why should I apologize for that? The Irish do not apologize for the Irish base. The Jews do not apologize for the Jewish base. The Italians do not apologize for the Italian base. The Polish do not apologize for the Polish base. So why should I apologize for the Black base?

Don't let them make you get so sophisticated until you really believe that Harold Washington won because of the white liberal vote on the lakeshore. That's not true. Harold Washington won in 1983 because Black people in unprecedented numbers came out to vote for him, from the Black base. It was that Black base that elected Richard J. Daley over and over again. It was the same Black base that elected Bilandic in 1977. It was the same Black base that elected Jane Byrne in 1979. If the Black base was all right for Daley, all right for Bilandic, all right for Byrne, then why in the hell isn't all right for Harold Washington?

This political movement is built on a Black base! I don't apologize for that. I'm sick and tired of all of this mess. I want some new clothes. I'm tired of the way they treat us. I want some new clothes. I don't want no old clothes no more. I want some new clothes. I'm tired of having to deal with leftover, warmed over, reconditioned and made-over white folks. I want one of my own. I would rather have a small piece of Harold Washington than all of anybody else.

When it looks like we're going to play the game, when it looks like we're going to win the game, they change the rules. And then they change the game. Oh, that's what's been happening in America. Anybody but Harold. That's what they say. Nobody but Harold. That's what we must respond. That's what this referendum is all about. They want to change the rules.

Has Harold Washington been a good mayor? He's been an outstanding mayor. Has Harold Washington been fair? He's been fairer than fair. Has Harold Washington been equal? He's been more equal than equality. You see we always are willing to try to do everything we possibly can. Oh, but white America will never accept us. But that's all right. It's our responsibility to save America. Just as we've always had to save America. Because Black people believe in democracy more than white folks. We believe in justice more than white folks. We believe in equality.

Why is the white leadership panicking? It ain't the white little folks. It ain't the little folks on the Northwest Side or the Southwest Side. It's the white leadership. The little white folks didn't send a letter to Paul Kirk, chairman of the Democratic Central Committee in Washington,

> D.C. It was Edward R. Vrdolyak. Little white people are not trying to find a Democrat to switch to the Republican party. It's the white leadership. They want a white person.
>
> Oh, it's just like in Alabama, Mississippi and Georgia. The white bosses used the divide and conquer tactics between poor white people and Black people. But I want to stand here today and say to you I'm sick and tired. I'm sick and tired of the pinstripe bigots. I'm sick and tired. I'm sick and tired of the racists who've exchanged their white sheets for blue suits. I'm sick and tired. Hear me! I'm sick and tired of the empirical white folks. Those white folks who believe by virtue of their birthright and their family that they automatically will inherit an office. I will say to you, to the Daleys and to the Stevensons, never again. Never again! Never again!
>
> Women ought to vote for Harold Washington because Harold Washington increased the percentage of female positions in the top level of his administration from 12 to 34 percent.
>
> White folks should vote for Harold Washington. They should vote for Harold Washington because he's done more for white folks than his predecessors did before him. Before him, just a handful of white folks got contracts with the city. Harold Washington has spread them around to a lot of white folks. Some of us think he has been too good to too many white folks. But that's all right. We're always fairer than fair and more equal than equality.
>
> It never occurred to Richard J. Daley to have anything but a white corporation counsel. It never occurred to Daley to have anything but a white press secretary. White everything. Yet Harold Washington has blended. The corporation counsel is Jewish. His press spokesman is a white man. The parliamentarian is a white man. So Harold Washington has blended a rainbow, believing more in democracy than white people. But we have to be careful. Because sometimes while we're out looking for rainbows, white folks are looking for Rambos.

Tom Todd's speech drew fire from mayoral candidate Edward Vrdolyak. The alderman of the 10th Ward filed a complaint on Jan. 16, 1987, with John A. McDermott, chairman of conduct of the Committee on Decent Unbiased Campaign Tactics (CONDUCT). Vrdolyak had filed a complaint against Tom Todd two months earlier. Both complaints were based on Todd's statement that: "I am sick and tired of racists who turn in their white sheets for blue suits."

Joe Novak, Vrdolyak spokesperson, said Washington should be censured for Todd's "inflammatory" statements because Todd was speaking for Washington.

The attempt to make the mayor responsible for statements made by individuals outside of his administration did not wear well with Washington's former colleagues in Congress. Rep. Gus Savage (D-Ill.) read a statement he wrote on behalf of the Congressional Black Caucus lambasting "the Reaganite racists . . . who have launched an all-out effort to defeat Mayor

Washington. Reaganism and the neoracism it nurtures have made the re-election of Harold Washington, the first Black and most liberal mayor of Chicago, an imperative national concern."

Savage further said he intended to slam Vrdolyak. "I don't believe he is a Reaganite racist. I know he is."

During a meeting with members of the Black Caucus in the District of Columbia, Washington expressed concern that the election might be stolen from him:

> I am not proud of what I am going to say, but it should be known. We have tackled the machine. And we have beaten it down. It's not dead. It's still wounded. It slipped into the forest. It can bite you, and it can hurt you. It's going to die. The trouble is its dying too damn slowly. The thing that bothers me is it has the capacity to steal.

Richard Anderson, executive director of Election Watch '87, expressed his concern about vote fraud and the record number of requests for absentee ballot applications. "We know absentee ballots have been used in the past to control votes. 125,000 absentee ballot applications have been handed out and a first-ever second printing of another 100,000 is under way."

Anderson further disclosed that his group had discovered names of a number of people who should not be on the voting rolls in Edmund Kelly's 47th Ward on the Northwest Side. He said they included an aspiring actor who moved to California in October 1984, and two women who had moved out of Illinois whose names were never stricken from voting rolls. Votes continued to be cast in their names after they had moved.

Alderman Vrdolyak did not publicly respond to Anderson's statement, but he did go public on the remarks by Congressman Savage and Mayor Washington. In an emotional speech delivered before a predominantly Jewish group on the Far North Side, Vrdolyak argued that he was being held to a double standard, noting that Washington refused to denounce Louis Farrakhan, the Nation of Islam leader, for allegedly anti-Semetic remarks.

"But if I said something, I'm a racist," said Vrdolyak.

"I want to talk about what people think about and what's on their lips, but they never say. I want to talk about prejudice, double standards, bigotry in a our society as we know it."

Vrdolyak further complained about being referred as a "Reaganite racist" by a member of the Black Caucus.

He said he was particularly upset that he was asked whether he was responsible for a campaign flyer linking Washington to separatist statements by Farrakhan and the Rev. Jesse Jackson.

Vrdolyak pleaded:

> How do you defend yourself? What do you say? Where do you go? They put the badge on you. They put the star on you. They put the arm band on you. Identify you. You are bad. You are wrong. I didn't

put it out. Everybody knows I didn't put it out. I am not that stupid, nor that venal. Nor that vile. Nor that racist to any degree.

Chicago is changing it's reputation as the city of Al Capone to the most racist city in the country.

The alderman's comments were greeted with an awkward silence from the crowd of 250 people attending the meeting at the Bernard Horwich Jewish Community Center on West Touhy Avenue.

Mayor Washington appeared later that evening before the same group and sidestepped a question about Farrakhan. Instead, he denounced Vrdolyak by inference.

"There are people who would try to drive us apart. One of them was here this evening," Washington warned after recounting his own record in support of Jews and Israel.

My Jewish friends have told me to avoid the 'divisive trap' being set by Vrdolyak.

Vrdolyak has blamed 'Black anti-Semitism' for the defeat of former sheriff Richard J. Elrod in a similar attempt to divide two groups. Elrod, who is Jewish, won 85 percent of the Black vote.

I am not about to fall in a trap of that kind of acrimonious, insidious, divisive debate designed to stimulate animosity between the Jewish community and the Black community.

I abhor it. I won't countenance it. I won't contribute to it. And my Jewish friends have told me that I was right. 'Harold, don't get bogged down in that kind anti-acrimony. It's not healthy for this city.'

The Jewish vote that was so critical to Harold's slim margin of victory over Bernard Epton in 1983 would be equally important in his 1987 re-election. However, as of Jan. 25, 1987, the mayor and Byrne were running neck and neck, according to a Gallup Poll conducted for the Sun-Times and Channel 7 between January 13 and January 18.

The poll indicated that if the primary were held on Jan. 25, 1987, Jane Byrne would receive 44 percent of the vote, Washington would get 43 percent, and 1 percent would go to Sheila Jones, the LaRouche supporter.

According to the poll, Washington would receive 87 percent of the Black votes, compared with his 99 percent Black support when he beat Bernard Epton in the previous mayoral election, and 14 percent of the white vote, compared with 18 percent in 1983. The race was tight: the poll's overall margin of error was plus or minus 4 percentage points.

By January 31, the political climate had become so tense that a lecture given by Illinois Appellate Court Justice R. Eugene Pincham at Operation PUSH on the eve of Black History Month promoted an onslaught of criticism. The section of his speech that drew the attacks follows:

Now, it's not enough for you to say, 'Well, I cast my ballot.' We have got to create an atmosphere. We've got to create an aroma. We've got to

> create an attitude of victory by February 24. We must do this. We must be dedicated to making certain that everybody we know goes to the polls on February 24. And those of us who might be inclined to be traitors, you see, there are still some who have slave mentalities. Those of us who are inclined to be traitors, who suspect that because you go into the secrecy of a voting booth, that you can vote for whom you want to vote for, we know who you are and be not confused about it. When a ballot comes out, we're going to count—100 percent, not 99 percent of the votes cast, not 90 percent of the votes cast. Any man south of Madison Street who casts a vote in the February 24 election and who doesn't cast that vote for Harold Washington *ought to be hung as those in New York.*

Two disparate groups, the campaign watchdog CONDUCT, and a state judiciary inquiry board, launched inquiries into the appropriateness of the remarks from an appellate court judge.

Judge Pincham insisted that his comments as reported in the media were "certainly taken out of context and inflated." He added, "Biases, bigotry and prejudice, like beauty, are in the eye of the beholder."

The judge contended that his speech did not belong in the area of "political activities" prohibited by the Illinois Supreme Court's judicial ethic rule, which was put into effect Jan. 1, 1987.

One blatant distortion in particular colored media coverage of Pincham's speech. It is significant that all reports stopped with the phrase, "ought to be hung," omitting the end of the sentence which was, "as those in New York."

That sentence referred to the hanging of Blacks on May 11, 1741, during the rebellion in New York. The judge and his audience were appalled when the message they considered appropriate to discussions of Black history were taken out of context to fuel the fires of racism.

Frederick Sperling, president of the Chicago Council of Lawyers, said his group was disturbed by Pincham's comments. "No judge should engage in conduct that would cause people to question the independence and neutrality of the judiciary. And we feel Justice Pincham's remarks will do just that."

On Saturday, Feb. 7, 1987, more than 1,400 individuals filled Operation PUSH headquarters at 930 E. 50th St. for "Judge R. Eugene Pincham Day." The meeting was held as a protest of the popular jurist being cited by the watchdog group Conduct.

The Rev. Jesse Louis Jackson rallied Washington supporters in defense of Justice Pincham and accused CONDUCT the campaign watchdog group, of "cultural bias." He also criticized the press and said he would create an alternative citizens' organization "that reflects the makeup of the entire city."

Jane Byrne used the Pincham statement as the centerpiece of her campaign on the Southwest Side.

"Who is this man that believes he can intimidate, frighten and divide the people of Chicago? That is not slang," Byrne said while standing on a fire truck outside of Pressman's Hall, 5717 S. Kedzie. She repeated her demand that Mayor Washington repudiate Pincham and apologize for some of his own remarks.

The mayor ignored Byrne's request and demanded that she withdraw a new television commercial that attempts to capitalize on the controversy. In an effort to cool things down, Washington called on a group of CTA workers to help him keep the lid on raucous conduct and divisiveness of all kinds.

Vernon Jarrett, the *Chicago Sun-Times* columnist, captured the essence of Mayor Byrne's newest commercial in his Feb. 12, 1987 column, which was entitled "Byrne Adds New Color to Pincham Quote." He wrote:

> Jane Byrne quoted Pincham as 'any Black man south of Madison Street who doesn't vote for Mayor Washington should be hung.' Byrne's TV quote is not exactly what Pincham said in that Pincham said 'any man' rather than Byrne's 'any Black man' south of Madison Street. Yet, I presume, as did Byrne, Alderman Ed Vrdolyak (10th) and many media critics, that Pincham's address did have an appeal to 'Black voters.' Yet, it's only a presumption since several largely white wards such as the 11th, 12th, 13th, 14th and 19th are south of Madison Street. And if Pincham wanted to really be 'racist,' he could have named many Black wards on the South and West Sides of the city.
>
> My problem with my media friends is not that they read a racial message in Pincham's speech; it's that they do not read a constantly racial message in the content and the language of the all-white crusade to defeat Chicago's first Black mayor.
>
> For example, when the white backers of candidate Thomas C. Hynes and the white backers of Vrdolyak accuse each other of being spoilers, why is there no demand that they also apologize? Everybody in town knows that when both sides shout 'spoiler' they mean you are dividing us whites and we should 'gang up on that Black man.'
>
> The naked truth is that this whole election reeks of racism. And it demonstrated every hour in the fact that we have two prominent Democrats, the county assessor and the party's county chairman running under two new phony party labels, rather than vying as Democrats.
>
> Could we not presume (as we have done on the Pincham issue) that their patent purpose is to give any 'white hope' a better chance in the February 24th primary? And just in case Byrne doesn't make it, there are two other Democrats, running under foreign party labels, seeking a second chance as white hopes in the April 7th general election. And on the Republican side, is there not another Democrat, Donald H. Haider, running as a backup fourth 'white hope?'
>
> Is is not too much for us to presume also that all of this scurrying about is an unabashed appeal to racial prejudice?

Five days after Jarrett's column appeared, Jane Byrne replaced her controversial television commercial with one whose closing plea was, "I want Chicago to smile."

CONDUCT asked Byrne to cancel the commercial that attacked Washington for likening her to Hitler and failing to disavow the remarks by Judge Pincham. Byrne said it had been her plan from the beginning to close the campaign on a high note, and that her withdrawal of the lightning rod television ads had nothing to do with criticism from Mayor Washington and the watchdog group.

Two days before elimination date, the Chicago Board of Elections indicated that 1.1 million voters were expected to go to the polls on Feb. 24. Mayor Washington was viewed as a narrow favorite to win the nomination over Jane Byrne, according to the strategists in both camps. Washington's daily tracking polls indicated that he had broadened his political base by attracting more support among whites and Hispanics than he received in the 1983 election. The mayor's polls also suggested that Washington was gaining strength along the city's northern lakefront, running almost even with Jane Byrne there.

The predictions of Washington's victory were almost scuttled in a ballot-switching ballet on election day.

The Democratic ballot was green, the Republican ballot was yellow and the Solidarity ballot was beige. In some Black wards, Democratic voters were not given the green ballot to vote for Harold Washington, but were handed a beige ballot for Vrdolyak in a green envelope. The confusion in those polling places apparently resulted from a well-orchestrated effort to sabotage the election. Once again, Harold's frequent observation, "Dragons die slow," proved prophetic.

Washington emerged from the chaos of February 24 as the victor over Jane Byrne, establishing himself as a early favorite for the April 7th general election.

"I think we have driven the spike of reform deep into the turf of this great city," Washington said. "I say to Democrats all over the city, it's time that we come together."

The Honorable Charles E. Freeman, justice of the Appellate Court of Illinois, administers the oath of office to the Honorable Harold Washington as the 43rd mayor of Chicago. At the far left is his fiancee, Chicago school teacher Mary Ella Smith; directly behind her is the mayor's brother, Ramon Price. At right, foreground is Alderman Eugene Sawyer; the Reverend Brady is at the far right. At right, background is Cook County Assessor Thomas C. Hynes.

CHAPTER

25

The Main Event

"We have faced their champ," chortled Harold Washington, bubbling with joy after winning the 1987 primary victory over Jane Byrne.

The ecstatic mayor was revved up and ready to take on Alderman Edward R. Vrdolyak (10th) and Cook County Assessor Thomas C. Hynes as Democratic turncoats. He also warned that he was not about to let Donald H. Haider, another Democrat who had just crossed over to Republicanism, escape from punishment.

"It makes me no difference," Harold asserted. "I am going to run against whoever runs. Singles, doubles, triples—and if they can find a fourth person, I will run against him, too."

Back at the starting gate, Vrdolyak and Haider were urging Hynes to get out of the race. Hynes and his aides were busy trying to persuade anyone who would listen that Vrdolyak did not have a snowball's chance in hell of beating Harold Washington. Hynes' pollster, Tom Carey, said that exit polls on the Northwest and Southwest Sides and along the lakefront indicated that Hynes would be the strongest opponent to field against Washington.

On the lakefront, Hynes finished first, Washington second, Haider third and Vrdolyak "dead last," Carey said.

Vrdolyak dismissed the pollster's numbers, claiming that he should be permitted to run alone against Washington. "I am the best person to stand face to face with him, and I will take him in April. He is not going to give me any of that hocus pocus he gave to Jane Byrne."

Joe Novak, press secretary for Vrdolyak, said: "You have an opportunity for these two guys (Washington and Vrdolyak) to go out and settle it in the alley. That's what the people want."

Vrdolyak, Hynes and Haider all saw Washington as an edible, freshly-cooked charcoal broiled steak because the mayor had beat Jane Byrne by a margin of only 78,158 votes out of more than 1 million cast. Although a 53.6 percent victory was convincing to many, their racist remarks fanned the belief that Harold was ripe to be devoured. They gained credence by pointing out that more than one-half million Chicagoans voted against Washington and another 100,000 voters stayed away from the polls on election day.

The mayor's response to the fact that so many people voted against him was typical: "Everybody doesn't love me. Sometimes it boggles the imagination to realize it, but it's true. I mean some people voted against FDR." To extend Washington's analogy, the author reminded him that some people did not like Jesus Christ.

Harold Washington's likability factor was higher among the general voting population than it was within the regular Democratic Organization, where it was practically zero. Although he had backed Harold in the 1983 general election against the Republican mayoral candidate, Bernard Epton, Rep. Dan Rostenkowski (D-Ill.) withheld his support from Washington in 1987.

Rostenkowski said: "Until such time as we know who's going to stay in the race for mayor of the city of Chicago, I think I will withhold my endorsement." The congressman subsequently endorsed Thomas Hynes.

Roman Pucinski, whose Northwest Side Ward voted heavily for Byrne in the primary, said that he was in no hurry to choose among challengers in the April 7 contest. "In the primary, we got exactly what we've been talking about for four years: a one-on-one race against Washington, and we still lost," he said. "It's hard to convince ourselves that three opponents are going to do worse."

Alderman Edward M. Burke (14th), a longtime ally of Vrdolyak, said he would probably sit out the mayoral race, but try to help some aldermanic candidates who might be able to swing council control back to the opposition.

Alderman Joseph Kotlarz (35th), a Democratic ward committeeman, said, "I'm looking at everyone. My ward had a 75 percent turnout in February. I doubt if a similar turnout can be obtained in April. I'm not pessimistic, just realistic. I predict that if Washington wins re-election, the Council Wars, a conflict that marked the mayor's first term, will abate."

Alderman Richard Mell (33rd), though firmly aligned with the Vrdolyak anti-administration bloc in the council, had a history of throwing in with winners when the election smoke clears. He planned to meet with Washington to discuss whether a truce can be reached. "With Vrdolyak in the race, Hynes can't win. So, it doesn't make any sense to make war with the mayor," he said. "My precinct captains are urging me to go with Washington. They are saying, 'Why not be with a winner?' "

Mayoral candidate Thomas C. Hynes received hearty support from State's Attorney Richard M. Daley, his friend and political ally. "I am fully endorsing Tom Hynes," Daley said. "I personally and publicly always endorsed Tom Hynes for public office. I have known him for many, many years."

"The votes are there to defeat Harold Washington and we're going to put them together and we will win on April 7," Hynes said,

From the other corner of the ring, Edward Vrdolyak blasted Daley: "The Daley endorsement of Hynes is from the same fellows who four years ago gave us Harold Washington. The Daley camp represented the same class who said that four years ago no one could win but them. Unfortunately, they were wrong then and quite unfortunately, they are wrong now."

Vrdolyak himself was wrong to ignore his own mayoral polls, which indicated that two out of three Chicago voters did not like him. One of Vrdolyak's top aides admonished: "With four candidates on the ballot, what's the point? There is no way Harold can lose a four-way match."

"Washington can't lose," said State Rep. Alfred G. Ronan, (D-Chicago), the director of Byrne's primary campaign, who hinted that he would throw his support behind Washington.

A fundraiser for Harold Washington at the Conrad Hilton Hotel on March 30, 1987 drew 4,000 supporters. They roared approval when former mayor Byrne proclaimed, "The battle is over. I wholeheartedly endorse Harold Washington."

In a TV commercial prepared for the Washington campaign, Jane Byrne stood before the city's skyline and asserts, "During my campaign, I spoke of the need for unity in our city. I believe that today as deeply as I did then."

"Harold will be the next mayor of Chicago. He has my vote and my support. . . . It's time to unite behind Harold Washington."

Byrne later said that the endorsement came after a month of consultation with her backers and was in keeping with her pledge to support the winner of the Democratic party.

On the day before Jane Byrne's appearance, Mayor Washington's political juggernaut picked up endorsements from two members of the opposition bloc in the Chicago City Council. Alderman Bernard Hansen (44th) and Alderman Eugene Schulter (47th) became the first of the anti-administration aldermen to announce support for the mayor.

Buoyed by his broadening support and the latest poll results, Washington left his two leading challengers, Vrdolyak and Hynes, fighting in the back of the pack over who would get the silver medal and who would get the bronze.

At 5:15 on Sunday afternoon, April 5, Cook County Assessor Hynes declared, "I love Chicago enough not to be mayor," before a crowd of supporters at a get-out-the-vote rally at Plumbers Hall, 1340 W. Washington. The shocking announcement twisted a cheerful crowd into one of despair. Standing by Tom's side were his wife Judy, his mother Kathleen, two of his three sons, Dan and Matthew, and his daughter Leah. Another son, Tom, was away at school. Their broken hearts were reflected in their grim faces.

State Sen. Jeremiah E. Joyce (D-Chicago), Hynes' campaign manager, said Hynes decided to withdraw after meeting with a core group of advisers that included Joyce, Hynes' brother Robert, and aides William Colson, Frank Kruesi and Phil Krone.

Joyce said Hynes had dropped out of the race because "he was not interested in pursuing a silver medal, as they say. He had said that from the outset he would not stay in the race if he believed that he was not going to win. This race cannot be won with more than a one-on-one."

"The withdrawal came late because we were not convinced until yesterday that Vrdolyak was not getting out under any circumstances," Joyce said.

"Hynes was always in it for first place," said Robert Benjamin, Hynes' press secretary. "The polls indicated, however, that the assessor was slipping and could have come in third."

Mayor Washington chided Hynes for "lacking the grace that he likes by asking for Haider or Vrdolyak to drop out to guarantee a Washington defeat." He boasted that Hynes "missed something. We got the votes no matter who drops out."

The mayor had dubbed his opponents Wynken, Blynken and Nod throughout the campaign. "Guess who dropped out?" he asked. "It was Nod. Nod dropped out. Nobody was surprised by that."

The Wednesday, April 8, 1987, *Chicago Sun-Times* headline screamed: "Harold Again."

> Mayor Harold Washington, claiming "a mandate for a movement" overpowered two challengers in the general election and established himself as the dominant political force of the post-Richard J. Daley era.
>
> In the process, Washington gained a clear majority of the City Council, with two members of the opposition losing two mayoral allies. He also consolidated his position as a major player in the state and national Democratic party.
>
> Washington became the first mayor since Daley to win a second term by forging a winning coalition that included a monolithic support among Blacks, increased support among whites and Hispanic voters. The mayor received 95 percent of the Black vote, about one-fifth of the white vote, and 60 percent of the Hispanic vote.
>
> With 97 percent of the city's 2,900 precincts reporting, Washington was leading with 580,336 votes (53 percent), Illinois Solidarity candidate Edward R. Vrdolyak had 459,426 (42 percent), and Republican Donald H. Haider, 46,567 (4 percent). Cook County Assessor Thomas Hynes, who withdrew Sunday, received about 1 percent of the votes.
>
> The voter participation in the general election dropped almost 10 percent from the record 82 percent of the 1983 general election. The turnout was higher in predominantly Black precincts than in white ethnic wards, a reversal of the February 24 Democratic primary.

Harold Washington's political coattail was long enough to enable him to knock off two opposition incumbents in the 31st and 46th Wards, and replace them with Raymond A. Figuerua (31st) and Helen Shiller (46th). The mayor now commanded a solid voting base of 25 in a 50-member council and a potential 29, when including four unaligned aldermen.

Mayor Washington intended to use his expanded city majority to dechair some of the hardcore former "29"ers from committee chairmanships. Alderman Burke was a major target caught in the middle of the sight on his political rifle, but the coup had to be accomplished so covertly that the opposition would not be given a rallying point from which to renew the Council Wars.

The mayor signified that he intended to bring peace to "Beirut on the Lake" when he chose the wide-open green space in Grant Park in front of the Petrillo Band Shell as the location for his second inauguration. He wanted it to be truly a people's inauguration where everyone felt welcome, unlike his 1983 inauguration at Navy Pier where invitations were required because of the size of the hall.

The author was a guest co-anchor with Bill Kurtis, Walter Jacobson and Linda McClennan on the Channel 2 (CBS) live coverage of the event. We broadcast from an elevated tower on the edge of the throng. The ceremony took place on May 4, a shiny, chilly afternoon. The strong Lake Michigan breeze constantly reminded us of why Chicago is known as the Windy City.

The program speeded up because many spectators and participants were dressed more for the month of May than for the winds of March.

President Pro Tempore Alderman Eugene Sawyer introduced the Honorable Charles E. Freeman, Justice of the Appellate Court of Illinois, who administered the oath of office to the Honorable Harold Washington. The oath, prescribed by statute, was subscribed to by the mayor and filed in the Office of the City Clerk.

The mayor thereupon addressed the City Council and assembled guests:

> One hundred and fifty years ago, not far from where we stand, a small company of Americans came together to create our city of Chicago.
>
> These Chicagoans faced the challenge of physical danger and economic disaster. They had to struggle to keep their town alive. But they weren't afraid of a fight. They had pledged themselves to a partnership, to create a new city by the lake.
>
> Through all their hardship, they had a spirit—aggressive, competitive, yet seasoned by cooperation; a spirit that was the essence of a youthful republic; a spirit that one day would define America's most American city: the Spirit of Chicago.
>
> Today, only 15 decades later, we live in one of the great cities in the history of man. The Spirit of Chicago, 'city of broad shoulders,' breathes into each of us new life every day and shines through our architecture and art, our parks and avenues, the vigor of our commerce and the vitality, the diversity of our people.
>
> And yet, once again, we are living in a time of challenge. More than ever, we need to call forth that determination and dedication that is the Spirit of Chicago. Like those early pioneers, we stand at a fork in the road. We may choose the risk and the opportunity and the sacrifice that will restore our city, or we may fall into the path of least resistance, down the road of decline.
>
> Today, here in a setting framed by our city's grand skyline and glorious lakefront, I want to reflect on the Spirit of Chicago, on the challenges we face today, on the partnership we will need to overcome the present danger, and on the promise that is ours if we prevail.

Four years ago, we inaugurated a new chapter in the history of Chicago. Chicago had suffered from two decades of decline. We were deeply in debt, and our management was in shambles. Our schools had been bankrupt, our public housing was falling deeper into a billion-dollar hole. City revenue collections were haphazard or nonexistent. Contract and personnel records were a mess.

Worse, we were a city deeply divided by class and race and ethnic differences. Many Chicagoans had become dispirited, despaired of change.

Despite that climate, we began a process of renewal—changing not only how we do business, but how we view ourselves and the world around us.

In the true Spirit of Chicago, we opened city government to the fullest access by the greatest number. We affirmed the most fundamental American principles of fairness—by word and by action—righting the balance to bring an ever wider participation to the business and governance of our city.

We fought for and won the right of Chicago's minorities to full representation in City Council.

We substituted administrators for political workers, and brought modern management to our municipal affairs—to an enterprise which had grown, from those cabins and shops 15 short decades ago, into a $2 billion corporation, on which the livelihoods of perhaps 8 million Chicagoans and their neighbors must depend.

We worked with community leaders to reinvest $300 million in the rebuilding of our neighborhoods, taking care, even in times of financial hardship, to maintain our heritage and provide for new generations.

We worked with business leaders for the prosperity of our downtown commercial district, which has grown at the rate of a billion dollars a year over this decade.

We worked with organized labor to bring fair and orderly collective bargaining practices to city employment.

We worked with the legal community and civic leaders to pass ethics legislation, seeking to eliminate both the temptation and the opportunity for corruption in public office.

We fought to empower new partnerships—of citizens, community groups, business organizations, churches and schools, and professional associations—to work alongside city government in the modernization of Chicago management.

Those four years were well spent. We have witnessed amazing change in our city, in four short years.

Across the country and around the world, we've made it clear: there's a new Spirit of Chicago, building on the old.

Chicago is not simply the City that Works. The word is out: Chicago Works Together.

We fought for this economic and social and spiritual renewal at a critical time, and we won that struggle just in time.

Because Chicago in 1987, like every other major American municipality, is facing unprecedented challenges to its survival as a world city.

Everywhere we look, across our land, we see the American city in peril—endangered by economic challenge from abroad, and threatened by a failure of the will from within.

You hear the story over and over, in every major city in America: the cities whose greatness made America great, are losing ground. In the name of a flawed and suspect ideology, their needs are being ignored and disdained by the federal administration.

General Revenue Sharing, the fair return of your income tax to support your city, is gone. Grants and tax breaks for social services and for economic development have been drastically cut.

Funds for the hungry, the homeless, needy, elderly and disabled, women and children, as well as millions of middle-class families who depend on their cities for quality of life, are being made to suffer for failed federal economic policies that have added a trillion dollars to our national debt.

Over the past four years, we have taken the lead in demanding a fair return of your tax dollar, to keep our cities healthy and strong. Chicago has become recognized as a leader in the national struggle for an urban policy in the federal agenda.

Now, more than ever, Chicago is challenged to take the lead. Just as we are finally able to leave local petty political bickering behind us, the new Spirit of Chicago is aroused to greater trials, perhaps the most important challenges our generation will face.

In 1837, the same year our city was incorporated, a great national depression nearly ruined Chicago, and many other cities, wiping out land holdings and life savings.

In 1847, when we were only 10 years old and only 16,000 in number, even before we had paved streets, we were host to America's first great national protest meeting. Twenty thousand people came to Chicago, from East and West, North and South, cosmopolitans like Horace Greeley of the *New York Tribune,* and country lawyers like young Abraham Lincoln from downstate Illinois. They came together in this place to protest federal neglect of the cities and towns across America. They helped to focus federal priorities on the development of a continent of cities.

In the years between their protest and our contemporary plight, the federal government did indeed develop a partnership with the cities. And through mutual support, the prosperity of those cities created for America the richest, most productive society our planet has ever known.

Now, the partnership is falling apart. Cities are treated like failed industries, cut off from the central economy, left to sink or swim if they can, the survivors urged to "vote with their feet" and migrate to defense industries in the Sun Belt, the halt and the lame callously discarded like so much worn-out furniture.

Now, once again, our way of life is in trouble—and it is in our cities where we know that firsthand. America is bleeding, in our streets and alleys, in our stairwells and in the corridors of our schools. America's cities are on the critical list, and we must not be timid or halfway in our response.

We have found that we must act to save ourselves, not just in Chicago, but all across that entire commonwealth of cities that has created an urban America.

We have mobilized, through the United States Conference of Mayors, the League of Cities, and other coalitions, to take care of our people.

We have acted urgently, because the need is great.

Today, almost one-fourth of our children are living in poverty. Two-fifths of Hispanic children, over one-half of Black children, little ones younger than seven years old, wake up each morning suffering the physical abuse of hunger. These are the highest rates we've ever seen, ever in the history of this country. Their hunger is unacceptable.

Nationally, one-fourth of our graduating classes are not graduating, an incalculable waste for our society. In Chicago, almost half of our boys and girls never finish school, a tragic human loss for them and their families, and an economic injury for our city and our nation. That dropout rate is unacceptable.

Mothers and babies, children and youth, the elderly, all those whose shelter depends on federal assistance, are threatened by the prospect that they may join the ranks of the homeless, as 70,000 units of public housing are abandoned each year; it is reported that 900,000 federally subsidized but privately owned apartments could vanish in the next decade. That destruction of our homes is unacceptable.

The economic inequality worsens: while the overall poverty rate in America is at 11 percent, it is 32 percent for Blacks, and 25 percent for Hispanic people. The inequality, that "We the people" versus "They the people," is unacceptable.

We do not accept the abandonment of the people of America's cities. We will not allow our citizens to be written off as bad debts.

Throughout Chicago history, when we have faced such crises, we have summoned our resources, and developed partnerships. We have reawakened the power to redirect our priorities. Now, once again we are called to the challenge. We must apply the lessons of the past to the challenges of today.

If we have learned one thing in this generation in Chicago, it is that bossism is not leadership, and leadership is not bossism.

The leadership that made Chicago great was not the dictate of any individual leader at any time in our history. It was not the operations of a cabal, in a smoke-filled room.

The leadership that made Chicago great, from its earliest origins, was the partnership of every sector of our city's society, working together. That partnership is the leadership that our times requires.

The partnership of our full body politic must, by any means necessary, press our case at the federal and state levels. We, the leaders of Chicago, have an obligation to recover for our people the fair share of our federal taxes to which Chicago is due. Not as charity or welfare, but as investment, and as a fair return.

But it is not enough to press our claims. We must also do for ourselves. We must, each of us, find that priority where our skills are of use, roll up our sleeves and take action. We must join together and do for ourselves what must be done.

We must plan and coordinate, improvise, innovate, recombine and reinvent, and leave no options unexplored, to provide at least temporary solutions while we press our case.

The city government can't do that alone. The cities, for three generations, prospered under an active partnership with the federal government. Our institutions evolved around that traditional American partnership.

Now that American tradition is no longer dependable, and even as we work to restore it, we must build on the new partnerships we have developed at the local level.

Although our greatest problems are truly national in origin, and national in scale; nonetheless they are local in their impact. And though we must take a role in the grand strategies laid in Washington, we are the ones who will have to carry the fight here, in the trenches, on the front lines, in our cities.

With every Chicagoan, and every Chicago institution, together at the wheel, we can turn this thing around.

Our most urgent need is for jobs. Give us jobs and we'll take care of the rest. Jobs will rebuild self-esteem; jobs will restore community pride; jobs will cut down the drop-out rate; jobs will slow down the cycles of crime, youth gangs, drugs, child abuse and abuse of women; jobs will reaffirm the justice of our economic system; jobs will reduce teenage pregnancy; jobs will ultimately end the human tragedy of welfare dependency.

We must not be satisfied with anything that can be achieved on the local level alone. We must work to change America's priorities, to turn our welfare programs into jobs programs, to redirect defense spending into domestic spending that creates jobs.

But we must also do for ourselves: We must apply ourselves, in partnership across our city, to the successful jobs programs we have created, in Hire the Future and Chicago First; and small business loan programs that have created or retained 20,000 jobs in our city over the past four years.

Jobs are our top priority—for unless the young and the working-age city dwellers go back to work again, nothing else will matter.

An equal priority is our educational system. We need the full partnership of the body politic to recognize their stake in the success of our schools; to join in the effort to provide a supportive environment for the very young; reinforcement for those in the middle grades, with special attention to problems of literacy; and career counseling with job incentives for high school students.

Every student who drops out of high school is a personal tragedy for whom each of us must feel personal reponsibility.

We must work with the state of Illinois to provide the network of resources the challenge requires. And we must respond to the national crisis in education and work with other cities to insist on new funds from the federal level. But we must also do for ourselves. We must work together over the next four years, through our Educational Summit, and the Learn-Earn incentives and a host of new church and community and corporate efforts, to help our young people excel in school.

The problems of housing are no less urgent—created by the failed attempt, a generation ago, to seal off our housing problems in monolithic cellblocks—badly designed and underfunded, then stripped and robbed in the financial marketplace.

The crisis in housing affects not only the poor condemned to substandard shelter. It also touches everyone who lives in our city, in every neighborhood of Chicago. For who among us can be serene and secure in our own home when we know that our brother and sister are living in such sad discomfort?

We must press for the needed funds from the state and federal level, for these Illinoisans, these Americans, who deserve affordable housing. But we must also do for ourselves: develop new programs like our successful Chicago Housing Partnership to leverage the resources of the private sector. And we must bring Chicago once again into the forefront of modern housing construction techniques, to accelerate the rehabbing of our housing stock. We must find ways to combine efforts and create jobs to solve our housing problems.

Jobs, education, housing, transportation, health, environmental concerns, including the preservation of our beautiful lakefront: although these are all national issues, affecting every city, beyond the resources of each alone, it is still in our individual cities where we feel the pain.

And so, it is in the cities where we must do for ourselves. We must recognize our responsibility, gather our forces, summon the spirit that made us great and fight for fundamental change.

The promise and the potential of Chicago requires no less of us. The Spirit of Chicago compels us. It is a spirit we must fight to sustain.

But our motivation is more basic than just idealism and altruism. We are also mindful of the self-interest that inspires us.

Chicago, in four years, has brought together Black and white, Asian and Hispanic, male and female, the young, the old, the disabled, gays and lesbians, Moslems, Christians and Jews, business leaders and neighborhood activists, bankers and trade unionists—all have come together to mix and contend, to argue and to reason, to confront our problems and not merely to contain them.

We didn't come together out of love for one another. Where that is lacking, that will follow. A civil society—a civilization—a city that works—requires simply that we behave well toward each other. And our present danger requires even more, that we work together, and do for ourselves.

And so, citizens of Chicago, I ask every man, woman and child of you, for your help over the next four years, as we do for ourselves to realize the promise that is Chicago.

I ask you to join with me in the national movement to restore our cities as American priorities. I ask you to exercise your rights as Illinoisans and Americans, to win Chicago's fair share at the state and federal level. But I also ask you to roll up your sleeves, so we can do for ourselves.

To the millions of our neighbors outside our city, who depend on a healthy Chicago for your quality of life, I ask you to join with us, to support us both in our fight for a fair share and in our effort to do for ourselves.

To the leaders of business, industry and trade, foundations and philanthropic societies, city, state and federal government, community organizations, schools at all levels, churches, professional associations, organized labor, educators and the media, I ask you to become directly, personally involved in the programs that address Chicago's most pressing needs, to help us do for ourselves.

To the political leaders at every level of government, I ask you to consider the importance of a healthy Chicago to your constituency, to your party, to your own responsibilities of public office, and lend your efforts to our cause, to join forces, to strengthen our effort to do for ourselves.

To every man, woman and child listening to me today, I ask you to consider the need and examine your skills, and find a way to contribute to the salvation of your city. Together we must form a human safety network that provides, in time and talent, what Chicago could never afford in its taxes and budgets.

In return for your investment, in return for your sacrifice, I promise you this: that you will be the richer for what you invest, that you will be the happier for the troubles you absorb, that you will be the healthier for the afflictions you confront, for the sake of your city, Chicago.

And that you will remember until you're past remembering, and you will take pleasure every time you recall, that you responded to your city in her hour of greatest need. That you found injustice and inequity unacceptable. That you fought for a fair share. And that you joined in, rolled up your sleeves, and helped Chicago do for ourselves.

Following the eruption of a rousing standing ovation for Mayor Harold Washington, Alderman Sawyer then introduced the Reverend J. M. Stone, pastor of the Stone Temple Baptist Church, who offered the benediction. Alderman Tim Evans then moved that the City Council adjourn, and the motion prevailed.

Left to right, Cleveland Walker, Mayor Harold Washington and Dempsey J. Travis, standing on a bridge in Kyoto, Japan. In the background is the garden and pools of Kin-Kaku-ji Temple, once a shogun's mountain villa converted into a Buddhist Temple. The picture was taken on Aug. 26, 1985.

CHAPTER

26

Harold's Last Miles, With Some Detours

Harold Washington was a man who needed very little sleep. He could be recharged with as little as four hours of sleep, and when the occasion demanded it, he could get by with even less. His days usually began before 6 a.m. and ended about midnight. In the more than 50 years I knew him, I never fully appreciated his high energy level until Aug. 23, 1985. On that day, I joined him and a small delegation of Chicago officials and civic leaders for a 16-day trip to the Far East. Our mission was to drum up trade and promote cultural exchange between Chicago and her sister cities, Osaka, Japan and Shenyang, China.

It was in Japan that I observed Harold hour after hour speaking in meeting after meeting and exchanging ideas with our many hosts throughout the day and late into the night. I must admit that I became fatigued by simply watching him work.

By any standard other than Harold's, I am considered a very high energy, goal-oriented person. However, by the eighth day, I was more tired than a junkyard dog who had been running and barking all night long. Therefore, I was truly happy to see Harold board the plane for China because his absence afforded me the only day I had to rest during our stay in Japan. I had begged off of the trip to China before we left Chicago because the mayor's plans called for his small entourage to cover in eight days what it had taken my wife Moselynne and me one month to cover the year before. Without a doubt, Harold had the physical stamina and the intellectual curiosity to be stimulated by China and its people.

David Canter, one of Harold's lawyers and statisticians, recalls Harold's phenomenal memory for numbers. Harold displayed almost total recall in citing the percentages and the number of votes cast in elections that had taken place 40 or 50 years earlier. His appetite for literature was unlimited, and he quoted long passages from the works of literary giants of the past and present. Washington frequently engaged in discussions with a college lad who was the night receptionist in his residence. They would philosophize and talk about philosophers. Plato's *Allegory of a Cave* was a favorite.

Harold's love of books and philosophy sometimes caused him to reschedule business appointments. Canter, during an interview, reflected on a 6:30 a.m. date he had with Harold for breakfast. When Canter arrived at the building, the receptionist said, "There is no way you are going to disturb the mayor now, because he just went upstairs to go to bed." The young man knew where of he spoke—he and Harold had been up all night discussing books and philosophy. Canter's experience was not unique. My wife and I often delayed dinner parties after telephoning Harold at his home to discover that he had gotten lost in the pages of a book.

The late William McCarthy, president of Kroch's and Brentano's bookstore chain in Chicago, told me that he never had to look at a calendar to know when it was Friday because whenever Harold was in town on that day of the week, he would come into Kroch's Wabash Avenue store, browse around by himself, and buy from one to a half-dozen books each time. Many of the books Washington purchased were biographies and autobiographies. McCarthy told me that Harold was the only Chicago mayor in the store's 80-plus-year history who visited the store on a regular basis. Gov. James Thompson was also a frequent visitor at Kroch's, he said.

One of Harold's lifelong habits was reading books throughout the night. Evan Canter, David's son, was Washington's legislative intern when Harold was in Congress. When Harold was too busy to go to a bookstore, he frequently gave Evan a list of books to buy. Some mornings, at a staff breakfast, Harold would discuss some of the books. Evan, a young law student on summer vacation from Benjamin Cardoso Law School in New York, would protest, " But, I just gave you the books that you are talking about late yesterday afternoon." Harold would reply, "Son, I have to confess that I spent the entire night reading them."

Harold's reading habits were familiar to his legislative colleagues in Springfield, Ill., and in Washington. Often, when a bill required serious scrutiny, they would ask Harold to read it because they knew he would do it thoroughly.

Former Alderman Leon Depres, the City Council parliamentarian during Mayor Washington's administration, observed:

> "Washington was a genuine intellectual and a tremendous reader. People would say he had a great vocabulary, used long words. Well, the way you get to use long words is you do a lot of reading and thinking and talking. Harold would respond to literary allusions. For example, I'd say to him, 'Sitting here (in the City Council) is like the general in *War and Peace* sitting under the trees at the Battle of Barziano, not knowing which way it's going because the great forces are running everything.'

Alderman Leon Despres (Fifth Ward).

Well, the mayor would respond to the allusion by quoting passages from the book. He'd also talk about the trouble he initially had reading *War and Peace* and how he finally finished it. Well, Daley never read *War and Peace.* I can guarantee you that. I doubt if Byrne did or Bilandic. And certainly not Mayor William Hale Thompson, who sat on the fifth floor for three terms.

Washington had a conception of government for the people. He didn't have a conception of government as something you make money out of, something that you use to your advantage. He had very high ideals and certainly no desire for personal wealth. That's something new and refreshing in politics.

Harold is kind of a Camelot legend, because we will look back at the Washington administration as ideal. He was an underrated mayor. He was much better as a mayor than he was ever generally given credit for. Without a question, he was the best mayor of Chicago in my lifetime of some 70-plus years. He put the city's welfare ahead of his party affiliations. The only other mayor that I can think of who came close to that idealism was William Devers, a Democrat who served as mayor of Chicago from 1923 to 1927.

Reading was a habit that Harold acquired very early in life. Allie Jackson, a high school student and the nephew of Harold's stepmother Arlene, lived with them in the Washington apartment at 111 E. 44th St. from Monday through Friday, and then go to his parents' home on the weekends. Allie's assignment in the Washington household was to make sure that Harold and his brother Edward did not get into any fights or cause any destruction. Harold was 12 years old and Edward was 14. Allie recalls:

> When Harold came home from school, he would head straight for the icebox and then go and curl up in a corner with a book. You wouldn't hear a peek from Harold for the rest of the afternoon and into the evening. Edward, his brother, who had a crutch, would move back and forth through the apartment fast and recklessly. I frequently became annoyed with Edward. Harold was quiet and introspective, whereas Edward was loud and mischievous.
>
> I didn't see Harold again for years and years. As a matter of fact, the next time I saw him was at Arlene Jackson Washington's funeral. He came up to me and said, 'You look the same as you did when I was this big,' holding his hand down about waist level. That made me feel old.

Margaret Ferguson, a young lady from Arkansas who came to Chicago via Kansas City, moved into Arlene Washington's second floor apartment at 4941 S. Michigan, shortly after Roy Washington Sr. died in November 1953. From her vantage point across the hall from Harold, Margaret interpreted his ferocious appetite for reading day and night was a sign of laziness. She wondered why he was sitting around reading when he should have been running his late father's law business from the office at 466 E. 47th St. The author understands Margaret's mindset. A neighbor once asked me, while I was a student at Roosevelt University why didn't I drop out of school and do something practical, like get a job.

Harold was basically getting his mind together when he retreated into reading, but he never let his intellectualism get in the way of his common touch and deep feelings of compassion for the young, old and those in between. For example, on May 4, 1987, the day of Washington's second inauguration, my 90-year-old mother fell and broke her arm in several places. In addition, she suffered some minor head injuries. Later that day, at a celebration dinner held at the Westin Hotel on North Michigan Avenue, I casually mentioned to him that his girlfriend, (the name he affectionately called my mother), was in the hospital. Harold, the man my mother called her second son, asked me where. I told him she was in the Mitchell Pavilion at the University of Chicago Hospital complex. The next afternoon, after spending the day with my mother, I called the hospital to find out how she was. She told me that she did not have time to talk to me because the mayor's office had just called and said that he was on his way to visit her. I was surprised and pleased that he would take time out of his hectic schedule to see her when a telephone call would have been sufficient. To this day, two of the highlights in my mother's life are the day when Harold spent more than an hour talking with her at bedside in the hospital, and her 89th birthday, when the mayor called her from Toyko to wish her a happy birthday.

Herman Cromwell Gilbert, author of a novel entitled, *The Negotiations,* executive vice president and editorial director of Path Press, and former administrative assistant to Illinois Congressman Gus Savage.

Harold, like his father, could be as soft as butter and as hard as steel. I know my mother was not unique among persons who found the hands of Harold Washington on their shoulders. I can identify many individuals to whom he extended a warm, helping hand until the day that his hand was stilled in the coldness of death.

Harold Washington was a gentle but complex man. Though he meant different things to different people, he was always Harold. Some of his complexities may be best understood through the eyes of Herman Gilbert, a novelist and philosopher who was a close observer of Harold Washington for more than four decades. Gilbert said:

> Harold was a good man because he personified Blackness and Black people. Black people trusted him. He typified Blackness beyond his Blackness, if you were defining Blackness from the Black nationalist perspective. Yet, he was not a Black nationalist. Harold was a Democrat who believed in ethnic cooperation. To the day he died, he was willing and trying to meet white people more than half way if they were willing to make any movement toward progress. He was willing to fight them if they were not willing to make any movement toward cooperation. But I think he enjoyed his Blackness. He exuded Blackness, Black machoism and things of that sort. He could talk that talk with the best of them. That's one reason why Black people trusted him.
>
> The second reason Harold was considered a good person is because

he prepared himself. He really was an expert in most areas of government. He truly knew government. Moreover, he knew white people respected his knowledge. And he also had their respect based on his dedication. You must remember that year after year, term after term, he won the best legislative awards, whether he was a state representative or a state senator. The reason is because he lived equally from the inside of his mind as from the outside. Some people live within but they have to try to translate or transfer that knowledge to the real world. They can't do it. But Harold was equally good in both worlds. He could sit down and argue with the intellectuals. He could talk to the pragmatists. He could talk to the visionaries and the dreamers, and hold his own in each category. But when he got ready, and the time came to do something, he could. He was as good as any of the activists. He was one of the few people that I've met in my 60-plus years who was a visionary, a theorist, a strategist and an activist, all with about equal ability.

On the flip side of Harold the theorist and strategist was Harold the humorist. He was as quick with a joke as he was with a smile. Few people could be in his presence very long without responding to his infectious personality.

It was his genuine good nature and sense of humor that enabled him to survive the Council Wars.

Leon Depres said that he saw Harold irritated only once during the four years and six months he worked with him. That incident was sparked by a remark by Edward Vrdolyak that implied there was a question about the mayor's manhood. The mayor appeared so enraged on the five o'clock news that I thought he would come off the dais and punch Eddie out on the council floor.

On another occasion, when Councilman Edward Burke said something mean spirited, the mayor diffused the situation by referring to Burke as "Buster." Burke objected to being called "Buster" and everyone on the council floor erupted in laughter.

Being mayor also seemed very natural for Harold. He was the "same old Harold" that I knew as president of the student council at Roosevelt University. He was the "same old Harold" who used to sit in the back of the 101 Philosophy class with Gus Savage and me and whisper about what we were going to be when we finished school. Harold always said he was going to be a lawyer and a politician, Gus said he was going to write the great definitive novel, and I said I was going to be rich. Those fantasies of our young minds were realized in ways we could not have foreseen. Gus became a newspaper publisher, columnist and later a congressman, I became a best-selling author in addition to making my fortune in the real estate business but not in that sequence, and Harold became the mayor of Chicago. Mayor Washington would often tell that story whenever he discovered I was in the audience.

The late William Goldsborough was a student at Roosevelt University when Harold and I were there. Bill frequently talked about Harold Washington's leadership talents with his wife, Evelyn. After Bill's untimely death, Eve-

Mayor Harold Washington with the Chicago Bears Refrigerettes, doing the, ''We are No. 1,'' ditty.

lyn became a real estate property manager and an owner. She was the resident manager at the Wilmington Apartments, located at 4901 S. Drexel Blvd., in 1961 when Harold Washington moved into one of the building's 2 1/2 room apartments.

Evelyn, like most good resident managers, observed the movement of the tenants in and out of the building. She noted that Harold was quiet but friendly, and he waved whenever he saw her. She usually closed her office about 7:30 p.m., and often glimpsed Harold coming in from work with a briefcase and several newspapers under his arm.

On the few occasions Evelyn entered Harold's apartment to make inspection or accompany some tradesman who was making a minor repair, she observed that it was sparsely furnished, bereft of pictures or other adornments, and noted only his large collection of books and newspapers. Her 39-year-old tenants apparently had little interest in acquiring an extensive wardrobe or in accumulating possessions. During this period, Washington would comment: "I have more to say than I have to show."

After Harold moved from the Wilmington apartment, their paths did not cross until 20 years later, when he rented a one-bedroom, second floor condominium that Mrs. Goldsborough owned in the Hampton House at 5300 South Shore Drive. Although his new apartment was more spacious than the one he occupied at the Wilmington, Evelyn observed that Harold had acquired very little material goods, and that books and papers far outnumbered his other possessions.

Although Harold's career path had escalated from hearing officer on the

Illinois Industrial Commission to U.S. representative of the 1st Congressional District, he maintained an austere lifestyle and friendly attitude. His voice still radiated a sincerity and warmth, she said, while his face wore that perpetual smile on his face and his eyes sparkled with a childish twinkle.

The main event took place at the real estate office shortly after Harold Washington was elected mayor of Chicago. Around May 1, 1983, two plain clothesmen walked into the Parker-Holzman office, looked around and left, unrecognized. Soon afterward, Mayor Washington walked in to pay his rent. Mrs. Goldsborough recalled:

> You would not believe the way people in our office were fumbling and falling over themselves while the mayor was there. The mayor was cool. He simply sat down and wrote his rent as he always had in the past. The mayor acted as if nothing had changed in his life. He jokingly told me before he left that his security people would not permit him to pay his rent in person anymore because they considered it too much of a risk.

Later in the month, Evelyn was advised that Harold must move to larger quarters, and would also need a second apartment directly across the hall from his for his security people.

Harold continued to pay rent for his old apartment after he moved up to apartment 66 on the sixth floor in the same building. When Evelyn asked the mayor's secretary when he was going to give up the second-floor apartment and return the keys, she was told he would surrender the apartment as soon as he could put his papers and books in some order. Evelyn suggested that the mayor call on his secretary, Delores Woods, to accomplish that task. Everybody agreed that that was a good idea, but there were still papers and things that the mayor wanted to make a decision on before anybody other than himself touched those papers.

Evelyn obtained the keys from Delores Woods several times over the next four years whenever some type of maintenance was required in the apartment. On those occasions, she found it contained only a couple of the mayor's old suits hanging in the closet and the inevitable stacks of books and papers all over the place, mirroring his love for reading.

The mayor also loved to play poker, but this was a pleasure that he reserved for his out-of-town trips, when he played poker with his security guards. The stakes in those games were 300 pennies, which were kept in a sock and divided among the players at the beginning of each game. Harold frequently admonished his poker partners: "Don't let Ink, Stink, or any of those other writers hear about our game because they will write that we are out here in California playing with a $100,000 pot."

These poker games were the times when Harold would kick off his shoes, open his shirt and relax, becoming the antithesis of his Chicago persona. In "Sweet Home, Chicago," Harold assumed a paternal role toward his beloved city. It was as though the sole responsibility for the city rested on his shoulders alone.

Delores Woods, secretary to Mayor Harold Washington for 20 years, and currently the secretary for Mayor Eugene Sawyer.

Those of us who saw poker as an escape mechanism for Harold said: "Thank God for poker." Frank Lee and Howard Saffold, both leaders on the mayor's security team, said that the mayor was a pretty good poker player. They said the mayor greatly enjoyed mimicking Wallace Berry, a MGM movie star during the 1930s and '40s, during their poker game.

Frank describes how Harold played the Wallace Berry role to the hilt:

> All the cards are in and the pot is in the middle of the table. Harold would stare everybody down around the table. He would then put his left hand to his nose and twist it a bit. At the same time, he is putting his right hand inside the waste band of his pants as if he had a gun. He would then say, 'If it's yourn, pick it up.' In the movie, when the guy reached for the pot, Wallace Berry shot him. Harold loved those old Western movies and Wallace Berry.

In reality, unlike the movies, Harold never shot the other guy. He shot himself by neglecting his health. A few of the people close to him tried their damndest to get him to cut down on his food intake and get some exercise. His secretary, Delores Woods, was also concerned and she asked me to intercede in attempting to get him to see a doctor. I set up appointments for him with my own doctors at least four times, and he always managed to cancel at the last minute.

In December 1985, I tackled the mayor's obesity problem by giving him an exercise bike for Christmas. He was very pleased with the present and promised me he would use it. That was a promise he never kept. I checked the milage every time I visited with him, and it was pretty much the same. He had put only a few miles on the bike over a period of several months.

Then I remembered that Harold had been an all-city track star at DuSable High School and I decided to take another route for Christmas of 1986. I gave him an exercise treadmill, on which he could walk or run. To my regret, he used the treadmill even less than he had used the exercycle.

Howard Saffold was also waging his own war with the mayor about his weight. His only reward was Harold's refusal to speak to him for several days after one of their arguments about his weight. The mayor frequently admonished Saffold to, "Remember, I have been taking care of myself for 65 years." Then, he would turn and pick up one of those chocolate doughnuts that he loved so much.

His friends wished he had loved himself as much as he loved those doughnuts.

I remember listening to Harold on a radio program called "Ask the Mayor," which was aired over WJPC (95 AM), WVON (1450 AM) and WBMX (102.5 FM), approximately six months before his death. You could hear him gasping for breath between sentences during the broadcast, a condition he also suffered when he walked up a single flight of steps. The indications that his health was endangered were as obvious as blinking neon stoplights.

Harold knew he was ill, and I suspect that he knew he was near the end because in the latter part of October, or the first part of November, he uncharacteristically began to plan for his retirement. He looked closely at the deferred compensation plans and other benefits he would be eligible for from the city. He talked generally about beneficiaries, but never identified them.

Harold Washington finished his last mile at 11:00 Wednesday morning, Nov. 25, 1987. At approximately 11:05, I received a call from City Hall informing me that the mayor had had a heart attack. I informed Renault Robinson, who was seated at my conference table, and he immediately grabbed a phone to determine where the mayor would be taken.

Our destination was Northwestern Memorial Hospital. Renault drove like a crazy man at the rate of 75 miles per hour northbound on the Outer Drive. While Renault was driving like hell, I was crying like hell because I knew in my heart that Harold was dead.

Shortly after I arrived at the hospital, Don Johnson of Channel 2 (CBS), grabbed me by the arm and said, "Come with me. I want you to join Walter Jacobson and Bill Kurtis in telling our audience what is happening."

For almost an hour, I talked with the CBS anchors on the air about my friend Harold. Suddenly, about 1:30 p.m., Jacobson started speaking of Harold in the past tense. I rose from my chair in the middle of the telecast and removed the microphone from my tie. I knew that Jacobson had heard the official pronouncement of Washington's death.

Waiting for Harold.

Flowers for Harold that couldn't be delivered.

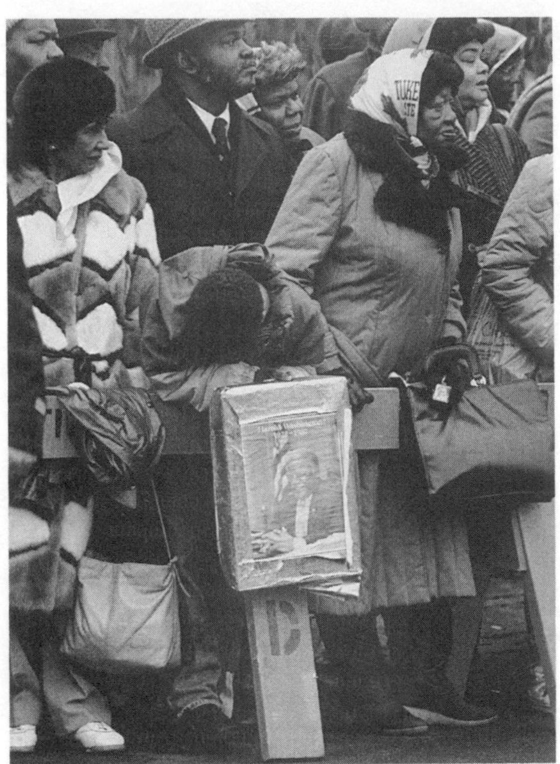

Mourning for Harold.

Harold's final address.

A father and son share a piece of history.

Harold's last ride.

Members of the Washington family. Left to right: Ernestine Price Scott, Elaine Price Lake, and Richard Lake.

Harold on my mind.

A "Harold" that we will always remember.

BIBLIOGRAPHY

CHAPTER 1

BOOKS

Drake, St. Clair and Horace R. Cayton, *Black Metropolis: A Study of Negro Life in a Northern City,* Volume I & II, New York: Harper & Row, 1945.

Holli, Melvin G. and Paul M. Green, *The Making of a Mayor:* Chicago, 1983, Grand Rapids, Michigan: William B. Eerdmans Publishing Company, 1984.

Levinsohn, Florence H., *Harold Washington: A Political Biography,* Chicago: Chicago Review Press, 1983.

Travis, Dempsey J., *An Autobiography of Black Chicago,* Chicago: Urban Research Institute, Inc., 1981.

________, *An Autobiography of Black Jazz,* Chicago: Urban Research Press, Inc., 1983.

________, *An Autobiography of Black Politics,* Chicago: Urban Research Press, Inc., 1987.

NEWSPAPERS

"Mayor Yule Rooted An Old Time Religion," *Chicago Sun-Times, 25 December 1983.*

"A Walk Down Memory Lane," Chicago Defender, 18 September 1984.

"The Mayor's Dad, His Only Hero," *Chicago Defender,* 19 September 1984.

"Harold The Man, Politician and Mayor," *Chicago Defender,* 22 September 1984.

"A Bitter Showdown," *Chicago Sun-Times,* 19 January 1986.

"Cities Stand Out Credits of Good Start," *Chicago Sun-Times,* 27 March 1986.

MAGAZINES

"Mayor Harold Washington's Commemorative Issue," *Dollars and Sense,* June 1983.

"Black Politics: The New Road to Freedom," *Ebony,* August 1984.

Chicago Tribune Magazine, November 15, 1986.

"Harold Washington: The Black Mayor Everybody Knows," *Ebony,* December 1987.

"In Memory of a Hero, Harold Washington: 1922–1987, Chicago's First Black Mayor," *Dollars and Sense,* February/March 1988.

INTERVIEWS

Brown, Albert, A Track Teammate of Mayor Washington at DuSable High School, Personal Interview, Chicago, 6 August 1984.

Cheefus, John, Boyhood Friend of Mayor Washington, Personal Interview, Chicago, 11 September 1984.

Harewood, Richard A., Former Municipal Judge, Personal Interviews, Chicago, 2 January 1985, 10 February 1985.

Plique, Eddie, Boxing and Sports Promoter, Personal Interview, Chicago, 13 September 1983.

Washington, Harold, Mayor of Chicago, Personal Interviews, Chicago, 23 April 1983, 31 April 1983, 31 May 1983, 22 January 1984, 16 April 1984, 12 May 1984, 19 May 1984, 17 July 1984, 24 April 1985, 11 August 1985, 24 August 1985, 22 September 1986, 15 October 1986.

Washington, Roy Lee Jr., Brother of Mayor Washington, Personal Interviews, Chicago, 5 May 1984, 20 May 1984.

NOTES

Notes from the Personal Diary of Dempsey J. Travis for the years between 1937 and 1985.

CHAPTER
2

BOOKS

Drake, St. Clair and Horace R. Cayton, *Black Metropolis: A Study of Negro Life in a Northern City,* Volume I & II, New York: Harper & Row, 1945.

Travis, Dempsey J., *An Autobiography of Black Chicago,* Chicago: Urban Research Institute, Inc., 1981.

________, *An Autobiography of Black Jazz,* Chicago: Urban Research Press, Inc., 1983.

________, *An Autobiography of Black Politics,* Chicago: Urban Research Press, Inc., 1987.

1939 Red and Black DuSable High School Annual.

1940 Red and Black DuSable High School Annual.

NEWSPAPERS

"Mayor Yule Rooted An Old Time Religion," *Chicago Sun-Times,* 25 December 1983.

"A Walk Down Memory Lane," *Chicago Defender,* 18 September 1984.

"The Mayor's Dad, His Only Hero," *Chicago Defender,* 19 September 1984.

MAGAZINES

"Mayor Harold Washington's Commemorative Issue," *Dollars and Sense,* June 1983.

"Black Politics: The New Road to Freedom," *Ebony,* August 1984.

Chicago Tribune Magazine, November 15, 1986.

"Harold Washington: The Black Mayor Everybody Knows," *Ebony,* December 1987.

"In Memory of a Hero, Harold Washington: 1922-1987, Chicago's First Black Mayor," *Dollars and Sense,* February/March 1988.

INTERVIEWS

Black, Timuel, Professor at Harold Washington (Loop) College, Personal Interview, Chicago, 28 April 1984, 12 January 1988.

Brown, Albert, A Track Teammate of Mayor Washington at DuSable High School, Personal Interview, Chicago, 6 August 1984.

Cheefus, John, Boyhood Friend of Mayor Washington, Personal Interview, Chicago, 11 September 1984.

Davis, Theodore, Chicago Police Officer, A DuSable grad who served with Mayor Harold Washington in the South Pacific during World War II, Personal Interview, Chicago, 11 November 1985.

Denoms, Carl, Former DuSable track star with Harold Washington, Personal Interview, Chicago, 29 January 1988.

Harewood, Richard A., Former Municipal Judge, Personal Interviews, Chicago, 2 January 1985, 10 February 1985.

Herrick, Mary, DuSable High School teacher, Personal Interviews, Chicago, Various Dates: 1979, 1980, 1981, 1982 and 1983.

Logan, Albert N., Former DuSable student, currently trustee of the University of Illinois Board, Personal Interview, Chicago, 30 January 1988.

Plique, Eddie, Boxing and Sports Promoter, Personal Interview, Chicago, 13 September 1983.

Washington, Harold, Mayor of Chicago, Personal Interviews, Chicago, 23 April 1983, 31 April 1983, 31 May 1983, 22 January 1984, 16 April 1984, 12 May 1984, 19 May 1984, 17 July 1984, 24 April 1985, 11 August 1985, 24 August 1985, 15 October 1986, 22 September 1986, 15 October 1986.

Washington, Roy Lee Jr., Brother of Mayor Washington, Personal Interviews, Chicago, 5 May 1984, 20 May 1984.

CHAPTER 3

BOOKS

Allen, Walter C. *Henderson: The Music of Fletcher Henderson and His Musicians.* Highland Park, NJ: Jazz Monograph, 1973.

Ewen, David. *American Popular Songs: From the Revolutionary War to Present.* New York: Random House, 1966.

Morris, Herman C. and Harry B. Hennison, editors. *World War II in Pictures, Volumes I and II,* New York: Journal of Living Publishing Corp., 1942.

Time-Life Books, editors. *This Fabulous Century, Vol. 5 1940-1950,* New York: Time-Life, 1969.

Travis, Dempsey J., *An Autobiography of Black Chicago,* Chicago: Urban Research Institute, Inc., 1981.

________, *An Autobiography of Black Politics,* Chicago: Urban Research Press, Inc., 1987.

Washington, Harold, editor. *The History of the 1887th Engineer Aviation Battalion.* October, 1945.

Winick, Charles and Paul M. Kinsie. *The Lively Commerce: Prosecution in the United States.* Chicago: Quadrangle Books, 1971.

INTERVIEWS

Davis, Theodore, Chicago Police Officer, A DuSable grad who served with Mayor Harold Washington in the South Pacific during World War II Personal Interview, Chicago, 11 November 1985.

Washington, Harold, Mayor of Chicago, Personal Interviews, Chicago, 23 April 1983, 31 April 1983, 31 May 1983, 22 January 1984, 16 April 1984, 12 May 1984, 19 May 1984, 17 July 1984, 24 April 1985, 11 August 1985, 24 August 1985, 15 October 1986, 22 September 1986, 15 October 1986.

NOTES

Notes from the Personal Diary of Dempsey J. Travis for the years between 1937 and 1985.

CHAPTER 4

BOOKS

Herrick, Mary J., *The Chicago School: A Social and Political History,* Beverly Hills, California: Sage Publication, 1971.

Levinsohn, Florence H. *Harold Washington: A Political Biography.* Chicago Review Press: 1983.

Travis, Dempsey J., *An Autobiography of Black Chicago,* Chicago: Urban Research Institute, Inc., 1981.

________, *An Autobiography of Black Politics,* Chicago: Urban Research Press, Inc., 1987.

NEWSPAPERS

"Kennelly Declares There Will Be No Housing Stalling," *Chicago Defender,* 5 April 1947.

"West Side Tenants Owners Triples Rent On Flat Without Water or Heat," *Chicago Defender,* 5 April 1947.

"Experts Clash on Housing And City Council Hearings," *Chicago Defender,* 12 April 1947.

"Martin H. Kennelly Takes Oath of Office," *Chicago Defender,* 19 April 1947.

"Racial Restrictive Covenant Boundaries in Chicago," *Chicago Defender,* 2 August 1947.

"Mayor Demands Cops Make Arrest In Troubled Areas," *Chicago Defender,* 16 August 1947.

"Wendell E. Green First Choice Bar Association," *Chicago Defender,* 18 November 1947.

ROOSEVELT TORCH ARTICLES

"Ten Roosevelt Delegates Back From National Student Association Regional Meeting at University of Illinois," February 23, 1948.

"Democracy is Topic of New Contest Sponsored by Drew Pearson," March 29, 1948.

"Savoy's Big Names Sport Kenton Jazz," March 29, 1948.

"New Roosevelt College Delegation Elects Frank London Brown Leader of Delegation," May 3, 1948.

"Fall Registration Figures Top 5,800," September 27, 1948.

"Campaign Fight Begins: 40 Seats Hot Election Issue," October 4, 1948.

"St. Clair Drake Presents Fall Lecture Series," October 4, 1948.

"Students Don Wallace Pins," October 8, 1948.

"Harold Washington Will Conduct Membership Drive for Wallace," October 8, 1948.

"The Council Seat No Bed of Roses," October 8, 1948.

"Battle of Ballots to Last 3 Days," October 11, 1948.

"Harold Washington Elected President," October 22, 1948.

"Judge Samuel Hellar Tells the Washington Group to 'Get Hot'," November 1, 1948.

"Laskie Plans Return to Roosevelt," November 22, 1948.

"Committee Reveals Full Social Program," November 22, 1948.

"Harold Washington Clarifies Council Issue," December 6, 1948.

"City Council Acts on Discrimination," December 6, 1948.

"Hail to the Student Council," January 17, 1949.

"Delegates Attend National Student Association Convention," February 14, 1949.

"Aims of College Given New Students," February 14, 1949.

"Present Ideals of Roosevelt College as Student Lives Them," February 21, 1949.

"President James Sparling Sends Settlement Plan to Roosevelt College's Student Council," February 28, 1949.

"Birth of a Nation Showing Stirs Comments; Pro, Con," February 28, 1949.

"Council Votes Over Birth of a Nation," March 7, 1949.

"State Senator Broyle's Probe Boils Down," March 14, 1949.

"Leys Views Probe, Bill-To Issues," March 14, 1949.

"Student Council Rejects Probe, Adopts Poor Proposal, Commerce Bloc Walks Out," March 14, 1949.

"CORE, City Community Blast Local Discrimination," March 14, 1949.

"Annes and Students Differ on Views," March 21, 1949.

"Laskie Here Tonight: Man Plans Lecture," April 4, 1949.

"G.J. Annes Promises No Bias," April 4, 1949.

"Student Council Gives Job Office Confidence Vote: In spite of Charges By Young Progressives," April 23, 1949.

"Council Tables Torch Revision," April 25, 1949.

"Louis Roundtree New Editor," April 25, 1949.

"Pontius Watson Elected Post in Scholars Group," May 9, 1949.

"Student Council Stiffed by Faculty," May 23, 1949.

"Split Plus Will Jones Equals Victory: Jones Elected on Second Ballot," October 31, 1949.

"Cut in Student Activity Fund Hit by Critics," October 31, 1949.

"State Representative Charles J. Jenkins Invited to Speak to the January 1950 Graduation Class," December 12, 1949.

"Annes Sets Up 6-Point Plan to Combat Discrimination," October 1, 1951.

INTERVIEWS

Despres, Marion, teacher at Roosevelt University, Personal Interview, Chicago, 30 May 1984.

Goldsborough, Evelyn, Former student at Roosevelt University, Personal Interview, Chicago, 12 March 1988.

Johnson, Bennett, Executive of Path Press and Political Activist, Personal Interview, 20 March 1985, 13 August 1986, 24 September 1986, 25 March 1988.

Kennedy, Winston, Personal Interview, Chicago, 16 February 1988.

Logan, Albert N., Former DuSable student, currently trustee of the University of Illinois Board, Personal Interview, Chicago, 30 January 1988.

Partee, Cecil, Chicago City Treasurer and former President of Illinois Senate, Personal Interview, Chicago, 28 December 1984, 14 December 1985, 21 December 1985.

Pincham, R. Eugene, Appellate Court Judge in the First District of Illinois, Personal Interview, Chicago, 31 July 1986, 5 August 1986.

Roundtree, Louis, Personal Interview, Chicago, 15 February 1988.

Savage, Gus, Member of U.S. House of Representatives, Personal Interview, Chicago, 22 April 1984, 13 December 1985, 14 January 1986, 2 April 1988.

Washington Jr., Roy Lee, Brother of Mayor Washington, Personal Interview, Chicago, 5 May 1984, 20 May 1984.

CHAPTER 5

BOOKS

Davis, Corneal A., *Corneal A. Davis Memoirs, Volume I & II,* Springfield, Illinois: Oral History Office, Legislative Studies Center of Sangamon State University, 1984.

Partee, Cecil, *Cecil A. Partee's Memoirs, Volume I & II,* Sprinfield, Illinois: Oral History Office, Legislative Studies Center of Sangamon State University, 1982.

Travis, Dempsey J., *An Autobiography of Black Politics,* Chicago: Urban Research Press, Inc., 1987.

NEWSPAPERS

"Alderman Holman Helps People and They Help Him," *Chicago Defender,* 21 February 1943.

"The Political Pot," *Chicago Defender,* 6 March 1954.

"Congressman Dawson: Chicago Democrat With Clout," *Chicago Sunday Tribune,* 6 February 1955.

"Mayor at Rites For General Dawson," *Chicago Defender,* 14 May 1955.

"Cite Salk, Mrs. Roosevelt, Warn," *Chicago Defender,* 4 June 1955.

"Representative Dawson Reports Total That Rivals National Debt," *Chicago Daily News,* 30 December 1957.

"Bentley Backers See Landslide," *Chicago Defender,* 29 March 1958.

"Near Split In Democratic Unit," *Chicago Defender,* 20 June 1960.

"Two Aldermen Clash In City Zoning Hearing," *Chicago Tribune,* 1 February 1963.

"B.G.A. Endorses Two Democrats, Eight Republicans," *Chicago Sunday Tribune,* 3 February 1963.

"Leon Despres in Fifth Ward," *Chicago Tribune,* 11 February 1963.

"Chew Backers Find Seventeenth Ward Alderman Unknown," *Chicago Defender,* 14 February 1963.

"Tribunes Choices For City Council," *Chicago Tribune,* 17 February 1963.

"Chew Charges Race Bating By Seventeenth Alderman," *Chicago Defender,* 20 February 1963.

"Seventeenth Ward Incumbent Caught In Squeeze of Racial Change," *Chicago Sun-Times,* 25 March 1963.

"Chew Attributes His Victory To Children," *Chicago Daily News,* 3 April 1963.

"Seventeenth Ward Revolt Knocks Out Slight," *Chicago Daily News,* 3 April 1963.

"Aldermanic Run-Off Race Totals," *Chicago Daily News,* 3 April 1963.

"Two New Aldermen Shun Block Vote In BLOC," *Chicago Daily News,* 3 April 1963.

"Campbell Leans As Top Negro Leader In City Council," *Chicago Daily News,* 3 April 1963.

"There Is A Scrapper In City Council Now," *Chicago Daily News*, 5 April 1963.

"Mayor Daley Congratulates Chew On The Election Victories," *Chicago Defender*, 6 April 1963.

"Chew, Political Dark Horse, Upsets Slight in Seventeenth Ward," *Chicago Defender*, 6 April 1963.

"Chicago Negro Alderman Stung By Criticism of Rights' Failures, Blasts Illinois NAACP Official," *Associated Negro Press*, 10 July 1963.

"Robichaux Wins Nod In 21st; Charges Fly," *Chicago Defender*, 14 November 1963.

"Political Explosion Rocks 21st Ward In Committeemanship Fight," *Chicago Defender*, 18 November 1963.

"Shannon Out In The Seventeenth Ward," *Chicago Defender*, 11 February 1964.

UNPUBLISHED MATERIAL

Hirsch, Arnold R., *Politics and The Interracial Struggle for Living Space in Chicago After World War II*, New Orleans: Department of History in School of Urban and Regional Studies, University of New Orleans, 1984.

INTERVIEWS

Black Jr., Timuel, Professor at Harold Washington (Loop) College, Personal Interview, Chicago, 24 November 1984, 28 April 1984.

Caldwell, Lewis A. H., Former State Representative, Personal Interviews, Chicago, 23 June 1984, 22 April 1985, 16 November 1985.

Campbell, Kenneth, Alderman, Personal Interview, Chicago, 23 May 1987.

Chew Jr., Charles, State Senator, Personal Interview, Chicago, 10 October 1984.

Davis, Corneal, Former State Representative and current Commissioner of Voter Registration, City of Chicago, Personal Interview, Chicago, 30 July 1984, 19 August 1984, 14 November 1984, 4 December 1984, 5 January 1985, 16 November 1985.

Dawson, Ira, Attorney and nephew of Congressman William L. Dawson, Personal Interviews, Chicago, 12 January 1985, 25 November 1985.

Despres, Leon, Former alderman and current Parliamentary to the Mayor, Personal Interviews, Chicago, 30 May 1984, 28 July 1984, 13 December 1985.

Eskridge, Chauncey, Attorney, Personal Interview, Chicago, 7 January 1985.

Ferguson, Margaret, Personal Interview, Chicago, 17 February 1988.

Frost, Wilson, Alderman, Personal Interviews, Chicago, 21 September 1985, 7 January 1986.

Gilbert, Herman, Executive Vice President and Editorial Director of Path Press, Personal Interviews, Chicago, 24 November 1984, 28 April 1984, 19 December 1985, 19 March 1988.

Harris, William F., Commissioner of Building and Zoning in Cook County, Personal Interviews, Chicago, 13 August 1984, 10 November 1985, 5 December 1985, 15 December 1985.

Johnson, Bennett, President of Path Press, Personal Interview, Chicago, 20 March 1985, 13 August 1986, 24 September 1986, 25 March 1988.

Korshak, Marshall, State Senator, Personal Interview, Chicago, 12 December 1985.

Metcalfe, Faye, Widow of Congressman Ralph Metcalfe, Personal Interview, 1 August 1984.

Montgomery, James D., Chicago Corporation Counsel, Personal Interview, Chicago, 28 December 1985.

Neal, Earl L., Personal Interview, Chicago, 19 January 1985.

Newhouse, Richard, State Senator, Personal Interviews, Chicago, 23 October 1984, 20 December 1985.

Partee, Cecil, Chicago City Treasurer and former President of Illinois Senate, Personal Interviews, Chicago, 28 December 1984, 14 December 1985, 21 December 1985.

Patch, Sam, Personal Interview, Chicago, 18 June 1984.

Rayner Jr., A. A. (Sammy), Former alderman, Personal Interview, Chicago, 23 October 1984, 29 January 1988.

Savage, Augustus A., Congressman, Personal Interview, Chicago, 22 April 1984, 13 December 1985, 2 April 1988.

Stroger Jr., John H., Cook County Commissioner, Eighth Ward Committeeman, Personal Interview, Chicago, 20 June 1984.

Washington, Harold, Mayor of the City of Chicago, Personal Interviews, Chicago, 23 April 1983, 31 April 1983, 31 May 1983, 16 April 1984, 22 January 1984, 12 May 1984, 19 May 1984, 17 July 1984, 24 April 1985, 11 August 1985, 24 August 1985, 22 September 1986, 15 October 1986.

CHAPTER 6

BOOKS

Ebony, eds., *The Negro Handbook,* Chicago: Johnson Publishing Co. Inc., 1966.

Holli, Melvin G. and Paul M. Green, eds., *The Making of a Mayor:* Chicago, 1983, Grand Rapids, Mich.: William B. Eerdmans Publishing Co., 1984.

Ebony, eds., *The Ebony Handbook,* Chicago: Johnson Publishing Co. Inc., 1974.

Howell, Paul, ed., *The 1965–66 Illinois Blue Book,* Springfield, Ill: State of Illinois, 1966.

Illinois General Assembly Oral History Program, *Cecil A. Partee Memoir Vol. 1,* Springfield, Ill: State of Illinois, 1982.

Levinsohn, Florence H., *Harold Washington: A Political Biography,* Chicago: Chicago Review Press, 1983.

McClory, Robert, *The Man Who Beat Clout City,* Chicago: Swallow Press, Inc., 1977.

O'Connor, Len. *Clout: Mayor Daley and His City,* Chicago: Contemporary Books, Inc., 1975.

Rakove, Milton L., *We Don't Want Nobody Sent,* Bloomington, Ind: Indiana University Press, 1979.

Royko, Mike, *Boss: Richard J. Daley of Chicago,* New York: E.P. Dutton & Company, Inc., 1971.

Travis, Dempsey J., *An Autobiography of Black Chicago,* Chicago: Urban Research Institute, 1981.

________, *An Autobiography of Black Politics,* Chicago: Urban Research Press, 1987.

NEWSPAPERS

"King's Birthday to be Marked in Schools," *Chicago Defender,* 5 January 1970.

"Rep. Harold Washington Tells Saga of King's Birthday Bill," *Chicago Defender,* 25 July 1973.

"Frost Ducks Mayor Issue," *Chicago Defender,* 15 May 1974.

"Metcalfe Won't be a Candidate for Mayor in '75," *Chicago Sun-Times,* 4 December 1974.

"Metcalfe Sees a Black Well Spring of Discontent," *Chicago Sun-Times,* 7 December 1974.

"Metcalfe About to Jump into Race," *Chicago Tribune,* 10 December 1974.

"How Richard Newhouse Became Mayor," *Chicago Defender,* 4 January 1975.

"Newhouse Nickels Help Keep Campaign Alive," *Chicago Defender,* 13 January 1975.

"McNeil Needs 50,000 Names," *Chicago Defender,* 14 January 1975.

"Charge Mayoral Sellout: Row Splits Top Leaders," *Chicago Defender,* 14 January 1975.

"72 Dems Fight, Jesse, Singer Win Suit," *Chicago Defender,* 16 January 1975.

"More Votes in Line Despite Defections," *Chicago Defender,* 20 January 1975.

"Newhouse Gains As McNeil Slips," *Chicago Defender,* 22 January 1975.

"Metcalfe Severs Daley Ties, Backs Singer for Mayor," *Chicago Tribune,* 26 January 1975.

"Newhouse: Calls Foe Faithless," *Chicago Defender,* 27 January 1975.

"18th Ward Hopeful Backs Newhouse," *Chicago Defender,* 28 January 1975.

"McNeil Backs Newhouse," *Chicago Defender,* 29 January 1975.

INTERVIEWS

Hayes, Charles, Member of U.S. House of Representatives, Personal Interview, Chicago, 16 April 1984, 5 June 1984, 22 February 1988.

Johnson, Bennett, Publisher and Civil Rights Activist, Personal Interview, Chicago, 20 March 1985, 13 August 1986, 24 September 1986, 25 March 1988.

Metcalfe, Fay, Widow of Congressman Ralph Metcalfe, Personal Interview, 1 August 1984.

Washington, Harold, Mayor of Chicago, Personal Interview, Chicago, 23 April 1983, 31 April 1983, 31 May 1983, 22 January 1984, 16 April 1984, 12 May 1984, 19 May 1984, 17 July 1984, 24 April 1985, 11 August 1985, 24 August 1985, 7 July 1986, 22 September 1986, 15 October 1986.

LETTERS

Letters from Charles Hayes, chairman of the Committee for a Black Mayor, to the following persons, dated September 6, 1974. To wit: Harold Washington, Ralph Metcalfe, A.A. Rayner, Richard H. Newhouse, Roland Burris, Joseph Bertrand, Cecil Partee, Wilson Frost, Thomas N. Todd, Edward Allen and E. Duke McNeil.

Letters from Charles Hayes, chairman of the Committee for a Black Mayor, to the following persons, dated February 5, 1975. To wit: Dr. Perry English, Daryl Grisham, George Johnson, Dr. T.R.M. Howard, Harvey Collins, John H. Johnson, Elijah Muhammad, Earl Dickerson, and Dempsey J. Travis.

DOCUMENTS AND MEMORANDA

Election schedule for mayoral and aldermanic races.

Suggested names to be called for mayoral interviews.

CHAPTER 7

BOOKS

Bush, Rod. ed. *The Black Vote: Politics and Power in Four American Cities,* San Francisco: Synthesis Publications, 1984.

Ebony, eds., *The Ebony Handbook,* Chicago: Johnson Publishing Co. Inc., 1974.

Ebony, eds., *The Negro Handbook,* Chicago: Johnson Publishing Co. Inc., 1974.

Holli, Melvin G. and Paul M. Green, eds., *The Making of a Mayor: Chicago, 1983,* Grand Rapids, Michigan: William B. Eerdmans Publishing Co., 1984.

Editor Paul Howell, *The 1965–66 Illinois Blue Book,* Springfield, Ill: State of Illinois, 1966.

Elliott, Jeffrey M., *Black Voices in American Politics,* New York: Harcourt Brace Jovanich, Publishers, 1986.

Fish, John Hall, *Black Power-White Control: The Struggle of the Woodlawn Organization in Chicago,* Princeton, N.J.: Princeton University Press, 1973.

Illinois General Assembly Oral History Program, *Cecil A. Partee Memoir Vol. 1,* Springfield, Ill: State of Illinois, 1982.

Kilian, Michael, Connie Fletcher and F. Richard Ciccone, *Who Runs Chicago?,* New York: St. Martin's Press, 1979.

Landers, James H. and Richard M. Quinn, *Jesse Jackson and the Politics of Race,* Ottawa, Ill.: Jameson Books, 1985.

Levinsohn, Florence H., *Harold Washington: A Political Biography,* Chicago: Chicago Review Press, 1983.

McClory, Robert, *The Man Who Beat Clout City,* Chicago: Swallow Press, Inc., 1977.

O'Connor, Len, *Clout: Mayor Daley and His City,* Chicago: Contemporary Books, Inc., 1975.

Powell, Paul, ed. Secretary of State, *The 1965–66 Illinois Blue Book,* Springfield, Ill. Printed by Authority of the State of Illinois.

Rakove, Milton L., *We Don't Want Nobody Sent,* Bloomington, Ind: Indiana University Press, 1979.

Royko, Mike, *Boss: Richard J. Daley of Chicago,* New York: E.P. Dutton & Company, Inc., 1971.

Travis, Dempsey J., *An Autobiography of Black Chicago,* Chicago: Urban Research Institute, 1981.

________, *An Autobiography of Black Politics,* Chicago: Urban Research Press, 1987.

NEWSPAPERS

"Newhouse Vote Dispute Has Been Damaged in Court," *Chicago Defender,* 4 February 1975.

"Westside Clerics Again Back Daley," *Chicago Defender,* 11 February 1975.
"Jesse Says Newhouse is Our Inspiration," *Chicago Defender,* 24 February 1975.
"See Record Black Vote," *Chicago Defender,* 24 February 1975.
"Mayor Wins: Three Wards Upset," *Chicago Defender,* 26 February 1975.
"Moral Victory for Newhouse," *Chicago Defender,* 27 February 1975.
"Newhouse Charges: 'Remap Hurts Blacks'," *Chicago Defender,* 19 April 1975.
"Newhouse Map Adds Black Rep," *Chicago Defender,* 17 May 1975.
"Metcalfe-France Duel Takes Shape," *Chicago Tribune,* 7 January 1976.
"Metcalfe Allies Become Turncoats," *Chicago Tribune,* 16 January 1976.
"Campaign Brings France out of Shell," *Chicago Tribune,* 18 January 1976.
"Black Caucus Here to Stump for Metcalfe," *Chicago Defender,* 14 February 1976.
"Third Ward Vote Tally Haunts Daley 'Machine'," *Chicago Defender,* 4 March 1976.
"Political Revolt Stirs in 24th," *Chicago Defender,* 13 March 1976.
"Stand for Metcalfe, He Stands for You and Needs Your Vote," *Chicago Defender,* 13 March 1976.
"Metcalfe Fighting Down to Election Wire," *Chicago Defender,* 13 March 1976.
"Metcalfe Winner by a Landslide," *Chicago Sun-Times,* 17 March 1976.
"Metcalfe: A Dream Win; France Loses in a Landslide," *Chicago Daily News,* 17 March 1976.
"A Message in Metcalfe's Victory," *Chicago Defender,* 20 March 1976.
"Metcalfe Victory—Is it Black Omen for Daley?," *Chicago Tribune,* 21 March 1976.
"Metcalfe Rips Daley After Win in Ward," *Chicago Tribune,* 28 March 1976.
"Getting Metcalfe's Identity Straight," *Chicago Tribune,* 9 July 1976.
"Illinois First in New Equal Hiring Law," *Chicago Defender,* 2 October 1976.
"Candidates Speak Out on Ethics," *Chicago Defender,* 3 October 1976.
"Okay $14 Million for Provident," *Chicago Defender,* 7 December 1976.
"Pick Mayor Today: Will Frost Run?," *Chicago Tribune,* 20 December 1976.
"Battle to Succeed Daley," *Chicago Tribune,* 24 December 1976.
"Blacks Gain Under 'Big Bill'," *Chicago Defender,* 25 December 1976.
"Police Guard Frost, Quinlan Homes," *Chicago Defender,* 27 December 1976.
"Bilandic Will be Interim Mayor," *Chicago Tribune,* 27 December 1976.
"Frost Declares He's Still In Race for Acting Mayor," *Chicago Sun-Times,* 28 December 1976.
"Frost: 'No Deals'; Seek Court Action," *Chicago Defender,* 28 December 1976.
"Frost Now Says He's Back in Mayor Race," *Chicago Sun-Times,* 28 December 1976.
"The Opportunity That Slipped Away," *Chicago Tribune,* 29 December 1976.
"Realism Carries the Day," *Chicago Daily News Editorial,* 29 December 1976.
"Wilson Frost Winner in City Hall (Non-Fight)," *Chicago Independent Bulletin,* 30 December 1976.
"Black Mayor Called on by Blacks," *Citizen Newspaper,* 31 December 1976.
"Did McMill Move to Support France?," *Chicago Defender,* 31 December 1976.
"The Culprit is Racism," *Citizen Newspaper,* 31 December 1976.
"Fifty to Recommend Black Candidate," *Chicago Defender,* 5 January 1977.
"Leaders Push for Mayor," *Chicago Defender,* 6 January 1977.
"Group Will Insist on a Black Mayor," *Chicago Tribune,* 7 January 1977.
"Who Should Select a Black Mayor," *Chicago Tribune,* 9 January 1977.
"Renault Explains Mayoral Moves," *Chicago Defender,* 10 January 1977.
"Mayoral Search Group Multiplies," *Chicago Defender,* 12 January 1977.
"Gaines Bids for Black GOP Ties in Mayor Hunt," *Chicago Defender,* 13 January 1977.
"Newhouse is Willing," *Chicago Defender,* 18 January 1977.
"Black Candidate Found—But," *Chicago Defender,* 18 January 1977.
"Has Mayoral Backing, Senator Washington Says," *Chicago Daily News,* 19 January 1977.
"Blacks Favor Mayor Bid by Washington," *Chicago Tribune,* 20 January 1977.
"Washington Quits Race After a Metcalfe

'No'," *Chicago Sun-Times,* 22 January 1977.
"Hint Washington 'Reconsidering'," *Chicago Tribune,* 24 January 1977.
"Representative Washington Bows Out, New Candidate 'Emerges'," *Chicago Defender,* 24 January 1977.
"What to Talk About During a Long Ride," *Chicago Tribune,* 26 January 1977.
"Newhouse Wins Defender Poll," *Chicago Defender,* 31 January 1977.
"Blacks Square Off in Mayoral Contest," *Chicago Defender,* 31 January 1977.
"Why Black Leaders Snub Newhouse," *Chicago Defender,* 1 February 1977.
"Washington Shafted, Savage Says," *Chicago Defender,* 8 February 1977.
"Tucker Denies Misuse of Merit Funds," *Chicago Defender,* 8 February 1977.
"Washington Changes Mind, Will Run in Mayoral Primary," *Chicago Tribune,* 19 February 1977.
"Senator Washington Enters Mayoral Race After 'Draft'," *Chicago Tribune,* 20 February 1977.
"Senator in Switch on Mayoralty," *Chicago Defender,* 21 February 1977.
"Washington Vows Candid Campaign," *Chicago Defender,* 22 February 1977.
"Washington's Mini-Machine in the Works," *Chicago Defender,* 7 March 1977.

MAGAZINES

"Congressman Ralph Metcalfe: A No Vote for the Daley Machine," *Chicago Tribune Magazine,* November 28, 1976.

INTERVIEWS

Depres, Leon, Former Alderman and Current Parliamentary to the Mayor, Personal Interview, Chicago, 30 May 1984, 28 July 1984, 13 December 1985, 15 July 1986.
Frost, Wilson, Alderman, Personal Interview, Chicago, 21 September 1985, 7 January 1986.
Hayes, Charles, Member of U.S. House of Representatives, Personal Interview, Chicago, 16 April 1984, 5 June 1984, 22 February 1988.
Johnson, Bennett, Publisher and Civil Rights Activist, Personal Interview, Chicago, 20 March 1985, 13 August 1986, 24 September 1986, 25 March 1988.
Metcalfe, Fay, Widow of Congressman Ralph Metcalfe, Personal Interview, 1 August 1984.
Ordower, Sid, Civil rights activist, Personal Interview, Chicago, 24 April 1984.
Neal, Earl L., Attorney, Personal Interview, Chicago, 19 January 1985.
Savage, Gus, Member of U.S. House of Representatives, Personal Interview, Chicago, 22 April 1984, 13 December 1985, 14 January 1986, 2 April 1988.
Washington, Harold, Mayor of Chicago, Personal Interview, Chicago, 23 April 1983, 31 April 1983, 31 May 1983, 22 January 1984, 16 April 1984, 12 May 1984, 19 May 1984, 17 July 1984, 24 April 1985, 11 August 1985, 24 August 1985, 7 July 1986, 22 September 1986, 15 October 1986.

LETTERS AND MAILGRAMS

Letters from Charles Hayes, chairman of the Committee for a Black Mayor, to the following persons, dated September 6, 1974. To wit: Harold Washington, Ralph Metcalfe, A.A. Rayner, Richard H. Newhouse, Roland Burris, Joseph Bertrand, Cecil Partee, Wilson Frost, Thomas N. Todd, Edward Allen and E. Duke McNeil.
Letters from Charles Hayes, chairman of the Committee for a Black Mayor, to the following persons, dated February 5, 1975. To wit: Dr. Perry English, Daryl Grisham, George Johnson, Dr. T.R.M. Howard, Harvey Collins, John H. Johnson, Elijah Muhammad, Earl Dickerson, and Dempsey J. Travis.
Mailgram from Charles Hayes and Al Boutte to Dempsey J. Travis dated January 11, 1977.
Letter from Charles Hayes to members of the Committee for a Black Mayor, dated January 11, 1977.
Mailgram from Alvin J. Boutte and Charles Hayes to Dempsey J. Travis, dated January 19, 1977.
Letter from Charles Hayes to Committee for a Black Mayor, dated February 25, 1977.

DOCUMENTS AND MEMORANDA

Statement outlining the criteria for a Black mayor delivered before the Committee for a Black Mayor by State Representative Washington, dated September 14, 1974.

Pamphlet prepared by the Chicago League of Negro Voters, dated June 1962.

Sample ballot for a Black mayor prepared by Dr. T.R.M. Howard, dated August 14, 1974.

Criteria for a Black Mayor prepared by the Committee for a Black Mayor, undated.

Press statement by Charles A. Hayes, delivered on Tuesday, July 9, 1974.

List of leaders who attended the first Black mayor's meeting in June 1974.

Memorandum from Edward C. "Bill" Berry to Congressman Ralph H. Metcalfe, dated January 8, 1975.

Ten-page questionnaire for mayoral candidates for a Black mayor prepared by the Committee for a Black Mayor.

Position paper, prepared by the Committee for a Black Mayor, undated.

Working paper, Committee for a Black Mayor, undated, prepared by Committee on Agenda and Platform: chairman-Thomas Todd, ex-officio-Charles Hayes, Larry Bullock, Tim Black, Lenora Cartwright, William Cousins, James Montgomery, Bill Smith.

Election schedule for mayoral and aldermanic races.

CHAPTER 8

BOOKS

Bush, Rod, ed., *The New Black Vote: Politics and Power in Four American Cities,* San Francisco: Synthesis Publications, 1984.

Ebony, eds., *The Ebony Handbook,* Chicago: Johnson Publishing Co. Inc., 1974.

Ebony, eds., *The Negro Handbook,* Chicago: Johnson Publishing Co. Inc., 1974.

Green, Paul M. and Melvin G. Holli, eds., *The Mayors: The Chicago Political Tradition,* Carbondale and Edwardsville, Ill.: Southern Illinois University Press, 1987.

Holli, Melvin G. and Paul M. Green, eds., *The Making of a Mayor: Chicago, 1983,* Grand Rapids, Michigan: William B. Eerdmans Publishing Co., 1984.

Editor Paul Howell, *The 1965–66 Illinois Blue Book,* Springfield, Ill: State of Illinois, 1966.

Illinois Blue Book, 1975-1976, ed. by Michael J. Howlett, Secretary of State.

Illinois Blue Book, 1977-1978, ed. by Alan J. Dixon, Secretary of State.

Illinois Blue Book, 1979-1980, ed. by Alan J. Dixon, Secretary of State.

Illinois Blue Book, 1981-1982, ed. by Jim Edgar, Secretary of State.

Illinois General Assembly Oral History Program, *Cecil A. Partee Memoir Vol. 1,* Springfield, Ill: State of Illinois, 1982.

Levinsohn, Florence H., *Harold Washington: A Political Biography,* Chicago: Chicago Review Press, 1983.

McClory, Robert, *The Man Who Beat Clout City,* Chicago: Swallow Press, Inc., 1977.

O'Connor, Len. *Clout: Mayor Daley and His City,* Chicago: Contemporary Books, Inc., 1975.

Rakove, Milton L., *We Don't Want Nobody Sent,* Bloomington, Ind: Indiana University Press, 1979.

Royko, Mike, *Boss: Richard J. Daley of Chicago,* New York: E.P. Dutton & Company, Inc., 1971.

Travis, Dempsey J., *An Autobiography of Black Chicago,* Chicago: Urban Research Institute, 1981.

________, *An Autobiography of Black Politics,* Chicago: Urban Research Press, 1987.

NEWSPAPERS

"Pick Mayor Today: Will Frost Run?," *Chicago Tribune,* 20 December 1976.

"Battle to Succeed Daley," *Chicago Tribune,* 24 December 1976.

"Police Guard Frost, Quinlan Homes," *Chicago Defender,* 27 December 1976.

"Bilandic Will be Interim Mayor," *Chicago Tribune,* 27 December 1976.

"Frost Declares He's Still In Race for Acting Mayor," *Chicago Sun-Times,* 28 December 1976.

"Frost: 'No Deals'; Seek Court Action," *Chicago Defender,* 28 December 1976.

"Frost Now Says He's Back in Mayor Race," *Chicago Sun-Times,* 28 December 1976.

"The Opportunity That Slipped Away," *Chicago Tribune,* 29 December 1976.

"Realism Carries the Day," *Chicago Daily News Editorial,* 29 December 1976.

"Wilson Frost Winner in City Hall (Non-Fight)," *Chicago Independent Bulletin,* 30 December 1976.

"Black Mayor Called on by Blacks," *Citizen Newspaper,* 31 December 1976.

"The Culprit is Racism," *Citizen Newspaper,* 31 December 1976.

"Fifty to Recommend Black Candidate," *Chicago Defender,* 5 January 1977.

"Leaders Push for Mayor," *Chicago Defender,* 6 January 1977.

"Group Will Insist on a Black Mayor," *Chicago Tribune,* 7 January 1977.

"Who Should Select a Black Mayor," *Chicago Tribune,* 9 January 1977.

"Renault Explains Mayoral Moves," *Chicago Defender,* 10 January 1977.

"Mayoral Search Group Multiply," *Chicago Defender,* 12 January 1977.

"Gaines Bids for Black GOP Ties in Mayor Hunt," *Chicago Defender,* 13 January 1977.

"Hynes Offers Political Plums in Bid to Win Senate Seat," *Chicago Tribune,* 17 January 1977.

"Newhouse is Willing," *Chicago Defender,* 18 January 1977.

"Black Candidate Found But," *Chicago Defender,* 18 January 1977.

"Hynes Tells Dem Power Picks and Moves to Sway Votes," *Chicago Tribune,* 18 January 1977.

"Have Mayoral Backing, Senator Washington Says," *Chicago Daily News,* 19 January 1977.

"Dissident Dems Reject Hynes Offer," *Chicago Tribune,* 19 January 1977.

"Blacks Favor Mayor Bid by Washington," *Chicago Tribune,* 20 January 1977.

"Washington Quits Race After a Metcalfe 'No'," *Chicago Sun-Times,* 22 January 1977.

"Hint Washington 'Reconsidering'," *Chicago Tribune,* 24 January 1977.

"Representative Washington Bows Out, New Candidate 'Emerges'," *Chicago Defender,* 24 January 1977.

"What to Talk About During a Long Ride," *Chicago Tribune,* 26 January 1977.

"End Senate Deadlock," *Chicago Tribune,* 28 January 1977.

"Newhouse Wins Defender Poll," *Chicago Defender,* 31 January 1977.

"Blacks Square Off in Mayoral Contest," *Chicago Defender,* 31 January 1977.

"Why Black Leaders Snub Newhouse," *Chicago Defender,* 1 February 1977.

"Washington Shafted, Savage Says," *Chicago Defender,* 8 February 1977.

"Tucker Denies Misuse of Merit Funds," *Chicago Defender,* 8 February 1977.

"Hynes Finally Wins In Senate," *Chicago Tribune,* 17 February 1977.

"Washington Changes Mind, Will Run in Mayoral Primary," *Chicago Tribune,* 19 February 1977.

"Senator Washington Enters Mayoral Race After 'Draft'," *Chicago Tribune,* 20 February 1977.

"Senator in Switch on Mayoralty," *Chicago Defender,* 21 February 1977.

"Washington Vows Candid Campaign," *Chicago Defender,* 22 February 1977.

"Washington's Mini-Machine in the Works," *Chicago Defender,* 7 March 1977.

"Washington Train Picking Up Steam," *Chicago Tribune,* 9 March 1977.

"Bacon, Boutte to Back Washington," *Chicago Defender,* 21 March 1977.

"Cardiss, Rhodes in Row Over Mayor," *Chicago Defender,* 22 March 1977.

"IRS Says Washington File is Ready," *Chicago Defender,* 29 March 1977.

"Washington Reveals Plan, Blasts Media," *Chicago Defender,* 5 April 1977.

"Washington See Win by His Poll," *Chicago Defender,* 19 April 1977.

"Washington Threatens Vote Suit, It's Bilandic by a Landslide," *Chicago Defender,* 20 April 1977.

"Washington Vows to Challenge Vote," *Chicago Defender,* 29 April 1977.

"Bilandic Strolls to Mayoral Victory," *Chicago Defender,* 29 April 1977.

"Harold Washington: 'I'll Be a Candidate for Mayor in '79," *Chicago Defender,* 2 May 1977.

"Washington Takes Bilandic's Spot, Snubs Both Candidates," *Chicago Sun-Times,* 1 June 1977.

"Thompson, Scott Voice Block Support," *Chicago Sun-Times,* 3 June 1977.

"I'd Fire Rochford, Hire Civilian, Block Says," *Chicago Sun-Times,* 4 June 1977.

"Mayoral Campaign Fading Away," *Chicago Sun-Times,* 5 June 1977.

"Bilandic to Bat for Elderly, Children at Mayor's Parlay," *Chicago Sun-Times,* 7 June 1977.

"Bilandic, Block Vie at Polls Today," *Chicago Sun-Times,* 7 June 1977.

"Hoopla Only for the Winner," *Chicago Sun-Times,* 8 June 1977.

"Bilandic Beats Block in a Breeze," *Chicago Sun-Times,* 8 June 1977.

"Bilandic Ran Four Races to Become Elected Mayor," *Chicago Sun-Times,* 9 June 1977.

"Bilandic Stakes Out a New Hideaway," *Chicago Sun-Times,* 9 June 1977.

"Singer In Mayoral Race? Some Early Signs Surface," *Chicago Sun-Times,* 9 June 1977.

"The New Meaning of Political Asylum," *Chicago Tribune,* 27 November 1977.

"Newhouse Plans Takeover of Independents," *Chicago Defender,* 10 January 1978.

"Metcalfe Dead," *Chicago Defender,* 11 October 1978.

"Dems Name Alderman Stewart to Replace Metcalfe on Ballot," *Chicago Tribune,* 17 October 1978.

"Stewart Will Replace Metcalfe on November Ballot," *Chicago Sun-Times,* 17 October 1978.

"Ralph Metcalfe's Replacement," Editorial *Chicago Tribune,* 18 October 1978.

"Washington, Ewell Press Rep. Taylor in the 26th District, *Chicago Defender,* 12 January 1981.

"Accuses Washington of Selling Out," *Chicago Defender,* 26 January 1981.

"Court Orders Thompson to Hold New Election," *Chicago Defender,* 10 February 1981.

"Washington Denies Plot," *Chicago Defender,* 27 January 1981.

MAGAZINES

"Congressman Ralph Metcalfe: A No Vote for the Daley Machine," *Chicago Tribune Magazine,* November 28, 1976.

"The Road to City Hall," *Chicago Tribune Magazine,* November 16, 1986.

INTERVIEWS

Frost, Wilson, Alderman, Personal Interview, Chicago, 21 September 1985, 7 January 1986.

Gilbert, Herman, Executive Vice President and Editorial Director of Path Press, Personal Interviews, Chicago, 24 November 1984, 28 April 1984, 19 December 1985, 19 March 1988.

Hayes, Charles, Member of U.S. House of Representatives, Personal Interview, Chicago, 16 April 1984, 5 June 1984, 22 February 1988.

Johnson, Bennett, Publisher and Civil Rights Activist, Personal Interview, Chicago, 20 March 1985, 13 August 1986, 24 September 1986, 25 March 1988.

Lee, Frank, Personal Interview, Chicago, 22 February 1988.

McClain, Clarence, former District Administrator for Congressional Office of Harold Washington, Personal Interview, Chicago, 8 May 1985, 7 April 1988.

Metcalfe, Fay, Widow of Congressman Ralph Metcalfe, Personal Interview, 1 August 1984.

Newhouse, Richard, State Senator, Personal Interviews, Chicago 23 October 1984, 20 December 1985, 29 January 1988.

Ordower, Sid, Civil Rights Activist, Personal Interview, Chicago, 24 April 1984.

Robinson, Renault, Former President of the Afro-American Patrolmen's League and Currently a Member of the Board of Directors of the Chicago Housing Authority, Personal Interview, 6 June 1984, 6 July 1981, 16 December 1987.

Saffold, Howard, Security Coordinator for the Mayor's Office, Personal Interview, Chicago, 12 January 1988, 25 February 1988.

Savage, Gus, Member of U.S. House of Representatives, Personal Interview, Chicago, 22 April 1984, 13 December 1985, 14 January 1986, 2 April 1988.

Washington, Harold, Mayor of Chicago, Personal Interview, Chicago, 23 April 1983, 31 April 1983, 31 May 1983, 22 January 1984, 16 April 1984, 12 May 1984, 19 May 1984, 17 July 1984, 24 April 1985, 11 August 1985, 24 August 1985, 7 July 1986, 22 September 1986, 15 October 1986.

LETTERS AND MAILGRAMS

Letters from Charles Hayes, chairman of the Committee for a Black Mayor, to the following persons, dated September 6, 1974. To wit: Harold Washington, Ralph Metcalfe, A.A. Rayner, Richard H. Newhouse, Roland Burris, Joseph Bertrand, Cecil Partee, Wilson Frost, Thomas N. Todd, Edward Allen and E. Duke McNeil.

Letters from Charles Hayes, chairman of the Committee for a Black Mayor, to the following persons, dated February 5, 1975. To wit: Dr. Perry English, Daryl Grisham, George Johnson, Dr. T.R.M. Howard, Harvey Collins, John H. Johnson, Elijah Muhammad, Earl Dickerson, and Dempsey J. Travis.

Mailgram from Charles Hayes and Al Boutte to Dempsey J. Travis dated January 11, 1977.

Letter from Charles Hayes to members of the Committee for a Black Mayor, dated January 11, 1977.

Mailgram from Alvin J. Boutte and Charles Hayes to Dempsey J. Travis, dated January 19, 1977.

Letter from Charles Hayes to Committee for a Black Mayor, dated February 25, 1977.

DOCUMENTS AND MEMORANDA

Statement outlining the criteria for a black mayor delivered before the Committee for a Black Mayor by State Rep. Harold Washington, dated September 14, 1974.

Pamphlet prepared by the Chicago League of Negro Voters, dated June 1962.

Sample ballot for a Black mayor prepared by Dr. T.R.M. Howard, dated August 14, 1974.

Criteria for a Black Mayor prepared by the Committee for a Black Mayor, undated.

Press statement by Charles A. Hayes, delivered on Tuesday, July 9, 1974.

List of leaders who attended the first Black mayor's meeting in June 1974.

Memorandum from Edward C. "Bill" Berry to Congressman Ralph H. Metcalfe, dated January 8, 1975.

Ten-page questionnaire for mayoral candidates for a Black mayor prepared by the Committee for a Black Mayor.

Position paper, prepared by the Committee for a Black Mayor, undated.

Working paper, Committee for a Black Mayor, undated, prepared by Committee on Agenda and Platform: chairman-Thomas Todd, ex-officio-Charles Hayes, Larry Bullock, Tim Black, Lenora Cartwright, William Cousins, James Montgomery, Bill Smith.

Election schedule for mayoral and aldermanic races.

Suggested names to be called for mayoral interviews.

CHAPTER

BOOKS

Fitzgerald, Kathleen Whalan, *Brass, Jane Byrne and the Pursuit of Power,* Chicago: Contemporary Books, Inc., 1981.

Granger, Bill and Lori Granger, *Fighting Jane, Mayor Jane and the Chicago Machine,* New York: Dial Press, 1980.

Holli, Melvin G. and Paul M. Green, editors, *The Making of a Mayor: Chicago 1983,* Grand Rapids, Mich: William B.

Eerdmans Publishing Co., 1984.
Illinois Blue Book, 1965-1966, ed. by Paul Powell, Secretary of State.
Illinois Blue Book, 1975-1976, ed. by Michael J. Howlett, Secretary of State.
Illinois Blue Book, 1977-1978, ed. by Alan J. Dixon, Secretary of State.
Illinois Blue Book, 1979-1980, ed. by Alan J. Dixon, Secretary of State.
Illinois Blue Book, 1981-1982, ed. by Jim Edgar, Secretary of State.
Kleppner, Paul, *Chicago Divided: The Making of a Black Mayor,* Dekalb, Ill: Northern Illinois University Press, 1985.
Levinsohn, Florence H., *Harold Washington, A Political Biography,* Chicago: Chicago Review Press, 1983.
O'Connor, Len. *Clout: Mayor Daley and His City,* Chicago: Contemporary Books, Inc., 1975.
Royko, Mike, *Boss: Richard J. Daley of Chicago,* New York: E.P. Dutton & Company, Inc., 1971.
Travis, Dempsey J. *An Autobiography of Black Politics,* Chicago: Urban Research Press, 1987.
Worrill, Conrad, *Worrill's World,* Chicago, Ill: National Black United Front, 1986.

NEWSPAPERS

"Why Washington is Running," *Chicago Sun-Times,* 18 March 1977.
"Ready for a Black Mayor," *Chicago Defender,* 4 May 1977.
"Dirty Tricks Charge Invalid Switch," *Chicago Defender,* 31 January 1978.
"Renault's Clash with Cop Nearly Starts Race Riot," *Chicago Defender,* 31 January 1978.
"Washington Explains Role of Muslims in Campaign," *Chicago Defender,* 28 February 1978.
"Your Vote Will Diffuse Political Plot," *Chicago Defender,* 4 March 1978.
"Burris Win a Must: Analyst," *Chicago Defender,* 6 March 1978.
"Is Washington Target of Angry Party Bosses?," *Chicago Defender,* 7 March 1978.
"24th District Democratic Race a Tangled Toss-Up," *Chicago Tribune,* 7 March 1978.
"Dems Senate Contest Has Very Few Hurrahs," *Chicago Tribune,* 7 March 1978.
"Black Vs Black Threatens Power of Incumbents," *Chicago Defender,* 8 March 1978.
"Job Bill Faces Big Test," *Chicago Defender,* 8 March 1978.
"Blacks Have Power to Awaken the Sleeping Giant," *Chicago Defender,* 9 March 1978.
"Fist Fight on South Side," *Chicago Tribune,* 10 March 1978.
"Vote Tampering Charge," *Chicago Defender,* 13 March 1978.
"Primary to Prove Machine's Power," *Chicago Defender,* 14 March 1978.
"Is Taylor New Black Boss?," *Chicago Defender,* 16 March 1978.
"Power Struggle in 24th," *Chicago Defender,* 16 March 1978.
"Tribune's Primary Day Endorsements," *Chicago Tribune,* 19 March 1978.
"Test Black Voters Today," *Chicago Defender,* 21 March 1978.
"Dem Fractions Cost State Senate Seat," *Chicago Tribune,* 22 March 1978.
"Three Independent Incumbents Beat," *Chicago Tribune,* 22 March 1978.
"Regulars Have A Field Day," *Chicago Defender,* 23 March 1978.
"Four Chicago Independents Swept Out of Seats in House," *Chicago Tribune,* 23 March 1978.
"Despite Light Turnout, Blacks United," *Chicago Defender,* 27 March 1978.
" 'The End' in City Politics," *Chicago Defender,* 4 April 1978.
"The Outs on the Political Scene," *Chicago Defender,* 4 April 1978.
"Don't Count Taylor Out," *Chicago Defender,* 6 April 1978.
"West Side Politics: A Different Game," *Chicago Defender,* 6 April 1978.
"Is Chicago Ready for a Black Police Boss?," *Chicago Defender,* 10 April 1978.
"Legislators Denied VGA Funds Rap," *Chicago Defender,* 1 May 1978.
"Real Story Behind ERA Snub," *Chicago Defender,* 15 June 1978.
"Daley's Shoes Too Big for Bilandic," *Chicago Tribune,* 4 March 1979.

"Chicago Blacks Need A Lesson," *Chicago Tribune,* 4 March 1979.
"The High Cost of a Senator," *Chicago Tribune,* 31 December 1980.
"Three Chicagoans Take Oath of Office," *Chicago Defender,* 6 January 1981.
"Washington Gives Up State Post," *Chicago Defender,* 20 January 1981.
"Congressmen Boycott Reagan," *Chicago Defender,* 4 February 1981.

MAGAZINES

"The Machine is not dead. It is waiting for Richie Daley," *Illinois Issues,* February 18, 1981.
"Bilandic: How did you get the mayor's job?," *Illinois Issues,* July 30, 1977.
"A Transfer of Power," *Chicago Magazine,* May 1979.
"The Road to City Hall," *Chicago Tribune Magazine,* November 16, 1986.

INTERVIEWS

Hayes, Charles, Member of U.S. House of Representatives, Personal Interview, 16 April 1984, 5 June 1984, 8 June 1984, 22 February 1988.
Jackson, Reverend Jesse L., Former Staff Member of the Southern Christian Leadership Conference, President of Operation Breadbasket, 1984 & 1988 Presidential Candidate, An International Civil Rights Leader, and Founder and Past President of Operation PUSH, Personal Interview, 30 November 1984.
Johnson, Bennett, Executive of Path Press and Political Activist, Personal Interview, 20 March 1985, 13 August 1986, September 24 1986, 25 March 1988.
Newhouse, Richard, State Senator, Personal Interview, 23 October 1984, 20 December 1985, 29 January 1988.
Palmer, Lu, Journalist, Radio Host and Political Activist, Personal Interview, 13 March 1985.
Robinson, Renault, Former President of the Afro-American Patrolmen's League and Currently a Member of the Board of Directors of the Chicago Housing Authority, Personal Interview, 6 June 1984, 6 July 1981, 16 December 1987.
Sampson, Reverend Al, Pastor of Fernwood Methodist Church, Personal Interview, 17 August 1984, 23 August 1984, 19 October 1986.
Washington, Harold, Mayor of the city of Chicago, 23 April 1983, 31 April 1983, 31 May 1983, 22 January 1984, 16 April 1984, 12 May 1984, 19 May 1984, 17 July 1984, 24 August 1984, 24 August 1985, 22 September 1986, 15 October 1986.
Worrill, Conrad W., Professor at Northeastern University, Personal Interview, 18 October 1984.

CHAPTER 10

BOOKS

Fitzgerald, Kathleen Whalan, *Brass, Jane Byrne and the Pursuit of Power,* Chicago: Contemporary Books, Inc., 1981.
Levinsohn, Florence H., *Harold Washington, A Political Biography,* Chicago: Chicago Review Press, 1983.
Travis, Dempsey J., *An Autobiography of Black Chicago,* Chicago: Urban Research Institute, 1981.
________, *An Autobiography of Black Politics,* Chicago: Urban Research Press, 1987.

NEWSPAPERS

"Schedule Public Hearings on Black Home Assessments," *Chicago Defender,* 17 April 1979.
"Washington to Bid for Congress Seat," *Chicago Sun-Times,* 27 May 1979
"Black Homeowners Ask Tax Probe," *Chicago Sun-Times,* 18 June 1979.
"Don't Forfeit Your Right: Vote," *Chicago Sun-Times,* 17 September 1979.
"Stewart's Bill Seeks to Halt Condos," *Chicago Defender,* 19 September 1979.
"Rep. Stewart Seeks Cutback in Political Action Committees Donations," *Chicago Defender,* 19 September 1979.
"Currency Exchange Fees Limits OK'd," *Chicago Sun-Times,* 26 September 1979.

"Effort to Pack Illinois Summit Charged," *Chicago Sun-Times,* 10 October 1979.

"Black Legislators Rip Byrne Plug to Ted," *Chicago Sun-Times,* 2 November 1979.

"Obstacles Will Hinder Byrne," *Chicago Sun-Times,* 21 January 1980.

"Running Mad," *The Reader,* 22 February 1980.

"First District Race Provides Test of Byrne's Strength," *Chicago Sun-Times,* 5 March 1980.

"Washington is Upset Victor in First Congressional District," *Chicago Sun-Times,* 19 March 1980.

"A Primary Battering for Byrne Machine," *Chicago Sun-Times,* 20 March 1980.

"Dem Machine Stunned as Picks Lose on South Side," *Chicago Sun-Times,* 20 March 1980.

"Vigor of Independent Movement Confirmed," *Chicago Sun-Times,* 22 March 1980.

"Black Voters Send Message to Machine: You Need Us," *Chicago Sun-Times,* 24 March 1980.

"Blacks' Political Attitude Change," *Chicago Defender,* 3 May 1980.

"State Senate Panel OKs Mayor-Recall Legislation," *Chicago Sun-Times,* 9 May 1980.

"Byrne Recall Bill Fails in Senate," *Chicago Sun-Times,* 21 May 1980.

"GOP Senators Stall Mayor-Recall Measure," *Chicago Sun-Times,* 22 May 1980.

"PUSH's New Political Freedom Movement," *Chicago Defender,* 16 August 1980.

"Citizens for Washington Launch Fall Campaign," *Chicago Defender,* 20 September 1980.

"Editorial for the U.S. House," *Chicago Sun-Times,* 23 October 1980.

"Findley, Simon Caught in Tight Races," *Chicago Sun-Times,* 5 November 1980.

"Byrne Under New Attack by Washington," *Chicago Sun-Times,* 29 December 1980.

"Party Ties No Longer Key to Political Success," *Chicago Sun-Times,* 23 June 1980.

"Harold Washington: "Let the Word Go Forth," *Chicago Defender,* 14 July 1980.

"Metcalfe Jr. Bows Out of Congressional Race," *Chicago Defender,* 9 August 1980.

"Washington: Not the Time to Lose Elective Offices," *Chicago Defender,* 3 January 1981.

"Press Represented Taylor in 26th District," *Chicago Defender,* 12 January 1981.

"Hard Ball in the 26th District," *Chicago Sun-Times,* 13 January 1981.

"Washington Ending Springfield Fight," *Chicago Sun-Times,* 20 January 1981.

MAGAZINES

"The Road to City Hall," *Chicago Tribune Magazine,* November 16, 1986.

"O'Neill, Dixon Win Senate Primaries in Illinois," Congressional Quarterly 22 September 1980.

INTERVIEWS

Chew Jr., Charles, State Senator, Personal Interview, Chicago, 10 October 1984.

Hayes, Charles, Member of U.S. House of Representatives, Personal Interview, Chicago, 16 April 1984, 5 June 1984, 22 February 1988.

Jennings, Rose, Former Director of Marketing/Playboy Magazine, Personal Interview, Chicago, 23 April 1988.

Johnson, Bennett, Publisher and Civil Rights Activist, Personal Interview, Chicago, 20 March 1985, 13 August 1986, 24 September 1986, 25 March 1988.

Landry, Lawrence, President of Associate Consultants, Personal Interview, Chicago, 2 May 1988.

Ordower, Sid, Civil Rights Activist, Personal Interview, Chicago, 24 April 1984.

Passmore, Juanita, Civic Leader and Retired Officer of Johnson Products Company, Personal Interview, Chicago, 15 April 1988.

Savage, Gus, Member of U.S. House of Representatives, Personal Interview, Chicago, 22 April 1984, 13 December 1985, 14 January 1986, 2 April 1988.

Washington, Harold, Mayor of the city of Chicago, Personal Interviews, 23 April 1983, 31 April 1983, 31 May 1983, 22 January 1984, 16 April 1984, 12 May 1984, 19 May 1984, 17 July 1984, 24 August 1984, 24 August 1985, 22 September 1986, 15 October 1986.

Washington, Roy Lee Jr., Brother of Mayor Harold Washington, Personal Interview, Chicago, 30 April 1988.

Wilson, Charles, Owner of C.W. Limousine Service, Personal Interview, Chicago, 18 April 1988.

CHAPTER 11

BOOKS

Holli, Melvin G. and Paul M. Green, *The Making of a Mayor:* Chicago, 1983, Grand Rapids, Michigan: William B. Eerdmans Publishing Company, 1984.

Levinsohn, Florence H., *Harold Washington: A Political Biography,* Chicago: Chicago Review Press, 1983.

Travis, Dempsey J., *An Autobiography of Black Politics,* Chicago: Urban Research Press, Inc., 1987.

NEWSPAPERS

"Adequate Black Representation May Never Happen," *Chicago Defender,* 6 January 1981.

"Blacks Vow to Fight Racial Gerrymandering," *Chicago Defender,* 22 January 1981.

"Washington Named to Third Committee," *Chicago Defender,* 31 January 1981.

"Sociologists Warn: Blacks to Lose Clout in Remap," *Chicago Defender,* 11 February 1981.

"It's Not Playing Favorite, It's Playing Fair," *Chicago Sun-Times,* 24 March 1981.

"Black Group Sets Plan to Save House Seats," *Chicago Sun-Times,* 2 April 1981.

"Race Big Issue in Remapping for Congress," *Chicago Sun-Times,* 19 April 1981.

"Legislative Caucus Hears Testimony on Reapportionment," *Chicago Defender,* 5 May 1981.

"Gus Savage Rips IVI on Redistricting," *Chicago Defender,* 5 May 1981.

"Power Politics, Not Racism," *Chicago Sun-Times,* 14 May 1981.

"Blacks Had Good Reasons to Back GOP Map," *Chicago Sun-Times,* 21 May 1981.

"Black Legislator A Pariah to Her Fellow Democrats," *Chicago Sun-Times,* 28 May 1981.

"Coup by Rep. Washington," *Chicago Sun-Times,* 28 June 1981.

"Remap Bid Fail:Now Up to Court," *Chicago Sun-Times,* 30 June 1981.

"Legislative Remap Panel Appointed," *Chicago Sun-Times,* 11 July 1981.

"Mapping Sunset for Dawn," *Chicago Sun-Times,* 13 August 1981.

"Dems Win State Remap Drawing," *Chicago Sun-Times,* 26 August 1981.

"Talks Fail, Remap Now Up to Shapiro," *Chicago Sun-Times,* 22 September 1981.

"Vote Tally Low for Three Reps from Illinois," *Chicago Sun-Times,* 4 November 1981.

"Washington Hails Court Ruling," *Forge* (The Citizens for Washington Newspaper), December 1981.

INTERVIEWS

Canter, David, Lawyer and Confidant of Harold Washington, Personal Interview, Chicago, 19 April 1988.

Gilbert, Herman, Executive Vice President and Editorial Director of Path Press, Personal Interviews, Chicago, 24 November 1984, 28 April 1984, 19 December 1985, 19 March 1988.

Hayes, Charles, Member of U.S. House of Representatives, Personal Interview, 16 April 1984, 5 June 1984, 8 June 1984, 22 February 1988.

Johnson, Al, President of both Johnson Cadillac and the Political Action Conference of Illinois (PACI), and Dollar-A-Year Man for Mayor Washington, Personal Interview, 25 July 1984.

Johnson, Bennett, Executive of Pathe Press and Political Activist, Personal Interview, 20 March 1985, 13 August 1986, September 24 1986, 25 March 1988.

Ordower, Sid, Civil rights activist, Personal Interview, Chicago, 24 April 1984.

Savage, Gus, Member of U.S. House of Representatives, Personal Interview, Chicago, 22 April 1984, 13 December 1985, 14 January 1986, 2 April 1988.

Washington, Harold, Mayor of the city of Chicago, 23 April 1983, 31 April 1983, 31 May 1983, 22 January 1984, 16 April 1984, 12 May 1984, 19 May 1984, 17 July

1984, 24 August 1984, 24 August 1985, 22 September 1986, 15 October 1986.

CHAPTER 12

BOOKS

Holli, Melvin G. and Paul M. Green, *The Making of a Mayor: Chicago, 1983,* Grand Rapids, Michigan: William B. Eerdmans Publishing Company, 1984.

Levinsohn, Florence H., *Harold Washington: A Political Biography,* Chicago: Chicago Review Press, 1983.

Travis, Dempsey J., *An Autobiography of Black Politics,* Chicago: Urban Research Press, Inc., 1987.

NEWSPAPERS

"Washington's Heavy Load 30 Percent Heavier than Most," *Forge,* December 1981.

"First District Community Task Forces Focus on Key Issues," *Forge,* December 1981.

"Washington Hails Court Ruling," *Forge,* December 1981.

"The Players," *Chicago Sun-Times,* 10 January 1982.

"Savage Votes Pick Up, But He Still Gets No-Show Prize," *Chicago Sun-Times,* 10 January 1982.

"Democrats Win as High Court Upholds Illinois Congress Remap," *Chicago Sun-Times,* 12 January 1982.

"Hold Conference on Bloc Grants in First District," *Chicago Defender,* 14 January 1982.

"Washington Blasts Reagan Cuts as 'Holy War on Poor and Blacks'," *Forge,* February 1982.

"Reagan Budget is 'Voodoo' Economics," *Forge,* February 1982.

"Washington Predicts Reagan Setback On Cuts," *Chicago Sun-Times,* 22 February 1982.

"Washington Testifies on Voting Rights Act," *Forge,* March 1982.

"Victors Against Reagan on the Horizon," *Chicago Defender,* 2 March 1982.

"Democratic the Primary Ballot," *Chicago Defender,* 9 March 1982.

"Washington Attacks Reagan's Civil Rights Policy," *Chicago Defender,* 31 March 1982.

"Congress Politics: Shifts to the Extremes," *Chicago Sun-Times,* 5 May 1982.

"Pols Keep Guard Up," *Chicago Sun-Times,* 18 July 1982.

INTERVIEWS

Canter, David, Lawyer and Confidant of Harold Washington, Personal Interview, Chicago, 19 April 1988.

Chew Jr., Charles, State Senator, Personal Interview, Chicago, 10 October 1984.

Coleman, Slim, Editor-in-Chief of *All Chicago City News* and Chairperson of the Heart of Uptown Coalition, Personal Interviews, 16 June 1984, 17 October 1986, 25 May 1988.

Hayes, Charles, Member of U.S. House of Representatives, Personal Interview, 16 April 1984, 5 June 1984, 8 June 1984, 22 February 1988.

Johnson, Al, President of both Johnson Cadillac and the Political Action Conference of Illinois (PACI), and Dollar-A-Year Man for Mayor Washington, Personal Interview, 25 July 1984.

Johnson, Bennett, Executive of Path Press and Political Activist, Personal Interview, 20 March 1985, 13 August 1986, September 24 1986, 25 March 1988.

Ordower, Sid, Civil Rights Activist, Personal Interview, Chicago, 24 April 1984, 31 May 1988.

Robinson, Renault, Former President of the Afro-American Patrolmen's League and Currently a Member of the Board of Directors of the Chicago Housing Authority, Personal Interview, 6 June 1984, 6 July 1981, 16 December 1987.

Schiller, Helen, Personal Interview, 16 June 1984.

Washington, Harold, Mayor of the city of Chicago, Personal Interviews, 23 April 1983, 31 April 1983, 31 May 1983, 22 January 1984, 16 April 1984, 12 May 1984, 19 May 1984, 17 July 1984, 24 August 1984, 24 August 1985, 22 September 1986, 15 October 1986.

CHAPTER

13

BOOKS

Black Power in Chicago, A Documentary Survey of the 1983 Mayoral Democratic Primary, Chicago: People's College Press, 1983.

Holli, Melvin G. and Paul M. Green, *The Making of a Mayor: Chicago, 1983,* Grand Rapids, Michigan: William B. Eerdmans Publishing Company, 1984.

Levinsohn, Florence H., *Harold Washington: A Political Biography,* Chicago: Chicago Review Press, 1983.

Travis, Dempsey J., *An Autobiography of Black Politics,* Chicago: Urban Research Press Inc., 1987.

NEWSPAPERS

"Byrne vs. Daley: How They Compare," *Chicago Sun-Times,* 7 May 1982.

"Washington a Shoo-in," *Chicago Defender,* 6 July 1982.

"Committee Approves CHA Nominees," *Chicago Defender,* 22 July 1982.

"Swiebel Resigns," *All Chicago City News,* 23 July 1982.

"Commissioners Agree to Support Voter Registration," *All Chicago City News,* 23 July 1982.

"Council Approves CHA Appointments in Raucous Session," *Chicago Tribune,* 24 July 1982.

"Protesters Express Anger Over CHA Actions," *Chicago Defender,* 26 July 1982.

"Threaten Boycott of Chicago Fest," *Chicago Defender,* 27 July 1982.

"CHA Protest Gains Steam as Cleric Pledges His Resignation," *Chicago Defender,* 28 July 1982.

"Stevie Wonder First to Cancel in Fest Boycott," *Chicago Defender,* 29 July 1982.

"Jackson Praises Stevie's Decision," *Chicago Defender,* 29 July 1982.

"Blacks' Picketing Predicted at Chicago Fest," *Chicago Tribune,* 30 July 1982.

"Stymied Protest Against Byrne," *All-American News,* 6 August 1982.

"P.O.W.E.R. Wins Special Voter Registration-Will Create 51st Ward," *All Chicago City News,* 22 August 1982.

"Voter Fever Registration Theme," *Chicago Defender,* 1 September 1982.

"P.O.W.E.R. Drive Nets 12,500 Registered," *Chicago Defender,* 8 September 1982.

MAGAZINES

"Chicago is Not Dead. It's Waiting for Richie Daley," *Illinois Issues,* February 18, 1981.

INTERVIEWS

Black, Timuel, Professor at Harold Washington (Loop) College, Personal Interview, Chicago, 28 April 1984, 12 January 1988.

Braun, Carol Mosely, State Representative, Personal Interview, 4 March 1985.

Burris, Roland, Comptroller, State of Illinois, Personal Interview, 12 January 1985.

Canter, David, Lawyer and Confidant of Harold Washington, Personal Interview, Chicago, 19 April 1988.

Clements, George, Father of Holy Angels Church, Personal Interviews, 18 October 1984, 14 February 1986.

Coleman, Slim, Editor-in-Chief of *All Chicago City News* and Chairperson of the Heart of Uptown Coalition, Personal Interviews, 16 June 1984, 17 October 1986, 25 May 1988.

Davis, Danny, Alderman, Personal Interview, 6 October 1984.

Gardner, Edward, Chairman of the Board of Soft Sheen Products, Inc., Personal Interview, 17 July 1984.

Jackson, Jesse, Former Staff Member of the Southern Christian Leadership Conference, President of Operation Breadbasket, 1984 & 1988 Presidential Candidate, An International Civil Rights leader, and Founder and Past President of Operation PUSH, Personal Interview, 30 November 1984.

Jefferson, Nancy, Executive Secretary for the Midwest Community Council, Personal Interview, 3 July 1984.

Langford, Anna, Alderman, Personal Interview, Chicago, 19 April 1985.

Newhouse, Richard, State Senator, Personal Interviews, Chicago 23 October 1984, 20 December 1985, 29 January 1988.

Palmer, Lu, Radio Host, Journalist and Civil Rights Activist, 13 March 1985.

Robinson, Renault, Former President of the Afro-American Patrolmen's League and Currently a Member of the Board of Directors of the Chicago Housing Authority, Personal Interview, 6 June 1984, 6 July 1981, 16 December 1987.

Savage, Gus, Member of U.S. House of Representatives, Personal Interview, Chicago, 22 April 1984, 13 December 1985, 14 January 1986, 2 April 1988.

Stroger, John, County Commissioner, Eighth Ward Committeeman, Personal Interview, 20 June 1984.

Washington, Harold, Mayor of Chicago, Personal Interviews, 23 April 1983, 31 April 1983, 31 May 1983, 22 January 1984, 16 April 1984, 12 May 1984, 19 May 1984, 17 July 1984, 24 August 1984, 24 August 1985, 22 September 1986, 15 October 1986.

CHAPTER 14

BOOKS

Black Power in Chicago, A Documentary Survey of the 1983 Mayoral Democratic Primary, Chicago: People's College Press, 1983.

Bush, Rod, editor, *The New Vote, Politics and Power in Four American Cities,* San Francisco: Synthesis Publications, 1984.

Fitzgerald, Kathleen Whalan, *Brass, Jane Byrne and the Pursuit of Power,* Chicago: Contemporary Books, Inc., 1981.

Levinsohn, Florence H., *Harold Washington, A Political Biography,* Chicago: Chicago Review Press, 1983.

Travis, Dempsey J., *An Autobiography of Black Politics,* Chicago: Urban Research Press, Inc., 1987.

NEWSPAPERS

"Rep. Washington Promises Mayor Decision After Nov. 2," *Chicago Sun-Times,* 8 October 1982.

"Rep. Washington Fundraiser Heats Up Talk of Mayoral Bid," *Chicago Sun-Times,* 16 October 1982.

"Barr Hints a GOP Support of Washington for Mayor," *Chicago Sun-Times,* 31 October 1982.

"Mayoral Race Jockeying Begins," *Chicago Sun-Times,* 2 November 1982.

"Power-Full Mayor Race," *Chicago Sun-Times,* 3 November 1982.

"Daley Opens Race Today," *Chicago Sun-Times,* 4 November 1982.

"Rich Daley In Mayor's Race," *Chicago Defender,* 6 November 1982.

"Jane Byrne: Displaying A New Maturity," *Chicago Sun-Times,* 7 November 1982.

"Washington Mayoral Bid is Expected," *Chicago Sun-Times,* 8 November 1982.

"A New Political Factor: A Black With a Chance," *Chicago Tribune,* 8 November 1982.

"Washington in Mayor Race," *Chicago Tribune,* 8 November 1982.

"Blacks May Redo Mayor Script," *Chicago Tribune,* 8 November 1982.

"Expect Washington to Say 'Yes' Wednesday," *Chicago Defender,* 9 November 1982.

"Two Dem Leaders Back Washington," *Chicago Sun-Times,* 9 November 1982.

"Washington is Reluctant But Ready," *Chicago Sun-Times,* 9 November 1982.

"Washington Leaps into Race for Mayor," *Chicago Sun-Times,* 11 November 1982.

"Lu Palmer Loses Radio Show," *Chicago Sun-Times,* 11 November 1982.

"A Machine Creature Turned Maverick Keeps Going His Own Way," *Chicago Tribune,* 11 November 1982.

"Washington in Race for Mayor," *Chicago Tribune,* 11 November 1982.

"Washington-Popular, But A Puzzle," *Chicago Sun-Times,* 11 November 1982.

"It's Official: Washington in Mayoral Race," *Chicago Defender,* 11 November 1982.

"Chicago Ripe for a Black Mayor," *Chicago Defender,* 11 November 1982.

"Reaction to Washington's Mayoral Bid 'Exciting'," *Chicago Defender,* 11 November 1982.

"Washington Takes Jab at Democratic Bosses," *Chicago Sun-Times,* 12 November 1982.

"Washington Joins the Race," *Chicago Sun-Times,* 12 November 1982.

"Washington Declares A Candidacy for All," *Chicago Metro News,* 13 November 1982.

MAGAZINES

"The Machine is not dead. It is waiting for Richie Daley," *Illinois Issues,* February 18, 1981.

"Bilandic: How did you get the mayor's job?," *Illinois Issues,* July 30, 1977.

INTERVIEWS

Brown, Bob, Political Activist and Organizer, Personal Interview, 18 October 1984.

Clements, George, Father of Holy Angels Church, Personal Interview, 18 October 1984, 14 February 1986.

Coleman, Slim, Editor-in-Chief of *All Chicago City News* and Chairperson of the Heart of Uptown Coalition, Personal Interviews, 16 June 1984, 17 October 1986, 25 May 1988.

Hayes, Charles, Member of U.S. House of Representatives, Personal Interview, 16 April 1984, 5 June 1984, 8 June 1984, 22 February 1988.

Jackson, Reverend Jesse L., Former Staff Member of the Southern Christian Leadership Conference, President of Operation Breadbasket, 1984 & 1988 Presidential Candidate, An International Civil Rights Leader, and Founder and Past President of Operation PUSH, Personal Interview, 30 November 1984.

Johnson, Bennett, Executive of Pathe Press and Political Activist, Personal Interview, 20 March 1985, 13 August 1986, September 24 1986, 25 March 1988.

Newhouse, Richard, State Senator, Personal Interview, 23 October 1984, 20 December 1985, 29 January 1988.

O'Hare, George, Former Executive of Sears, Roebuck and Co., Radio Host of *Accent the Positive* and early volunteer in the Washington Campaign Personal Interview, 17 May 1985, 31 May 1985, 18 October 1986, 24 February 1988.

Palmer, Lu, Journalist, Radio Host and Political Activist, Personal Interview, 13 March 1985.

Robinson, Renault, Former President of the Afro-American Patrolmen's League and Currently a Member of the Board of Directors of the Chicago Housing Authority, Personal Interview, 6 June 1984, 6 July 1981, 16 December 1987.

Sampson, Reverend Al, Pastor of Fernwood Methodist Church, Personal Interview, 17 August 1984, 23 August 1984, 19 October 1986.

Washington, Harold, Mayor of the city of Chicago, 23 April 1983, 31 April 1983, 31 May 1983, 22 January 1984, 16 April 1984, 12 May 1984, 19 May 1984, 17 July 1984, 24 August 1984, 24 August 1985, 22 September 1986, 15 October 1986.

Worrill, Conrad W., Professor at Northeastern University, Personal Interview, 18 October 1984.

Wyatt Jr., Reverend Claude, Pastor of Vernon Park Church of God, Personal Interview, 4 August 1984, 28 August 1984.

Wyatt, Addie, Union Executive, Personal Interview, 4 August 1984.

CHAPTER 15

BOOKS

Black Power in Chicago, A Documentary Survey of the 1983 Mayoral Democratic Primary, Chicago: People's College Press, 1983.

Bush, Rod, editor, *The New Vote, Politics and Power in Four American Cities,* San Francisco: Synthesis Publication, 1984.

Fitzgerald, Kathleen Whalan, *Brass, Jane Byrne and the Pursuit of Power,* Chicago: Contemporary Books, Inc., 1981.

Granger, Bill and Lori, *Fighting Jane, Mayor Jane and the Chicago Machine,* New York: Dial Press, 1980.

Holli, Melvin G. and Paul M. Green, editors, *The Making of a Mayor: Chicago 1983,* Grand Rapids, Mich: William B. Eerdsman Publishing Co., 1984.

Kleppner, Paul, *Chicago Divided: The Making of a Black Mayor,* Dekalb, Ill: Northern Illinois University Press, 1985.

Levinsohn, Florence H., *Harold Washington, A Political Biography,* Chicago: Chicago Review Press, 1983.

Travis, Dempsey J., *An Autobiography of Black Politics,* Chicago, Ill: Urban Research Press, Inc., 1987.

Worrill, Conrad, *Worrill's World,* Chicago, Ill: National Black United Front, 1986.

NEWSPAPERS

"Washington Mayoral Bid Expected," *Chicago Sun-Times,* 8 November 1982.

"Expect Washington to Say 'Yes' Wednesday," *Chicago Defender,* 9 November 1982.

"Chicago Headed for a Rousing Four-Way Battle for Mayor," *Chicago Tribune,* 9 November 1982.

"Washington is Reluctant But Ready," *Chicago Sun-Times,* 9 November 1982.

"Two Dem Leaders Back Washington," *Chicago Sun-Times,* 9 November 1982.

"I Am A Candidate," *Chicago Defender,* 11 November 1982.

"Washington Leaps Into Race for Mayor," *Chicago Sun-Times,* 11 November 1982.

"Byrne Boasts of Black Gains," *Chicago Sun-Times,* 11 November 1982.

"Lu Palmer Loses Radio Show," *Chicago Sun-Times,* 11 November 1982.

"Chicago Ripe for Black Mayor," *Chicago Defender,* 11 November 1982.

"Washington Joins the Race," *Chicago Sun-Times,* 12 November 1982.

"Washington: 'My Life is as Open as Anyone Elses'," *Chicago Defender,* 13 November 1982.

"Reaction to Washington's Mayoral Bid 'Exciting'," *Chicago Defender,* 13 November 1982.

"A Black Mayor? Definite (Maybe)," *Chicago Sun-Times,* 14 November 1982.

"Look at What is in Their Heads," *Chicago Tribune,* 14 November 1982.

"Voting for Mayor Not So Black and White," *Chicago Tribune,* 14 November 1982.

"Daley Touted as Early Favorite in Upcoming Mayoral Derby," *Chicago Tribune,* 14 November 1982.

" 'It's Our Turn-Washington'," *Chicago Sun-Times,* 15 November 1982.

"Washington Gets Thunderous Applause at Bethel AME Meeting," *Chicago Defender,* 16 November 1982.

"Race For Mayor Free-For-All," *Chicago Defender,* 16 November 1982.

"Black Politicians Choose Up Sides in Mayor's Race," *Chicago Defender,* 16 November 1982.

"Daley Gains Support With Scott Backing," *Chicago Defender,* 16 November 1982.

"Byrne to Run: Dems Slating Likely," *Chicago Sun-Times,* 17 November 1982.

"Harold, Richie to Ignore Democratic Slate Makers," *Chicago Defender,* 18 November 1982.

"A New Kind of Election," *Chicago Tribune,* 18 November 1982.

"Bare Move to Draft Vrdolyak," *Chicago Sun-Times,* 18 November 1982.

"Stroger Defends Support for Daley," *Chicago Defender,* 18 November 1982.

"I Paid Penalty for Tax Error-Washington," *Chicago Sun-Times,* 19 November 1982.

"Washington Now Leads the Field, Vrdolyak Says," *Chicago Tribune,* 20 November 1982.

"Washington Takes Jab at Democratic Bosses," *Chicago Sun-Times,* 21 November 1982.

"Committeemen's Positions," *Chicago Sun-Times,* 21 November 1982.

"Washington Vows to Cut City's Patronage Jobs," *Chicago Tribune,* 22 November 1982.

"Won't Let Race Become Issue, Byrne Declares," *Chicago Tribune,* 22 November 1982.

"Harold's Petitions to be Filed Dec. 6," *Chicago Defender,* 23 November 1982.

"Age of Independence? Masking Truth," *Chicago Sun-Times,* 23 November 1982.

"Ward Bosses, Washington in 'Secret' Meet," *Chicago Defender,* 23 November 1982.

"Daley Backers Charge Park District Pressure," *Chicago Tribune,* 24 November 1982.

"Byrne Splits Machine," *Chicago Defender,* 24 November 1982.
"Mayoral Politics and Polish," *Chicago Tribune,* 24 November 1982.
"Charges Black Paid Less," *Chicago Defender,* 27 November 1982.
"Chicago Machine is Squeaking," *Chicago Tribune,* 28 November 1982.
"The Racial Truth of Politics," *Chicago Tribune,* 29 November 1982.
"Washington Raps Racial Dividers," *Chicago Sun-Times,* 29 November 1982.
"Washington Takes Pitch to North Side," *Chicago Tribune,* 29 November 1982.
"Byrne Workers Accused of Improper Soliciting of Mayoral Petitions," *Chicago Defender,* 1 December 1982.
"Daley Best for Blacks Aide Says," *Chicago Tribune,* 2 December 1982.
"Washington: 'Make Chicago Fair to the Neighborhood'," *All Chicago City News, 3 December 1982.*
"Racial Anger Flares Up," Chicago Sun-Times, 5 December 1982.
"Report 100,000 Signatures Collected for Washington," *Chicago Defender,* 6 December 1982.
"Ward Bosses 'Mug' Mayor," *Chicago Tribune,* 12 December 1982.

INTERVIEWS

Clements, George, Father of Holy Angels Church, Personal Interview, 18 October 1984, 14 February 1986.
Coleman, Slim, Editor-in-Chief of *All Chicago City News* and Chairperson of the Heart of Uptown Coalition, Personal Interviews, 16 June 1984, 17 October 1986, 25 May 1988.
Cotton, Rev. Jesse W., Pastor of Greater Institutional AME Church, Personal Interview, 31 August 1984.
Hayes, Charles, Member of U.S. House of Representatives, Personal Interview, 16 April 1984, 5 June 1984, 8 June 1984, 22 February 1988.
Hicks, Jr., Odell, Certified Public Accountant, Personal Interview, 19 January 1985, 5 April 1988.
Jefferson, Nancy, Executive Secretary for the Midwest Community Council, Personal Interview, 3 July 1984.
Johnson, George, President and Chief Executive Officer of Johnson Products, Personal Interview, 25 July 1984.
Robinson, Renault, Former President of the Afro-American Patrolmen's League and Currently a Member of the Board of Directors of the Chicago Housing Authority, Personal Interview, 6 June 1984, 6 July 1981, 16 December 1987.
Sampson, Reverend Al, Pastor of Fernwood Methodist Church, Personal Interview, 7 August 1984, 23 August 1984, 19 October 1986.
Sive-Thomashefsky, Rebecca, Public Relations Director and Member of Board of Directors of Chicago Park District, Personal Interview, 12 September 1984.
Washington, Harold, Mayor of the city of Chicago, Personal Interviews, 23 April 1983, 31 April 1983, 31 May 1983, 22 January 1984, 16 April 1984, 12 May 1984, 19 May 1984, 17 July 1984, 24 August 1984, 24 August 1985, 22 September 1986, 15 October 1986.
Worrill, Conrad W., Professor at Northeastern University, Personal Interview, 18 October 1984.
Wyatt, Addie, Union Executive, Personal Interview, 4 August 1984.

CHAPTER 16

BOOKS

Black Power in Chicago, A Documentary Survey of the 1983 Mayoral Democratic Primary, Chicago: People's College Press, 1983.
Bush, Rod, editor, *The New Vote, Politics and Power in Four American Cities,* San Francisco: Synthesis Publications, 1984.
Holli, Melvin G. and Paul M. Green, editors, *The Making of a Mayor: Chicago 1983,* Grand Rapids, Mich: William B. Eerdsman Publishing Co., 1984.
Kleppner, Paul, *Chicago Divided: The Making of a Black Mayor,* Dekalb, Ill: Northern Illinois University Press, 1985.
Levinsohn, Florence H., *Harold Washing-*

ton, A Political Biography, Chicago: Chicago Review Press, 1983.

Travis, Dempsey J., *An Autobiography of Black Politics,* Chicago, Ill: Urban Research Press, Inc., 1987.

Worrill, Conrad, *Worrill's World,* Chicago, Ill: National Black United Front, 1986.

NEWSPAPERS

"Byrne Issues Challenge to Debate," *Chicago Sun-Times,* 25 November 1982.

"Democratic Mayoral Trio Nears First Set of Hurdles," *Chicago Sun-Times,* 28 November 1982.

"Three Prominent Coaches Join Washington," *Chicago Sun-Times,* 5 December 1982.

"Washington Files the Mayoral Petitions," *Chicago Defender,* 7 December 1982.

"The Chicago Mayoral Race," *Chicago Independent Bulletin,* 9 December 1982.

" 'Say Cheese' and Debate: Speak Up Rich," *Chicago Sun-Times,* 9 December 1982.

"If He Can Talk–Debatable Boss," *Chicago Sun-Times,* 12 December 1982.

"Washington Announces Blue Ribbon Team," *Chicago Defender,* 14 December 1982.

"Daley Agrees to Mayoral Debates, Promises Full Airing of Real Issues," *Chicago Tribune,* 16 December 1982.

"Issues and the Debate," *Chicago Tribune,* 17 December 1982.

"Washington's Camp Wooing Ex-Byrne Aides," *Chicago Sun-Times,* 18 December 1982.

"1,000 Washington Buttons Stolen From Parked Car," *Chicago Defender,* 20 December 1982.

"Daley Seeks Debates with Limits," *Chicago Sun-Times,* 20 December 1982.

"Washington Hires Media Advisors for Campaign Ads," *Chicago Sun-Times,* 22 December 1982.

"Three Rivals OK Sun-Times Debate," *Chicago Sun-Times,* 25 December 1982.

"Washington Wins Top Spot on Mayoral Primary Ballot," *Chicago Defender,* 28 December 1982.

"Byrne, Daley OK Debate on Jan. 18," *Chicago Sun-Times,* 30 December 1982.

"Four Mayoral Debates Lined Up, But Daley Still Uncertain," *Chicago Tribune,* 31 December 1982.

"Six Campaign Sites for Washington," *Chicago Sun-Times,* 10 January 1983.

"Coalition Tells Political Targets," *Chicago Defender,* 11 January 1983.

"Washington Bares His Financial Skeletons," *Chicago Defender,* 12 January 1983.

"Washington Details Troubles, Wins Sympathy," *Chicago Sun-Times,* 12 January 1983.

"Byrne, Washington Pull Out; Debate Off," *Chicago Sun-Times,* 12 January 1983.

"Washington Debate Aide Quits," *Chicago Sun-Times,* 12 January 1983.

"Turnabout on Debates," *Chicago Sun-Times,* 12 January 1983.

Let's Have a Mix of Debates," *Chicago Sun-Times,* 13 January 1983.

"Mayor Debates Okay," *Chicago Sun-Times,* 14 January 1983.

"Four Debates Set After Week of Squabbling," *Chicago Tribune,* 14 January 1983.

"Chicago's Gladiatorial Debates," *Chicago Tribune,* 14 January 1983.

"Three Dem Mayoral Aspirants Agree to Debate Four Times," *Chicago Sun-Times,* 15 January 1983.

"Washington is Mounting a Campaign of Confusion," *Chicago Tribune,* 16 January 1983.

"Washington Bill: It's a Gas," *Chicago Sun-Times,* 28 January 1983.

"Rich Daley Campaigns the Old Way," *Chicago Sun-Times,* 1 February 1983.

"Washington Solidifies Base," *Chicago Sun-Times,* 2 February 1983.

"Byrne Runs Hot With Cool," *Chicago Sun-Times,* 3 February 1983.

"Hartigan to Buck Party, Back Daley for Mayor," *Chicago Tribune,* 4 February 1983.

"Fifteen Thousand at Rally for Washington," *Chicago Defender,* 7 February 1983.

"Fifteen Thousand Means Momentum in Mayoral Marathon," *Chicago Observer,* 12 February 1983.

"Washington Wins, Heavy Black Turnout Key to Victory," *Chicago Tribune,* 23 February 1983.

"Representative Washington, Chicago Victor, Sets Ambitious City Hall Agenda," *New York Times,* 24 February 1983.

INTERVIEWS

Alter, Joanne, Commissioner of Chicago Metropolitan Sanitary District, Personal Interview, 2 October 1985.

Black, Timuel, Professor at Harold Washington College (Loop), Personal Interview, Chicago, 28 April 1984, 12 January 1988.

Brookins, Howard, State Representative, Personal Interview, 3 April 1986.

Brown, Bob, Civil Rights Activist, Personal Interview, 18 October 1984.

Clements, George, Father of Holy Angels Church., Personal Interviews, 18 October 1984, 14 February 1986.

Coleman, Slim, Editor-in-Chief of *All Chicago City News* and Chairperson of the Heart of Uptown Coalition, Personal Interview, 16 June 1984, 17 October 1986, 25 May 1988.

Cotton, Jesse, Pastor of Greater Institutional AME Church, Personal Interview, 31 August 1984.

Davis, Danny, Alderman, Personal Interview, 6 October 1984.

Dunne, George W., President of the Cook County Board, Personal Interview, 14 August 1985.

Gilbert, Herman, Executive Vice President and Editorial Director of Path Press, Personal Interviews, Chicago, 24 November 1984, 28 April 1984, 19 December 1985, 19 March 1988.

Hayes, Charles, Member of U.S. House of Representatives, Personal Interview, 16 April 1984, 5 June 1984, 8 June 1984, 22 February 1988.

Hicks Jr., Odell, Certified Public Accountant, Personal Interview, 19 January 1985, 5 April 1988.

Jackson, Jesse L., Former Staff Member of the Southern Christian Leadership Conference, President of Operation Breadbasket, 1984 & 1988 Presidential Candidate, An International Civil Rights Leader, and Founder and Past President of Operation PUSH, Personal Interview, 30 November 1984.

Johnson, Al, President of Johnson Cadillac, the Political Action Conference of Illinois (PACI), and Dollar-A-Year Man for Mayor Washington, Personal Interview, 25 July 1984.

O'Hare, George, Public Relations Consultant, Radio Host and Civil Rights Activist, Personal Interview, 17 May 1985, 31 May 1985, 18 October 1986, 24 February 1988.

Sampson, Al, Pastor of Fernwood Methodist Church, Personal Interview, 17 August 1984, 23 August 1984, 19 October 1986.

Savage, Gus, Member of U.S. House of Representatives, Personal Interview, Chicago, 22 April 1984, 13 December 1985, 14 January 1986, 2 April 1988.

Washington, Harold, Mayor of the city of Chicago, Personal Interview, 23 April 1983, 31 April 1983, 31 May 1983, 22 January 1984, 16 April 1984, 12 May 1984, 19 May 1984, 17 July 1984, 24 August 1984, 24 August 1985, 22 September 1986, 15 October 1986.

Worrill, Conrad, Professor at Northeastern University, Personal Interview, 18 October 1984.

CHAPTER 17

BOOKS

Black Power in Chicago, A Documentary Survey of the 1983 Mayoral Democratic Primary, Chicago: People's College Press, 1983.

Bush, Rod, editor, *The New Vote, Politics and Power in Four American Cities,* San Francisco: Synthesis Publications, 1984.

Holli, Melvin G. and Paul M. Green, editors, *The Making of a Mayor: Chicago, 1983,* Grand Rapids, Mich: William B. Eerdsman Publishing Co., 1984.

Kleppner, Paul, *Chicago Divided: The Making of a Black Mayor,* Dekalb, Ill: Northern Illinois University Press, 1985.

Levinsohn, Florence H., *Harold Washington, A Political Biography,* Chicago: Chicago Review Press, 1983.

McClain, Leanita, *A Foot in Each World,* Evanston, Ill: Northwestern University Press, 1986.

Travis, Dempsey J., *An Autobiography of Black Politics,* Chicago, Ill: Urban Research Press, Inc., 1987.

Worrill, Conrad, *Worrill's World,* Chicago, Ill: National Black United Front, 1986.

NEWSPAPERS

"Washington and Patronage," *Chicago Defender,* 1 March 1983.

"Majerczyk Bolts Dems, Say He Will Back Epton," *Chicago Sun-Times,* 1 March 1983.

"Majerczyk: Hero in the 12th," *Chicago Sun-Times,* 2 March 1983.

"Epton Dems Hide Faces," *Chicago Tribune,* 3 March 1983.

"Third Party Tells $1 Million Bid for Its Ballot Slot," *Chicago Tribune,* 4 March 1983.

"Democrats Studying the Mayoral Options," *Chicago Tribune,* 6 March 1983.

"Byrne Plans Turnout for Epton," *Chicago Sun-Times,* 6 March 1983.

"Discipline Dissidents, Henry Urges Vrdolyak," *Chicago Defender,* 7 March 1983.

"Black GOP Ward Committeemen Endorse Bernie Epton," *Chicago Defender,* 7 March 1983.

"Puchinski Withholds Support," *Chicago Defender,* 8 March 1983.

"Vrdolyak Snubs Washington's Unity Lunch," *Chicago Sun-Times,* 8 March 1983.

"Endorsements Piling Up for Washington," *Chicago Sun-Times,* 10 March 1983.

"James Taylor, Top Black in House Quits Post," *Chicago Tribune,* 10 March 1983.

"Forget Ward Bosses: Clout Goes 'Pifft'," *Chicago Sun-Times,* 10 March 1983.

"Labor Pays Debt to Rep. Washington," *Chicago Defender,* 10 March 1983.

"Vrdolyak May Ask Party Backing of Washington," *Chicago Sun-Times,* 11 March 1983.

"What was Behind Rumors of Byrne Switch to GOP," *Chicago Defender,* 14 March 1983.

"Dem Chiefs Meet, Weigh Epton Backing," *Chicago Tribune,* 15 March 1983.

"Epton Makes Pitch for Support of Cops," *Chicago Tribune,* 15 March 1983.

"Washington, Epton Agree to One TV Debate," *Chicago Tribune,* 15 March 1983.

"Washington Expects Support Despite Rumors of Defection," *Chicago Defender,* 16 December 1983.

"Washington's Talk Falls on Deaf Ears," *Chicago Tribune,* 16 March 1983.

"Top City Clergy Urge Unbiased Election," *Chicago Tribune,* 16 March 1983.

"Dems Say Byrne to Seek Re-election as Write-In," *Chicago Tribune,* 16 December 1983.

"Jane's Deal: 'Compromise City, Party'," *Chicago Defender,* 17 March 1983.

"Byrne Wants to Destroy Party," *Chicago Defender,* 17 March 1983.

"Washington Gets a Cool Party OK," *Chicago Tribune,* 25 March 1983.

"Vrdolyak Aide Organizing Voters for Epton," *Chicago Tribune,* 29 March 1983.

MAGAZINES

"Race in the Race, The Candidates and Their Strategies," *Chicago Reporter,* March 1983.

"Chicago: A Dream Come True," *Newsweek,* March 7, 1983.

"Mayor Jane Byrne Bad Sport," *Newsweek,* March 28, 1983.

DOCUMENTS

United States of America, plaintiff vs. Harold Washington, defendant Case #1 CR 292 Transcript for proceedings before Honorable Joseph Sam Perry, judge. United States of America, Northern District of Illinois, Eastern Division.

INTERVIEWS

Brown, Bob, Civil Rights Activist, Personal Interview, 18 October 1984.

Coleman, Slim, Editor-in-Chief of *All Chicago City News* and Chairperson of the Heart of Uptown Coalition, Personal Interview, 16 June 1984, 17 October 1986, 25 May 1988.

Cotton, Jesse, Pastor of Greater Institutional AME Church, Personal Interview, 31 August 1984.

Dunne, George W., President of the Cook County Board, Personal Interview, 14 August 1985, 25 January 1988.

Gardner, Edward, Chairman of the Board of Soft Sheen Products, Inc., Personal Interview, 17 July 1984.

Jackson, Jesse L., Former Staff Member of the Southern Christian Leadership Conference, President of Operation Breadbasket, 1984 & 1988 Presidential Candidate, An International Civil Rights Leader, and Founder and Past President of Operation PUSH, Personal Interview, 30 November 1984.

Jefferson, Nancy, Executive Secretary for the Midwest Community Council, Personal Interview, 3 July 1984.

Johnson, George, President and Chief Executive Officer of Johnson Products, Personal Interview, 7 December 1984.

Kennon, Lawrence, Attorney, Personal Interview, 20 June 1984.

Washington, Harold, Mayor of the city of Chicago, Personal Interview, 23 April 1983, 31 April 1983, 31 May 1983, 22 January 1984, 16 April 1984, 12 May 1984, 19 May 1984, 17 July 1984, 24 August 1984, 24 August 1985, 22 September 1986, 15 October 1986.

CHAPTER 18

BOOKS

Black Power in Chicago, A Documentary Survey of the 1983 Mayoral Democratic Primary, Chicago: People's College Press, 1983.

Bush, Rod, editor, *The New Vote, Politics and Power in Four American Cities,* San Francisco: Synthesis Publications, 1984.

Holli, Melvin G. and Paul M. Green, editors, *The Making of a Mayor: Chicago, 1983,* Grand Rapids, Mich: William B. Eerdsman Publishing Co., 1984.

Kleppner, Paul, *Chicago Divided: The Making of a Black Mayor,* Dekalb, Ill: Northern Illinois University Press, 1985.

Levinsohn, Florence H., *Harold Washington, A Political Biography,* Chicago: Chicago Review Press, 1983.

McClain, Leanita, *A Foot in Each World,* Evanston, Ill: Northwestern University Press, 1986.

Travis, Dempsey J., *An Autobiography of Black Politics,* Chicago, Ill: Urban Research Press, Inc., 1987.

Worrill, Conrad, *Worrill's World,* Chicago, Ill: National Black United Front, 1986.

NEWSPAPERS

"Epton, Washington Trade Charges," *Chicago Sun-Times,* 26 February 1983.

"Mayoral Rivals Rip One Another," *Chicago Sun-Times,* 18 March 1983.

"Byrne Leads, But Only in Parade," *Chicago Sun-Times,* 18 March 1983.

"Epton Blasts Media in Vitriolic Attack," *Chicago Tribune,* 26 March 1983.

"Callers Blast Church Over Washington Incident," *Chicago Tribune,* 29 March 1983.

"Puchinski Snubs Party, Backs Epton," *Chicago Tribune,* 1 April 1983.

"Washington Debate Bid Rejected by Epton," *Chicago Sun-Times,* 2 April 1983.

"Won't Tell All Details of Health-Epton," *Chicago Sun-Times,* 2 April 1983.

"Washington's Transition Team," *Chicago Sun-Times,* 4 April 1983.

"Police and Mayor's Race," *Chicago Tribune,* 6 April 1983.

"Brzeczek Quits: Move Seen as Boost for Epton," *Chicago Tribune,* 6 April 1983.

"A Racial Issue Puts City in U.S. Spotlight," *Chicago Tribune,* 7 April 1983.

"Flurry of New Charges Hits Washington," *Chicago Tribune,* 7 April 1983.

"Word War: Chicago Candidates' Advisors Clash as Showdown Nears," *Washington Post,* 7 April 1983.

"Ugliness of Election Can't Taint Entire City," *Chicago Tribune,* 7 April 1983.

"Readers' Views on Chicago Mayoral Campaign," *Chicago Tribune,* 7 April 1983.

"Angry Washington Vows to Fight Lies," *Chicago Sun-Times,* 8 April 1983.

"Jane on TV, But What's Her Line?," *Chicago Sun-Times,* 8 April 1983.

"Why Top Blacks Back Washington," *Chicago Tribune,* 8 April 1983.

"An Ugly Smear Campaign," *Chicago Tribune,* 8 April 1983.

"Epton is Low Key, Upbeat," *Chicago Sun-Times,* 8 April 1983.

"Vrdolyak: Bitter Election After Taste Seen," *Chicago Sun-Times,* 8 April 1983.

"His Kind of Town, *Chicago Ain't,"* *Chicago Sun-Times,* 8 April 1983.

"Irate Washington Retaliates," *Chicago Tribune,* 8 April 1983.

"Three Northwest Side Rallies Give Epton Giant Boosts," *Chicago Sun-Times,* 9 April 1983.

"Bitter Flurry Capping Brutal Campaign Here," *Chicago Sun-Times,* 9 April 1983.

"Dirty Tricks Continue," *Chicago Defender,* 9 April 1983.

"Who Are the Real Culprits in Election," *Chicago Defender,* 9 April 1983.

"Rumors Traced to Byrne Guards, Washington Says," *Chicago Sun-Times,* 9 April 1983.

"Chicago Voters Show Desperation, Determination," *Washington Post,* 10 April 1983.

"Washington Blasts Dems: Epton Cools It," *Chicago Sun-Times,* 10 April 1983.

"If Harold Loses, He Will Have Himself to Blame," *Chicago Sun-Times,* 10 April 1983.

"Election May Hinge on Ethnic Turnout," *Chicago Sun-Times,* 10 April 1983.

"The Countdown: Bitter Mayoral Race Goes Down to the Wire," *Chicago Tribune,* 10 April 1983.

"Question of Racism Full of Gray Area," *Chicago Tribune,* 10 April 1983.

"A Candid Look at the Candidates," *Chicago Sun-Times,* 10 April 1983.

"Washington Works Lakefront, Blacks; Epton Keeps Low Profile," *Chicago Tribune,* 10 April 1983.

"City's 'Bigot' Label Came from Outside," *Chicago Tribune,* 11 April 1983.

"Racist Literature Traced to Epton," *Chicago Defender,* 11 April 1983.

"Chicago Election Reviewed," *Chicago Defender,* 11 April 1983.

"Racial Politics and the Black Backlash," *Chicago Defender,* 11 April 1983.

"Blacks Urged Get Smart, Not Mad Tonight," *Chicago Defender,* 11 April 1983.

"Washington: Raps Rich Foe," *Chicago Sun-Times,* 11 April 1983.

"Epton Dems Push Turnout," *Chicago Sun-Times,* 11 April 1983.

"Eight Council Seats May Go To Independents," *Chicago Sun-Times,* 11 April 1983.

"Mayoral Unity Vowed," *Chicago Sun-Times,* 12 April 1983.

"Fraud Fighters In Force for Vote Today," *Chicago Sun-Times,* 12 April 1983.

" 'No More' Campaign-Weary Chicagoans Say," *Chicago Sun-Times,* 12 April 1983.

"One Vote Against Hatred and Fear," *Chicago Sun-Times,* 12 April 1983.

"U.S. Poll Cites Washington Legal Troubles," *Chicago Sun-Times,* 12 April 1983.

"Time to Choose," *Chicago Sun-Times,* 12 April 1983.

"1.3 Million Expected to Elect Mayor Today," *Chicago Tribune,* 12 April 1983.

"Critics Say Chicago Establishment Fumbled Mayoral Campaign," *Washington Post,* 12 April 1983.

"Is Chicago Really So Important?," *Washington Post,* 12 April 1983.

"Blacks Here Raise Funds for Out of Towners," *Washington Post,* 12 April 1983.

MAGAZINES

"Good Intentions, Negative Results," *The Christian Century,* April 13, 1983.

"Race and Politics: Chicago's Ugly Election," *Newsweek,* April 11. 1983.

"Harold Washington Wins Hot Race to Become First Black Mayor of Chicago," *Jet,* May 2, 1983.

"Mayor Harold Washington: Changing of Guard in Chicago," *Ebony,* July 1983.

INTERVIEWS

Brown, Bob, Civil Rights Activist, Personal Interview, 18 October 1984.

Black, Timuel, Professor at Harold Washington College (Loop), Personal Interview, Chicago, 28 April 1984, 12 January 1988.

Braun, Carol Mosely, State Representative, Personal Interview, 4 March 1985.

Clements, George, Father of Holy Angels Church., Personal Interview, 18 October 1984, 14 February 1986.

Coleman, Slim, Editor-in-Chief of *All Chicago City News* and Chairperson of the Heart of Uptown Coalition, Personal Interview, 16 June 1984, 17 October 1986, 25 May 1988.

Cotton, Jesse, Pastor of Greater Institutional AME Church, Personal Interview, 31 August 1984.

Dunne, George W., President of the Cook County Board, Personal Interview, 14 August 1985, 25 January 1988.

Gilbert, Herman, Executive Vice President and Editorial Director of Path Press, Personal Interviews, Chicago, 24 November 1984, 28 April 1984, 19 December 1985, 19 March 1988.

Hayes, Charles, Member of US House of Representatives, Personal Interview, 16 April 1984, 5 June 1984, 8 June 1984, 22 February 1988.

Jackson, Jesse L., Former Staff Member of the Southern Christian Leadership Conference, President of Operation Breadbasket, 1984 & 1988 Presidential Candidate, An International Civil Rights Leader, and Founder and Past President of Operation PUSH, Personal Interview, 30 November 1984.

Jefferson, Nancy, Executive Secretary for the Midwest Community Council, Personal Interview, 3 July 1984.

Kennon, Lawrence, Attorney, Personal Interview, 20 June 1984.

Washington, Harold, Mayor of the city of Chicago, Personal Interview, 23 April 1983, 31 April 1983, 31 May 1983, 22 January 1984, 16 April 1984, 12 May 1984, 19 May 1984, 17 July 1984, 24 August 1984, 24 August 1985, 22 September 1986, 15 October 1986.

CHAPTER 19

BOOKS

Black Power in Chicago, A Documentary Survey of the 1983 Mayoral Democratic Primary, Chicago: People's College Press, 1983.

Bush, Rod, editor, *The New Vote, Politics and Power in Four American Cities,* San Francisco: Synthesis Publication, 1984.

Holli, Melvin G. and Paul M. Green, editors, *The Making of a Mayor: Chicago 1983,* Grand Rapids, Mich.: William B. Eerdsman Publishing Co., 1984.

Kleppner, Paul, *Chicago Divided: The Making of a Black Mayor,* Dekalb, Ill.: Northern Illinois University Press, 1985.

Levinsohn, Florence Hamlish, *Harold Washington, A Political Biography,* Chicago: Chicago Review Press, 1983.

Travis, Dempsey J., *An Autobiography of Black Chicago,* Chicago: Urban Research Press, 1981.

________, *An Autobiography of Black Politics,* Chicago: Urban Research Press, 1987.

Worrill, Conrad, *Worrill's World,* Chicago: National Black United Front, 1986.

NEWSPAPERS

"Washington Moves to City Hall," *Chicago Independent Bulletin,* 28 April 1983.

"Mayor Harold Washington: April 29, 1983," *Chicago Independent Bulletin,* 29 April 1983.

"It's Washington's Day, But Battle for Power Looms," *Chicago Tribune,* 29 April 1983.

"VIPs, Family to See New Mayor Bow In," Chicago Sun-Times, 29 April 1983.

"Washington's Tax Debt Paid," *Chicago Sun-Times,* 29 April 1983.

"Washington Battles Council on Key Jobs," *Chicago Sun-Times,* 29 April 1983.

"Gala to Usher in New Mayor," *Chicago Sun-Times,* 29 April 1983.

"Tale of Two Chicagos, One White, One Black," *Chicago Sun-Times,* 29 April 1983.

"Washington's Challenge," *Chicago Sun-Times,* 29 April 1983.

"Inaugural Surprises Some, Pleases Others," *Chicago Tribune,* 30 April 1983.

"Inauguration Finds Epton in Another World," *Chicago Tribune,* 30 April 1983.

"A Day of Celebration for Chicago's 42nd Mayor," *Chicago Tribune,* 30 April 1983.

"Conciliatorial Note is Tone of the Day for Brightest Hero," *Chicago Tribune,* 30 April 1983.

"Washington Takes Office; Vows Layoffs, Pay Slashes," *Chicago Sun-Times,* 30 April 1983.

"Reactions: Emotions at Fever Pitch," *Chicago Sun-Times,* 30 April 1983.

"Mayor Comes in Firing," *Chicago Tribune,* 30 April 1983.

"Byrne's Calm Turns to Pain Under Successor's Attack," *Chicago Tribune,* 30 April 1983.

"Washington's Inauguration in Chicago," *Washington Post,* 30 April 1983.

"Emotions Rip Washington's Audience," *Chicago Sun-Times,* 30 April 1983.

"What Washington Inherited," *Chicago Tribune,* 1 May 1983.

"Mayor: Budget May Run $150 Million in the Red," *Chicago Sun-Times,* 1 May 1983.

"City Now More Than Half Minorities," *Chicago Tribune,* 1 May 1983.

"Mayor Cuts His Pay 20%," *Chicago Tribune,* 1 May 1983.

"Council Infighting Begins," *Chicago Tribune,* 1 May 1983.

"Mayor Seeks Compromise; Aldermen 'Hang Tough' " *Chicago Sun-Times,* 1 May 1983.

"For Mayor Washington, the Major Battles are Still to Come," *Chicago Tribune,* 1 May 1983.

"Washington's Crowning Brings Emotional Tears," *Chicago Defender,* 3 May 1983.

"Citizens Reflect on Chicago's 42nd Mayor," *Chicago Defender,* 3 May 1983.

"Mayor Washington's Heavy Burden," *Chicago Tribune,* 4 May 1983.

"Boycott for Freedom in Fairness of News," *Chicago Tribune,* 18 May 1986.

MAGAZINES

"Chicago Says Its Had Enough," *Progressive,* April 1983.

"The New Black Politics," *Newsweek,* April 11, 1983.

"Good Intentions, Negative Results," *The Christian Century,* April 13, 1983.

"The Activist," *Chicago Tribune Magazine,* April 17, 1983.

"Job Now: Put Chicago Back Together," *U.S. News and World Report,* April 25, 1983.

"Harold's Needed Victory," *New Republic,* May 2, 1983.

"The Winds Shift in Chicago," *Progressive,* June 1983.

"Washington's Inaugural: Pomp, Pageantry and Promise of a New Chicago," *Dollars and Sense,* Special Issue, June 1983.

"The Winds Shift in Chicago," *Progressive,* June 1983.

"Mayor Harold Washington: Changing of the Guards in Chicago," *Ebony,* July 1983.

INTERVIEWS

Black, Timuel, Professor at Harold Washington (Loop) College, Personal Interviews, Chicago, 18 April 1984, 12 January 1988.

Braun, Carol Moseley, State Representative, Personal Interview, 4 March 1985.

Coleman, Slim, Editor-in-Chief of *All Chicago City News* and Chairperson of the Heart of Uptown Coalition, Personal Interviews, 16 June 1984, 17 October 1986, 25 May 1988.

Cotton, Jesse, Pastor of Greater Institutional AME Church, Personal Interview, 31 August 1984.

Davis, Danny, Alderman, Personal Interview, 6 October 1984.

Ellis, Morris, Musician and Orchestra Leader, Personal Interviews, 18 February 1986, 31 July 1988.

Gilbert, Herman, Executive Vice President and Editorial Director of Path Press, Personal Interviews, Chicago, 24 November 1984, 28 April 1984, 19 December 1985, 19 March 1988.

Goldsborough, Evelyn, Former student at Roosevelt University and owner of Harold Washington's condominium #27 at Hampton House, Personal Interview, 12 March 1988.

Hayes, Charles, Member of U.S. House of Representatives, Personal Interviews, 16 April 1984, 5 June 1984, 8 June 1984, 22 February 1988.

Hicks Jr., Odell, Certified Public Accountant, Personal Interviews, 19 January 1985, 5 April 1988.

Lee, Frank, Member of the Mayor's Security Detail, Personal Interview, Chicago, 22 February 1988.

McClain, Clarence, District Administrator for Congressional Office of Harold

Washington, Personal Interviews, Chicago, 8 May 1985, 7 April 1988.
O'Hare, George, Public Relations Consultant, Radio Host and Civil Rights Activist, Personal Interviews, 17 May 1985, 31 May 1985, 18 October 1986, 24 February 1988.
Saffold, Howard, Member of the Mayor's Security Detail, Personal Interviews, 12 January 1988, 25 February 1988, 27 July 1988.
Savage, Gus, Member of U.S. House of Representatives, Personal Interviews, Chicago, 22 April 1984, 13 December 1985, 14 January 1986, 2 April 1988.
Walls II, Bill, Mayor's Aide, Personal Interview, 7 January 1988.
Washington, Harold, Mayor of the city of Chicago, Personal Interviews, 23 April 1983, 31 April 1983, 31 May 1983, 22 January 1984, 16 April 1984, 12 May 1984, 19 May 1984, 17 July 1984, 24 August 1984, 24 August 1985, 22 September 1986, 15 October 1986.
Wyatt, Addie, Union Executive, Personal Interview, 4 August 1984.
Wyatt, Claude, Pastor of Vernon Park Church of God, Personal Interview, 4 August 1984.

CHAPTER 20

BOOKS

Kleppner, Paul, *Chicago Divided: The Making of a Black Mayor,* Dekalb, Ill.: Northern Illinois University Press, 1985.
Travis, Dempsey J., *An Autobiography of Black Politics,* Chicago: Urban Research Press, 1987.
Worrill, Conrad, *Worrill's World,* Chicago: National Black United Front, 1986.

NEWSPAPERS

"Mayor Seeks Compromise; Aldermen 'Hang Tough'," *Chicago Sun-Times,* 1 May 1983.
"City Now More Than Half Minorities," *Chicago Tribune,* 1 May 1983.
"For Mayor Washington, the Major Battles are Still to Come," *Chicago Tribune,* 1 May 1983.
"Mayor Cuts His Pay 20 Percent," *Chicago Tribune,* 1 May 1983.
"What Washington Inherited," *Chicago Tribune,* 1 May 1983.
"Mayor's People Claim Enough Votes to Organize Concert," *Chicago Sun-Times,* 2 May 1983.
"The Mayor Takes A Powder, Shocks Chicago City Council," *Washington Post,* 3 May 1983.
"Vrdolyak 'Coup' Ripped by Mayor," *Chicago Sun-Times,* 3 May 1983.
"Chicago Mayor and His Rivals Meet After Tumultuous Clash," *New York Times,* 4 May 1983.
"Behind the Council Coup," *Chicago Sun-Times,* 5 May 1983.
"Chicago Mayor's Smoldering Bid To Control City Council Flares Up," *New York Times,* 7 May 1983.
"Round Two, Vrdolyak Scores Again in His Brawl with Mayor," *Chicago Tribune, 8 May 1983.*
"Mayor Asks Council to Negotiate," Chicago *Tribune,* 9 May 1983.
"Accord is Reached on Chicago Parks," *New York Times,* 11 May 1983.
"A Tinderbox in the City Council," *Chicago Tribune,* 11 May 1983.
"City Council Set for A Donnybrook," *Chicago Tribune,* 11 May 1983.
"Chicago Democrats Fail to Heal Rift," *New York Times,* 11 May 1983.
"Mayor Lists Top Points of First Days," *Chicago Sun-Times,* 12 May 1983.
"The Spoils of Chicago's Political War: Money and Power Go To the Winners," *New York Times,* 14 May 1983.
"City That Worked Does, As Council Feuds," *Chicago Sun-Times,* 15 May 1983.
"Victory for Vrdolyak," *Chicago Sun-Times,* 17 May 1983.
"Mayor Appeals Court Ruling; Feud Goes On," *Chicago Defender,* 17 May 1983.
"Why Washington Fumbled A Victory," *Chicago Sun-Times,* 20 May 1983.
"Open Power Struggle in Chicago," *Chicago Tribune,* 21 May 1983.
"How Did Council Wars Affect the City Business?" *Chicago Sun-Times,* 22 May 1983.
"Kenner Weeps As Jury Finds Him Guilty of Extortion, Fraud," *Chicago Tribune,* 25 May 1983.

"Failure at City Hall," *Chicago Sun-Times,* 25 May 1983.

"Three-Week City Council Crisis of Chicago, Still at Impasse," *New York Times,* 26 May 1983.

"Washington Calls Council Division 'War,'" *Chicago Tribune,* 26 May 1983.

"Chicago's New Political Base," *Chicago Tribune,* 29 May 1983.

"Independence is Key Word for Vrdolyak 29," *Chicago Sun-Times,* 29 May 1983.

"Power Struggle or Racism, Voters Frown On Council's Feuding," *Chicago Tribune,* 29 May 1983.

"Let City Council Get to Work, The Vrdolyak 29 Urge Court," *Chicago Sun-Times,* 15 June 1983.

"Vrdolyak Bloc Victory," *Chicago Sun-Times,* 28 June 1983.

"Chicago Power Struggle in New Stage," *New York Times,* 28 June 1983.

"Burke Says Washington Backers Ready to Defect," *Chicago Sun-Times,* 2 July 1983.

"Chicago Compromise: Budget Breaks New Ground," *New York Times,* 31 December 1983.

"Chicago Mayor Regrets Time Spent on His Rival," *New York Times,* 23 April 1984.

"Foes of Chicago Mayor Say He Has Forfeited His Office," *New York Times,* 24 May 1984.

"Cool Off, Burke Advises, As Council Session Sizzles," *Chicago Tribune,* 14 July 1984.

"Chicago 'Council Wars' Drag Into Intermission," *New York Times,* 14 July 1984.

"Southwest Side Fuming Over Council Feud," *Chicago Tribune,* 15 July 1984.

"Mayor May Sue 29 Over Appointments," *Chicago Defender,* 18 August 1984.

"'I Won't Submit to Blackmail'–Mayor," *Chicago Defender,* 1 September 1984.

"Vrdolyak Talking Tough Again," *Chicago Tribune,* 1 July 1985.

"Unratified City Nurses' Pact Called 'Hostage' to Council Wars," *Chicago Tribune,* 1 July 1985.

"Mayor and Opposition Leaders Meet On Aide Tie-Up," *Chicago Sun-Times,* 2 July 1985.

"Can Berry Free City Hall Hostages?" *Chicago Tribune,* 3 July 1985.

"Compromise, Vrdolyak-Style," *Chicago Tribune,* 8 July 1985.

"A Refuge for Lame Ducks," *Chicago Tribune,* 9 July 1985.

"Direct From City Hall, It's Dem Streetfighters," *Chicago Tribune,*12 July 1985.

"Burrell Indicted, Charged with Bugging the Mayor's Apartment," *Chicago Defender,* 25 July 1985.

"Vrdolyak's Accused of Blocking Bills," *Chicago Sun-Times,* 30 July 1985.

"Chicago War Goes Global," *Chicago Tribune,* 7 September 1985.

"Overrule Mayor's Dismissal of Spicer," *Chicago Defender,* 12 September 1985.

"Council Fights Over Port; Witch Hunting Charged," *Chicago Sun-Times,* 28 September 1985.

"Control of Boards Eludes Mayor," *Chicago Sun-Times,* 26 November 1985.

MAGAZINES

"When City Hall Becomes a Circus," *U.S. News & World Report,* May 23, 1983.

"The Battle for Chicago: It's the Old Machine Vs. New Mayor," *Time,* May 23, 1983.

INTERVIEWS

Coleman, Slim, Editor-in-Chief of *All Chicago City News* and Chairperson of the Heart of Uptown Coalition, Personal Interviews, 16 June 1984, 17 October 1986, 25 May 1988.

Davis, Danny, Alderman, Personal Interview, 6 October 1984.

Frost, Wilson, Alderman, Personal Interviews, Chicago, 21 September 1985, 7 January 1986.

Humes, Marian, Alderman of 8th Ward, Personal Interview, 29 April 1985.

Jones, Mark, Former Circuit Court Judge, Personal Interview, 19 August 1985.

Miner, Judson, Corporation Counsel for the City of Chicago, Personal Interview, 16 January 1986.

Montgomery, James, Attorney, Personal Interviews, Chicago, 28 December 1985, August 1986.

Newhouse, Richard, State Senator, Personal Interviews, Chicago 23 October 1984, 20 December 1985, 29 January 1988.

Pincham, R. Eugene, Appellate Court Judge in the 1st District of Illinois, Personal In-

terviews, Chicago, 31 July 1986, 5 August 1986, 8 December 1987.
Saffold, Howard, Member of the Mayor's Security Detail, Personal Interviews, 12 January 1988, 25 February 1988, 27 July 1988.
Sampson, Rev. Albert, Pastor of Fernwood Methodist Church, Personal Interviews, 17 August 1984, 23 August 1984, 19 October 1986.
Tillman, Dorothy, Alderman, 3rd Ward and Former Staff Member of Dr. Martin Luther King's Southern Christian Leadership Conference, Personal Interviews, 31 May 1985, 2 July 1988.
Washington, Harold, Mayor of the City of Chicago, Personal Interviews, 23 April 1983, 31 April 1983, 31 May 1983, 22 January 1984, 16 April 1984, 12 May 1984, 19 May 1984, 17 July 1984, 24 August 1984, 24 August 1985, 22 September 1986, 15 October 1986.

CHAPTER 21

NEWSPAPERS

"U.S. Weighs Appeal of Chicago Remap," *Chicago Defender,* 1 January 1983.
"Streeter: 'We Got Screwed on Remap,' " *Chicago Metro News,* 1 January 1983.
"Chicago Coalition Arises," *Chicago Tribune,* 9 January 1983.
"Mayor's Backers Plan '84 Primary Slate," *Chicago Sun-Times,* 31 May 1983.
"Remap May Increase Vote Power," *Chicago Defender,* 2 November 1983.
"Mayor Ties Remap to Early Vote," *Chicago Sun-Times,* 19 May 1984.
"Local Wards Affected by Court Ordered Remap," *Lawndale News,* 20 May 1984.
"New Ward Map Sets Up Struggle for Early Election," *Chicago Tribune,* 20 May 1984.
"Hit '29' Remap Appeal," *Chicago Defender,* 21 May 1984.
"Remap Orders Stalls City," *Chicago Sun-Times,* 22 May 1984.
"Local Wards Affected by Court Ordered Remap," *Northwest Herald,* 23 May 1984.
"Council Majority in Hand of the Court," *Chicago Sun-Times,* 24 May 1984.
"Council Split on Appeal of Ward Remap Decision," *Chicago Defender,* 5 June 1984.
"Council Lawyers Out in Remap Conflict," *Chicago Sun-Times,* 7 June 1984.
"Washington Tactics Aim to Speed Council Elections," *Chicago Tribune,* 7 June 1984.
"End Remap Battle," *Chicago Sun-Times,* 8 June 1984.
" 'Firing' Fails to Deter Appeal of City Remap," *Chicago Tribune,* 8 June 1984.
"Alderman Appeal Ward Remap," *Chicago Sun-Times,* 8 June 1984.
"Remap Appeal Sought," *Chicago Defender,* 9 June 1984.
"No Refunds for Remap Fight," *Chicago Tribune,* 9 June 1984.
"City Pushes in Court For Prompt Ward Remap," *Chicago Sun-Times,* 9 June 1984.
"The Litmus Test," *All Chicago City News,* 16 June 1984.
"Mayor Urges New Elections in Ward Remapping," *All Chicago City News,* 16 June 1984.
"City Remap War Erupts," *Chicago Sun-Times,* 20 June 1984.
"Mayor Predicts Remap Victory," *Chicago Sun-Times,* 27 June 1984.
"Alderman Sherman Irks Hispanics," *Chicago Defender,* 28 June 1984.
"Cheers, Jeers Greet City Filers of Ward Remap Votes," *Lawndale News,* 28 June 1984.
"Hispanics Unite to Fight For a New Ward Map and Elections," *All Chicago City News,* 30 June 1984.
"Republicans Mull Bid to Elect Aldermen-at-Large," *Chicago Northwest Press,* 11 July 1984.
"Alderman Santiago Backs Ward Remap Plans," *Chicago Sun-Times,* 29 August 1984.
"Appellate Panel Affirms Ward Redistricting Order," *Chicago Sun-Times,* 12 September 1984.
"U.S. Appeals Court Reaffirms City Wards Must Be Remapped," *Chicago Tribune,* 12 September 1984.
"Party Won't Finance Remap Appeal," *Chicago Defender,* 18 September 1984.

"Punish Dems Who Oppose Redistricting, Mayor Urges," *Chicago Sun-Times,* 21 September 1984.

"No Gerrymandered Wards," *Chicago Tribune,* 22 September 1984.

"Operation PUSH Enters 1981 Ward Remap Fight," *Chicago Defender,* 17 October 1984.

"Council Asks High Court to Block Ward Remap," *Chicago Tribune,* 19 October 1984.

"Court Temporarily Bars Ward Remap," *Chicago Tribune,* 23 October 1984.

"Stevens Blocks Ward Remaps," *Chicago Sun-Times,* 23 October 1984.

"Mayor Wins Ward Remap Squirmish," *Chicago Tribune,* 6 July 1985.

INTERVIEWS

Braun, Carol Moseley, State Representative, Personal Interview, 4 March 1985.

Cerda, Maria B., Assistant to the Mayor for Employment and Training, Personal Interview, 25 October 1985.

Collazo, Migadalia, Candidate for alderman in 31st Ward, Personal Interview, 15 October 1985.

del Valle, Miguel, member of the Mayor's Advisory Council on Latino Affairs and currently state senator in the 5th District, Personal Interview, 15 October 1985.

Garcia, Jesus, Democratic committeeman and alderman of the 22nd Ward, Personal Interview, 16 October 1985.

Goitia, Andy, Personal Interview, 17 October 1985.

Gutierrez, Luis, Committeeman and alderman of 26th Ward, Personal Interview, 19 October 1985.

Hayes, Charles, Member of U.S. House of Representatives, Personal Interviews, 16 April 1984, 5 June 1984, 8 June 1984, 22 February 1988.

Jackson, Jesse, Former Staff Member of the Southern Christian Leadership Conference, President of Operation Breadbasket, 1984 & 1988 Presidential Candidate, An International Civil Rights leader, and Founder and Past President of Operation PUSH, Personal Interview, 30 November 1984.

Johnson, Al, President of Johnson Cadillac Co. and of the Political Action Conference of Illinois (PACI), and Dollar-A-Year Man for Mayor Washington, Personal Interview, 25 July 1984.

Miner, Judson, Corporation Counsel for the City of Chicago, Personal Interview, 16 January 1986.

Montgomery, James, Attorney, Personal Interview, Chicago, 28 December 1985, 4 August 1986.

Savage, Gus, Member of U.S. House of Representatives, Personal Interviews, Chicago, 22 April 1984, 13 December 1985, 14 January 1986, 2 April 1988.

Torres, Maria, Director of the Mayor's Advisory Committee on Latino Affairs, Personal Interview, 22 October 1985.

Washington, Harold, Mayor of the city of Chicago, Personal Interviews, 23 April 1983, 31 April 1983, 31 May 1983, 22 January 1984, 16 April 1984, 12 May 1984, 19 May 1984, 17 July 1984, 24 August 1984, 24 August 1985, 22 September 1986, 15 October 1986.

CHAPTER 22

NEWSPAPERS

"Remap of Wards; Vrdolyak May Face Test," *Chicago Sun-Times,* 4 June 1985.

"Court Upholds Remap of Wards," *Chicago Tribune,* 4 June 1985.

"Remap Verdict: A New Day in Wards," *Chicago Sun-Times,* 6 June 1985.

"New Ball Game," *Chicago Sun-Times,* 6 June 1985.

"Latinos Key to Council Realignment," *Chicago Sun-Times,* 6 June 1985.

"Hispanics Hail Supreme Court's Hands-Off Ruling," *Lawndale News,* 6 June 1985.

" '29' Run From Council Vote on Ward Remap—Force Adjournment," *All Chicago City News,* 7 June 1985.

"Remap Fight Likely to go the Distance," *Chicago Tribune,* 9 June 1985.

"Minorities Seek Fast Action on Ward Remap," *Chicago Sun-Times,* 20 June 1985.

"Judge Sets Deadline in Remap Case," *Chicago Sun-Times,* 22 June 1985.

"Ward Remap Fight in Court," *Chicago Tribune,* 22 June 1985.

"Ward Remap Election Won't Unfold in '85," *Chicago Tribune,* 3 July 1985.

"Mayor Wins Ward Remap Skirmish," *Chicago Tribune,* 6 July 1985.

"City Council Unit Quietly Approves Community Projects Budget," *Chicago Sun-Times,* 9 July 1985.

"Jane Byrne Denies Any Association with Remap," *Chicago Sun-Times,* 22 July 1985.

"Paying for Party Fights," *Chicago Tribune,* 23 July 1985.

" '29' Continue to Fight Court-Ordered Remap," *All Chicago City News,* 26 July 1985.

"Long Battle Over City Ward Map Worth Millions—To Lawyers," *Chicago Sun-Times,* 1 November 1985.

"Ward Remap in Judge's Hands," *Chicago Tribune,* 1 November 1985.

"Aldermen Scramble: Remap Spurs Interest in County Board Seats," *Chicago Sun-Times,* 1 November 1985.

"Dispute in 15th Ward Threatens Remap Plan," *Chicago Sun-Times,* 2 November 1985.

"Ward Remap Catches Up to Changing City," *Chicago Tribune,* 3 November 1985.

"Council Factions Courting Hispanics," *Chicago Sun-Times,* 3 November 1985.

"Remap Brawl Splits Eddie's '29' " *Chicago Sun-Times,* 4 November 1985.

"Ward Battle Lines Drawn," *Chicago Sun-Times,* 5 November 1985.

"City Council Stokes Remap Fire," *Chicago Tribune,* 7 November 1985.

"Mayor Presses for Ward Elections," *Chicago Sun-Times,* 9 November 1985.

"FBI Mole Gave Aldermen Cash," *Chicago Tribune,* 26 December 1985.

"Swindler Sparked FBI Probe," *Chicago Tribune,* 27 December 1985.

"Aldermen, Contractors Feel Heat," *Chicago Tribune,* 28 December 1985.

"FBI Mole's Credo: 'Let's Make A Deal,'" *Chicago Tribune,* 29 December 1985.

"Businessman Links Informer to McClain," *Chicago Tribune,* 30 December 1985.

"McClain Must Go, Mayor Told," *Chicago Tribune,* 31 December 1985.

"No Guarantees in the Wards," *Chicago Tribune,* 8 January 1986.

"Victory in Remap, Judge Orders March Special Election," *All Chicago City News,* 10 January 1986.

"Changing Hats at City Hall," *Chicago Tribune,* 14 January 1986.

"Eddie Tried to Rewrite History of Ward Remap," *Chicago Sun-Times,* 22 January 1986.

"Remap Lawyers Seek $2 1/2 Million in Fees," *Chicago Tribune,* 30 January 1986.

"Chicago's Mayor Seeks Federal Voter Observers," *New York Times,* 12 March 1986.

"Changing Sides Barred in Remap," *Chicago Sun-Times,* 28 March 1986.

"Three Remap Lawyers Lose Out on Fees," *Chicago Tribune,* 28 March 1986.

"Judge Orders Election for 18th, 15th, Wards," *Southwest News Herald,* 2 July 1986.

INTERVIEWS

Braun, Carol Moseley, State Representative, Personal Interview, 4 March 1985.

Cerda, Maria B., Assistant to the Mayor for Employment and Training, Personal Interview, 25 October 1985.

Collazo, Migadalia, Candidate for alderman in 31st Ward, Personal Interview, 15 October 1985.

Coleman, Slim, Editor-in-Chief of *All Chicago City News* and Chairperson of the Heart of Uptown Coalition, Personal Interview, 16 June 1984, 17 October 1986, 25 May 1988.

del Valle, Miguel, member of the Mayor's Advisory Council on Latino Affairs and currently state senator in the 5th District, Personal Interview, 15 October 1985.

Davis, Danny, Alderman, Personal Interview, 6 October 1984.

Frost, Wilson, Alderman, Personal Interview, 21 September 1985, 7 January 1986.

Garcia, Jesus, Democratic committeeman and alderman of the 22nd Ward, Personal Interview, 16 October 1985.

Gardner, Edward, chairman of the board of Soft Sheen Products Inc., Personal Interview, 17 July 1984.

Goitia, Andy, Personal Interview, 17 October 1985.

Gutierrez, Luis, Committeeman and alderman of 26th Ward, Personal Interview, 19 October 1985.

Humes, Marian, Alderman of the 8th Ward, Personal Interview, 29 April 1985.

Jones, Mark, Former Circuit Court Judge, Personal Interview, 19 August 1985.

Miner, Judson, Corporation Counsel for Chicago, Personal Interview, 16 January 1986.

Montgomery, James, Attorney, Personal Interview, 28 December 1985, 4 August 1986.

Newhouse, Richard, State Senator, Personal Interviews, 23 October 1984, 20 December 1985, 29 January 1988.

Pincham, R. Eugene, Appellate Court Judge in the 1st District of Illinois, Personal Interview, 31 July 1986, 5 August 1986, 8 December 1987.

Saffold, Howard, Officer in Mayor Harold Washington's security detail, Personal Interview, 12 January 1988, 25 February 1988, 27 July 1988.

Sampson, Rev. Albert, Pastor of Fernwood Methodist Church, Personal Interview, 17 August 1984, 23 August 1984, 19 October 1986.

Tillman, Dorothy, Alderman, 3rd Ward and Former Staff Member of Dr. Martin Luther King's Southern Christian Leadership Conference, Personal Interview, 31 May 1985, 2 July 1988.

Torres, Maria, Director of the Mayor's Advisory Committee on Latino Affairs, Personal Interview, 22 October 1985.

Washington, Harold, Mayor of the City of Chicago, Personal Interviews, 23 April 1983, 31 April 1983, 31 May 1983, 22 January 1984, 16 April 1984, 12 May 1984, 19 May 1984, 17 July 1984, 24 August 1984, 24 August 1985, 22 September 1986, 15 October 1986.

CHAPTER 23

NEWSPAPERS

"Mayor Captures Committees," *Chicago Tribune,* 7 June 1986.

"Two Aldermen Explain Why They Walked," *Chicago Sun-Times,* 2 June 1986.

"Ailing Alderman Aides Mayor's Council Coup," *Chicago Sun-Times,* 7 June 1986.

"Hutch, Humes Answer Critics," *Chicago Defender,* 2 June 1986.

"Humes Excuse Doesn't Impress Jesse," *Chicago Defender,* 9 June 1986.

"Alderman Walk Stalls Appointees," *Chicago Sun-Times,* 31 May 1986.

"Humes, Stroger Trade Blows," *Chicago Defender,* 3 June 1986.

"Humes Vows Vote for Mayor's Choices," *Chicago Tribune,* 4 June 1986.

"Chicago Mayor's Bloc Has it Debut," *New York Times,* 10 May 1986.

"Aldermen, Contractors Feel Heat," *Chicago Tribune,* 28 December 1985.

"City Deal?" *Chicago Sun-Times,* 25 December 1985.

"Council Wars Open a New Front in Court," *Chicago Sun-Times,* 13 June 1986.

"Mayor Gets Way on Nominees," *Chicago Tribune,* 10 May 1986.

"Mayor's Opponents' Solidarity Begins to Melt Away," *Chicago Sun-Times,* 11 May 1986.

"Three Years Later, It's the Mayor's Round," *Chicago Sun-Times,* 10 May 1986.

"City Hall Hostage Battle Looms," *Chicago Sun-Times,* 5 May 1986.

"A Cheap Victory for Mayor's Allies," *Chicago Tribune,* 31 July 1986.

"Mayor Sprints Past Fast Eddie," *Chicago Sun-Times,* 1 May 1986.

"Hispanic Squirmish Highlights Changes in Council Make-Up," *Chicago Tribune,* 2 May 1986.

"The Chicago Machine," *Chicago Tribune,* 3 May 1986.

"Chicago Mayor Calls Machine Dead," *New York Times,* 1 May 1986.

"Mayor Feels Power Shifting His Way," *Chicago Tribune,* 30 May 1986.
"Some Allies Break with Eddie," *Chicago Sun-Times,* 1 May 1986.
"Mayor Flexes Muscle," *Chicago Sun-Times,* 1 May 1986.
"Ward Races Hold Hidden Meaning," *Chicago Tribune,* 29 April 1986.
"City Lawyers in Polls," *Chicago Defender,* 29 April 1986.
"Campaign Door to Door to Settle 26th Ward," *Chicago Tribune,* 28 May 1986.
"Results in 26th Ward Still Tilt Toward Mayor," *Chicago Tribune,* 22 March 1986.
"26th Ward Race Still in Doubt," *Chicago Tribune,* 23 March 1986.
"Vrdolyak Candidate Wants New Election," *Chicago Tribune,* 25 March 1986.
"Gutierrez A Victor," *Chicago Sun-Times,* 22 March 1986.
"Mayor's Choice Leaps Ahead," *Chicago Sun-Times,* 21 May 1986.
"Backs Marlene in 15th Ward," *Chicago Defender,* 2 April 1986.
"Chicago Voting Battle Yields a Split Decision," *New York Times,* 20 March 1986.
"Mayor's Man Leads in the 26th," *Chicago Tribune,* 21 March 1986.
"Mayor, Vrdolyak Show Their Muscles," *Chicago Tribune,* 20 March 1986.
"Mayor's Council Gains May Be Hollow Victory," *Chicago Tribune,* 20 March 1986.
"Judge Tells Some Polls to Close Late," *Chicago Tribune,* 19 March 1986.
"Mayor Stops Short of Goal," *Chicago Tribune,* 19 March 1986.
"Gutierrez Seeks Nardulli Ouster," *Chicago Tribune,* 14 April 1986.
"Gutierrez Asks Judge to Set New Election," *Chicago Tribune,* 3 April 1986.
"Election Judges Facing Purge," *Chicago Tribune,* 25 April 1986.
"Latinos Crucial to New Council," *Chicago Defender,* 28 April 1986.
"Chicago Mayor Seeks Federal Voting Observers," *New York Times,* 12 March 1986.
"Soliz, Machine Fight Three in 25th," *Chicago Sun-Times,* 11 March 1986.
"Six Challenge Brady in 15th Ward Race," *Chicago Sun-Times,* 12 March 1986.
"Trash Cans at Issue in 22nd Ward Fight," *Chicago Sun-Times,* 13 March 1986.
"Giles, Myles Lead a Field of Nine Blacks in the 37th," *Chicago Sun-Times,* 14 March 1986.
"Splits Within Splits in Fractured Primary," *Chicago Sun-Times,* 16 March 1986.
"Sun-Times Choices in Tuesday's Vote," *Chicago Sun-Times,* 16 March 1986.
"Supporters Rally Around the Mayor," *Chicago Sun-Times,* 11 March 1986.
"It's a New Day at City Hall," *Chicago Sun-Times,* 26 March 1986.
"Leaders Charge Stealing in Vote Race," *New York Times,* 19 March 1986.
"Gun Shot and Bomb Threats Plague End of Chicago Council Race," *New York Times,* 18 March 1986.
"New Council Sworn In With One Seat Tied Up in Court," *New York Times,* 26 March 1986.
"No Hispanic Bloc," *Chicago Sun-Times,* 24 March 1986.
"Washington's Choice Whips Rep. Bullock," *Chicago Sun-Times,* 19 March 1986.
"Ballots Held," *Chicago Sun-Times,* 19 March 1986.
"Runoff is Aim in 18th, 31st," *Chicago Sun-Times,* 15 March 1986.
"26th Ward Feels 11th Hour Heat," *Chicago Sun-Times,* 18 March 1986.
"Mayor Beats the Drums for Hispanic Ward Allies," *Chicago Sun-Times,* 17 March 1986.
"Aldermanic Choices," *Chicago Sun-Times,* 14 March 1986.
"Mayor Gains Two Seats on Council," *Chicago Sun-Times,* 10 March 1986.
"Council Control Waits on 26th Ward," *Chicago Sun-Times,* 20 March 1986.

INTERVIEWS

Braun, Carol Moseley, State Representative, Personal Interview, 4 March 1985.
Cerda, Maria B., Assistant to the Mayor for Employment and Training, Personal Interview, 25 October 1985.
Coleman, Slim, Editor-in-Chief of *All Chicago City News* and Chairperson of the Heart of Uptown Coalition, Personal In-

terviews, 16 June 1984, 17 October 1986, 25 May 1988.

Collazo, Migadalia, Candidate for alderman in 31st Ward, Personal Interview, 15 October 1985.

del Valle, Miguel, member of the Mayor's Advisory Council on Latino Affairs and currently state senator in the 5th District, Personal Interview, 15 October 1985.

Garcia, Jesus, Democratic committeeman and alderman of the 22nd Ward, Personal Interview, 16 October 1985.

Goitia, Andy, Personal Interview, 17 October 1985.

Gutierrez, Luis, Committeeman and alderman of 26th Ward, Personal Interview, 19 October 1985.

Davis, Danny, Alderman, Personal Interview, 6 October 1984.

Evans, Timothy, Alderman, Personal Interview, 17 June 1985.

Frost, Wilson, Alderman, Personal Interview, 21 September 1985, 7 January 1986.

Gardner, Edward, chairman of the board of Soft Sheen Products Inc., Personal Interview, 17 July 1984.

Humes, Marian, Alderman of the 8th Ward, Personal Interview, 29 April 1985.

Jones, Mark, Former Circuit Court Judge, Personal Interview, 19 August 1985.

Miner, Judson, Corporation Counsel for the City of Chicago, Personal Interview, 16 January 1986.

Montgomery, James, Attorney, Personal Interviews, 28 December 1985, 4 August 1986.

Newhouse, Richard, State Senator, Personal Interviews, 23 October 1984, 20 December 1985, 29 January 1988.

Pincham, R. Eugene, Appellate Court Judge in the 1st District of Illinois, Personal Interviews, 31 July 1986, 5 August 1986, 8 December 1987.

Saffold, Howard, Member of the Mayor's Security Detail, Personal Interviews, 12 January 1988, 25 February 1988, 27 July 1988.

Sampson, Rev. Albert, Pastor of Fernwood Methodist Church, Personal Interviews, 17 August 1984, 23 August 1984, 19 October 1986.

Tillman, Dorothy, Alderman, 3rd Ward and Former Staff Member of Dr. Martin Luther King's Southern Christian Leadership Conference, Personal Interviews, 31 May 1985, 2 July 1988.

Todd, Thomas N., Attorney, Personal Interviews, 15 August 1985, 6 June 1986, 29 July 1986.

Torres, Maria, Director of the Mayor's Advisory Committee on Latino Affairs, Personal Interview, 22 October 1985.

Washington, Harold, Mayor of the City of Chicago, Personal Interviews, 23 April 1983, 31 April 1983, 31 May 1983, 22 January 1984, 16 April 1984, 12 May 1984, 19 May 1984, 17 July 1984, 24 August 1984, 24 August 1985, 22 September 1986, 15 October 1986.

CHAPTER 24

NEWSPAPERS

"Rusty Backs Non-Partisan Mayor Vote," *Chicago Sun-Times,* 28 December 1985.

"Scrapping the Chicago Machine," *Chicago Tribune,* 3 March 1986.

"A Cheap Victory for Mayor's Allies," *Chicago Tribune,* 31 July 1986.

"Election Board Could Have Spared Us This Confusion," *Chicago Tribune,* 5 January 1987.

"Hynes Out of Primary–It's Mayor vs. Byrne," *Chicago Sun-Times,* 8 January 1987.

"Eddie's Moves Aid Byrne, Hurt Hynes," *Chicago Sun-Times,* 8 January 1987.

"State Pols Make Their Pick," *Chicago Sun-Times,* 9 January 1987.

"Mayor Confirms It-He Will Run As Dem vs. Byrne," *Chicago Sun-Times,* 10 January 1987.

"Challenge May Push Epton Off GOP Ballot," *Chicago Sun-Times,* 12 January 1987.

"Daley Ally Lipinski Swings Over to Byrne," *Chicago Sun-Times,* 15 January 1987.

"Chicago Voters on Decline," *Chicago Tribune,* 16 January 1987.

"Vrdolyak Files Complaint," *Chicago Sun-Times,* 17 January 1987.

"Three Daley Allies in Byrne Camp," *Chicago Sun-Times,* 19 January 1987.

"Voter Apathy Lifts Mayor's Primary Hope," *Chicago Sun-Times,* 20 January 1987.

"Vrdolyak Slugs Away at Hynes," *Chicago Sun-Times,* 23 January 1987.

"Vrdolyak, Hynes Bids 'Foolish' Byrne Says," *Chicago Sun-Times,* 24 January 1987.

"Mayor, Byrne Running Even," *Chicago Sun-Times,* 25 January 1987.

"Hynes' Candidacy Faces Legal Attacks," *Chicago Sun-Times,* 25 January 1987.

"Mayor Ally Bids to Block Votes of Hynes Petitions," *Chicago Sun-Times,* 27 January 1987.

"Two Aides of Hynes Say They Will Work for Byrne in Primary," *Chicago Sun-Times,* 27 January 1987.

"Hynes Signers Win First Round," *Chicago Sun-Times,* 29 January 1987.

"Hynes Tells Plan to Boost Revenue Collections," *Chicago Sun-Times,* 30 January 1987.

"Byrne Vows Revival of Fest at Pier," *Chicago Sun-Times,* 30 January 1987.

"Vrdolyak Insists He's No Racist, Blasts Double Standard," *Chicago Sun-Times,* 30 January 1987.

"Vrdolyak Seeking a Jewish, Black Split, Says Mayor," *Chicago Sun-Times,* 31 January 1987.

"Old Friends Kick In for Byrne Campaign," *Chicago Sun-Times,* 31 January 1987.

"Pincham Draws Scrutiny," *Chicago Sun-Times,* 3 February 1987.

"Jesse Rallies Backing for Pincham as Byrne Fumes," *Chicago Sun-Times,* 8 February 1987.

"South Side Church Gives Byrne Hearing," *Chicago Sun-Times,* 9 February 1987.

"Mayor Rips Byrne on Contract Donors," *Chicago Sun-Times,* 9 February 1987.

"Byrne Cements Ties to Daleys; Mayor Breaks Sod for Airline," *Chicago Sun-Times,* 10 February 1987.

"34th Ward Hopefuls Feeling Impact of Former Alderman Frost," *Chicago Sun-Times,* 11 February 1987.

"Byrne Adds New Color to Pincham Quote," *Chicago Sun-Times,* 12 February 1987.

"Crossover Votes Seen as Key in Primary," *Chicago Sun-Times,* 12 February 1987.

"Many Convicts Registered by Jackson May be Ineligible," *Chicago Sun-Times,* 13 February 1987.

"Byrne Raps Mayor for Atlanta Link," *Chicago Sun-Times,* 13 February 1987.

"Mayor's Backers Hounded by Second Term Jinx," *Chicago Sun-Times,* 16 February 1987.

"Freedom Riders Hit, Hail," *Chicago Sun-Times,* 18 February 1987.

"Washington Has Already 'Peaked,' Byrne Contends," *Chicago Sun-Times,* 18 February 1987.

"Thousands Pack Pavilion in Rally for Washington," *Chicago Sun-Times,* 18 February 1987.

"Byrne Shifts to a 'Smile' TV Strategy," *Chicago Sun-Times,* 18 February 1987.

"Ruling to Reinstate Voters if Pols Appeal," *Chicago Sun-Times,* 19 February 1987.

"Mayor's Aides Fear Low Turn Out, Step Up Drive," *Chicago Sun-Times,* 19 February 1987.

"Washington, Byrne Work Same Street," *Chicago Sun-Times,* 22 February 1987.

"Mayor Given Edge," *Chicago Sun-Times,* 22 February 1987.

"Absentee Votes Worry Mayor Aides," *Chicago Sun-Times,* 23 February 1987.

"Even At 8-5 Odds, Beware a Bet Against Byrne," *Chicago Sun-Times,* 23 February 1987.

"Turn Out Key to Victory," *Chicago Sun-Times,* 24 February 1987.

"It's Harold," *Chicago Sun-Times,* 25 February 1987.

"Colored Ballot Stirs Fury," *Chicago Defender,* 25 February, 1987.

"Byrne, Vrdolyak Spurred Black Vote Sign Ups," *Chicago Sun-Times,* 25 February 1987.

"A Special Vote Tally Ordered," *Chicago Sun-Times,* 25 February 1987.

"Mayor Wins Another Close One, Calls for Dem Unity," *Chicago Sun-Times,* 25 February 1987.

"Mayor Headquarters Shares Hugs and 'Slapping Five,' " *Chicago Sun-Times*, 25 February 1987.

SPEECHES

Thomas N. Todd speech, Operation PUSH, August 25, 1984.

Harold Washington speech, Bethel AME Church, November 29, 1986.

Thomas N. Todd speech, Bethel AME Church, November 29, 1986

Justice R. Eugene Pincham speech, Operation PUSH Headquarters, January 31, 1987.

INTERVIEWS

Pincham, R. Eugene, Appellate Court Judge in the 1st District of Illinois, Personal Interviews, Chicago, 31 July 1986, 5 August 1986, 8 December 1987.

Saffold, Howard, member of the mayor's security detail, Personal Interviews, 12 January 1988, 25 February 1988, 27 July 1988.

Sampson, Rev. Albert, Pastor of Fernwood Methodist Church, Personal Interviews, 17 August 1984, 23 August 1984, 19 October 1986.

Tillman, Dorothy, 3rd Ward alderman, and former staff member of Dr. Martin Luther King's Southern Christian Leadership Conference, Personal Interviews, 31 May 1985, 2 July 1988.

Todd, Thomas N., Attorney, Personal Interviews, 15 August 1985, 6 June 1986, 29 July 1986.

Washington, Harold, Mayor of Chicago, Personal Interviews, 23 April 1983, 31 April 1983, 31 May 1983, 22 January 1984, 16 April 1984, 12 May 1984, 19 May 1984, 17 July 1984, 24 August 1984, 24 August 1985, 22 September 1986, 15 October 1986.

CHAPTER 25

NEWSPAPERS

"Confident Hynes Starts Push for Mayoral Election," *Chicago Sun-Times,* 25 February 1987.

"Vrdolyak Revved Up and Ready to Take on the Mayor," *Chicago Sun-Times,* 25 February 1987.

"Mayor Shows He Can Go One on One," *Chicago Sun-Times,* 26 February 1987.

"Mayor 'Squeaked' in Hynes Says," *Chicago Sun-Times,* 26 February 1987.

"Pressure on Vrdolyak to Quit Race," *Chicago Sun-Times,* 26 February 1987.

"Mayor Still Can Lose–And Here's How," *Chicago Sun-Times,* 26 February 1987.

"Vrdolyak Launches 'Emotional' Bid," *Chicago Sun-Times,* 26 February 1987.

"Mayor Pledges Heat on Hynes, Vrdolyak," *Chicago Sun-Times,* 26 February 1987.

"Placing the Blame in Ballot Foul Up," *Chicago Sun-Times,* 26 February 1987.

"Byrne to Talk About Unity at Dem Lunch," *Chicago Sun-Times,* 28 February 1987.

"Byrne Offers Mayor 'Unity,' Not Support," *Chicago Sun-Times,* 1 March 1987.

"Hyncs Maps Plan to Oust Mayor," *Chicago Sun-Times,* 2 March 1987.

"Hynes Foes Fighting Endorsement," *Chicago Sun-Times,* 3 March 1987.

"Mayor Rips Vrdolyak, Hynes as Purveyors of the Past," *Chicago Sun-Times,* 3 March 1987.

"Top Byrne Aide, Ronan, Says He May Back Mayor," *Chicago Sun-Times,* 3 March 1987.

"Why Byrne is Reaching Out to Washington," *Chicago Sun-Times,* 4 March 1987.

"Rosty Bucks on Mayor," *Chicago Sun-Times,* 4 March 1987.

"Vrdolyak Runs Strong for Number 2 Spot," *Chicago Sun-Times,* 5 March 1987.

"Pullout Deadline for Eddie, Hynes," *Chicago Sun-Times,* 6 March 1987.

"Vrdolyak Sign is Vowed: Won't Quit," *Chicago Sun-Times,* 7 March 1987.

"Word War Ends Post-Primary Lull," *Chicago Tribune,* 10 March 1987.
"Mayor Charges Hynes 'Duplicity' on Bonds," *Chicago Sun-Times,* 10 March 1987.
"Hynes Payroll is Packed with Pals, Neighbors," *Chicago Sun-Times,* 11 March 1987.
"Gloves Come Off, Hynes, Washington Pull No Punches," *Chicago Sun-Times,* 11 March 1987.
"Explain Hiring Pals, Mayor Tells Hynes," *Chicago Sun-Times,* 12 March 1987.
"Hurdler Harold Sprints by Foes," *Chicago Sun-Times,* 12 March 1987.
"Vrdolyak Raps Hynes, Mayor and – Sun-Times," *Chicago Sun-Times,* 13 March 1987.
"Mell Hints He Will Back the Mayor," *Chicago Sun-Times,* 14 March 1987.
"Hynes Given Endorsement by Pal Daley," *Chicago Sun-Times,* 15 March 1987.
"City Democratic Stalwarts Head for the Sidelines," *Chicago Tribune,* 15 March 1987.
"Brawl for City Hall has Lighter Side," *Chicago Sun-Times,* 16 March 1987.
"More Council Foes Marching to Mayor," *Chicago Sun-Times,* 17 March 1987.
"Mayor's Race – 'Contest for Silver Medal,' " *Chicago Sun-Times,* 19 March 1987.
"Ballot Foul Up Has Angry Charges, Lawsuits Flying," *Chicago Tribune,* 25 March 1987.
"Hey, Eddie, Harold: Anti-Semitism is No Issue," *Chicago Sun-Times,* 26 March 1987.
" 'White Mayor' Remark Trips Haider," *Chicago Sun-Times,* 27 March 1987.
"Thompson Boasts for Haider," *Chicago Sun-Times,* 27 March 1987.
"Two Council Foes Back the Mayor," *Chicago Tribune,* 30 March 1987.
"A Hard Choice Between Losers," *Chicago Tribune,* 31 March 1987.
" 'Battle Over,' Byrne Backs Mayor," *Chicago Sun-Times,* 31 March 1987.
"Black Activist Accuses Vrdolyak of Libel in Ad," *Chicago Sun-Times,* 1 April 1987.
"Mayoral Debaters Do More Infighting," *Chicago Sun-Times,* 1 April 1987.
"Byrne Faces Up to Reality in Backing Mayor," *Chicago Sun-Times,* 1 April 1987.
"Vrdolyak 29 Fading Away," *Chicago Sun-Times,* 2 April 1987.
"Hynes Aid is Gloomy, Mayor Sees a Big Win," *Chicago Sun-Times,* 3 April 1987.
"Combative Hynes Irks Some on Lakefront," *Chicago Sun-Times,* 3 April 1987.
"Final Four go to Wire," *Chicago Sun-Times,* 5 April 1987.
"Mayor Aiming for Mandate," *Chicago Sun-Times,* 5 April 1987.
"Bombshell Surprises Voters," *Chicago Sun-Times,* 6 April 1987.
"Pull Out a Sour Note for Some Hynes Backers," *Chicago Sun-Times,* 6 April 1987.
"Hynes Out," *Chicago Sun-Times,* 6 April 1987.
"Vrdolyak Ready to Make History," *Chicago Sun-Times,* 7 April 1987.
"Haider Basks in Glow of Renewed Attention," *Chicago Sun-Times,* 7 April 1987.
"Harold Again," *Chicago Sun-Times,* 8 April 1987.
"Burke Vows to Keep Fighting," *Chicago Sun-Times,* 8 April 1987.

CHAPTER 26

INTERVIEWS

Canter, David, Lawyer and Confidant of Harold Washington, Personal Interview, Chicago, 19 April 1988.
Childs, Josie, Friend of Harold Washington for 34 years and currently a member of the staff of the Chicago Department of Special Events, Personal Interview, 3 March 1988.
Despres, Leon, Former alderman and current Parliamentary to the Mayor, Personal Interviews, Chicago, 30 May 1984, 28 July 1984, 13 December 1985, 16 January 1988.
Ferguson, Margaret T., Family friend and retired financial coordinator for the Xerox Corporation. Personal Interview, 17 February 1988.
Gilbert, Herman, Executive Vice President and Editorial Director of Path Press, Personal Interviews, Chicago, 24 November

1984, 28 April 1984, 19 December 1985, 19 March 1988.

Goldsborough, Evelyn, Former student at Roosevelt University and owner of Harold Washington's condominium fi7 at Hampton House, Personal Interview, 12 March 1988.

Jackson, Orville, Thaddeus and Allie, Nephews of Arlene Jackson Washington, Harold Washington's stepmother, Personal Interview, 11 February 1988.

Lee, Frank, Member of the Mayor's Security Detail, Personal Interview, Chicago, 22 February 1988.

Miller, Alton, Press Secretary to Mayor Washington, Personal Interview, 28 April 1988.

Saffold, Howard, Member of the Mayor's Security Detail, Personal Interviews, 12 January 1988, 25 February 1988, 27 July 1988.

Walls II, Bill, Mayor's Aide, Personal Interview, 7 January 1988.

OTHER MATERIALS

"The Journey to the Orient," August 23–September 8, 1985. Pamphlet chronicled by Harry Golden Jr., *Chicago Sun-Times.*

The Journal of the City Council of Chicago, May 4, 1987.

INDEX

C

D

E

F

G

H

I

J

K

L

M

N

O

P

Q

R

S

T

U

V

W

Y

Z